PEIRCE

The Arguments of
the Philosophers

EDITOR: TED HONDERICH

Professor of Philosophy, University College, London

The group of books of which this is one will include an
essentially analytic and critical account of each of the
considerable number of the great and the influential
philosophers. The group of books taken together will
comprise a contemporary assessment and history of the
entire course of philosophical thought.

Already published in the series

Bentham Ross Harrison
Berkeley George Pitcher
Butler Terence Penelhum
Descartes Margaret Dauler Wilson
Gottlob Frege Hans D. Sluga
Hegel M. J. Inwood
Hume Barry Stroud
Kant Ralph C. S. Walker
Kierkegaard Alastair Hannay
Karl Marx Allen Wood
Meinong Reinhardt Grossman
Nietzsche Richard Schacht
Plato J. C. B. Gosling
Karl Popper Anthony O'Hear
The Presocratic Philosophers (2 vols) Jonathan Barnes
Russell R. M. Sainsbury
Santayana Timothy L. S. Sprigge
Sartre Peter Caws
Schopenhauer D. W. Hamlyn
Socrates Gerasimos Xenophon Santas
Wittgenstein Robert J. Fogelin

PEIRCE

Christopher Hookway

Department of Philosophy,
University of Birmingham

Routledge & Kegan Paul
London, Boston, Melbourne and Henley

First published in 1985
by Routledge & Kegan Paul plc

14 Leicester Square, London WC2H 7PH, England

9 Park Street, Boston, Mass. 02108, USA

464 St Kilda Road, Melbourne,
Victoria 3004, Australia and

Broadway House, Newtown Road,
Henley-on-Thames, Oxon RG9 1EN, England

Set in Garamond 10/12
by Columns of Reading
and printed in Great Britain

Library of Congress Cataloging in Publication Data

Hookway, Christopher.
Peirce.
(The Arguments of the philosophers)
Bibliography: p.
Includes index.
1. Peirce, Charles S. (Charles Sanders), 1839-1914.
I. Title. II. Series.
B945.P44H66 1985   191   84-13315

British Library CIP data also available

ISBN 0-7100-9715-8(c)

FOR JO

Contents

Preface

Many people share the opinion that Charles S. Peirce is a philosophical giant, perhaps the most important philosopher to have emerged in the United States. Most philosophers think of him as the founder of 'pragmatism' and are aware of doctrines – about truth and meaning, for example – which they describe as 'Peircean'. But, curiously, few have read more than two or three of his best-known papers, and these somewhat unrepresentative ones. On reading further, one finds a rich and impressive corpus of writings, containing imaginative and original discussions of a wide range of issues in most areas of philosophy: he appears to have anticipated many important philosophical discoveries of the last eighty years. However, the interest of Peirce's work does not consist simply in these detailed examinations of philosophical problems, for he was, above all, a systematic philosopher. Inspired by his reading of Kant, he devoted his life to providing foundations for knowledge and, in the course of doing so, he brought together a number of different philosophical doctrines: the new logic of relations and quantifiers invented independently by Frege in Germany and Peirce himself in the United States; sophisticated insights into the structure of science and the logic of probability; a systematic theory of meaning and interpretation; a developed philosophy of mathematics; a general theory of value; and a metaphysics incorporating an ambitious evolutionary cosmology. It is not wholly surprising that he is not read more widely. As the reader will see from the introduction, he never produced a unified and coherent presentation of the system. We have to work from a mass of papers, sets of lecture notes, reviews, and manuscripts, and on that basis – helped by his many programmatic statements – reconstruct the structure and development of his system. For that reason, this book is probably more concerned with exegesis than others in the series: I have set myself the task of writing the book which I had looked for when I started to read Peirce – hopefully, a clear presentation of his views on the topics of principal concern to him, and an explanation of how the whole is supposed to fit together. While I have not eschewed criticism, the main focus throughout has been upon providing a guide that will enable people to read Peirce's works with an understanding of what he is up to and why he presents his doctrines as he does.

Much of the work on the book was carried out during the academic year 1981–2 when I was a Fulbright Scholar at Harvard University. This enabled me to work on the Peirce manuscripts in the Houghton Library, and gave me valued leisure to think and write. The trip was made possible by the award of an American Studies Fellowship, jointly funded by the American Council of Learned Societies and the United States–United Kingdom Educational Commission (Fulbright–Hayes), and I am pleased to have this opportunity to thank them for their support. I am grateful to Leon Pompa and my colleagues at Birmingham for allowing me to take leave to make use of this opportunity. I have discussed Peirce's views with many people, at Harvard and Birmingham, and when I have given talks and papers at conferences and university philosophy departments in Britain and the United States, and I have always profited from these discussions. I cannot thank all of these people individually here, but I would like to acknowledge my colleague Nick Dent whose conversation while the final draft was being prepared and detailed written comments on several chapters have produced substantial improvements. Finally, I hope that my wife, Jo, can feel that the finished book compensates for the separations and stresses of its production. But for her support and encouragement, it would never have been finished.

Note on references

References to works by authors other than Peirce are by author and date to the list in the bibliography. The one exception to this is that references to Kant's *Critique of Pure Reason* simply take the familiar form: 'A' followed by a page number for quotations from the first edition; 'B' followed by a page number for quotations from the second edition. Throughout, I use Kemp Smith's translation (1933, London: Macmillan).

It is necessary to make use of a number of different sources for Peirce's own writings. References to these take the forms indicated in the following list:

Collected Papers of Charles Sanders Peirce, volumes 1–6 edited by C. Hartshorne and P. Weiss, 1931–1935, volumes 7 and 8 edited by A. W. Burks, 1958. Cambridge, Mass: Belknap Press.
References take the form n.m indicating volume and paragraph number: thus, 5.378 refers to paragraph 378 of volume 5. Copyright material from these volumes is reprinted by permission of the Harvard University Press.

Writings of Charles S. Peirce: a Chronological Edition, volume 1, edited by M. Fisch et al., 1982. Bloomington: Indiana University Press.
References of the form CW1 followed by a page number are to this work.

The New Elements of Mathematics, four volumes in five, edited by C. Eisele, 1976. The Hague: Mouton.
References are by volume and page number, e.g. NE iv 375.

Semiotic and Significs edited by C. Hardwick, 1977, Bloomington: Indiana University Press.

References to this work, which contains the correspondence of Peirce and Victoria, Lady Welby, take the form 'SS' followed by a page number.

Charles Sanders Peirce: Contributions to 'The Nation', compiled and annotated by K. L. Ketner and J. E. Cook. Three volumes, 1975–1979, Lubbock: Texas Tech Press.

This work is referred to as CTN; references indicate volume and page.

Finally, I have made use of the many thousands of Peirce manuscripts in the Houghton Library at Harvard University. These are in the process of being renumbered in the new chronological edition of Peirce's works. I employ the numbering given in Richard Robin's *Annotated Catalogue of the Papers of Charles S. Peirce*, 1967, Amherst: University of Massachusetts Press. References of the form Rn are to these manuscripts, which are available on microfilm from the Widener Library at Harvard. I am grateful to the Department of Philosophy at Harvard University for permission to use these papers.

There are several anthologies of Peirce's philosophical writings, edited by Buchler, Wiener, Moore, and others. Since all of these collections omit works that I take to be of central importance, I have decided not to give references to these sources although they may be more accessible to the average philosophical reader. Where appropriate, I have referred to major works by title to help readers using these anthologies to track down references.

Introduction

Charles Sanders Peirce (1839–1914) can seem one of the most modern or contemporary of philosophers. If many of his views are controversial or implausible, still, on reading his work, we are likely to feel that many of his problems are close to the issues that are philosophically pressing today. Like Frege, he recognizably inhabits our philosophical world, forging tools and concepts which are still central to philosophical debate. One of the founders of the quantificational logic which is the staple of contemporary textbooks in the subject, we find him groping towards an understanding of the philosophical underpinnings of logic, and discussing the implications of the new logic for our grasp of thought and reality. He appears to attach great importance to the philosophical analysis of meaning which is to occupy a foundational role for logic and the rest of philosophy. In his discussions of pragmatism, the doctrine for which he is best known, we find familiar themes concerning the extent to which our grasp of abstract concepts can be articulated as an understanding of the conditions in which the assertion of a proposition is justified by available evidence. Furthermore, he appears to be concerned with familiar problems about truth and verification, attempting to reconcile the view that reality has an objective character which is independent of our view of it with the claim that this character is available to us if we conduct our inquiries efficiently or correctly. He offers sophisticated and informed treatment of complex and modern issues in the philosophy of science. It is no accident that the literature contains frequent claims that Peirce has anticipated this or that doctrine which became a focus of concern in the twentieth century. One can readily see the force of Rorty's claim, in Rorty (1961); that 'Peirce's thought envisaged, and repudiated in advance, the stages in the development of empiricism which logical positivism represented, and that it came to rest in a group of insights and a philosophical mood

1

much like those we find in the *Philosophical Investigations*' (pp. 197–8).

But a closer reading of Peirce's texts reveals material which seems to conflict with this sort of interpretation. We find him developing a speculative evolutionary cosmology which explains how the law-governed world studied by the sciences evolved out of nothing, or out of pure possibility; and we find a defence of a form of objective idealism, which holds that all matter is 'effete mind'. We are assured that logic and epistemology must be grounded in aesthetics. We encounter the mind-numbing claim that the elements of experience and reality may be classified into firstness, secondness and thirdness. And there is a commitment to a systematic, structured form of first philosophy, drawing on none of the natural or human sciences, which sits poorly with a widespread popular conception of Peirce as a defender of naturalism, the doctrine that philosophy is continuous with psychology and other sciences, able to draw on them in order to provide an adequate account of man and his place in nature. It is difficult to produce a unified treatment of a philosopher who seems to incorporate the anti-metaphysical prejudices of a critical philosopher of language, with a predisposition to speculative mataphysics derived from Hegel and the German idealists. Some twenty years after writing the passage quoted above, we find Rorty claiming that Peirce contributed no more than a name to pragmatism, and was still in the grip of the traditional conception of the task of philosophy which the other pragmatists (most notably James and Dewey), as well as the author of the *Philosophical Investigations*, did much to overthrow (Rorty, 1982, p. 161).

In an influential study published in 1950, Thomas Goudge is forced to acknowledge two Peirces. He finds a reasonable, tough-minded naturalistically inclined philosopher who tends to lapse into indefensible 'transcendentalism' when he turns to aesthetics, spinning metaphysical stories and speculating about the reality of God. Other scholars have tried to avoid this unwelcome hypothesis by stressing the extent to which Peirce's thought evolved, finding a succession of different philosophical systems and no finished view (e.g. Murphey, 1968). Others claim that Peirce's underlying motivations were always in speculative metaphysics, that he was an heir to Hegel and Schelling (Esposito, 1980); while yet others, for example, Skagestadt (1981) have recommended that interpretation should focus on Peirce's contributions to relatively small concrete issues, with attempts to grasp the systematic importance of his thought being postponed. This last approach cannot but distort the character of Peirce's thought: he was the most systematic of philosophers, and one can only understand his discussions of, for example, relatively concrete issues in the logic of science if the systematic structure of his thought is kept in mind. And although interests in metaphysics and in reconciling science and religion were always

2

important to him, we shall not understand his arguments unless we see that his metaphysics was, in an important sense, subordinate to his work in logic and epistemology. However, the variety of interpretations in the literature may make one despair of making sense of Peirce's philosophy.

I shall argue that in important respects Rorty's description of Peirce as a traditional philosopher is correct. He was a systematic philosopher concerned with the sorts of problems about science, truth and knowledge which exercised Descartes and Kant. He wanted to provide a demonstration that, if we conduct our inquiries properly, we can obtain knowledge of an objective reality. Although the term is vague, the description of him as sympathetic to 'naturalism' is bound to sow confusion: in most of his writings, Peirce seeks for a 'first philosophy', a discipline which makes use of no materials derived from the sciences but rather offers an independent justification of science. In fact, he is more sensitive than most philosophers about the character that such a first philosophy must have; and many of the writings that Goudge would describe as 'transcendental' are occupied with the sensitive treatment of the epistemology of philosophy itself. As we shall see in chapters II and III, the discussion of firstness, secondness and thirdness as well as the attempt to ground logic in aesthetics are accompanied by philosophical discussions of the epistemological grounding that these studies have, and are motivated by the need to construct an adequate account of truth that can be appealed to in justifying methods of inquiry employed in the sciences. Properly understood, these doctrines are less wildly speculative – and less alien to the styles of modern philosophy – than may, at first glance, appear. The interest of Peirce's work lies in the ways in which, within a traditional conception of the task of philosophy, he transformed how the problems arose and used his new logic and claims about meaning to resolve them. He tried to undermine a host of mistaken beliefs about reality – he called them 'nominalism' – which had disfigured the discussions of earlier philosophers. For some of the thinkers that Rorty admires, the traditional problems and aspirations of philosophy vanish when these errors are exposed; for Peirce, they remained but became tractable.

An understanding of the problems that concerned Peirce requires a consideration of the intellectual climate in which his views were first formed.[1] Peirce grew up in an academic environment at a time of considerable intellectual ferment for educated New Englanders. His writings about knowledge and reality, and his pragmatism, represent a response to problems about scepticism, science and religion which exercised intellectual Boston in the middle years of the nineteenth century. It is easily forgotten that by that time the United States had centres of academic and intellectual excellence to match those of the Old World. Darwin supposedly claimed that Cambridge, Massachussetts,

3

contained enough brilliant minds in the 1860s to furnish all the universities of England; and Bruce Kuklick has stressed that the cultured classes of nineteenth century Boston were intensely intellectual, concerned with religious and philosophical issues. Peirce's own family, residents of the Boston area since John Pers came from England in 1637, were at the hub of this intellectual activity, his father a key figure in the scientific establishment of the United States. Benjamin Peirce was arguably the leading American mathematician of the time and was Professor of astronomy and mathematics at Harvard – Peirce's elder brother was eventually to succeed to this chair. Actively involved in campaigning for funding for scientific research, a founding member of the National Academy of Sciences, involved in the running of the United States Coastal Survey, Benjamin Peirce was a man of wide interests, considerable influence and great ability – there is evidence that Charles always felt that he was in his shadow. Emerson, Longfellow and Oliver Wendell Holmes were friends of the Peirce family, and their home seems to have been a frequent centre for discussions among the leading scientific figures of Cambridge. Charles was to emerge from this family environment to graduate from Harvard in 1859 and, after a short spell gaining practical experience with the Coastal Survey, he entered the Lawrence Scientific School at Harvard, becoming the first student to graduate *summa cum laude* in Chemistry in 1863. Although at this stage he may have thought himself headed for a scientific career – and continued for many years to describe himself as a chemist or chemical engineer – Peirce's interests in logic and philosophy had already been awakened. Deeply influenced by reading Schiller and Kant while an undergraduate, and already well read in logic, he wrote a number of metaphysical essays around 1860 in which hindsight can find some hints of the interests and doctrines that he was later to develop (CW1 37–94).

The people of Boston were mostly Unitarians, and they looked to the philosophers of Harvard to provide the intellectual foundations that their faith required. Already troubled during the 1850s, these foundations were rocked by two books published during the following years. One of these, predictably, was Darwin's *Origin of Species*, which appeared in 1859; and six years later came J. S. Mill's *Examination of Sir William Hamilton's Philosophy*. Although they did not go so far as to hold that belief in God was to be grounded solely in the claim that He provided the best explanation of the order and variety discovered by the sciences, still they believed that 'nature's laws represented the usual mode of action of the divine power' (Kuklick, 1977, p. 7). We could come to know the nature of God through scientific activity; and the ordered nature of the laws discovered by the sciences was bound to reinforce one's faith. Bostonians were prepared to allow that God may occasionally employ miracles, but as the nineteenth century developed, less importance was attached to these. Emerson and the other transcendentalist thinkers, based in Concord some few miles inland from Cambridge, attacked the Unitarians' attempt to integrate reason and religion: religious truth was apprehended by the soul, and concerned the feelings rather than reason. So long as the Harvard philosophers – people like Peirce's teacher Francis Bowen – could provide secure foundations for the Unitarian position, these criticisms had little influence. But, the work of Darwin and Mill made those foundations seem unsatisfactory. The bearing of the *Origin of Species* on the matter should be obvious. If natural selection reflects the usual mode of working of God, then He brings about order and diversity through a process that seems wasteful, cruel and inefficient. Moreover, if an evolutionary explanation can be offered of how laws and regularities of behaviour emerge, there is little scope for seeing these regularities as expressive of God's nature. During the 1860s, Darwin's theory was a topic of constant debate among the Harvard scientific community, Asa Gay, professor of natural history, championing the new ideas in the face of the opposition of the great zoologist Louis Agassiz. As elsewhere, a principal focus of the debate was the question whether a scientist could consistently adopt the Darwinian theory and hold on to his religious belief (as Gay proposed and Agassiz denied).

Peirce was certainly interested in this debate. He studied with Agassiz in the early 1860s and, although he made use of evolutionary ideas, was always lukewarm about the Darwinian position. However, we shall understand better the springs of his thought when we notice the impact of Mill's book. The Unitarian position held that through scientific inquiry we could discover the laws which govern reality; and it was clear to them that this required an epistemological grounding. They thought that they required an assurance that science discovered the properties of an independent realm of things in themselves. If Humean scepticism could not be defeated; or if we could only have knowledge of our own ideas or experiences; or if we only know the world of appearance, things in themselves being beyond our grasp; in all these cases, we could not hold on to the thesis that science reveals the action of God in nature. Intellectual security for the people of New England rested upon the belief that the Scottish philosopher Sir William Hamilton had provided them with the epistemology they required; he was regarded as one of the great philosophers, an equal of Aristotle or Kant, and his influence was considerable. I shall not describe his position in any detail, just noting that it was a curious mixture of the common-sense position of Reid that we have immediate knowledge of things in themselves and the Kantian insight that this knowledge was coloured or conditioned by our cognitive constitution. Mill's critique removed the epistemological prop that sustained the religious beliefs of educated New England. Hence the need for a new attempt to justify the pretensions of the sciences to provide knowledge of reality, and to reconcile science and religion.

It would be a mistake to think that Peirce was awakened from Hamiltonian confusions by Mill's book. Although one can find hints of some of Peirce's subsequent claims about signs and mental action in Hamilton, there is no evidence that Hamilton was ever an important influence upon him. Already by 1859, Kant was the major source of his ideas. Indeed, when, in 1862, Peirce married his first wife Melusina, an early American feminist, he was confirmed an Episcopalian and acknowledged the Trinity. His early attempts to develop a Kantian system of three categories are given a context which suggest that he is attempting to relate them to the Trinity. He was probably closer to the common-sense position after 1900 than he ever was during the 1860s. However, we can understand the problems that occupied him by noting the consequences of Mill's attack on Hamilton. A natural result both of Darwin's theory of evolution and of Mill's position is a philosophical outlook that we can call 'naturalism'. The former can suggest that, if we want to understand a human practice such as scientific inquiry or morality or religion, we should undertake a scientific investigation which indicates its history, explaining why it evolved as it did. We can have no assurance in advance that these practices are designed to take us to the truth, promote human happiness or nobility, or put us into contact with the ground of our being. The consequence is likely to be a sceptical mistrust of our cognitive faculties, and the claim that biology, psychology or some other sciences are the only sources of understanding of our nature and practices. Mill's sceptical empiricism has a similar consequence. We must give up the attempt to justify our methods of inquiry, to show that they will provide us with knowledge of reality. We must rest content with a description of our practices, and a list of the forms of inference that we find plausible.

As Murphey has stressed, one response to the challenge of Darwin and Mill was a return to the history of philosophy to find sources of inspiration for a new vindication of science, and a new attempt to reconcile science and religion. Francis Bowen turned to Berkeley, but others turned to Kant. When Peirce was invited to give several series of lectures at Harvard in the late 1860s, we can see him providing a broadly Kantian response to the sort of naturalism we have been discussing. These lectures resulted in a famous series of papers in the *Journal of Speculative Philosophy*. In chapter I below, I introduce central themes of Peirce's thought by examining both the structure of argument that led to sceptical naturalistic conclusions and the central conceptions that Peirce uses in his response. Thinking of the challenge that was offered to

Unitarian thought in the 1860s, we can note three respects in which Peirce's philosophical project is profoundly conservative and in line with the philosophical tradition. Earlier philosophers had hoped for a 'first philosophy', prior to any of the natural or human sciences, which would provide a general account of man and his place in nature, and which would explain the legitimacy of the methods we use for uncovering the character of reality. Many had attached a peculiar value to the activity of inquiry, claiming that it is only through scientific inquiry that we can truly fulfil ourselves: the scientist has the most meaningful kind of life available to us. We can see such a thought present in the Unitarian's claim that scientific investigators discern the normal working of the ground of their being. As will become clearer in chapter II, it is impossible to understand Peirce's work without seeing his endorsement of this philosophical ideal. He too seeks a first philosophy; and he too sees the single-minded pursuit of knowledge as a supreme form of human flourishing; and he too wants to find close connections between science and religion – in later work, he seems to hold that a non-believer cannot participate in a scientific investigation of reality. We can read Peirce as part of a Kantian backlash against the psychologism and naturalism that threatened logic and philosophy in the latter half of the nineteenth century.[2]

The differences of interpretation partly reflect the particular difficulties of working on Peirce. He never produced the finished statement of his position that he aspired to. Where the student of Descartes or Kant can undertake to understand a number of central texts, appealing to lesser works for the light they throw upon the central texts, any attempt to specify a canon of central Peircean texts is likely to be controversial. Moreover, as Murphey's classic work indicates, Peirce's views were constantly developing, leaving it unclear when we can appeal to a later work as clarifying, and when repudiating, an earlier draft. The eight-volume *Collected Papers* contained a selection of published and unpublished work; but they were not ordered chronologically, and they omit much that now seems to be of great importance. Moreover, the papers that are most often anthologized or reprinted are mostly either early papers from before 1870 or pieces which, like 'Fixation of Belief' and 'How to Make our Ideas Clear', Peirce soon repudiated. The chronological edition of Peirce's writings now being published will make Peirce study much easier, but for the present it is necessary to make use of a number of different published sources, and to study his many fascinating unpublished manuscripts in the Houghton Library at Harvard.[3]

Although he was writing continuously from the 1860s until after 1910, important landmarks are provided by a number of series of papers, sets of lectures and, complete and incomplete, drafts of logic treatises which reflect the development of his thought. We can use these to provide a skeleton for a sketch of the rest of Peirce's biography. I have already mentioned the lectures which, as a promising young scholar, he was invited to give at Harvard in the second half of the 1860s and the papers which resulted from these. In the years around 1870, he met constantly with a number of other scholars in what he later called a 'Metaphysical Club'. His fellows included William James, Chauncey Wright (a slightly older man and a defender of Mill and Darwin who was venerated by James and Peirce as their 'boxing master'), and the young lawyers Nicholas St John Green and Oliver Wendell Holmes junior. Peirce's Harvard classmate Francis Abbot was an occasional visitor. It was in these discussions that pragmatism was born, and several members of the group contributed to the development of the doctrine. At the same time, Peirce was struggling to set out his developing views in a textbook, the 'Logic' of 1873; although this was never completed, many of the views it contained appeared in the second of his major series of papers, a sequence of six in the *Popular Science Monthly* in 1878–9. Entitled *Illustrations of the Logic of Science*, the series contains Peirce's two best-known papers, 'The Fixation of Belief' and 'How to Make our Ideas Clear'; although the doctrine is not mentioned by name, these contain the first full published treatment of pragmatism.

By the end of the 1870s, Peirce's marriage had failed; Melusina Fay Peirce left him, and, having divorced her in 1883, he remarried, his second marriage enduring and sustaining him through many difficult years till the end of his life. Still working part-time for the Coastal Survey, he obtained in 1879 his only orthodox university post, as a lecturer in logic at the Johns Hopkins University in Baltimore. Johns Hopkins had recently set up the first graduate school in the country, and had attracted a remarkable mathematics faculty, as well as providing able and stimulating students. Most of Peirce's writings of this time deal with issues in formal logic and mathematics. In 1884, he published a volume of *Studies in Logic*, by himself and his students, which contains the paper by O. H. Mitchell which introduces the Peircean version of quantificational logic, which was of great importance for the development of his ideas about language, thought and reality. However, this stimulating time in an exciting intellectual environment was brought to a premature close in 1884. Under the prompting of a scandal the causes of which are still somewhat obscure, the faculty at Johns Hopkins was reorganized, with, apparently, the single intention of easing Peirce from his post as inconspicuously as possible. From that time it seems to have been clear that Peirce could never expect another orthodox university post. After an initial attempt to earn his living as a consulting chemical engineer, he spent the rest of his life writing prodigiously but in a state of considerable poverty. William James, Josiah Royce and other admirers from Harvard arranged for him to give some lectures there; he wrote many reviews for *The Nation*; and he relied upon the help of his friends and former colleagues. His post with the Coastal Survey was ended in 1891, and he built himself a house in Milford, Pennsylvania, where he spent the rest of his life, in some isolation.

The years 1892–3 are the next landmark. Freed from his professional duty to devote much of his time to formal logic, Peirce had been working for some time elaborating his metaphysical conception of reality. His writings had contained little that was obviously metaphysical since the 1860s, and this development may reflect his having the leisure to pursue topics which had been held in abeyance for a while – although, as we shall see in chapter III, the logical discoveries of the early 1880s put strains upon his philosophical programme which prompted a more serious concern with metaphysics. *The Monist* contained a series of papers in 1891 and 1892 which presented the metaphysical positions that he had been developing; he was drawn towards an evolutionary cosmology which did not ground the evolutionary developments in natural selection, and a form of objective idealism which must have owed something to the transcendentalists and the German idealist tradition. But, at the same time, Peirce was attempting a general statement of his logical doctrines. The manuscript of a large logic text from 1893 remains, and Peirce also made plans to republish many of the papers he had written during the preceding twenty-five years under the self-consciously Cartesian title *Search for a Method*.

However, he was already entertaining doubts about the foundations of his logic, and in the following years, through several series of lectures, drafts of books and published articles, we can see him moving towards his final attempt to provide systematic foundations for a system of first philosophy. In 1898 and again in 1903, he delivered fascinating lectures to the Lowell Institute near Harvard University; and in the latter year he gave his Pragmatism lectures at Harvard which offered a systematic defence of his doctrine, drawing on the ideas developed during the previous decade. His work came to public attention when James credited him with the paternity of pragmatism in his own defence of the position in 1898. Peirce wished to exploit the fashionability of pragmatism to obtain a new hearing for his own doctrine but was appalled at much that the pragmatists had to say. As I have indicated, he was much closer to the ambitions of traditional philosophy than they were – indeed, many took pragmatism to be a tool for undermining the aspirations of traditional conceptions of the philosopher's task. Thus, in the 1903 lectures, in a sequence of papers published in *The Monist* a few years later, and in endless unpublished drafts, he attempted to formulate his version of the doctrine and show that it could receive a rigorous *proof*. Much of his later work was devoted to justifying the philosophical tools to be used in this proof. Still influenced by Kant, he believed that philosophy should defend and make use of a system of extremely general conceptions which could be known to have application to all possible objects of experience, a system of categories. Although the germ of his theory was probably present in juvenilia from around 1860, it was reformulated several times during his life, and he constantly rethought the problem of how we could establish that a system of concepts had this universal applicability. Many of his later writings are concerned with the 'phenomenological' grounding he sought for his categories after the later 1890s. Many more discuss the theory of signs. Drawing on doctrines from the nominalist tradition – which, in its central claims, he repudiated – Peirce sought a general theory of signs, a semiotic theory, which would provide him with a philosophical account of thought and language. For many scholars, it is his groundbreaking work in semiotics which justifies Peirce's place as a great philosopher. Many of these ideas were developed in correspondence with an Englishwoman, Victoria Lady Welby, who wrote a number of short books on signs. This lasted from 1903 to 1912, and it was Peirce's principal intellectual contact during the last years of his life. Even in his final decade, he was attempting to write the final synthesis of all the elements of his position. Drafts of logic books are found which date from as late as 1910. The most important of these are the 'Grand Logic' from 1903 and some later fragments on 'Logic conceived as Semiotic'. In some ways even more interesting, however, is an application that Peirce made to the Carnegie Foundation in 1902: he sought funding to write a series of thirty-six 'memoirs' which summed up his views on a variety of topics. The (unsuccessful) application summarizes the contents of these memoirs, and provides an invaluable guide to the structure of Peirce's thought.

He seems to have been an arrogant, irascible and difficult man. In his early years, his father pushed him forward as something of a prodigy, and it is reported that he was the sort of teacher who put material across in a complex manner likely to bemuse less able students; in a candid assessment of his own powers as a logician, he placed himself alongside Aristotle and Leibniz, and the only contemporary for whom he seems to have had unreserved admiration was Cantor. Although often offensive, improvident and eccentric, it is impossible not to be impressed by the single-minded love of the truth which motivated Peirce's writings. He was marked by the 'devotion to the pursuit of truth for truth's sake', which, he insisted, was required for scientific work.

This volume is divided into two parts. Roughly, the first seeks a general description of Peirce's philosophical project, the task he set himself. Since this is to show that the methods employed in the sciences are adequate to discover the character of reality, the part is primarily concerned with examining the substantive account of truth or reality that Peirce relies upon. In the course of doing this, it is necessary to provide a general explanation of two of Peirce's most important doctrines, his theory of categories (chapter III) and his theory of signs (chapter IV). Part Two examines how perception, deductive reasoning and the different forms of ampliative inference are involved in the growth of knowledge: by chapter VIII, we can consider Peirce's philosophical 'theorem' that continued use of the scientific method would provide us with knowledge of reality, that, in the long run, continued use of induction would reveal the nature of reality to us. The final two chapters discuss the nature of Peirce's pragmatism and his metaphysics; each chapter stresses the role of the doctrine in question in the vindication of the 'method of science' provided in chapter VIII. Thus, the second part looks at the execution of the project described in the first four chapters; it contains more detailed treatments of more concrete subjects; and it provides useful illustrations of the applications of the claims about categories and signs which were previously discussed in general terms.

As should be obvious by now, Peirce's views changed and it is necessary to say something about how they evolved. This is mostly done in Part One. The very first chapter examines Peirce's first published views from the late 1860s, with the aim of giving a general account of a number of Peircean themes. Although Peirce's thinking soon progressed beyond the views expressed in those papers, they are still among his most widely read writings and we can see in them many of the themes which emerge in more developed form in later writings. Chapter II discusses views about truth from two periods. First the well-known discussion from the *Popular Science Monthly* articles from the late 1870s, and the second the arguments from around 1900 which ground a definition of truth in studies in ethics and aesthetics. The latter discussion was a response to what Peirce had early seen to be deeply inadequate in the earlier work, an unintended but essential reliance on psychological theories in a philosophical discussion. This bifurcation into 'early and late' Peirce is the most important chrónological division for the understanding of his thought, but chapter III fills out the chronology a bit further. We there consider three distinct arguments that Peirce uses to defend his theory of categories. Although he attached importance to all three to the end of his life, they enter his writings at different times; and we can understand something about the development of his thought by noticing what prompts him twice to seek additional defence for his categories. We see development in his philosophical views by finding development in the arguments for his categories.

Peirce was exceptionally well read in the history of philosophy, and much of his work can be read as a commentary upon earlier thinkers. The most important of these influences is Kant, and we shall see subsequently just how pervasive Kantian themes are in his thought: his description of his position as 'Kantism without things in themselves' is fair and accurate. But he also mentions Spinoza and Berkeley as adherents to pragmatism and draws heavily upon Aristotle, Hegel, Scottish philosophers such as Thomas Reid, and mediaeval logicians like Ockham and Scotus. He was aware too of much contemporary philosophical writing: although he appeared to know little of the work of Frege and displayed a very sketchy understanding of Russell's *Principles of Mathematics* (for his review of this work, see CTN, vol. 3,143), Peirce was well read in modern developments in logic; he responded to the work of other pragmatists such as William James and Josiah Royce (whose position Peirce claimed to be closest to his own); and, in his articles in *The Nation*, he discussed many new books on philosophy and related subjects. However, for much of his life, he worked in a vacuum, confident that he had reached the truth and intolerant of others who could not see it. He forged his own technical terminology, and produced lectures and papers which were not accessible to his contemporaries. We can understand James's response to a lecture in 1903 that it contained 'flashes of brilliant light relieved against Cimmerian darkness'. After he left Johns Hopkins he was never to achieve his ideal of being a member of a community of inquirers united in a single-minded pursuit of the truth.

PART ONE

Peirce's Project: the Pursuit of Truth

I

Logic, Mind and Reality: Early Thoughts

---

1 Logic and psychology

By 1868, the results of Peirce's logical and philosophical investigations during the 1860s were in print; the material that was covered in his two series of lectures on the Logic of Science, at Harvard in 1865 and the Lowell Institute the following year, emerged in five technical papers in the *Proceedings* of the American Academy of Arts and Sciences and in an important and brilliant series of three papers in the *Journal of Speculative Philosophy*.[1] These three papers contain a single unified argument, presenting an account of mind and reality which enabled Peirce, in the third paper, to explain the validity both of deductive reasoning and of ampliative inference. In the course of explaining the possibility of knowledge they introduced many of the pervasive themes in Peirce's thought; ideas were used which, developed and transformed, were retained throughout the development of his philosophy. So, a survey of these early papers will provide us with an overview of the problems that prompted Peirce's philosophical work and the sorts of approach to them that he favoured. We shall also be able to understand the difficulties that stimulated the subsequent changes in his doctrines. Therefore, this chapter will offer an account of the arguments and conclusions of the three papers:

'Questions Concerning Certain Faculties Claimed for Man' (5.213ff);
'Some Consequences of Four Incapacities' (5.264ff);
'Grounds of Validity of the Laws of Logic: Further Consequences of Four Incapacities' (5.318ff).

I shall refer to them as QFM, CFI and GVL respectively.

Peirce begins both of the series of lectures by defending the autonomy of logic against those – the 'Anthropological Logicians' such as James

Mill and John Stuart Mill – who 'think that Logic must be founded on a knowledge of human nature and requires a constant reference to human nature' (CW1 361). As we shall see in the following chapter, this rejection of psychologism – in fact, the denial that any information from the sciences can have a bearing upon logic or epistemology – was a fundamental feature of Peirce's work; it places him in a common tradition with Frege and much of twentieth-century philosophy. Thus, he would deny the claim of J. S. Mill that the object of Logic was 'to attempt a correct analysis of the intellectual process called Reasoning or Inference, and of such other mental operations as are intended to facilitate this' (Mill, 1891, p. 23). However, he did not divorce logic from 'intellectual processes' completely, for he claimed that logic was 'the science whereby we are enabled to test reasons' (CW1 358). This does not mean, as Mill claimed, that logic is simply 'a collection of precepts or rules for thinking, grounded on a scientific investigation of the requisites for valid thought' (Mill, 1868, vol. 2, p. 146). Rather, logic is the 'classifying science' which underlies the practice of testing reasons.

> if we wish to be able to test arguments, what we have to do is take all the arguments we can find, scrutinize them and put those which are alike in a class by themselves and then examine all those different kinds and learn their properties. (CW1 359)

The 'formal' logician, such as Peirce, denies that psychological information is relevant to such classifications; the logician works on the 'products of thought' such as linguistically expressed sentences and arguments directly, and has no need to study the 'constitution of the human mind'.

He employs many sorts of arguments to defend this view, and I shall not consider all of them here. A claim that he places some stress upon is that the logical forms shared by arguments that are classified together should not be thought of, primarily, as forms of *thought*. Consider this printed argument:

> All conquerors are butchers.
> Napoleon is a conqueror.

So, Napoleon is a butcher.

Peirce insists that this argument has a distinctive form, which anyone can recognize: the logical form is realized in a linguistic object, so it is perverse to think of the form as solely a form of thought (CW1 165). He grants that the linguistic object only has the form it does because it can be understood and thought in a certain way, but holds that that does not make the form any the less a real property of the inscription. The case is parallel to that of colour: no one doubts that the letters in the printed argument are black, yet the concept of blackness ascribes a character to

16

things which they only have 'in so far and because they can be seen' (CW1 165).[2] It is a real and objective property of the sign that it will affect us in a certain way. Another objection to Peirce's position stresses, not that such arguments have to be understood by people, but that they are typically produced by human agents. However, this involves a form of the genetic fallacy. Like the 'tester of reasons', the flour tester requires a system of classifications to be used in his evaluations of flour samples.

> There are many curious and important facts about flour which are of no consequence at all to the inspector of flour. What proportions of the chemical elements enter into the composition of the best flour, whether Nitrogen or Phosphorus should be present in large amounts is of no practical moment to him. (CW1 359)

> [All] information as to the forces which produce things of any kind is quite irrelevant to the business of classifying those things. The inspector of flour does not care to know by what agencies wheat grows. (CW1 361)

The logician similarly has no need to take an interest in the production of arguments and the origins of logical concepts. A little later, in an 1869 lecture series on British logicians, Peirce stresses his 'somewhat singular' opinion that the question whether an inference is a good one simply concerns the 'real fact' of whether, if the premises are true, the conclusion is also: information about how the inference arises in the mind, or how the argument was produced can have no bearing upon this (R 584 – this should be in CW2). The non-psychological approach has other advantages too. It makes it easier to avoid errors, and relies upon fewer suspect capacities in obtaining its knowledge; it does not rely upon introspection, or upon some curious faculty for discerning the normative rules which govern the correct or ideal functioning of the mind (CW1 166ff).

Thus, Peirce defines logic, not as a descriptive or normative theory of human thought and inference, but as part of a general study of representations such as propositions and arguments. It restricts itself to a particular set of the facts about representations – those involved with the reference of words and predicates, the truth conditions of sentences and the validity of arguments, and classifies arguments in ways that are relevant to our concerns with discovering the truth. Since linguistic objects and thoughts are alike representations – this will receive further discussion in section 4 of this chapter – the study of representation will yield information about the 'forms of thought': however, logic benefits from abstracting from this aspect of them and studying publicly accessible linguistic expressions of arguments.

Peirce's project extends beyond providing a 'formal' non-psychological account of the validity of the different forms of deductive inference.

17

He wants to provide an explanation of the inferences that are central to the growth of scientific knowledge, to classify the different kinds of ampliative argument and provide an objective explanation of their validity. The importance he attaches to this task is evident from GVL.

> According to Kant, the central question of philosophy is 'How are synthetical judgments *a priori* possible?' But antecedently to this comes the question how synthetical judgments in general, and still more generally, how synthetical reasoning is possible at all. When the answer to the general problem has been obtained, the particular one will be comparatively simple. This is the lock upon the door of philosophy. (5.348)

Peirce sees that the strongest argument in favour of the psychological approach to logic rests on the claim that a formal logic of induction is not possible, and he is aware of considerations that seem to support that claim. One can see him facing an unpalatable dilemma which suggests that either the logic of induction must rest content with describing the inductive strategies that we find it reasonable to adopt, or else it must ground induction in some metaphysical principle such as the benevolence of God. Neither horn is compatible with the autonomy of logic as Peirce conceives it: the first leads straight to psychologism, the second to grounding logic in suspect reasonings which seem themselves to cry out for logical scrutiny. The aim of the three papers in the *Journal of Speculative Philosophy* is to overcome this dilemma and unlock the door of philosophy. The final paper uses the results of the other two to explain the validity of induction. In the earlier papers, he attacks the assumptions upon which the dilemma rests, and provides an account of mind and reality which rests upon a rejection of these assumptions. In the following section, I shall elaborate the set of Cartesian and nominalistic assumptions which support the dilemma – they represent tendencies of thought which, according to Peirce, have tainted most European logic and epistemology.

Peirce's underlying motivations are metaphysical. As will become clearer in the third chapter, he saw his work as part of an attempt to carry through successfully the project that Kant attempted in the first *Critique*: much of his work in logic was prompted by the recognition that it would be necessary to correct Kant's logic before an adequate system of categories could be constructed. In one of the papers in the *Proceedings* of the American Academy, the points are given a straightforwardly Kantian cast. The motivation for having a non-psychological logic was that Peirce shared the opinion of 'several great thinkers' that the only successful method of inquiry in metaphysics 'yet lighted upon is that of adopting our logic as our metaphysics' (CW1 490). Thus, our logic will provide a non-psychological examination of the forms of human thought; and the account of synthetic inference will explain how we are able to unify the manifold of our experience. And, in advancing to explain the 'grounds of validity of the laws of logic', both deductive and inductive, Peirce presents a distinctive and original metaphysical view.

Let us now turn to some of the details of the position Peirce defended in these papers. I should stress, once again, that these are early papers. They reflect views not yet fully formed, and, in spite of Peirce's subsequent admiration of them, we must recognize that they contain a lot that is sketchy, confused and obscure; many of the positions we find in them were quickly superseded. Since their influence has been considerable, they cannot be ignored in a book-length treatment of Peirce's philosophy. Moreover, offering a reading of them serves two further purposes: it enables us to introduce some important elements in Peirce's thought and display some of their systematic connections; and it provides helpful background for understanding the ways in which his ideas developed after 1870. The discussion in this chapter will be concerned with describing and understanding the general themes that characterized Peirce's thought at this time; I shall not evaluate the details or probe the intentions underlying some of the more gnomic remarks that the papers contain. In this respect, the discussion is still introductory, preparing for the examination of Peirce's mature doctrines in subsequent chapters.

2 Nominalism and the spirit of Cartesianism

The first section of the second of the 1868 papers, CFI, repudiates the 'spirit of Cartesianism': Cartesianism is distinguished from scholastic philosophy by four errors about the nature of knowledge and philosophical method. Each of the four distinctive marks of Cartesianism represents a departure from a truth which had earlier been acknowledged.

(1) It teaches that philosophy must begin with universal doubt; whereas scholasticism had never questioned essentials.
(2) It teaches that the ultimate test of certainty is to be found in the individual consciousness; whereas scholasticism had rested on the testimony of sages and the Catholic church.
(3) The multiform argumentation of the middle ages is replaced by a single thread of inference depending often upon inconspicuous premisses.
(4) Scholasticism had its mysteries of faith, but undertook to explain all created things. But there are many facts which Cartesianism not only does not explain but renders absolutely inexplicable, unless to

say that 'God makes them so' is to be regarded as an explanation.
(5.264)

Peirce claims that 'modern science and modern logic' require that the
Cartesian assumptions be rejected and call for something closer to the
scholastic outlook. His four counterclaims represent doctrines that he
often restated. Universal doubt is a fiction, and we should not pretend
to doubt what we have no real reason for doubting. We should
contribute to the progress towards knowledge of a community of
inquirers, trusting to the 'multitude and variety' of our reasonings rather
than to the strength of any one. Our reasonings 'should not form a
chain that is no stronger than its weakest link, but a cable whose fibres
may be ever so slender, provided they are sufficiently numerous and
intimately connected' (5.265). Finally, philosophy should never allow
that anything is absolutely inexplicable. Peirce presents an attractive
picture of philosophy as a fallible communal form of inquiry. However,
simply as a set of claims, what he says does not undermine
Cartesianism. Cartesians are likely to deny that the method of doubt is
unmotivated or impossible, and point to the first *Meditation* as
providing a justification for the strategy. Moreover, they will hold that
communal and fallible methods cannot answer to the sorts of problems
that concern the philosopher or logician. So, do Peirce's remarks have
any argumentative weight at all?

One way to take them is as a reminder that, according to the
Cartesian, the methods to be employed in philosophy are very different
from those employed in other fields of inquiry; the burden of proof lies
with someone who holds that philosophy is subject to the Cartesian's
special constraints. The Cartesian assumptions are not built into the way
that central philosophical problems present themselves; additional
argument is required to persuade us that the question 'How is synthetic
inference possible?' cannot be approached in the fallibilist spirit that we
normally employ in theoretical inquiries. Now, Peirce believed that
certain not implausible assumptions – those that make up the picture he
described as 'nominalism' – could be used to support the Cartesian
outlook. It is these assumptions that yield the dilemma mentioned in the
previous section: indeed, that dilemma can be seen as a case of clause 4
of the definition of Cartesianism – the validity of induction is either
inexplicable or attributable to something like the benevolence of God.
Thus, the first of the papers is, largely, devoted to undermining these
assumptions, and the second to elaborating a framework which does not
incorporate them. As is suggested in 5.265, Peirce does not have to be
constrained by the requirements of the Cartesian method in attacking
the assumptions which make that method attractive.[3]

What Peirce is criticizing is a *picture* which is manifested in a wide variety of philosophical theories; hardly any major philosopher escapes being called a nominalist by Peirce at some stage in his career. Since it is not possible to capture such a picture in a simple list of doctrines, I shall illustrate what Peirce has in mind by sketching a typical and familiar form that it can take. This will involve briefly pointing out a few central doctrines of the form of empiricism which Peirce encountered in the work of Mill and others. First, it draws a distinction between two faculties: one is a receptive faculty of perception through which we are confronted with particular objects and states of affairs; and the other is employed when we use reasoning to compare our perceptions and formulate general laws and theories to explain them and predict their future course. In typical forms, the impressions of sense are wholly singular. We are acquainted with, for example, particular red objects or particular persons but we are not acquainted with the general character of redness or personhood. Our awareness of what we perceive as instantiating general properties reflects the activity of the second faculty. The second element is a distinctive conception of reality. By the time he wrote an important review of Berkeley's works in 1870, Peirce was convinced that this concept of the real was the essential feature of the nominalist picture. It thinks of reality as what is encountered in perception, as the efficient cause of our sensations. A proposition is true if it fits the world that acts upon the first of the two faculties to produce our sensations or impressions. Thus, according to the nominalist, our thoughts

> have been caused by sensations, and those sensations are caused by something out of the mind. This thing out of the mind, which directly influences sensation, and through sensation thought, because it *is* out of the mind, is independent of how we think it, and is, in short, the real. (8.12)

In the 1868 papers, these doctrines are captured in the claim that we have 'intuitions'. QFM begins,

> Throughout this paper, the term *intuition* will be taken as signifying a cognition not determined by a previous cognition of the same object, and therefore so determined by something out of the conscious-
> ness. . . . *Intuition* here will be nearly the same as 'premiss not itself a conclusion'; the only difference being that premisses and conclusions are judgments, whereas an intuition may, as far as its definition states, by any kind of cognition whatever. (5.213)

So, an intuition is a cognition – a judgment or a sensation – whose content reflects not the other cognitions which produced it but the direct action of the 'thing as it is in itself'. As we shall see, the principal aim of QFM is to establish that there are no intuitions.

21

It is easy to see that, once this view is adopted, the role of the second faculty in providing us with knowledge of reality is wholly problematic: what reason can we have for thinking that *reasoning* can establish truths about a world that is only known through its effects in sensation. It provides the means that *we* use for coping with our experience, but there seems no reason to suppose that it guides us to new facts about the reality which prompts our perceptions. Unless the faculty is backed up by a metaphysical guarantee provided by a benevolent deity, there seems to be no task left to the logician apart from providing some sort of description of the laws governing the normal functioning of this faculty, perhaps the laws of the association of ideas. For example, since all we know of reality consists in representations of *singular* objects and states, we have no guarantee that the general laws and properties that we 'discover' have anything corresponding to them in reality at all. Thus, the picture leads both to a nominalistic construal of laws and general concepts, and to a sceptical psychologism which defends the psychological approach to logic as all we have left, since Peirce's desire for an autonomous objective account of synthetic reasoning cannot be satisfied.

The links between this picture and the Cartesian approach to philosophy are straightforward. If we desire to hold only true beliefs, and we hold to the nominalist view of reality, then we have a reason to doubt any belief which results from our cognitive activity. We cannot adopt fallibilistic methods because we cannot trust to reasoning to remove or correct errors which may emerge at a certain state of inquiry; any self-correction that relies upon general propositions is suspect. The only way to keep a grip on reality is to venture as little as possible from the security of our intuitions, employing only steps of reasoning which carry no risk of transforming truth into falsehood. Indeed, as Descartes recognized through his use of the malignant demon hypothesis, once the nominalist picture is adopted, scepticism can extend to our intuitions themselves. If the intuition is solely determined by the action of the external object upon it, how can we be justified in supposing that it accurately reproduces the character of reality? Peirce remarks on several occasions that nominalism leads directly to a picture of reality as a realm of unknowable things in themselves (5.312; 6.492).

Peirce traced the development of this nominalist picture from mediaeval nominalists such as Ockham, through Hobbes, Berkeley, Locke and Hume to nineteenth-century epistemologists such as James Mill and John Stuart Mill; subsequently, as we shall see below, he even came to see Kant as an heir to this tradition. His perception of this history is clear from the discussion in the 1870 Berkeley review (8.7ff), and from a fascinating review of a new edition of James Mill's *Analysis of the Phenomena of the Human Mind* – 'a really great Nominalistic book' (8.37) – in *The Nation* (CTN, vol. 1, p. 32). I lack the space to discuss

Peirce's understanding of mediaeval philosophy here, but the reader will find a useful discussion of it in Boler (1963, 1980). We must now turn to Peirce's attempt to undermine this picture.

3 Four denials

In CFI, Peirce reports that the first paper in the series has issued in four major conclusions, each a denial that we have a capacity which many philosophers claim that we have. The four conclusions – which are presented as provisionally established, and to be further tested in the attempt to construct a positive account of mind and reality – are:

(1) We have no power of introspection, but all knowledge of the internal world is derived by hypothetical reasoning from external facts.
(2) We have no power of intuition, but every cognition is determined logically by previous cognitions.
(3) We have no power of thinking without signs.
(4) We have no conception of the absolutely incognizable. (5.265)

Point (1) fixes the terms for the subsequent discussion and enables Peirce to override our 'introspective' assurance that something like the nominalist picture must be correct. (2) and (4) between them challenge fundamental parts of the picture, the doctrine of intuition and the concept of reality that the nominalist uses. (3) has a dual role: it provides a premiss for the development of an applicable non-psychological logic, and is also used (as we shall see in the next section) in order to deny that there are absolutely singular impressions involved in experience. Establishing (1) – (4) provides the room for developing Peirce's alternative account of knowledge, and we must now look at the arguments for the four denials. (To avoid confusion, note that (1) – (4) are *not* simply the denials of the four marks of Cartesianism discussed above.)

He prepares for these arguments by arguing that we lack three specific intuitive capacities; recall that an intuition is a cognition not grounded as or determined by an earlier thought. First – and this, again, is setting the terms for subsequent discussion – he claims that we do not know intuitively whether a given cognition is an intuition. The hypothesis that something is an intuition is only to be accepted if it enables us to make explanatory sense of phenomena. Notice that this is a weaker claim than denial (1), for it is compatible with our having an introspective sense, analogous to the outer ones, which reveals to us distinctive phenomena which our hypotheses must explain – (1) denies this. Secondly, he denies that we are intuitively acquainted with our private selves – there is no intuitive self-consciousness. And thirdly, we have no intuitive access to the 'subjective' elements of our cognitions. Consider a state such as a belief, which can be described using a sentence of the form

23

A believes that p.

Peirce contrasts the object of this state – that p – with the subjective attitude that is held towards that object – in this case, of belief. What he denies is that we need to ascribe an intuitive capacity to an agent in order to explain his ability to tell whether he is judging that p, supposing that p, wondering whether p, etc. In the light of the first point mentioned above, his strategy is to claim that positing such intuitive capacities does not enable us to explain anything which could not have been explained otherwise. Since they introduce themes that were important for Peirce – and also because they represent a rejection of the Cartesian stress on the certainty of our knowledge of our own existence and of the nature of our minds – we shall look briefly at the arguments employed to reach these conclusions.

The four conclusions and three preliminary claims together represent negative answers to seven questions about our capacities. In the paper, Peirce discusses each question in turn. He thinks that the only reason there is for supposing that we can tell intuitively whether a cognition is an intuition is that we feel that we have this capacity (5.214), and he provides a mass of psychological evidence designed to show that this confidence is misplaced. For example, he points out that somebody who, fooled by a magician's trick, swears that *he* saw one solid ring pass through another and denies that this impression involves interpretation is unaware that his cognition is not an intuition. Moreover, we might suppose that the perception of three-dimensional space, or the hearing of a tone, were intuition. But in each case, an enormous amount of processing, which we can think of as unconscious inference, is involved in transforming the two-dimensional state of the retina, or the succession of vibrations of the eardrum, into what we experience. It is not essential to the argument to describe this as inference; rather, he is insisting that the tone heard, or the three-dimensional world, do not determine the character of our experience directly. Our experience reflects our processing, and the information has been coded in distinct ways *en route* from the external object to our experience of it. He also instructs us in how to identify the blind spot on the retina, thus showing that our conception of our confronting a continuous unified visual field rests upon interpretation. There can be little doubt that the variety of examples he introduces suffice to establish that we should have recourse to intuitive capacities only when it is clear that our explanatory needs will not be met if we do not do so. (For these discussions, see 5.213–224.)

So, Peirce offers an explanation of the origin of the concept of the self that shows it to be introduced, not as a name for an object of acquaintance, but as an explanatory notion.

A child hears it said that the stove is hot. But it is not, he says; and, indeed, that central body (which it finds especially important) is not touching it, and only what that touches is hot or cold. But he touches it, and finds the testimony confirmed in a striking way. Thus he becomes aware of ignorance, and it is necessary to suppose a *self* in which this ignorance can inhere. (5.233)

The child can think about the world and act in it, but it is only when it has to deal with testimony that it requires a concept of the self, in order to contrast what it thinks from what is actually the case. The concept is introduced inferentially to explain some anomalous phenomena. In a similar vein, Peirce explains our abilities to distinguish imaginings from experience, beliefs from supposals, in order to show that no intuitive capacity for discerning the subjective elements of thoughts is required. As with the previous case, the arguments move very quickly and raise more questions than they settle; for example he simply asserts that differences in the objects of (say) dreams and experiences – presumably the greater coherence of the latter – provide a sufficient basis for distinguishing them. Beliefs, he announces, are distinguished from other cognitions both on the basis of an accompanying sense of 'conviction' and because they are cognitions that guide action: he claims – although he would hardly have done so a few years later – that it is a verbal matter which of these characteristics we take as essential, which as accidental. Plainly, if a belief is, say, a disposition to behave in certain ways, 'it may be discovered by the observation of external facts and by inference from the sensation which usually accompanies it' (5.242). If we adopt the other convention, then, since a sensation is an *object* of consciousness, our view about the subjective element of consciousness is grounded in an inference from a belief about the objective element: we reason, 'That state is accompanied by a feeling of conviction, so it is a belief.'

We can now move on to the first of Peirce's 'four denials', the claim that we have no power of introspection (5.244–9). As we have no intuitive access to the subjective elements of our cognitions, it is necessary to consider the explanatory role that positing such a power would occupy. As noted above, this does not simply deny that we have intuitive knowledge of our own inner states; rather he claims that our knowledge of our own inner states should not be thought of as obtained by the use of an 'inner sense' thought of as analogous to such senses as sight and hearing. Peirce seems to be claiming that our ordinary avowals of our pains and thoughts rest upon an inference from outer behaviour, which seems very implausible – there is no obvious inconsistency in the claim that many of the *concepts* we use in making introspective reports have an important function in explaining external behaviour. So, it is rather surprising that Peirce does not offer an account of our ordinary first-person avowals. Indeed, in the following passage he seems to concede the point at issue.

> There is one sense in which any perception has an internal object, namely, that every sensation is partly determined by internal conditions. Thus, the sensation of redness is as it is, owing to the constitution of the mind; and in this sense it is the sensation of something internal. Hence, we may derive a knowledge of the mind from a consideration of this sensation . . . (5.245)

The continuation does not seem to remove the thought that we have introspective knowledge of the sensation.

> . . . but that knowledge would, in fact, be an inference from redness as a predicate of something external.

If we grant that 'red' has its primary employment in describing public objects, we do not seem to be committed to the conclusion that it cannot also be used introspectively.

Peirce may be guided by the thought that if we have the introspective capacity, then there should be a range of predicates whose primary employment is in describing what we introspect; any sense creates its own set of secondary properties. This is suggested by the fact that he turns to an examination of the emotions which 'appear to arise in the first place, not as predicates at all and to be referable to the mind alone' (5.245): my anger is something which is found only through inner observations.

> It must be admitted that if a man is angry, his anger implies, in general, no determinate and constant character in its object. But on the other hand, it can hardly be questioned that there is some relative character in the outward thing which makes him angry, and a little reflection will show that his anger consists in his saying to himself, 'this thing is vile, abominable, etc.' and that it is rather a mark of returning reason to say, 'I am angry'. (5.247)

The recognition that I am angry reflects a hypothesis formulated to explain my tendency to have thoughts of a particular kind – although this correct observation does not entail, as Peirce supposes, that the anger cannot be manifested in thoughts about *inner* objects, such as pains. This suggests that Peirce might have it in mind that my judgment that I have a sensation of red, or that I am angry, can always be an inference from my wanting to make certain public utterances – that something is red or vile. But surely introspection would be required to establish that I have these dispositions or make these judgments, so the argument seems inconclusive.

The argument could perhaps be rescued along these lines, using

Peirce's account of the self. The premisses from which one begins are of the form

That object is red.

The advance to the first person

That looks red to me.

uses a theoretical notion introduced, as we saw, to explain facts. And the sensation, or emotion, is introduced to explain the thoughts one judges oneself to have. Now, as an account of ordinary avowals, this seems very implausible, but there is more to be said for it as an account of concept formation – it resembles accounts advanced by Sellars (1963, ch. 5) Reichenbach (1938, ch. 3) and others. If the claim is that all psychological predicates are introduced to explain public phenomena, and are answerable to public criteria, then Peirce offers a sample of two cases as part of a (weak) inductive argument for the conclusion. I suspect that this is all the conclusion that he requires for his subsequent discussion. To reach the stronger conclusion, he requires either a plausible treatment of ordinary avowals which does not introduce an introspective faculty, or a demonstration that the thesis about concept formation is incompatible with the existence of such a faculty.

The thesis about concept formation is required for establishing denial (3); we have no capacity for thinking without signs. Roughly, the claim is that all thought takes the form of overt linguistic activity, conscious inner dialogue, or unconscious inference which is modelled on linguistic behaviour. This doctrine is important for Peirce, and its acceptability will turn on whether it can be elaborated in a satisfactory fashion. The argument in QFM is brief. From the premiss that ('plainly') the only thoughts evidenced in external facts are in signs, Peirce exploits denial (1) to infer that the only thoughts that are knowable are those that are in signs. He helps himself to the assumption that anything which exists is knowable, in order to derive the stronger conclusion that all thought is in signs (5.251). Denial (1) is required to block the claim that we are aware of other sorts of thoughts in introspection: but since, as I noted, it is an induction from a sample of two it cannot offer much support to a conclusion about other sorts of cognitions.

Peirce next moves on to the claim that we have no conception of the absolutely incognizable (5.254–8). He glosses this as the thesis that 'cognizability (in its widest sense) and being are not merely metaphysically the same, but are synonymous terms' (5.257): and we can see it as an early appearance of the verificationist doctrine that we can make no sense of there being objects that we cannot have knowledge of, properties whose presence we could never confirm, or true propositions that cannot be known to be true. This is the first move towards the account of truth and reality which, as we shall see below, Peirce wants to oppose to the nominalist picture. There is little point dwelling over the arguments he offers here, beyond noting that they employ two general strategies. He deflects the counterexample provided by generalizations such as

All ruminants are cloven-hoofed.

which, since they cover a possible infinity of cases, cannot be verified conclusively, by asserting that inductive support can provide them with a weaker but legitimate degree of justification. He gestures towards a *semantic* argument which should show that, since the function of concepts is to enable us to make sense of experience, and since concepts are acquired by abstraction from what is experienced, we could not conceive of a state of affairs as one which would transcend our capacities for verification.

Finally, we can examine the argument for denial (2) in the final section of QFM. The conclusion is that we have no reason to suppose that there are any intuitions at all; every cognition is determined logically by earlier cognitions. As Peirce notes, there is strong *prima facie* support for the doctrine of intuition in the fact that if all our cognitions are determined by earlier *thoughts*, it is hard to see how perception, for example, can be a source of new information. But, in line with his earlier conclusions, the burden of proof is with the defender of intuitions to show that they must be invoked to explain 'external' facts. In line with earlier remarks about the meaning of 'intuition', we can take it that the examples of cognition that Peirce is here most concerned with are sensations rather than conceptual thoughts – typical forms of the nominalist picture hold that sensations result immediately from the action of the object of thought on the mind. Reason then describes and theorizes about these sensations. QFM employs three major arguments: first, Peirce claims that the doctrine of intuition offers a *non*-explanation of the character of the intuition; second, he holds that it is impossible that we should ever identify an intuition, so they are 'incognizable objects'; and third, that the opponent of intuitions is not powerless to account for the introduction of new information into thought. The first of these is familiar from arguments from the nominalist picture to scepticism. The character of the 'thing as it is in itself' is invoked to explain the character of the intuition, but our only access to the explanans is through its effect upon the explanandum. It is a plausible constraint upon explanation that there should be evidence for the existence of the explaining event independently of the existence of what it explains (5.260). Thus, the defender of intuition claims to explain something in terms which cannot explain anything. It would not do for the nominalist to support his explanation by invoking his theoretical beliefs about the nature of reality, thus providing independent support for his hypothesis, because the claim of those theoretical beliefs to describe the 'thing as it is in itself' is wholly problematic.

The other two arguments exploit the claim that cognition is continuous, that our mental life does not consist in a discrete series of distinct cognitive events one after another. This stress upon continuity will recur throughout this discussion – it is the core of Peirce's doctrine of synechism. For the present, note simply that its plausibility when our examples of intuitions are sensations or sense data, is much greater than if we think of them as primarily full-fledged judgments. My sensory experience of looking at a red book seems to be a continuous phenomenon, and not broken into discrete elements. However, there is justice in the complaint of many commentators, that Peirce does not argue for the claim that this cognition is continuous. Peirce then argues that it is only at the instant at which the new cognition comes into consciousness that it is an intuition – in which case, any apprehension of it would itself have to take no time, which is not possible. (See 5.262 for this obscure argument.)

The argument with which the first paper finishes is supposed to undermine the suspicion that there must be something analogous to a first premiss, which would have to be an intuition. It is an attempt to suggest a picture whereby, given the continuity of cognition, the claim that there must be absolute first premisses involves a fallacy analogous to that involved in Zeno's paradoxes of motion; the argument is found at 5.263 and also, an earlier version, at CW1 489. Roughly, Peirce offers a picture of a sensation or experience 'growing' very rapidly to full consciousness, passing through a continuous process of mental organiza- tion through which it becomes steadily clearer. Since this process is continuous, there need be no first member of the series of cognitions which is actually in consciousness. 'And the only ultimate premiss is the matter of fact itself which is not in the consciousness' (CW1 489). Moreover, we are to think of this as a process whereby later stages are logically determined by earlier stages in the growth of the sensation. At this stage, our only response must be that the picture needs to be worked out in much greater detail before we can begin to evaluate it. Both thinking of this as a continuous process of growth and explaining it in terms of logical determination are very unclear; and the metaphor of 'ultimate premiss' for the external state of affairs requires substantial unpacking.

I have not thought it worthwhile to discuss all of these arguments in detail both because many of them are presented in a sketchy fashion, and because I am more interested in letting them introduce themes which will be pursued more fully in subsequent chapters. The negative arguments certainly do not refute the nominalist picture, although they

29

raise important problems for someone who wants a developed defence of it.

The picture can only be replaced by providing an adequate and defensible alternative, and we must now turn to the leading moves involved in Peirce's first sustained attempt to meet this challenge.

4 The logical conception of mind

In this section, we shall encounter three of Peirce's central doctrines: the fundamental classification of arguments he employs at the basis of his logic; his account of representation; and his alternative to the nominalist account of reality. Building on the results of QFM, he attempts, in the earlier sections of CFI, to construct an account of mind which will enable him to avoid the dilemma posed at the end of section 1. It must provide room for the vindication of synthetic inference; it must allow that an autonomous logic studies the forms of thoughts and provides results applicable in the evaluation of human reasoning; and it must allow that there are no intuitions. Tenuously claiming to be drawing the consequences of the denials of the first paper, he claims:

All mental events are inferences.
In fact, all mental events are *valid* inferences.
All mental phenomena are signs or representations.

We may grant him that (valid) inferences are evidenced in external behaviour, and that claiming that every mental event is an inference provides that there are no intuitions: but his theory goes well beyond those acceptable claims. The first step towards understanding it is to introduce some of the ideas in Peirce's theory of inference.

(a) Deduction, induction and hypothesis

If mental events are all valid inferences, then a classification of basic forms of valid inference will provide a classification of mental events. Throughout his writing, Peirce held that there were three fundamental kinds of inference: deduction, induction, and hypothesis (later often called abduction or retroduction). His ideas on the essential characteristics of the three kinds developed, and here I shall simply indicate how the distinction was drawn in 1868, using straightforward syllogistic examples of arguments.[4] Recall the example we used above, the parts of which Peirce would label thus:

Rule All conquerors are butchers.
Case Napoleon is a conqueror.
Result Napoleon is a butcher.

The conclusion is the result of applying the rule provided by the major premiss to the case given in the minor premiss. As we shall see in more detail below, Peirce saw the general proposition as a rule which licenses the substitution of 'butcher' for 'conqueror' in the minor premiss. Peirce often refers to deductively valid reasoning as 'necessary reasoning' meaning that the conclusion follows from the premisses of necessity: it is not possible that the premisses be true and the conclusion false.

Induction and hypothesis are distinct forms of ampliative inference; Peirce sided with those who said the hypothesis was a distinct kind of argument.[5] A typical inductive argument would take the form

x, y and z are all dogs.
x, y and z are all mammals.
_____

So, (probably) all dogs are mammals.

As Peirce remarks, we can view this as deriving a rule from knowledge of a case and a result: the second premiss can be derived from the conclusion and the first premiss by a straightforward deductive argument (2.479, 2.619ff (1878)). Analogously, hypothesis can be viewed as deriving the case from knowledge of the rule and the result. An example of the form would be

All Frenchmen are F1, F2, F3.
Napoleon is F1, F2, F3.
_____

So, (probably) Napoleon is a Frenchman.

The second premiss could have been derived from the first premiss and the conclusion by an inference in Barbara. In the conclusion, we apply a predicate to the subject which unifies a manifold of properties applied to that subject in the second premiss: the conclusion is plausible because it makes the second premiss unsurprising. Peirce would have held that this analysis holds quite generally; it does not just apply to arguments involving singular statements among the premisses and conclusions, and it continues to apply when we deal with more complex relational propositions.

Peirce holds that both induction and hypothesis can be looked upon as inferences from samples to the character of the population from which they are drawn. In the inductive example, the conclusion that all dogs were mammals was drawn from the claim that a sample of dogs (x, y and z) were all mammals. In the example of hypothesis, the conclusion that Napoleon has all the properties shared by all Frenchmen, was drawn from the premiss that a sample of Napoleon's properties (F1, F2 and F3) were among the properties shared by all Frenchmen. According to Peirce, their ampliative character is reflected in the fact that whether

31

an inductive or hypothetical argument is a good one depends upon the *non-existence* of some other knowledge (5.270; Peirce distinguishes the three kinds of arguments and gives further examples in 5.269–279). Induction 'proceeds as though all the objects which have certain characters are known' (5.272): the argument is one we can rely on only if we do not know anything about any other objects that are dogs and are known to be, or not to be, mammals. Hypothesis analogously requires that we know nothing about whether Napoleon has other properties which no Frenchman shares. The lock on the door of philosophy is the problem of explaining how such sampling can be successful.

The claim that all mental action is *valid* inference is, at first glance, implausible: it seems to preclude any explanation of human irrationality. It receives only very weak support from the observation that agents tend to accept obvious logical consequences of their beliefs. Stronger support is available from the observation – stressed by a number of philosophers – that we try to understand the behaviour of other people by rationalizing it, by showing that it represents a reasonable and rational course of action in their circumstances. That such charity is constitutive of what is involved in understanding behaviour is suggested by Peirce's own response to the problems of irrationality. He takes several examples of human irrationality, claiming that they exhaust the kinds of irrationality that occur, and suggests that we make sense of such phenomena by assimilating it to deductive reasoning based upon false premises or valid but exceedingly weak inductive or hypothetical reasoning. We understand human irrationality only so far as we can rationalize it. (5.280–2)

(b) Thoughts and signs

CFI contains a brilliant and extended study of Peirce's account of what is involved in one thing being a sign of another and of his claim that all thoughts can be understood as signs. Since chapter IV is devoted to a detailed discussion of Peirce's theory of representation, I shall content myself here with introducing some of the central themes. The fundamental thought Peirce uses is that when clouds signify rain, or an utterance signifies that snow is white, there is more involved than a simple dyadic relation between the clouds and the rain, the utterance and the colour of snow. The fact that we can always ask, 'To whom do the clouds signify rain?' brings out the fact that our idea of one thing signifying another incorporates the idea of the first thing being understood or *interpreted* as a sign of the second. Of course, a sign may not actually be interpreted by anyone, but it would not be a sign unless it were capable of being interpreted, or understood in a certain way. The meaning of a sign is a power to determine observers of the sign to interpret it in a determinate fashion. Peirce expresses this by saying that the signification relation is an irreducibly *triadic* relation; its most straightforward employment is in sentences of the form

    X interprets Y as a sign of Z,
or
    Y is a sign of Z to X.

The semantical relation between a sign and what it signifies is not determined by the material quality of the sign – for example, the colour of the ink and shape of the letters – nor is it determined by any straightforward physical or temporal relation between the two. Rather it depends upon our *using* or *understanding* such objects as signs of such things – or upon its being possible for us to do so. The link between the sign and what it signifies is mediated through subsequent thoughts which serve as *interpretants* for the sign.

When Peirce claims that all thoughts are signs, he means that the analytical framework introduced to account for the working of ordinary natural, conventional and linguistic signs can be used to describe and explain mental phenomena. Suppose that I judge

    Napoleon was a conqueror.

The link between that thought and its object is mediated through subsequent thoughts which interpret it as a thought about Napoleon. A characterization of a thought in terms of its intentional content attributes to it a power to produce certain sorts of interpreting thoughts; to ascribe a content to a thought is to ascribe it a complex relational property. This receives a less abstract formulation when we apply it to the claim that all thought takes the form of inference. If I believe that all dogs are mammals, then my deriving

    Fido is a mammal.

by applying that general belief as a rule to a particular judgment is a way of interpreting the judgment as having the content

    Fido is a dog.

Drawing this conclusion from that premiss also manifests my interpretation of the general belief as having a particular meaning. The sign theory links together the view the mental states are, in some way, analogous to utterances and the claim that all mental action is valid inference to provide what we might recognize as a sort of functionalist account of mental states: an ascription of a psychological predicate to an event or state assigns to it a complex temporal relational character which determines its role in the process of inference. It also provides support for the idea that all mental action is *valid* reasoning by making that a condition of a judgment having a clear content: we determine the content of a judgment by seeing what is validly inferred from it. If much reasoning was invalid, we should need a criterion for judging that some 'interpretations' of a judgment in thought were misinterpretations, and this would require an independent access to the content of the judgment.

In the example just given, the judgment that Fido was a mammal secured its reference to Fido through the premiss from which it was inferred: we might gloss the conclusion

Fido, that dog, is a mammal.

thus indicating that the judgment is an inference. Of course, it refers to Fido, through the earlier judgment, only because it is itself interpreted in subsequent thought as referring, through that earlier thought about Fido, to Fido. The upshot of Peirce's denial of intuition is that all reference is interpreted as secured via earlier thoughts about the same thing. It will be evident that a problem for the kind of theory that Peirce defends is that of breaking out of the network of judgment – judgment connections – and indicating what it is that makes the thought one about a particular real dog. The metaphorical talk of the real state of affairs as an ultimate premiss that is out of consciousness does no more than indicate the problem that has to be solved. It will be discussed at several points in later chapters.

In order to see how this conception of mind, which Peirce probably derived in part from Wundt, functions, we shall note some of the remarks he makes about sensation. The strategy is to construe ideas as judgments, and interpret the association of ideas as proceeding according to patterns of inference. First, he likens the felt quality of a sensation to the material quality of a written or spoken sign; a flow of feeling functions as a vehicle for inner dialogue. The analogy is rather strained, however, for he acknowledges that we cannot describe or re-identify this feeling (5.289), and that all of our psychological self-ascriptions make use of functional characterizations. So, it is unclear that feeling can guide understanding of a thought as the material character of a spoken or written utterance does. Secondly, he claims that a sensation of tone, for example, can be seen as a kind of hypothetic inference: the idea is that through unconscious inference, a sequence of distinct vibrations of the eardrum are unified into a single experience, the sensation unifying a manifold of vibrations just as a hypothesis unifies a variety of data. This suggestion that we think of sensations as analogous to predicates is supported by rejecting the nominalist assumption that sensations are wholly *singular* representations. If an image or representation is wholly singular, Peirce believes that for any property p, the situation represented would either be represented as one in which p was realized or as one in which it was not. The state of affairs would be determinate. The 'generality' of sensory images is revealed in their vagueness: for example, we can see a speckled surface without seeing it as having a definite number of speckles; our sensation is applicable to a variety of distinct states of affairs so is implicitly general. Peirce suggests that all perceptual images display this kind of generality. Chapter V will discuss these views more fully.

(c) Reality and the validity of induction

Finally, we must introduce the earliest formulations of the conception of reality which Peirce proposed to set against the nominalist account. We employ the notion to create the possibility of a discrepancy between what we think and what is actually the case; it is needed to make sense of ignorance and error. However, in line with the fourth denial, Peirce is anxious to account for reality in a way that does not divorce it from what is knowable. He takes his cue from his discussion of the emergence of the concept of the self.

> And what do we mean by the real? It is a conception which we must first have had when we discovered that there was an unreal, an illusion; that is, when we first corrected ourselves. Now the distinction for which alone this fact logically called, was between an *ens* relative to private inward idiosyncrasy, and an *ens* such as would stand in the long run. The real, then, is that which, sooner or later, information and reasoning would finally result in, and which is therefore independent of the vagaries of you and me. Thus, the very origin of the conception of reality shows that this conception involves the notion of an unlimited COMMUNITY, without definite limits and capable of a definite increase of knowledge. (5.311)

Reality is thus a *social* concept; the contrast on which it builds is that between my opinions and those of the community, and more generally, the contrast between our opinions and those of the unlimited community inquiring throughout time. Since truth and reality are here cashed in terms of what would be discovered if inquiry continued for long enough, the account accords with the fourth denial and does not allow that there are realities which are not (in a wide sense) knowable.

Much of Peirce's philosophical activity in the early 1870s was directed towards improving this account of reality: formulating it more clearly, providing better arguments in its support, and, most important, dealing with some difficulties that arise for this early formulation. The final section of this chapter will indicate some of these difficulties, in preparation for an extended discussion of the development of Peirce's ideas about reality in the next chapter. I want now to indicate how the theory bore upon Peirce's attempt to provide an objective vindication of induction. His strategy is to argue that according to this notion of reality, sampling inferences, such as both induction and hypothesis, meet a defensible standard of logical correctness. Moreover it is not necessary to accept dubious metaphysical principles, such as the principle of universal causation, in order to establish this. I shall not go into the details of Peirce's arguments; they will be examined at much greater length in chapter VII. The following remarks should indicate the kind of view he defends. He relies upon some facts about statistical sampling. Suppose that we draw samples from a population P in order to establish what proportion of the members of P have a particular property F; and suppose also that the methods we use for drawing our samples from P are 'fair' – in the long run, any member of P would be drawn as often as any other. Then, once we have drawn a fairly large number of samples, we can be confident that most of them will be genuinely representative of the character of the population – the generality of inductions from the character of a sample to the character of the population would have an approximately true conclusion. Also, once we have drawn a fairly large number of samples, the mean of the results obtained from the different samples will approximate the distribution of things with F in the population as a whole. Thus, successive inductions, averaging the results of the inductions we have so far used, will carry us closer and closer to the truth. This provides no guarantee of the short-run validity of sampling inferences, and relies upon the fairness of our sampling methods. This second point raises difficulties for employing such facts in order to provide a vindication of induction, for scepticism could be grounded in the thought that our observations constitute a most unrepresentative sample of the nature of reality. Peirce uses his conception of reality to argue that, in the long run, it could not be the case that our sampling was unrepresentative, since 'all the members of any class are the same as all that can be known' (5.350). That induction should not work in the long run requires that the population should have an unknowable character; whatever induction agrees is the character of the population in the long run is the reality.

Notice that such an argument provides no support for the short-run use of induction. In GVL, Peirce takes this to show that the employment of induction requires altruistic sentiments. We are justified in our inductions because we know that the use of induction will eventually lead to knowledge; but, since our own lifespans are limited, we have no logical assurance that induction will lead to *our* having knowledge. We employ inductions although we know that *ours* may be unsuccessful, for the sake of the growth of knowledge in the community. Thus, 'He who would not sacrifice his own soul to save the whole world is illogical in all his inferences, collectively. So, the social principle is rooted intrinsically in Logic' (5.354). Peirce stresses the 'logical necessity of complete self-identification of one's own interests with those of the community' (5.355); such self-identification – and the view that this community is the subject of the knowledge at which we aim – is a condition of being able to regard ampliative inference as logically grounded. Moreover, the guiding assumption here, that 'man or the community . . . shall ever arrive at a state of information greater than some definite finite information, is entirely unsupported by reasons' (5.357). We have no reason to suppose that inquiry will not die out with the human race sooner rather than later. It functions, Peirce writes, as a 'transcendent and supreme interest', 'so august and momentous' that it would be impertinent to subject it to rational scrutiny.

This strange doctrine introduces themes of central concern for Peirce, as we shall see in the next chapter. He divorces the motivations behind science from any concern with science's applications, and his defence of induction is a vindication of pure disinterested inquiry guided by a passionate concern for the truth. In later writings, the guiding assumptions are given a more precise formulation, and their epistemological status is adjusted; but the idea of the life of science as a selfless subordination of the self to the growth of something which transcends one's personal concerns and capacities remains a fundamental one.

5 Realism

In his 1870 review of Berkeley's works, Peirce calls his conception of reality the *Realist* conception. To the modern ear, this is somewhat surprising; his theory lacks what, following Dummett, we are inclined to suppose is the distinctive characteristic of realism, the idea that there are verification transcendent states of affairs or incognizables (Dummett, 1973, passim). The verificationist flavour of Peirce's denying that we can conceive of incognizables, and of his equating the real with the knowable allies him with those who defend a form of what is now called anti-realism. Peirce's 1868 description of his position as idealist seems more appropriate, and hardly compatible with the later claim to realism (5.310). The motivation for calling the view realist is that it permits Peirce to reject a nominalist view of universals or 'generals'. We must free ourselves from the nominalist prejudice that the only things that are real are objects or particulars; it is a sign that they are not free of this prejudice that many Platonists see the problem of universals as concerning whether there are abstract *particulars* such as *redness*. The realist picture enables us to see that the crucial issue concerns objectivity; if it is true (really the case) that the book in front of me is red then there are realities that involve generality.

> It is plain that this view of reality is inevitably realistic; because general conceptions enter into all judgments, and therefore into true opinions. . . . It is perfectly true that all white things have whiteness in them, for that is only saying, in another form of words, that all white things are white; but since it is true that real things possess whiteness, whiteness is real. It is a real which only exists by virtue of an act of thought knowing it, but that thought is not an arbitrary or accidental one dependent on any idiosyncrasies, but one which will hold in the final opinion. (8.14)

However, there are serious problems for the account of reality that Peirce offered in 1868. As is evident from 8.15, he is ambitious to obtain a sort of Kantian fusion of idealist and realist themes: the real is defined by reference to the process of inquiry, but that process is characterized in non-psychological terms and it is held that any concept which is necessary for coherent experience has objective validity. Reality is seen as the 'normal product of mental action'. Has he said enough to make this compatible with reality having an objective character?

One difficulty is that the account seems to restrict the scope of the real. Whereas we might suppose that all natural laws are discoverable in principle, there are many singular propositions – especially about the past – where we have reason to think that there is no possibility of future inquiry determining their truth values. It is a *prima facie* implausible feature of the doctrine that it suggests that there is no fact of the matter whether such propositions are true.

However, the difficulty I want to draw attention to here goes rather deeper than this. According to Peirce's position, what my thoughts are about and what the truth is depend upon the future course of inquiry. It is compatible with the definitions and explanations that he offers that what is to be a subject of future long-run agreement results from convention or decisions, that our decisions constitute what is true, rather than our investigations discovering what is true. In other words, we don't agree on p because it is true that p; rather it is true that p because that is what we agree on. Whatever we agree on is thus, ipso facto, true; somebody sufficiently skilful in the use of torture and intimidation might be able to make true the description of reality that he favours. The difficulty indicates, too, the importance of the guiding principle that inquiry will continue for long enough to ensure that the truth is reached. According to this picture, the continuance of inquiry is required not only in order that our inquiries should issue in knowledge, but also in order that there should be any truth at all; our belief that there is reality itself rests upon assumptions of the continuation of inquiry. It is not my claim that Peirce in 1868 defended this position; rather, he faces the challenge of explaining how his conception of reality is a conception of something more substantial. He must make sense of the idea that investigation is a process of *discovery*.

By the 1870 review, his formulation of the doctrine begins to engage with this difficulty. A number of idioms employed in 8.12 stress that 'human opinion universally tends in the long run to a definite form which is the truth'; 'there is a definite opinion to which the mind of man is, on the whole and in the long run, tending. On many questions the final agreement is already reached, on all it will be reached if time enough is given.' 'To assert that there are external things . . . is nothing different from asserting that there is a general *drift* in the history of human thought which will lead it to one general agreement, one catholic consent.' The claim is that there is a definite opinion on which different inquirers *would* converge *if* they inquired for long enough. The problem, however, is to make sense of this; on Peirce's philosophical principles, it is not sufficient to posit an inexplicable 'drift' in human opinion, and the 1870 paper makes little advance in accounting for this.

A related difficulty for Peirce's position in these early papers emerges when we notice that there is no consideration of how far whether we reach the truth depends upon how well we conduct our inquiries. It goes with our conception of reality as having an objective character that knowledge of it might be indefinitely postponed if we conduct our inquiries inefficiently or according to the wrong standards. Our reaction to agreement produced through torture and intimidation is likely to be that it does not count because it is obtained through the *wrong* methods. Such thoughts are not present at all in the papers of 1868; the need for them may be obscured by the claim that all mental action takes the form of *valid* inference, although room for them is created by the remarks about the need for self-identification with the community if inquiry is to be rational. (A poor inquirer may still draw only valid inferences: but he will rely upon false premises about the activity of inquiry and may rely upon very weak inductions.)

Moreover, Peirce is not clearly aware of the point in 1870 either. Thus, developing the point that the realist will not be inclined to doubt confident beliefs on hypothetical or spurious grounds, he produces the extraordinary remark:

> [According to the realist] it is a consensus or common confession
> which constitutes reality. What he wants, therefore, is to see questions
> put to rest. And if a general belief, which is perfectly stable and
> immovable, can in any way be produced, though it be by the fagot
> and the rack, to talk of any error in such a belief is utterly absurd. (8.16)

We can see a sense of the difficulty in some comments on Peirce's review by Chauncey Wright, published in *The Nation*. He is responding to Peirce's claim that although the reductionist approaches of modern science reflect the fact that scientists see what they are doing in a nominalist spirit, science is best understood and practised by adopting the realist doctrine. Wright remarks that the sceptical and nominalist tendencies of modern science should be seen as a response to the 'conservatism and dogmatism' of realists, and 'their desire to agree with authority' (CTN, vol. 1, p. 45).

During the early 1870s, Peirce was engaged in constant discussion with Wright and others in the Metaphysical Club in Cambridge, Mass. At the same time, he was working on revisions of his theory of reality. The manuscripts towards the 'Logic' of 1873, which issued in the famous *Illustrations of the Logic of Science* of 1878–9, reflect an attempt to construct an account of reality which avoided these difficulties. Explanations of the convergence of opinion are offered, and discovery of reality made to depend upon adoption of the correct methods; and realists are allowed to adopt a sceptical critical approach to their inquiries and to forswear conservatism, dogmatism and deference to authority. In the next chapter, we shall examine the development of Peirce's theory of reality during the 1870s, and the subsequent reassessment it received twenty years later.

II

Truth and the Aims of Inquiry

1 Introduction

After 1870, Peirce's manuscripts show that he was trying to rework his conception of reality. He was aware of the sorts of problems that we noted at the end of the previous chapter, and sought a theory which would enable him to avoid them. During the period that he was regularly attending meetings of the Metaphysical Club in Cambridge, the period when his pragmatism was born, Peirce was working on a treatise, the 'Logic' of 1873. This was never published, but we can trace the development of Peirce's thought about reality from the drafts that have survived. The views that it contained appeared in a series of papers, published in the *Popular Scientific Monthly* in 1877–8 under the running title *Illustrations of the Logic of Science*: the series contained his famous papers 'The Fixation of Belief' and 'How to Make our Ideas Clear.' He subsequently claimed that he had been deeply dissatisfied with this work from soon after its publication, and when he returned to epistemological issues after 1890, he offered new foundations for his theory of reality, treating logic as one of a trio of 'normative sciences'. In this chapter, we shall examine both the doctrines of the 1870s and Peirce's later claims about truth and reality.

By studying what prompted Peirce's change of view, we shall clarify his conception of philosophy and prepare for later chapters by establishing what philosophical tasks must be accomplished for him to ground our claims to knowledge.

2 The first stage: 1870–78

We can begin by noting three characters that distinguish the writings of the 1870s from those of 1868.[1] In the light of the problems raised in the previous chapter, they are not surprising. First, although Peirce does not return to the nominalist theory of truth, and still holds that reality is 'of the nature of a thought' (R 393), he places much greater stress upon the fact that reality *constrains* our opinions. Repeating the claim made in the 1870 review of Berkeley's *Works*, that reality is evident from a convergence in the opinion of distinct inquirers, he remarks,

> . . . to say that thought tends to come to a determinate conclusion, is to say that it tends to an end, is influenced by a *final cause*. The final cause, the ultimate opinion is independent of how you, I or any number of men think. (R 393 p. 1)

In 'How to Make our Ideas Clear,' in 1878, he stresses that the true opinion is one which is *fated* to be the object of ultimate consensus, and glosses this by saying that it is 'sure to come true, and can nohow be avoided' (5.407, 5.407n). One of his concerns is to make sense of this process of final causation.

Secondly, there is a new stress upon *justifying* methods of inquiry and rules of inference. Throughout the 'Logic' of 1873 and 'The Fixation of Belief', the method of science is compared with methods of inquiry that have been employed widely in the past, and still are, and is shown to be superior. There is evidence that Peirce thinks that it is only in the nineteenth century that we have come to a clear understanding of what the method of science involves and what it can achieve. This brings with it the thought that we might find a defence of a method which could be used to *convince* someone who was sceptical of its effectiveness that it was the correct method to use. In constructing such arguments, we have to be particularly sensitive about begging questions and about circularity: an attempted inductive demonstration of the acceptability of induction will not impress someone for whom there is genuinely a question of whether to use inductive inferences.

The third feature of the work of the 1870s is a distinction between observation and reasoning, apparently a reinstatement of the distinction into two faculties that Peirce had attacked in 1868. In a draft of the 'Logic', he announces that he has no objection to the claim that 'external reality causes the sensation, and through the sensation has caused all that line of thought which has finally led to the belief' (R 370). There is a new stress upon how hypotheses are tested against observations, and upon how we should subject our thinking to the control of perceptual facts. *Reasoning* is characterized as controlled deliberation, the kind of inference that can be brought to conform to standards, and carried out more or less well. In fact, there is no clash with the earlier view; his distinction is not between uninterpreted sensation and inferential processing, but between the perceptual input over which we have no *control*, and the practice of monitored deliberation that we can carry out with the results of observation. It is compatible with the distinction that sensation is the product of 'inference' over which we have no critical control. This distinction is obviously called for by the first two points mentioned: perceptual input provides part of an account of how our opinions are constrained by reality; and a practice of deliberate reasoning provides a focus for the evaluation and justification of methods.

Borrowing scholastic terminology, Peirce often contrasts *logica utens* and *logica docens*. Both are concerned with standards that may be employed in the evaluation and control of deliberation or reasoning. Anyone who reasons makes use of a set of, perhaps vague and inchoate, standards of reasoning which guide his own self-criticism and settle problems of how to proceed: this unformulated theory of logic, Peirce calls the agent's '*logica utens*'. *Logica docens* represents the carefully articulated and developed logical theories of the logicians. Thus, Peirce's writings are concerned with the development of a *logica docens*, but he is now concerned with understanding the functioning of, and with the critical evaluation of, the *logica utens* of the scientific investigator.

Peirce's conception of reality is carefully elaborated in the first two papers in *Illustrations of the Logic of Science*, 'The Fixation of Belief' and 'How to Make our Ideas Clear'. Before looking at the arguments of those papers in detail, we should consider the strategy Peirce employs in them; this is especially important because a misunderstanding of this has led many commentators to be puzzled by the paper's structure. The task Peirce is interested in is determining which 'guiding principles' are true: a guiding principle is a proposition which formulates a general rule of inference. If all of our reasoning employs true guiding principles, then our reasoning will be logically sound: it is only slight distortion to say that the prime component of our *logica utens* is a set of guiding principles. In 'The Fixation of Belief', at 5.369, Peirce raises the question of what resources should be employed in arguing for the truth of guiding principles. He suggests that there are certain beliefs which are presupposed by the very questions that logic asks; if we did not accept those beliefs, then the questions could not arise for us. There is a division between two sorts of facts, 'those which are necessarily taken for granted in asking whether a certain conclusion follows from certain premises, and those which are not implied in that question' (5.369). He says that it is clear that various facts are presupposed when asking a question of that kind. 'It is implied, for instance, that there are such states of mind as doubt and belief – that a passage from one to the other is possible, the object of thought remaining the same, and that this transition is subject to some rules which all minds are alike bound by' (5.369). Then, Peirce's procedure is guided by the thought:

> It is easy to believe that those rules of reasoning which are deduced from the very idea of the process are the ones that are most essential; and, indeed, that so long as it conforms to these it will, at least, not lead to false conclusions from true premisses. (5.369)

So Peirce is concerned to see what fundamental rules of inference can be derived from 'the assumptions involved in the logical question'; and, later in the series of papers, he claims to have derived the validity of induction from 'one of the facts with which logic sets out' (2.693).

The role of 'The Fixation of Belief' in the series is to establish that one of the presuppositions of logic is 'the Hypothesis of Reality':

> There are Real things, whose characters are entirely independent of our opinions about them; those realities affect our sense according to regular laws, and, though our sensations are as different as our relations to the objects, yet, by taking advantage of the laws of perception, we can ascertain by reasoning how things really are; and any man, if he have sufficient experience and reason enough about it, will be led to the one true conclusion. (5.384)

Amending the formulations slightly, the hypothesis holds that there are real things with the following properties:

(1) They do not depend upon the will or opinion of any individual or group of individuals.
(2) They will be the object of a consensus among people who have enough experience and conduct their inquiries correctly.
(3) Indeed, this consensus is not limited to a particular community but could include any rational agent.
(4) The consensus results from the action of external reality upon our senses and thus upon our opinions.

Peirce's logical investigations are directed towards showing what guiding principles should be adopted by an inquirer who believes that there are real things, and adopts as his aim the discovery of their properties. The question whether the hypothesis is *true* is distinct from that of whether it is a presupposition of logic. In 'The Fixation of Belief', Peirce is concerned with the second of these questions – he remarks in 5.369, that, since such claims are presuppositions of logic, little interest can remain for an investigation into their truth or falsity! So, we can view 'The Fixation of Belief' as investigating the *aim* that guides our inquiries and should be used in assessing the methods and guiding principles to be employed in inquiry.

Throughout his writings, Peirce insists that we cannot specify the aim of our inquiries simply as 'the truth'. In 1877 he makes this point by noting, in effect, that whatever we believe, we believe to be true. The advice 'believe only what you think to be true' is empty; and the advice 'believe only what is true' cannot be followed. In specifying the aim that controls our inquiries, Peirce wants a notion that is sufficiently substantive to provide a criterion to be used in selecting beliefs or selecting guiding principles. The elucidation of 'reality' will provide a notion that meets this condition. Nor will it do to gloss 'truth' in Kantian fashion as 'the conformity of a representation to its object'. He scouts the correspondence theory after 1900 in the Lowell lectures: the object to which the representation conforms must be something that possesses a certain character independently of whether that representation – or any representation – presents it as having that character; but we can only explain what is involved in an object possessing a character by saying that something is *true* of it, so no non-circular, substantive account of truth is provided (1.578). Thus, if, as Peirce sometimes does, we continue to say that inquiry aims at discovery of the truth, we must produce a substantive account of what having this aim consists in.

We must now turn to Peirce's claim that the hypothesis of reality is one of the presuppositions of logic. The argument of 'The Fixation of Belief' rests upon a comparison of four methods that can be employed in settling questions that arise: three of the methods are unsatisfactory and conflict in different ways with the hypothesis of reality, but the fourth satisfactory method incorporates this assumption. The first of the methods is the 'method of tenacity': we dogmatically stick by our chosen answer to a given question, 'taking any answer to a question which we may fancy, and constantly reiterating it to ourselves, dwelling on all that may conduce to that belief, and turning with contempt and hatred from anything which might disturb it' (5.377). If we adopt the 'method of authority', we do not claim the right to determine what belief to defend for ourselves, but rather defer to an authority, perhaps the state or the church, to define the belief that is to be defended at all costs. The *a priori* method does not allow what is to be believed to depend upon the will of any individual or group – the method itself determines what proposition is to be believed. 'Let the action of natural preferences be unimpeded, then, and under their influence let men, conversing together and regarding matters in different lights, gradually develop beliefs in harmony with natural causes' (5.382). We accept what, after consideration, we can all recognize to be an attractive and plausible belief. The fourth method is the method of science, and is supposed to ensure that our beliefs are determined, not by the will of an individual group, nor by what we collectively find it agreeable to believe but 'by some external permanency' (5.384). To adopt the method of science is, simply, to accept the hypothesis of reality, and to resolve to employ only those methods of inquiry that can be justified as leading to knowledge of reality so understood. The realist hypothesis is described by Peirce as the 'fundamental hypothesis' of the method of science; it provides the means for assessing all other rules for the conduct of our inquiries.

The first three methods all conflict with the hypothesis of reality. The first two methods allow what is true to be determined by the will of an individual or group; and while the second method may provide for consensus among those belonging to the community which acknowledges a particular authority, it cannot account for consensus involving every rational agent. The a priori method might seem to offer such a consensus, but it fails to incorporate the fourth clause of the hypothesis since it does not make the consensus rest upon the action of external things upon us. Thus, Peirce's choice of the three unsound methods for his discussion is not simply based upon his assurance that they have been widely adopted in science, philosophy and everyday life – although their links with what Wright saw as the vices of realism makes them appropriate targets for criticism as widespread but mistaken practices. Rather, they are chosen because each can be used to highlight a different element in the hypothesis of reality. However, since Peirce is trying to establish what the presuppositions of logic are, it will not suffice simply to point out that the three inadequate methods do conflict with this hypothesis. He needs a way of demonstrating their inadequacy which will show us that the source of their inadequacy is, in fact, their failing to take into account some proposition with the property that if we do not take it to be true, the 'logical question' does not arise. The conjunction of the propositions we uncover by these means will turn out to be the hypothesis of reality.

Peirce's discussion begins with a naturalistic account of what investigation or inquiry is, starting from a description of the difference between belief and doubt. If we believe a proposition, then 'we shall behave in a certain way when the occasion arises' (5.373). Beliefs 'guide our conduct and shape our actions' (5.371). If we doubt whether p is so, we are uncertain or agnostic about its truth value, then, according to Peirce, we are in a state whose primary influence upon conduct is to prompt inquiry into whether p, conduct designed to replace that doubt by a settled belief in p or its negation. To put it simply: believing that p is a state which prompts action on the assumption that p, but does not prompt further inquiry into whether p; doubting that p issues (in appropriate circumstances) in inquiry into whether p, but no action on the assumption that p. Inquiry into whether p is so is an activity, a 'struggle', prompted by a doubt over whether p is true, which aims to dispel that doubt, replacing it by a settled belief. The doubt may originate in experience which conflicts with our earlier settled opinion on the matter, or in the suspicion that an earlier investigation employed methods that were not logically sound, or the issue may be one over which we have always been ignorant which has now become pressing.

The assumption that Peirce wants to draw from this discussion is that 'the settlement of opinion is the sole end of inquiry' (5.376): we have no aim but to replace our doubt by a belief which can be stably defended and retained. Thus, the inadequacy of the three unsatisfactory methods is brought out by showing that they will not serve to replace doubt by settled belief, but contain within themselves the sources of new doubt.

Leaving critical discussion aside for the moment, we can examine how the evaluation of the different methods proceeds. The method of tenacity is doomed because 'the social impulse is against it' (5.378). Noticing that his fellows disagree with him on some matters, 'it will be apt to occur to' the inquirer that 'their opinions are quite as good as his own'. This arises from 'an impulse too strong in man to be suppressed, without danger of destroying the human species'; 'we shall necessarily influence each other's opinions' (5.378). Similar reflection upon the different opinions held by those not subject to our authority will shake confidence in the method of authority. So long as the authority cannot control every belief, so that some are due to 'natural causes', it is likely that someone will come to reflect that:

> it is the mere accident of their having been surrounded with the
> manners and associations they have, that has caused them to believe as
> they do and not far differently. And their candour cannot resist the
> reflection that there is no reason to rate their own views at a higher
> value than those of other nations and other centuries; and this gives
> rise to doubts in their minds. (5.381)

And they will see that the same doubt must attach to any belief that results from the will or caprice of an individual. The *a priori* method is more intellectually respectable, and has been widely adopted in metaphysics and science. However, its failure is clear.

> It makes of inquiry something similar to the development of taste; but
> taste, unfortunately, is always more or less a matter of fashion, and
> accordingly metaphysicians have never come to any fixed agreement,
> but the pendulum has swung backward and forward between a more
> material and a more spiritual philosophy, from the earliest times to
> the latest. (5.383)

Peirce is not just claiming that if we adopt one of these methods, the stable beliefs we arrive at may prove short lived, likely to dissolve in further doubt when we encounter other individuals or communities. I think that he supposes that reflection upon this fact must undermine the use of such methods. The fact that a belief results from one of these methods will itself be likely to prompt a doubt of it. The methods cannot be self-consciously employed to obtain settled beliefs. Reflection upon these inadequacies leads us to want beliefs which are determined by the external reality that they represent: we adopt the method of science.

A first worry about this argument can be introduced by noting the appeal to the 'social impulse' in the discussion of the method of tenacity. Is this just a psychological property of human beings: we cannot hold on to beliefs that other people confidently deny? If so, it is hard to see its relevance to a conclusion about the presuppositions of a logic which is presumably binding on all rational beings. Isn't Peirce descending to a form of psychologism which he had repudiated in 1868? His reference to the fundamental importance of this impulse is vague and unhelpful, and equally seems to be the view of an anthropological logician. We require an explanation of how such a psychological fact can have a role in an argument intended to demonstrate the logical presuppositions of inquiry. The first step towards a defence of Peirce's argument is to recognize that if the realist hypothesis is a presupposition of controlled inquiry, then anyone who has a *logica utens* accepts or presupposes the realist hypothesis, even if they do not articulate it clearly. And, anyone who accepted the realist hypothesis would be subject to the 'social impulse'; they would find that the disagreement of others would provide a *prima facie* challenge to their own confident beliefs, because it can sow doubt that the belief will be an object of general consensus. Thus, the fact that Peirce adduces is one that could be explained if Peirce's conclusion were correct, but we have no reason to suppose that it can be explained in no other way. In particular, it could be explained if everyone accepted the realist hypothesis, even if it were not a presupposition of logic.

The way that the argument is supposed to work becomes clearer from Peirce's response to the question of how we know that the realist hypothesis is true at 5.384. He sees that it would be question-begging to provide scientific support for it: 'If this hypothesis is the sole support of my method of inquiry, my method of inquiry must not be used to support my hypothesis.' And his response is to explain why he has no doubt of the proposition, why it would be futile to make it the object of inquiry. He makes four points: two are that everyone uses the scientific method much of the time, which shows that no one seriously doubts it, and that use of the method has impressed us with its richness rather than sown doubts about its effectiveness. The other two are more relevant here.

The first stresses that no doubts of the scientific method 'necessarily arise from its practice' and suggests that the use of the other methods does necessarily give rise to such doubts. This is because this method 'and the conception on which it is based remain ever in harmony'. However, the thought receives no amplification in 'The Fixation of Belief', and it is not easy to see how to apply the idea of a disharmony between method and underlying conception to the three earlier methods, because it is hard to identify the conceptions on which they are based. However, this is a thought which, I think, becomes more prominent in Peirce's later thought and I shall return to it below. The final point is again undeveloped but more suggestive. Adoption of any method of fixing belief presupposes that one finds it unsatisfactory that one's beliefs are inconsistent: if the predictions based upon my theories clash with experience, I am prompted to reassess my theories. One explanation of why we find inconsistent beliefs unsatisfactory is that they cannot all be true; 'but here already is a vague concession that there is some *one* thing to which a proposition should conform'. Unless I accept the realist hypothesis, it is unclear what motivation I have for removing inconsistencies or doubting what clashes with experience. Peirce uses this to suggest that nobody does doubt the realist hypothesis, but, if it works, it is an argument that would explain how the hypothesis could be a presupposition of logic. It would explain why we respond according to the social impulse and react against a method which makes the results of inquiry a matter of fashion.

As Peirce himself soon saw, many of the details of the argument of 'The Fixation of Belief' are obscure, hurried or unsatisfactory. The general strategy, I hope, is clear: starting from a characterization of the aim of inquiry as the settlement or fixation of belief, Peirce hopes to derive a statement of the 'presuppositions of the logical question' from a consideration of how certain methods of inquiry simply *cannot* be adopted. Simply asking 'How should I conduct my inquiries?' reveals my acceptance of propositions which help me to answer the question. One thing that is lacking is any general discussion of how such a derivation can proceed, and there is little commentary in the paper on just how the arguments that are offered are supposed to work. Before turning, in the next section, to further criticisms of this paper, it will be useful to provide a brief introduction to the doctrines of the paper that follows it in the *Illustrations of the Logic of Science*, the first explicit presentation of Peirce's pragmatism in 'How to Make our Ideas Clear'. In a later chapter the content of, and arguments for, the doctrine will be examined in detail; at present, it will be useful just to have some familiarity with its role in Peirce's thought.

I may have a grasp of a concept which enables me, unthinkingly, to apply it to elements of experience, or I may advance to a verbal definition of it which links it to other concepts. Peirce promises to derive, 'from the principles set forth in the first of these papers', a method for attaining a still higher grade of clarity in our use of concepts. A detailed discussion of Peirce's arguments will be provided in chapter VIII, and at this stage I shall present Peirce's view informally.

If I believe that some wine is sweet, then I expect that, under certain circumstances, if I were to drink it, I should have a sensation of a particular kind; if I believe that the fluid in a flask is acid, then I shall expect that if I place a piece of blue litmus paper in it, the paper will turn red. Beliefs guide actions by providing such conditional predictions which engage with our desires to make certain actions rational. Each of the conditionals I listed provided that certain experiences would follow a particular action: the action would be called for if the predicted experience accorded with what was desired. By making use of all my beliefs, I may be able to derive an indefinite number of such conditional predictions from a given belief; one mark of science progressing is that the set of such beliefs derivable from a given belief will grow. Plainly, if I become reflectively aware of what predictions of this kind can be derived from a certain belief, I have a clearer grasp of what the content of that belief is. And, I can attain a clearer grasp of my concept of C by reflecting upon what such predictions could be derived from any proposition saying that some particular thing is C. There is no suggestion that this clarification involves simply discovering that such predictions follow necessarily from the claim that something is C: rather, it consists in determining which such conditionals I take to be true – given my other general and theoretical beliefs. The pragmatist principle holds that were I to become aware of all of the conditional predictions that could be derived from a proposition of the form a is C, then I would have reached *complete* clarity about my concept or conception of C.

> Consider what effect, which might conceivably have practical bearing, we conceive the object of our conception to have. Then our conception of those effects is the whole of our conception of the object. (5.402)

This thesis connects with what has gone before in a number of ways. First, it provides a new formulation of the semantic arguments employed in 1868 to show that there can be no incognizables: if such predictions can be derived from a proposition, then it can be empirically tested by seeing whether they are satisfied; if no such predictions are available, then the proposition at issue is empty. Consequently, it allows that all realities are, at least in principle, knowable. Indeed, Peirce applies the method to the clarification of the concept of reality itself, and claims that when we take something to be really the case, we expect that it is 'fated to be agreed upon by all who investigate' (5.407). Secondly, it suggests how reality can constrain our opinions in the course of our inquiries. We derive conditional predictions from hypothesis and test them against experience; there can be no residue of meaning in a proposition which could mean that it was false although all of the testable predictions derivable from it were true. Moreover, we can conclude from the presuppositions of logic that it is sound methodological practice to seek this form of clarification of the content of our hypotheses, in order to test them efficiently.

3   Peirce's project: logic and naturalism

We shall now turn to critical assessment of the argument of 'The Fixation of Belief'. Initially, we must consider two features of the strategy that Peirce employs. First, he relies upon a fundamental claim about the aims of inquiry:

(I) The sole object of inquiry is the settlement of belief (5.375). The importance of this proposition for the argument should be clear, for I have argued that Peirce's grounds for claiming that the 'fundamental hypothesis' of the method of science is a presupposition of logic rest upon establishing that:

(II) Only the method of science *can* be self-consciously adopted as a method for the settlement of belief.

Here, we must examine more closely both the role that (I) occupies in this argument and, more important, why Peirce should suppose it to be true. Secondly, we must look at the sorts of grounds that Peirce offers for proposition (II), and consider the kind of impossibility that is involved in adopting the method of tenacity, the method of authority or the *a priori* method.

Two misunderstandings of proposition (I) can lead to reading it as expressing the kind of pragmatism associated with James and Dewey. It does not embody the sort of irrationalist doctrine that denies that we desire to make our beliefs conform to a fixed external reality. In fact, the argument using proposition (II) is supposed to persuade us that a rational and self-conscious investigator could only allow his beliefs to be settled by the use of methods which can be shown to enable him to reach a correct description of such a reality. Secondly, it does not reflect the view that the only function of inquiry is to settle practical doubts in order to enable us to pursue our ends. As will become clearer below, Peirce thinks that when we adopt the hypothesis of reality, we commit ourselves to the single-minded and disinterested pursuit of the truth. We are ready to sacrifice short-run settlement of opinion for the sake of an eventual consensus which will be stable and lasting – indeed, Peirce defends a conception of 'pure inquiry' which embraces *suspicion* of any attempts to apply scientific results for practical purposes. Thus, proposition (I) does not move Peirce away from the traditional idea of inquiry as a disinterested attempt to find out the nature of reality.

But, if Peirce is not stressing that inquiry always answers to our practical concerns, what is the point of proposition (I)? The best way to bring out its role in the argument is: accepting proposition (I) as providing a fundamental criterion for the evaluation of methods of inquiry already commits us to a realist, rather than a nominalist, conception of reality. Sceptical doubts which grow out of the nominalist picture, supposedly, will not disturb someone who adopts this proposition: he is not disturbed by the thought that, although his methods might produce a stable consensus on all empirical questions, they might fail to produce an accurate description of the external object which causes his experience. Hence, after pointing out in 5.375 that accepting the proposition 'sweeps away, at once, various vague and erroneous conceptions of proof', Peirce makes clear in 5.376 that it does so by freeing us of certain Cartesian and nominalist prejudices. We can understand how someone who accepts the claim about the object of inquiry will find hypothetical doubts fictitious or spurious. The proposition provides a substantial starting point for the investigation which reflects the realist's thought that reality is the natural product of our methods of inquiry: reality is the final cause of inquiry because it is reflected in the stable settled beliefs at which inquiry can rest.

However, if this provides an explanation of why Peirce found this a suitable starting point for his argument, there remains the question of why he thought that it was true. The argument of 'The Fixation of Belief' is brief, and rests upon the supposed truths that 'The irritation of doubt is the only immediate motive for the struggle to attain belief,' and that as soon as doubt is replaced by settled belief, both doubt and inquiry end. It is only plausible to take these as psychological generalizations: they reflect fundamental laws of human behaviour. Similarly, for all Peirce's claims about truths so fundamental that human life would be impossible without them, it is hard to escape the conclusion that proposition (II) is a psychological generalization as well: the social impulse seems to be either a psychological or biological force. In view of Peirce's insistence in his papers of 1868 that logic should make no use of psychology, it is surprising that the presuppositions of logic are argued for in this fashion: it raises the question whether the 1878 arguments represent an aberration on Peirce's part, or he became an 'anthropological logician' some time around 1870. Our diagnosis of the basis of these arguments is confirmed by Peirce's own subsequent explanation of why he could no longer accept the argument of 'The Fixation of Belief', which was that it traced its account of how we should proceed in inquiry back to a 'psychological principle'.

This naturalism – making use in logic of facts about the constitution of the human mind and human inquiry – is a pervasive feature of Peirce's writings from 1870 through to the 1880s. It partly reflected the influence of those in the Cambridge Metaphysical club such as

Chauncey Wright and Nicholas St John Green, and their concern with Darwinian ideas and the psychological theories of Bain. It also reflected what will be discussed in the following chapter, the development of Peirce's system of Kantian categories. Furthermore, it need involve no major break with the earlier work: in 1868, we find Peirce allowing that a philosopher may use any argument that gets his point across; and in 1878, his use of psychological materials does not prevent him employing an objective notion of validity, and studying arguments through the examinations of logical forms rather than through studying the natural tendencies of the mind. Hence in an unpublished review of a book by Royce, written around 1884, he spoke of 'formal logic in its new development, drawing nutriment from physiology and from history without leaving the solid ground of logical forms' (8.42). The arguments against psychologism of 1868 rested upon pointing out errors which often, but need not, accompany the use of psychological facts in logic. When Peirce returned to this issue after 1890, he was armed with fresh arguments which, he supposed, established in a more thorough and systematic manner, that logic can make *no use at all* of any facts drawn from the special sciences. It is to these that we must now turn.

The new arguments rely upon the fact that logic can provide a justification of rules to be employed in self-controlled reasoning or 'deliberation'. We look to logic to provide the standards used in controlling and criticizing our deliberations; we derive from logic our understanding of how we *ought* to reason. A first approximation to what is wrong with the 1878 argument is that it grounds a statement about what we *ought* to make the object of our reasonings, in a claim about what we naturally do aim for. If this were all there was to Peirce's argument, we should be unimpressed: first, even if it were accepted, it would not provide the general argument against any use of psychological materials in logic that Peirce is plainly looking for; and, second, the particular point that it relies on is not without problems. If it is a truth of psychology that the settlement of opinion is all that human investigators *can* pursue in their inquiries, the suggestion that they *ought* to pursue something else is empty. The psychological facts that Peirce adduces could easily be relevant to establishing what we should make our overriding aim in our inquiries. They establish psychological limits to be respected in fixing an aim that can be *realistically* recommended. In his later work, Peirce believes that the logician should not take this response seriously: he should not allow speculations about human capacities and incapacities to be reflected in the standards he sets up. We can see some force in this: why should we take these psychological facts as constraining what is involved in being rational, rather than illustrating the limits of the human capacity for rationality – especially because Peirce takes the results of logic to hold for all rational beings, and not just humans? Moreover, someone with a clear idea of how inquiry should be directed is unlikely to be shaken in his conviction by the suggestion that it specifies an end that is not psychologically possible, feeling, perhaps, that it is as probable that the psychological laws are incorrect as it is that his normative claim is false.

However, exactly how does Peirce justify his later resolute anti-psychologism? He does not rely simply on the claim that our scientific theories are fallible, but rather insists that their results are themselves subject to criticism employing the standards that logic provides. Once we have developed our logic, we may use it as the basis of a reassessment of our current psychological beliefs. Peirce employs the general principle that logic should make no use of any techniques or materials which might themselves be subject to logical criticism: nor should it rely upon beliefs obtained by such means. It is a special case of this principle that we should not make use of inductive arguments – or facts learned through inductive argument – in the logical theory which will be used to ground criticism of our inductive strategies. Thus, his understanding of logic relies upon a distinction between two sorts of knowlege – that which is subject to logical criticism and that which does not risk logical evaluation – and he claims that logic must provide for the evaluation of methods and arguments using no materials of the former kind.

Leaving aside the question what basis then remains for developing a logical theory, what exactly is wrong with using, in our logic, the results obtained in disciplines that are themselves 'consumers' of the standards of rational inquiry defended in logic? In order to answer this question, we must examine Peirce's view of *deliberation*, which he takes to involve rational self-control of methods of thinking and inquiry.

> To say that thinking is deliberate is to imply that it is controlled with a view to making it conform to a purpose or ideal. Thinking is universally acknowledged to be an active operation. Consequently the control of thinking with a view to its conformity to a standard or ideal is a special case of the control of action to make it conform to a standard, and the theory of the former must be a special determination of the theory of the latter. (1.573)

We seek an active rational control both of our actions and our reasonings, and logic is the source of the standards that make this control of our reasoning possible. Moreover, Peirce rejects the claim made by the psychological logicians – in later work it is chiefly Germans such as Sigwart and Schroeder that he has in mind – that the standards we employ in controlling our reasonings can receive no objective vindication (see, for example, NE iv 39; 3.422ff). Peirce holds that any intrusion of psychological materials in the arguments employed in logic would threaten our rational self-control of our reasoning, weakening our ability to distinguish standards which simply seem right to us from those, which, objectively, are right.

Although Peirce is not very explicit about his arguments, it is plausible that there are two lines of thought operative in his discussion. The first rests upon general consideration of the nature of rational deliberation. It is a point familiar from the work of Aristotle, Kant and others that, insofar as we view ourselves as engaged in controlled and rational deliberation, as reasoning in an autonomous and responsible fashion, we cannot look upon our ends as psychologically determined, but must see ourselves as free to adopt any standards or purposes that we think we ought to adopt. If we control our inquiries in a deliberate fashion, then we must claim the power to decide what our aims in inquiry are to be; if it has been observed that human inquirers have always aimed at the settlement of opinion, we cannot look on this as an immutable truth. We cannot rest content with establishing proposition (I) as a psychological law without compromising our claim to rational self-control. Thus, in a draft of his submission to the Carnegie Foundation, written in 1902, Peirce commented on taking the critical attitude to a process of reasoning:

> It supposes that this process is subject to the control of the will; for its whole purpose is correction, and one cannot correct what one cannot control. Reasoning, in the proper sense of the word, is always deliberate and, therefore, is always subject to control. (NE iv 42)

To allow the aim of inquiry, the ultimate standard to be used in our evaluations of our practice, to be fixed by psychological law, would compromise our autonomy: we should not accept limits to our control over our reasoning.

This argument does not establish that we cannot use psychological information when we consider how to order our reasonings; it shows only that we must not grant that our aims and standards are psychologically determined. The second argument tries to show that our autonomy as reasoners would be compromised if we used the special sciences at any stage of the investigation. One respect in which this would limit our autonomy as reasoners has already been mentioned: if we rely upon the fallible results of science in defending standards of inference, we must allow that, through ignorance, we might reasonably hold to be rational a procedure which is, in fact, not reliable. But, the real difficulty cuts deeper than this. For, if, guided by a false belief, we employ unsound procedures of inquiry, we have no assurance that the falsity of the scientific belief will be exposed; indeed, the false belief might lend support to procedures that are guaranteed to maintain that very mistaken opinion. In that case, even if we suppose that there are objective standards for the evaluation of arguments, we have no reason to suppose that we could ever discover what these are. Now, it is difficult to judge the best response to this argument. Some philosophers hold that we have no alternative but to use information drawn from the special sciences in our theory of how inquiry should proceed, and they draw from this either sceptical conclusions about the objectivity of scientific inquiry, or offer accounts of scientific progress which exploit the capacity of science to pull itself up by its own bootstraps and rid itself of error. Peirce by contrast offers a vindication of rationality which derives universally valid methods and argument forms from resources which are not drawn from the natural or human sciences. He offers a logic prior to all scientific knowledge which provides all the standards required to conduct scientific inquiry in a deliberate and rational fashion. If such a logic is actually possible, we can readily agree that it provides for a secure well-founded practice of logical self-criticism, making use of objective standards; doubts about its philosophical interest could only be based upon questioning its feasibility. Thus, whether or not we agree that it is the only way to provide a vindication of the claims to objectivity of scientific knowledge, we should be interested in Peirce's attempts to carry out his project.

As was indicated above, Peirce stresses the parallel between the rational evaluation of reasoning and of action (1.573, 1.606–7, 5.130). Both are 'active', both are criticized and corrected in the light of standards and ideals, and he speaks of both as forms of 'conduct'. In a passage from the Lowell lectures, he provides an impressionistic sketch of the elements in the deliberate control of action which also illustrates how he sees the evaluation of reasoning (1.592). Through reflection upon certain 'ideals of the general description of conduct that befits a rational animal in his particular station of life', the agent forms the *intention* that his own life be brought to conform to them – he may formulate vague and general rules of conduct, adopt general projects and plans, but his intentions are not directed at particular actions on particular occasions. He may intend to develop his talents, to learn to swim, to avoid precipitate inductions, etc. When he learns that a special occasion is imminent on which one of these general plans could be put into effect, he forms the *resolution* to perform an action of a general kind on that occasion – he might resolve to go to the swimming pool tomorrow afternoon, for example. This is still just a general idea, and will not effect his conduct unless it is transformed into a *determination* 'by which I mean a really efficient agency, such that if one knows what its special character is, one can *forecast* the man's conduct on the special occasion'. Once the resolution has been transformed into a determination, the action is, so to speak, out of the agent's hands; the decision or act of will, or whatever, has been put into effect. Having performed an action, I can evaluate it, investigating how far it accords with my resolution, how that conforms with my general intentions, and how far my intentions fit my ideals of the conduct fitting to someone like me. The leading principles, or other standards of inference entering into someone's *logica utens*, reflect his general inferential intentions – he intends only to use inferences and methods conforming to the general descriptions they provide. They too are evaluated according to more abstract standards, and they influence our inferential practice by prompting resolutions and determinations.

The forms of evaluation that I referred to in the previous paragraph were all criterial: an action or process of reasoning was evaluated by seeing how it accorded with a general principle, or a principle was evaluated by reference to a more abstract principle. However, as Peirce saw, it is not possible that all evaluations be criterial. When I evaluate an action with respect to an intention, I presuppose that the intention is a good one, and when I test my intentions against my ideals, I assume that the ideals are sound. Since there cannot be an infinite hierarchy of criteria, there is a problem about the status of the ultimate standards employed in such evaluations. Either we must just admit, as a brute fact about us, that we have certain ultimate standards, or else we must explain how we can establish the objective validity of such standards without showing that they satisfy independent criteria. If we take the first alternative, then we abandon the project of providing objective foundations for science and practical reasoning. Peirce saw clearly that he was required to show how there can be objectively valid ultimate standards employed in the evaluation of reasoning. What he tries to show is that this ultimate standard, which specifies the aim in terms of which we evaluate all of our deliberations, embodies a substantive analysis of truth and reality: it is proper for us to adopt only those rules of inference and methods which can be justified by being shown to contribute to our progress towards a correct description of reality. So, the endpoint of the argument is to be much the same as that of 'The Fixation of Belief': as self-controlled, rational deliberators, it is rational to adopt the hypothesis of reality, and to want to settle our opinions so that they correspond to the real.

I shall discuss what resources are available to the logician towards the end of the chapter, but we should note here that Peirce is committed to the claim that we can establish what are the ultimate standards to be used in evaluating reasoning without using methods of inquiry that could be subjected to logical criticism. He hopes to achieve this by providing a general account of how there can be ultimate ends for *conduct*, and an abstract description of what these ends for conduct are. The characterization of the aim of inquiry will then be obtained by applying this general theory to deliberation, which, as I mentioned above, can be viewed as a special kind of conduct. Admitting that this may distort customary usage, he uses the term 'ethics' for the discipline which discovers those truths which make possible the control of conduct generally; so he views logic as a special determination of ethics (1.611; NE iv 19). Hence, as the final development of a train of thought present when, in the 1868 papers, Peirce wrote that it was a necessary condition of being rational that one have altruistic concerns, we find Peirce making claims such as:

> [To] call an argument illogical, or a proposition false, is a special kind of moral judgement. (8.191)

> Truth, the conditions of which the logician endeavours to analyze, and which is the goal of the reasoner's aspirations, is nothing but a phase of the *summum bonum* which forms the subject of pure Ethics. (1.576)

4   Ultimate standards: ethics and aesthetics

Peirce's task is to explain how there can be objectively valid ultimate standards for the control of all forms of conduct, including deliberation. Since the standards are *ultimate*, he cannot do this by showing that they satisfy some goal specified in yet more abstract terms. The strategy that he employs to achieve this task parallels that of 'The Fixation of Belief' in one important respect: although he wants to establish truths about what ultimate ends *ought* to be adopted, most of his discussion is focused upon what ultimate aims rational deliberators *can* adopt. Thus, at 5.134 and elsewhere, he remarks that the problem of ethics is to ascertain what kind of ultimate end is possible. In 5.133 the two sorts of claims are linked in the suggestion that aims which *cannot* be adopted consistently by a reflective agent are bad. If this approach is to provide the required foundations for logic and escape the objections that faced the earlier argument, Peirce must show that the kind of possibility investigated by ethics is not psychological; the limitations on what we can aim at, which ethics describes, must not threaten our rational autonomy. Moreover, he must hope that the constraints upon what can be adopted as an ultimate aim will sufficiently limit our freedom of choice that the pursuit of a correct description of reality remains as the only possible ultimate aim for the control of inquiry. We shall arrive at our substantive analysis of reality and truth by seeking an account of what can be adopted as an ultimate aim for the evaluation of the practice of reasoning and inquiry.

Just as Peirce approaches the description of the ultimate end of deliberation through answering a more general question about the ultimate ends that can be adopted for the control of any kind of conduct, so he approaches this question by considering a yet more abstract one: he asks what it is possible to *admire* unconditionally. What sorts of states of affairs can we take pleasure in the contemplation of, our pleasure not being consequent upon the recognition that they conform to some standard that we have adopted? We shall discuss below how the results of this inquiry are applied to the problems of ethics and logic, but it is plausible that if an aim can be acknowledged to be unconditionally good, then what is aimed at must be unconditionally admirable. Ethics

> supposes that there is some ideal state of things which, regardless of how it should be brought about and independently of any ulterior reason whatsoever, is held to be good or fine. In short, Ethics must rest upon a doctrine which, without at all considering what our conduct is to be, divides ideally possible states of things into two classes, those that would be admirable and those that would be unadmirable, and undertakes to define precisely what it is that constitutes the admirableness of an ideal. (5.36)

This discipline, which studies what it is possible to admire *per se*, Peirce calls aesthetics. So, we are to proceed from a discussion of what can be admired unconditionally, to a consideration of what can be adopted as an end of conduct unconditionally, and from there to a specification of what can be adopted unconditionally as the ultimate standard or end for the direction of our reasonings and inquiries. The hope is that if our standards of inquiry can be accounted for in this way, they will be seen to have objective validity; the constraints upon what we can pursue will not challenge our autonomy as agents or deliberators.

Logic is the least fundamental of a trio of normative sciences, depending both on ethics and on the most basic of the three aesthetics.[2] To guard against misunderstanding, we should note Peirce's insistence that these normative sciences are theoretical, not practical disciplines. This means that we do not look to these disciplines to *justify* our choice of ultimate aim, or for guidance on what standards to adopt: if an aim is ultimate, it is adopted without justification. So, Peirce is not claiming that we have moral or aesthetic *reasons* for using our substantive conception of truth in evaluating our reasoning. Rather, the task is to understand how standards adopted *without justification* can have objective validity, to explain how we can reasonably hold that the standards we adopt without justification are not psychologically determined but hold for all rational agents. Consequently, the normative sciences attempt to provide an abstract and perspicuous description of the kinds of standards, of all kinds, that can be adopted unconditionally, thereby providing a vindication of the objectivity of the ultimate standards employed in aesthetic, ethical and logic evaluation. Peirce is aware that he excludes from the purview of ethics and aesthetics much that is normally included. Aesthetics offers just a general characterization of what we find admirable *per se*; it has nothing to say about the appreciation of natural beauty, or about our enjoyment of the arts, although its results could be applied to account for this. Similarly, the doctrine of rights and duties is not a part of philosophical ethics. In the *Minute Logic* of 1902, Peirce explains that in order to know my rights I also need wisdom, or 'knowledge which comes from reflection upon all the general facts of human life' and knowledge of the structure of human society (R 432).

The following quotations from the Pragmatism lectures of 1903 exemplify Peirce's view of the aesthetically good.

> [It] seems to me that while in esthetic enjoyment we attend to the totality of Feeling – and especially to the total resultant Quality of Feeling presented in the work of art we are contemplating – yet it is a sort of intellectual sympathy, a sense that here is a Feeling that one can comprehend, a reasonable feeling (5.113).

> [An] object to be esthetically good, must have a multitude of parts so related to one another as to impart a positive simple immediate quality to their totality; and whatever does this is, in so far, esthetically good, no matter what the particular quality of the total may be. (5.132)

The doctrine seems to be that we derive aesthetic pleasure in comprehending something as a unified structure, in finding that a complex of disparate phenomena can be experienced as a unified whole. These vague formulations, reminiscent of the views of Kant and others, do not receive a more detailed spelling out in Peirce's writings. The issue we should press here concerns the methods Peirce employs to reach his conclusions: are they sufficient to provide not just an autobiographical claim or generalization about the preferences of nineteenth-century Americans, but rather specify 'conditions which would make a form beautiful in any world, whether it contained beings who would be pleased with such forms or not' (NE iv 197). Why should these claims have any objective validity?

First, let us note the methods of rational reflection employed, both in determining for ourselves what we can regard as admirable *per se* and in other investigations within the normative sciences. Ultimately, we must use ourselves as measuring instruments, observing what we can admire unconditionally. However, we should not take our responses at face value, but should subject them to a rigorous rational interrogation. The following passage is actually about the methods used in ethics, but the point it makes has general application.

There is no ultimate source of evidence on these questions than our own heart or conscience. . . . But we are by no means to think that the utterances of this faculty are infallible. On the contrary, nobody needs to be told that nothing is more insincere or ignorant of itself than the human heart. It is a dull and mendacious witness that needs to be cross questioned and examined closely in order to extract from it the real truth. Anything that is usually desirable naturally comes to be regarded as desirable in itself. (*Minute Logic*, R 434)

Thus, using 'the heart as witness, the head as jury' (R 434), we interrogate our first descriptions of what we find admirable *per se*, often showing that the object is only conditionally admirable by proposing circumstances in which it could not be admired. The technique is illustrated by Peirce's objection to the suggestion that absolutely simple feelings ('the momentary satisfaction of momentary desires') could be absolutely admirable.

Now let it be supposed that it could be proved to you that, I will not say for a moment only, but for the entire duration of a millionth of a second, you were to enjoy a simple sensation, with no effects of any kind, and of course no memory of it . . . how much would you value it? How many years of purgatory would you be willing to endure for the sake of it? Come speak up. Would you endure five minutes of toothache? For the knowledge that you had, or were about to have, the strange experience, perhaps. But this would be an effect. (1.582)

Such reasoning exposes to us that what we may have supposed to be admirable unconditionally is only admirable in certain circumstances. Influenced by such rational criticism, we may also come to see that the effects of an object on the emotions might blind us to the fact that it is admirable *per se*: it may nauseate, scare or

otherwise disturb us to the point of throwing us out of the mood of esthetic enjoyment, out of the mood of simply contemplating the embodiment of the quality – just for example, as the Alps affected the people of old times, when the state of civilization was such that an impression of great power was inseparably associated with lively apprehension and terror. (5.132)

As so often with Peirce's philosophy, a comparison of his views with those of Kant will help us to focus on the issue. In the *Critique of Judgment*, Kant contrasts two kinds of judgment of taste. The first kind concerns what is *agreeable*, and Kant writes,

As regards the *agreeable* everyone concedes that his judgment which he bases on a private feeling, and in which he declares that an object pleases him, is restricted merely to himself personally. Thus he does not take it amiss if, when he says that Canary-wine is agreeable,

another corrects the expression and reminds him that he ought to say:
It is agreeable *to me*. (Kant, 1790, p. 212)

When someone judges something to be beautiful, on the other hand,

> when he puts a thing on a pedestal and calls it beautiful, he demands
> the same delight from others. He judges not merely for himself, but
> for all men, and then speaks of beauty as if it were a property of
> things, thus he says the thing is beautiful; and it is not as if he counted
> on others agreeing in his liking owing to his having found them in
> agreement on a number of occasion, but he *demands* this agreement.
> (ibid., pp. 212–13)

Kant speaks of the individual speaking with a 'universal voice' in making
this second sort of judgment which concerns the 'taste of reflection' –
the former concerns the taste of sense. Now, it is a condition of our
being able to make judgments of the taste of reflection that the demand
that others respond as we do is actually justified: the possibility of a
harmony of aesthetic response is a transcendental condition of the
possibility of making such judgments. But, it is one thing to show that
this demand is embodied in our practice of responding aesthetically to
objects, another to explain how this transcendental condition is satisfied:
Kant attempts a transcendental deduction of the principles that warrant
such judgments in later sections of the *Critique of Judgment*. It is
plausible that one thing involved in the objectivity of ultimate ideals of
taste and conduct, according to Peirce, is that in endorsing them we
speak with a universal voice and demand the agreement of all rational
agents. Although our belief that others will share these standards is not
simply the product of an empirical induction, our claim to be
autonomous rational agents controlling our own deliberations stands or
falls with our right to speak with a universal voice about the
acceptability of ultimate ends. Peirce does not explicitly discuss Kant's
views of aesthetic judgments, but there are passages which suggest that
this interpretation is correct: we could reasonably extrapolate from a
remark on his theory of categories that it would simply *never occur to*
an agent that the ultimate ends and ideals he adopts do not have
universal validity (see chapter III below), and that this should
somehow stop worries about universality.

However, even if we do demand to be taken to speak with a universal
voice, why should our claims for our ultimate ends and ideals be taken
seriously? Is there any reason to suppose that our claims to rational
autonomy are not psychologically conditioned and an illusion? We shall
not be able to answer this question in this chapter, although the
direction in which Peirce looks for a solution can be indicated.

Two aspects of Peirce's discussion bear on these questions. The first of these prepares us for the following chapter, for Peirce believes that the definitions provided by the normative sciences can be articulated in terms of a system of universal categories binding on all rational beings. So long as we are satisfied by the claim that these categories are universal, then the fact that what is admirable *per se* is describable in these very abstract formal categorial terms provides at least some support for the claim that the ultimate standards too have universal validity. However, we are not yet in a position to evaluate this aspect of Peirce's thought.

The second introduces a style of argument which is prominent in Peirce's later writings. As I have suggested, one way that Peirce tries to avoid the circularities of naturalism is to claim that certain disciplines are prelogical or 'acritical' – they are not subject to logical criticism. Thus, he is committed to the claim that the techniques we employ in inquiry in the normative sciences, and in vindicating his theory of categories, are not subject to logical criticism. But, this is not the only strategy that he uses. There are presuppositions of logic which cannot be vindicated in this fashion, and they cannot be introduced as empirical truths. It is conceivable that there will be no convergence in opinion, and it is conceivable that careful inquiry in the normative sciences will provide no stable accounts of the aesthetic, ethical and logical goods. We cannot vindicate our assurance that there is a reality, or that there are objective ultimate standards simply by saying that these truths are indispensable for logic.

> It may be indispensable that I should have $500 in the bank – because I have given checks to that amount. But I have never found that the indispensability directly affected my balance in the least. (2.113)

Rather, they function as *regulative hopes*.

> The true presuppositions are merely *hopes*; and as such, when we consider their consequences collectively, we cannot condemn scepticism as to how far they may be borne out by facts. (NE iv 19)

Peirce typically justifies such hopes along the following lines.

> When a hand at whist has reached the point at which one player has but three cards left, the one who has the lead often goes on the assumption that the cards are distributed in a certain way, because it is only on this assumption that the odd trick can be saved. That is indisputably logical . . . (2.113)

I shall not discuss all Peirce's applications of this technique here, nor his views on how such hopes must be vindicated in post-logical fields of inquiry. But, on at least one occasion, Peirce admits that our belief that there are objective ultimate ends functions as a regulative hope. In the

Pragmatism lectures at 5.136, he admits that we can have no guarantee that any ethically good end is possible. Employing the whist analogy, he remarks that it is reasonable to rely upon the hope that it is, because without it the aim of autonomous self-controlled conduct is unattainable.

We can now briefly note Peirce's views about ethics and the control of conduct. According to Peirce, the righteous man controls his passions in the name of an aim which has been deliberately adopted: indeed the only moral evil is not to have an ultimate aim (5.130–3). So, the task of ethics is to specify what sorts of ultimate aim *can* be deliberately adopted. When an end is proposed, the heart immediately declares itself for or against it, but the final choice rests with reason which must determine whether the end can or should be adopted as an ultimate end. Once adopted, the end is beyond all criticism, 'apart from the quite impertinent criticism of others': it is adopted as an ultimate criterion for assessing conduct, and there are no further criteria to use to assess it. The rational evaluation which precedes the adoption of the end does not directly employ criteria. It is concerned with whether it is an end which can genuinely be adopted, that can be sustained come what may: the end specifies how one is to act in all possible circumstances, and, in adopting it, one resolves to hold to it in all possible circumstances. If an agent is unable, or not prepared, to go by the requirements of an end in some unlikely but at least possible circumstances, he must recognize that the end is not a good one. As Peirce explains in 5.136, this means that we must guard against two kinds of disturbance that our resolve may have to face. First, we must provide for the 'free development of (our) own aesthetic quality': the phrase is vague, but means, I think, that we must not commit ourselves to realizing ends which, in the fullness of time, we shall cease to take pleasure in due to changes in our tastes. Second, we must be sensitive to the 'reactions of the outside world': if our ultimate end were one which changes in the environment or the responses of our fellows could render unviable, then it cannot be deliberately adopted. As noted above, Peirce claims that we have no guarantee but only grounds for hope that any end is available that can be sustained whatever may occur. Although Peirce does offer some rather vague and cryptic suggestions about what ultimate ends can be adopted for the control of our conduct, we shall not discuss these until we have introduced his claims about the control of inquiry.

What is involved in deciding whether an end can be adopted? Obviously, we must not rely upon the results of the special sciences. This has two distinct implications. First, we must not allow the special sciences to guide us in describing the possible contexts in which the aim must be sustained, for

> that would rest on a misconception of the nature of an ultimate aim, which is what *would be* pursued under all possible circumstances – that

is, even though the contingent facts ascertained by the special sciences were entirely different from what they are. Nor on the other hand, must the definition of such an aim be reduced to formalism.

Thus, the end must be tested even against what we would judge to be physically and psychologically impossible situations. Secondly, the issue cannot be about whether we can, psychologically, sustain the aim in given circumstances. We must assume that we can withstand all psychological constraints to maintain an aim that we have chosen. In that case, it is not clear what we are to do. We can, presumably, judge whether we would be *happy* with such an aim in such a situation; this is not a purely psychological matter, but reflects an aesthetic appraisal of our position. Then, the question could be whether, lacking any knowledge about how likely the state of affairs is, we are prepared to *risk* ending up in that position. If it were established that we should be *averse* to risk – that we should not risk an outcome that we should not accept if it were certain that it would result from our choice – then it is possible to see how Peirce's theory could work. A life plan is morally sound if it would or could be chosen behind a veil of ignorance – in ignorance of all scientific facts – using a particular kind of criterion of choice. However, when the position is spelled out in such terms, it becomes very implausible. If it does not deteriorate into mere 'formalism' – and this is by no means clear – then it is likely that we shall be forced to sacrifice what we can see to be a happier life for an ultimate end which will be adequate in a context which, we are sure, is physically impossible. Moreover, it is hard to find any *argument* for the restrictive criterion of choice that would be employed.

I am not certain that this is what Peirce has in mind. If it is, then it places him firmly within a tradition that runs from Kant to Rawls. The relation to the categorical imperative of Kant is obvious: we adopt an end only if we would endorse its adoption in any context, and we regard the end we adopt as valid for any rational agent. Like Rawls Peirce employs a thought experiment to locate the demands of reason upon conduct, focusing on the purely *rational* aspects of choice by restricting the information which can be taken into account in adopting ends. Unlike Rawls, Peirce believes in a first philosophy prior to all science, so he places more severe restrictions upon what information may be taken into account: Rawls permits appeal to general laws of nature but no reference to particular facts, but Peirce prohibits any reference to scientific discoveries.

How can these views be presented as an application of Peirce's view about the aesthetically good? He is largely silent on this, but I think that the following provides the most important perspective. When an agent exercises self-control, he emerges as a complex and varied creature unified in pursuing an ultimate aim. When he reflects upon the fact that his actions are unified by a guiding aim that can be sustained through any contingency, he can find his functioning as an agent 'admirable *per se*': if the account of the aesthetically good that Peirce has provided is correct, then we can understand how someone can think it proper that our conduct should be controlled by an ultimate aim deliberately adopted. This sails dangerously close to the ludicrous-sounding claim that we adopt an ultimate aim with a view to turning ourselves into aesthetically admirable totalities. It can, I think, be formulated in more temperate terms, however. We derive pleasure from achieving the kind of moral self-control that Peirce describes, and this pleasure is connected with the thought that we have ordered our conduct in a proper fashion. It would be false to say that this is simply aesthetic pleasure: the structure at which my pleasure is directed is more complex than normal objects of aesthetic pleasure, involving patterns of volition and perception. However, we can gain understanding of this pleasure and its objects by calling attention to analogies between the structures involved in ordinary aesthetic pleasures and those involved when we are pleased at how we have ordered our conduct. These analogies, especially because, as we shall see in the next chapter, points of both analogy and disanalogy can be described in terms of Peirce's universal categories, support the claim to objective validity of the results of normative science.

But aesthetics must also be involved in the ethical investigation in another way. For when I consider whether an end can be sustained come what may, my concern must *not* be with what is psychologically possible for me; if it was, then my rational autonomy would be compromised. The question must rather be whether I am prepared to commit myself to sticking by the standard whatever circumstances may ensue. This requires that I evaluate the consequences of acting in accordance with the proposed ultimate end in each conceivable circumstance, and consider whether I am now prepared to commit myself to so acting in those circumstances. This requires that I be able to evaluate the different consequences, and Peirce must hold that this evaluation has objective validity; and this evolution must be aesthetic since it determines how admirable the consequences of the hypothetical actions are.

5 Truth and the aims of inquiry

In the light of the discussion of the previous section, the way to arrive at a characterization of the ultimate goals that should control self-conscious deliberation is to ask what ultimate ends for the control of inquiry and reasoning are possible. However, this application of the results of ethics to logic is not wholly straightforward. In *Reason's Conscience*, a draft of a general work in logic produced after 1900, Peirce remarks that logic 'has problems of analysis of its own, and . . . its end appears in the light of phenomenology to involve an element of a higher nature than the moral end' (NE iv 198). This remark can only be elucidated fully when we have introduced Peirce's theory of categories, but its force is that the three normative sciences deal with the evaluation of things with different levels of complexity: aesthetics is concerned with the evaluation of feelings, ethics with that of actions on the world, and logic with the assessment of rules to be employed in a process of reasoning. The difference that this is supposed to make will, I hope, become clearer below. Unpublished sections of *Reason's Conscience* contain some hints about the nature of the logical good.

> Now I think that sound reasoning is constituted by its leading us to believe what will reduce our surprises to a minimum. (R 693 p. 164)

> The most logical way of reasoning is the method which while reaching some conclusion will the most ensure us against surprise, or, if you please, the method which while leading us as seldom as possible into surprise, produces the maximum of expectation, or again, which leads us by the shortest cut to the maximum of expectation and the minimum of surprise. (R 693 p. 166)

Methods are to be adopted which minimize the risk both of agnosticism and error. With the aid of his categories, Peirce aims to convert these remarks into a substantive characterization of truth, and then prove both that certain inductive methods will inevitably lead us to the truth, and that there are no truths which are not knowable by those of us who conduct our reasonings properly. My concern here is almost entirely with the initial characterization of truth and reality; the two theorems about induction and the openness of reality to our knowledge will be discussed more fully subsequently.

A useful clue to Peirce's understanding of the ultimate end to be employed in deliberation is provided by his many remarks about the nature of science; in the later work, as in 1878, he seems to have assumed that exercising full self-control over one's reasonings cannot be distinguished from adoption of the scientific method. As this might lead us to expect, Peirce does not characterize science as a body of certified truths or systematized knowledge. Rather, he begins by characterizing the 'scientific man', who has adopted a distinctive 'mode of life': what is crucial is that the scientist aims for critical control of his reasonings in the light of an ultimate aim. Thus, around 6.428, Peirce even suggests that knowledge is neither necessary nor sufficient for science: it is not sufficient because 'knowledge, though it be systematized, may be dead memory; while by science we all habitually mean a living and growing body of truth'; it is not necessary because we can take the activities of, for example, Ptolemy to be genuinely scientific although most of the propositions he defended were substantially false. The ultimate aim which the scientist is guided by, the 'dominant passion of his soul' (7.605), is to discover the truth, whatever that may be. All great scientists are marked by a 'devotion to the pursuit of truth for truth's sake'. Time and again, Peirce returns to stressing this point, and we should note some of the implications he took it to have. First, the scientific man is motivated not by the love of knowing, but by the love of learning.

> If a man burns to learn and set himself to comparing his ideas with experimental results in order that he may correct those ideas, every scientific man will recognize him as a brother, no matter how small his knowledge may be. (1.44)

> A problem started today may not reach any scientific solution for generations. The man who begins the inquiry does not expect to learn, in this life, what conclusion it is to which his labours are tending. (7.186)

Thus, the scientist sees himself as contributing to a growth of knowledge which transcends anything that he can expect to achieve himself or even to see achieved. Secondly, however skilful he may be, and however valuable his contributions may be, no 'scientific man' 'occupies himself with investigating the truth of some question for some ulterior purpose, such as to make money, or to amend his life, or to benefit his fellows' (1.45).

The third of the aspects of Peirce's view that I want to stress is already implicit in the second. The true Peircean pragmatist, who devotes his life to science, must have no concern with the practical applications of his discoveries; the scientist and the practical man are subject to totally different motivations. The latter is concerned with obtaining a reliable basis for effective and successful action. On the other hand,

> Nothing is *vital* for science; nothing can be. Its accepted propositions, therefore, are but opinions at most; and the whole list is provisional. The scientific man is not in the least wedded to his conclusions. He risks nothing upon them. He stands ready to abandon one or all as soon as experience opposes them. (1.635)

Once a proposition becomes vitally important, then it is 'sunk to the condition of a mere utensil', and unscientific 'because concerning matters of vital importance reasoning is at once an impertinence towards its subject matter and a treason against itself' (1.671). I shall return to this surprising suggestion that reasoning should not be employed in resolving practically important questions below. For the present, we should notice that Peirce often expresses these views by saying that scientists never *believe* their latest results or established theories. As we saw above, Peirce claims that beliefs are habits of action, to believe something is to be prepared to act in certain ways, conditional on what one desires – 'belief is the willingness to risk a great deal upon a proposition' (5.589).

> But this belief is no concern of science, which has nothing at stake on
> any temporal venture but is in pursuit of eternal verities (not
> semblances to truth) and looks upon this pursuit, not as the work of
> one man's life, but as that of generation upon generation indefinitely.
> (5.589, cf 7.606, 7.186 and many other places)

When a practical man, for example an engineer, makes use of a current scientific result, then he *converts* it into a belief; the scientist simply looked on it as 'the formula reached in the existing state of scientific progress' (7.186).

This point can be clarified if we think of the role of the pragmatist principle in Peirce's theory. As we saw above, this provides an explanation of the content of a concept by deriving from simple propositions embodying the concept conditional propositions concerning the experiential consequences of actions that the agent might perform. This can encourage the view that Peirce's view of science is that it is pursued for the sake of its practical applications: a true scientific theory would certainly be predictively valuable. However, if we are motivated by the true scientific spirit, we allow these conditionals to guide our *scientific activity* – the construction and interpretation of experiments, and the assessment of scientific observations – but we do not allow the elucidations of currently endorsed scientific propositions to guide us in activity which is not subordinate to the controlling aim of science.

Peirce sees science as a form of human flourishing – perhaps as the most complete and fulfilling one; the scientist views reality as 'something great, and beautiful, and sacred, and eternal and real' (5.589). In the Berkeley review of 1870, he eulogizes scholastic philosophers by comparing them with the builders of Gothic cathedrals.

> The men of that time did fully believe and did think that for the sake
> of giving themselves up absolutely to their great task of building or of
> writing, it was well worthwhile to resign all the joys of life. . . .
> Nothing is more striking in either of the great intellectual products of
> that age, than the complete absence of self conceit on the part of artist
> or philosopher. That anything of value can be added to his sacred and
> catholic work by its having the smack of individuality about it, is

what he has never conceived. (8.11; the whole paragraph is worth reading)

He plainly thinks that the modern scientist is possessed by a similar self-denying reverence for the works of nature. Scientific activity, he tells us, requires 'a true elevation of the soul' (1.576); and 'all history does not tell of a single man who has considerably increased human knowledge (unless theology be knowledge) having been proved a criminal' (1.576).

In order to understand the bearing of aesthetics and ethics upon Peirce's conception of the logical good, we must look for structured unities in the life and achievements of the 'man of science'. The first thing to notice, and this is worth spelling out in some detail, is that Peirce can see both knowledge and reality as admirable totalities. As is suggested by the quotations from *Reason's Conscience* at the beginning of this section, Peirce thinks that knowledge enables us to unify the manifold elements of our experience, which, through being brought under general rules, can be anticipated. That we cannot predict our experience – or that our predictions are surprised – shows that our experience is not fully unified. Thus, in 1901, Peirce wrote that any truth which 'affords the means of predicting what would be perceived under any conceivable conditions is scientifically interesting; and nothing which has not conceivable bearing on practice is so, unless it be the perceptual facts themselves' (7.186). Just as knowledge involves a unified manifold of opinions and experiences, so reality itself is known to be rationally ordered. The scientific interest lies in 'finding what we roughly call generality or rationality or law to be true independently of whether you and I and any generation of men think it to be so or not' (7.186). If knowledge is possible, then it is possible to find the entire cosmos to be an admirable structured whole. Knowledge puts us into a harmonious relation with our experience; it reveals to us the intrinsically pleasing structure of the cosmos. Having distinguished these two elements, however, we should quickly note that they are not wholly separate. Since we are a part of reality, our ability to know the truth turns out to be simply one aspect of the admirable character of reality. We can view ourselves as at home in, and in harmony with, our experience and our surroundings.

These remarks will suggest that Peirce defends a substantive theory of truth, which sees as true those propositions that enter into some ideally coherent body of opinions. If this is not to be wholly free-floating, then our rational autonomy must be constrained. It must not be up to us exactly what we believe and what criteria of coherence we employ. Thus, Peirce distinguishes the *acritical* elements of our practice – those which cannot be subjected to logical criticism – from those which are subject to logical criticism. The importance of these acritical elements becomes clear when we notice that a rough paraphrase of Peirce's theory of truth would be that a statement is true if and only if none of its perceptual consequence clash with experience. The notions of 'consequence' and 'clash with experience' seem to be used in formulating the doctrine. If consequence is to be explained in terms of the preservation of *truth*, and if a statement clashes with experience if it is known perceptually to be *false*, then the presence of these notions in the definition introduces circularity. The circularity seems particularly acute when we note that Peirce allows that our perceptual beliefs are fallible, and may be corrected in the light of subsequent experience. We shall discuss Peirce's response to these difficulties at length subsequently. However, we should note here that he claims that both perceptual judgments and deductive reasoning are *acritical*, i.e. we cannot control the ways that we conduct them. Our logical self-control is restricted to assessing our practices of ampliative reasoning – induction and abduction. Thus, in controlling our practice of reasoning, we employ rules that attempt to find hypotheses which make coherent sense of our experience, while respecting the criteria of coherence embodied in our practice of deductive reasoning. A further fixed element is provided by the opinions of others; we seek a harmony between our own opinions and those of our fellows, which enable us jointly to anticipate our joint experience and resolve disagreements.

But the picture is more complicated than this, because we have no reason to suppose that knowledge of reality is available to us *now*; in controlling our reasonings and directing our inquiries, we cannot adopt methods which will immediately provide us with knowledge. If this were otherwise, there would be no conflict between the concerns of theory and those of practice; practically applicable knowlege would be readily available. However, we can adopt methods which can be justified as contributing to the eventual progress of science towards the truth: we see ourselves as contributing to the discovery of truth, and thereby to the ordered reasonableness of the universe. The methods can only be justified as enabling us to contribute to the growth of knowledge; we have no reason to suppose that they will yield information that is reliable in the short run at all. This means that it is compatible with the adoption of such methods that nearly all of the hypotheses we propose should lead to perceptual surprise: the control of deliberation is possible only if it is guided by an ultimate aim that could be sustained even in that unfavourable case. Now, Peirce takes it, I think, that if our fundamental concern was for the practical applications of our theories, we should not be able to sustain our scientific endeavours in such circumstances; in practical inquiries, we risk disappointment and would not wish to sustain our practice of self-controlled inquiry in a situation in which we consistently 'risk all' and lose. If our concerns are purely theoretical, on the other hand, we risk nothing: surprises represent not the failure of our practical projects, but rather new opportunities to learn from experience and improve our theories. Hence 'The scientific man is not in the least wedded to his conclusions. He risks nothing upon them. He stands ready to abandon one or all as soon as experience opposes them' (1.635). The cost of having an ultimate aim for the conduct of inquiry which fits Peirce's ethical doctrine is that utter disdain for the achievements of the individual which, according to Peirce, characterizes the best scientific work. The whole of science functions as a form of ethical substance – the individual finds his aims compelling and his life meaningful only because he thinks of himself as essentially a part of a larger quasi-personal unity; his actions are of value because they contribute to the good of this larger whole.

Before attempting an evaluation of Peirce's position, there are three features of it that I should like to comment on further. First, the later views do not represent a total break with the argument of 'The Fixation of Belief'. First, there is a clear parallel between the claim that the critical self-control of deliberation requires that the thinker distance himself from the concerns of current practice, and the suggestion that when we adopt the method of science we sacrifice a concern with the short-run settlement of belief for the sake of a more stable long-run consensus which will reflect the nature of reality. Secondly, a reason is given for supposing that the settlement of belief would be acknowledged by any agent to be a good: it creates a harmony between expectation and perceptual judgment which, we have granted, is something it is possible to admire. Thirdly, similar remarks can be made about the 'social impulse': it is reasonable to desire to avoid the disruption of constantly finding public disagreement about the truth, so it is rational to want your beliefs to be ones that could form a public or universal consensus. Thus, if Peirce can make good his claim that the normative sciences describe the content of standards with objective validity, then he is in a position to avoid at least some of the psychological premises of the 1877 paper.

The second topic that I wish to mention is Peirce's *fallibilism*. He famously described himself as a 'contrite fallibilist' (1.14), and stressed that we have no reason to suppose that any of our opinions – theoretical, perceptual, even mathematical – might not involve error. Our methods of ampliative inference, in particular, are all fallible. Chapters V, VI and VII below will contain more detailed examinations of Peirce's claims about the fallibility of different sorts of knowledge. A moderate kind of fallibilism often presents itself in this way: although we cannot attain a sort of absolute or metaphysical certainty about any of our beliefs, we may still, if we are careful and responsible in our practice, obtain fallible beliefs of which we may, with reason, be fairly sure. Cartesians court scepticism because they make an unreasonable demand for absolute certainty; the moderate fallibilist lowers his sights, and settles, reasonably, for less. Many of Peirce's remarks resemble such a moderate fallibilism; for example, in an 1884 review of a book by Josiah Royce, he qualifies his fallibilism by saying,

[Upon] innumerable questions, we have already reached the final opinion. How do we know that? Do we fancy ourselves infallible? Not at all; but throwing off as probably erroneous a thousandth or even a hundredth of all the beliefs established beyond present doubt, there must remain a vast multitude in which the final opinion has been reached. Every directory, guide book, dictionary, history, and work of science is crammed with such facts. (8.43)

On several occasions, Peirce reaffirms that the final consensus has been reached on very many issues. Some scholars have suggested that he shared the widespread nineteenth-century view that, in broad outlines, science has completed the picture, with only details remaining to be worked out.

But Peirce's fallibilism is less moderate than this; it escapes scepticism only by a crucial hair's breadth. Someone may *believe* that most of our scientific opinions are correct; if this were not believed, practical men would make no applications of scientific knowledge. But there can be no philosophical demonstration that this is so; we cannot take this for granted in selecting an ultimate aim for the control of inquiry. Our commitment to the project of disinterested inquiry does not require the assurance that any of our scientific opinions are correct; it is a commitment that can be sustained in the least favourable situation where our opinions are wholly in error. As we shall see more fully in the chapter on ampliative inference, Peirce's fallibilism differs from scepticism only because he claims to be able to prove the theorem that, if we were to inquire efficiently enough, and for long enough, then we are guaranteed, eventually, to arrive at the truth. This provides no reassurance about our current cognitive grip upon reality. Logical investigations provide rational support for the scientist's reliance upon forms of ampliative inference; they provide no reassurance for the practical man who is concerned with making predictions here and now.

This leads to the third topic I wished to take up, the relation between theory and practice, and the role of reason in settling practical questions. We have already noted that Peirce thought it improper to attempt to resolve 'vital' questions through deliberation. If something is practically important, he thinks, we should trust to our instincts and rely upon common sense, and traditional wisdom. In 'The Fixation of Belief', there is already the suggestion that the methods of tenacity and authority and the *a priori* method have their own merits, and it is clear that in later works he thought that unless we are devoting our lives to the life of science, we must compromise our logical autonomy, exercise less than complete logical self-control, in order to have beliefs on which to base our actions. In a passage from a letter to Victoria Lady Welby, he stresses that, as a pragmatist,

> naturally and necessarily nothing can appear to me sillier than rationalism; and folly in politics cannot go further than English liberalism. The people ought to be enslaved; only the slaveholders ought to practise the virtues that alone maintain their rule. England will discover too late that it has sapped the foundations of culture.

The passage continues to predict that the 'labour organizations' are in the process of enslaving society, while those currently in power do nothing to resist them (SS 78–9). Elsewhere, we find criticisms of liberal institutions, attempts to curtail the powers of monopolies etc. In part, this should be read as the complaints of an embittered and arrogant old man, already weakened by the illness that caused his death. But, it also reflects a number of themes central to Peirce's thought. One of these is that rational self-control has no role in the settling of practically important issues: rationalism and liberalism look to reason for assistance where it can have no role. Another is that the kind of society that Peirce here admires is, above all, a structured unity with a hierarchical organization allowing for a wide variety of different kinds of social position unified by a highly structured and authoritarian political arrangement. He supposes that liberal institutions cannot unify the elements of society in the appropriate way. Insofar as such complex social arrangements are admirable, then, in adopting ultimate ends, it may well be rational to resolve to dedicate oneself to contributing to an admirable totality which is larger, more complex, and more admirable than oneself; the life of the slave is a possible ultimate end. Since Peirce says so little about ultimate ends for conduct, and about the settlement of practical and political questions, it is by no means clear that this is a consequence of his position. I mention it to indicate how Peirce's limiting the scope of controlled deliberation to the settlement of wholly theoretical issues leaves room for some rather distasteful political opinions.

The chief problem that I wish to raise, at this point, concerns the moral position of the 'man of practice'. According to Peirce, the standpoint of pure science reflects the only possible ultimate end for the control of deliberation; the autonomous reflective reasoner must commit himself to disinterested inquiry. In that case, as we have seen, the man of practice must compromise his rational autonomy; his control of his reasoning must be limited. In consequence, his control over his conduct as a whole is limited, in which case, he does not have an ultimate end. If Peirce is actually committed to this line of argument, then he must hold that only the 'man of science' is morally good; a dedication to the truth is a necessary component of any morally adequate life. The engineer and surgeon stand morally condemned. There are passages in 'The Fixation of Belief' which suggest this unsavoury conclusion; see, for example 5.387. But, any doctrine which claims that a surgeon must compromise his integrity in order to benefit mankind must surely be mistaken. Can we find a way for Peirce to avoid it?

A necessary component of any response to this difficulty must be the claim that one's decision to sacrifice one's 'integrity' as a reasoner can itself reflect one's control of one's conduct in the name of a higher ideal. Just as one can rationally decide to allow full rein to one's spontaneous passions or instinctive reactions, so one can defensibly decide to limit one's control over one's reasonings, using beliefs as a basis for practical activity without the support provided by a rational vindication of applied science. Moreover, one can do this with full knowledge of the concept of truth, and with a reflective awareness of what the critical control of reasoning requires. Perhaps, one's integrity is secure if one knowingly and reasonably compromises one's autonomy as a reasoner. But, if this response is to work, it will be necessary to specify an ultimate ideal for conduct, which can be sustained in all conceivable circumstances and which can warrant the life of the man of practice – or, of course, any of the other apparently fulfilling lives which are not devoted to laboratory activity. Unfortunately, Peirce says little about what would be a suitable ultimate ideal for conduct, and suggests just 'contributing to the growth of concrete reasonableness' (5.3): doing whatever falls to us to do which makes the world a more reasonable place. What this means is not very clear, but there is no reason why it should not allow for the sort of justification of the life of practice that we are considering: the practical man relies upon his instincts, and when they allow him to do so, he does what he can towards making the world a more intelligible and welcoming place.

However, if this approach to justifying forms of life other than that of the pure scientist works, then one may suspect that Peirce has not done enough to vindicate the life of science. Even if we grant that only the pure scientist evinces complete self-control of his reasonings, there remains a question about whether self-controlled reasoning can form part of an intelligible ultimate ideal for conduct generally. Peirce might reply that since the scientist does contribute to the growth of reasonableness, his activity fits the general ethical ideal. However, the following considerations suggest that, at the very least, there is a problem. In many conceivable situations, the contributions that we actually make to the growth of knowledge are very small: we may devote our energies to testing theories using an unrepresentative set of data, so that the results of our inductions are distorted; or we may investigate questions that have no determinate answer. This last point is important. Peirce holds that the reasoner has no guarantee that there are any realities at all; there is no assurance that opinion will converge on certain propositions. The belief that there are realities is another of those regulative hopes, adopted because they are necessary for achieving rational self-control. As we shall see later, Peirce denied that reality was wholly determinate: there is not a reality corresponding to every question that might arise. Although he admits in the 'Minute Logic' that any reasoner is likely to suppose that there are *some* realities on the basis of immediate experience, in general he is content to reduce the presumption 'all the way down to the single case that happens to have come up' (2.113). Whenever a question comes up as a topic for inquiry, it is rational to hope, and to proceed on the assumption that the question has a determinate answer.

> Logic requires us, with reference to each question we have in hand, to hope some definite answer to it may be true. That *hope* with reference to each case as it comes up is, by a *saltus* stated by logicians as a *law* concerning *all cases*, namely the law of excluded middle. This law amounts to saying that the (universe?) has a perfect reality. (NE iv xiii)

Peirce denies the law of the excluded middle: as we shall see in chapter VI, he thinks there are counterexamples to it in mathematics and in discourse about fictional entities; and, more important, his metaphysics claims that empirical reality is vague and indeterminate. But, whenever a question becomes the subject of inquiry, it is reasonable to *hope* that the instance of the law of the excluded middle which concerns that question is true. Unless we formed this hope, and made it the basis of our action, we should never be able to participate in inquiry, not least because, since science does not trade in beliefs, we could not be guided by the *belief* that the question has an answer.

Now, the hope is justified as necessary for the control of reasoning; it is not justified as necessary for living an integrated life. If we think that there are meaningful kinds of life in which the disinterested pursuit of truth is not the ultimate aim, in which the occasional critical control of one's reasoning is required as subordinate to some more inclusive goal, the instincts, passions and reason being integrated in a unified whole, then more needs to be said to justify adopting these regulative hopes in the course of adopting the life of science. And, when such possibilities are admitted, we may wonder why such single-minded dedication to science is required for the growth of knowledge. We may recognize what self-controlled reasoning requires, and use this to construct a conception of disinterested inquiry which is an idealization of our ordinary practices of common-sense inquiry. We may grasp the value of such inquiry, and follow Peirce in his account of how we may see the pursuit of knowledge as intrinsically worthwhile and not justified only on utilitarian grounds. But, compatible with this, we can understand the individual's contributions to inquiry as a part of an intelligible life plan which incorporates practical concerns and other sorts of interests. But, if this sort of position is adopted, the justification provided for the regulative hopes on which science rests may be more complex.

What I am querying is Peirce's sharp distinction of the concerns of theory from those of practice. If we are sure that scientific investigation is going to reach useful truths in the short run, then practical considerations might motivate us to participate in science. So long as we are aware of the nature of scientific inquiry, and do not allow our practical concerns to 'block the road of inquiry' (1.135), then it is just not obvious that our integrity while we are in the laboratory is compromised. However, even if these objections to Peirce's view of science are accepted, his general claims about the nature of deliberation, the intrinsic value of knowledge and learning, and the aims of science can be retained. We can reject the sharp distinction between the man of science and the man of practice without adopting a utilitarian view of science or rejecting most of Peirce's substantive claims about science.

6 Conclusion

This discussion of Peirce's conception of truth and reality has raised more questions than it has settled. In this section, I shall indicate some of the issues that have emerged, and thus provide a sketch map of the philosophical ground we shall cover in subsequent chapters. One of these issues has emerged several times, and concerns the dependence of Peirce's theory upon his theory of universal categories; if the theory of categories is to be used to provide a clear definition of the different species of the good, and to bolster the claim of the normative sciences to a kind of objective validity, then it must provide categories which genuinely reveal universal features of all experience without being itself subject to logical criticism. The study of the categories must be a pre-logical discipline, which uses only *acritical* methods. In the next chapter, we shall discuss a number of approaches to the categories, employed by Peirce at different times, including the final phenomenological approach which was supposed to ground the normative sciences. Peirce also requires to vindicate the kinds of reasoning used in the study of categories and the normative sciences; they too must not risk logical criticism. As we shall see in chapter VI, Peirce held that all of pure mathematics – in which he included our normal practice of deductive inference – was acritical: our mathematical practice neither requires logical foundations, nor does it risk logical criticism. It provides the acritical standards of coherence employed in providing a substantive conception of truth, and yields the forms of reasoning used in phenomenology and the normative sciences.

The disciplines mentioned in the previous paragraph provide the base of a hierarchical classification of disciplines which informs Peirce's later works. He arranges all sciences in a tree-like hierarchy, tracing relations of logical dependence; a discipline is subordinate to another in the classification if it draws upon it for principles or methods. I shall not go into Peirce's detailed discussions (see 1.176–283), but shall introduce the trunk of the (inverted) tree, the disciplines which are not themselves special sciences on which all of the special sciences depend. The most fundamental discipline, depending upon no other, is mathematics. The other philosophical sciences are arranged as follows:

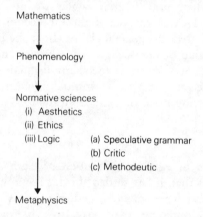

```
        Mathematics
             │
             ▼
       Phenomenology
             │
             ▼
     Normative sciences
        (i)  Aesthetics
        (ii) Ethics
        (iii) Logic        (a) Speculative grammar
             │             (b) Critic
             │             (c) Methodeutic
             ▼
        Metaphysics
```

The first branch of logic – which will be discussed further in chapter IV – contains a systematic account of representation, describing the different kinds of expressions, accounting for the logical forms of propositions, and providing a theory of meaning and reference. The substantive definition of truth is also constructed as a part of speculative grammar. Critic is primarily concerned with the validity of arguments, with deriving sound guiding principles from the ultimate goal of reasoning. Chapter VII will discuss Peirce's theory of ampliative inference and his theorem about the defensibility of induction. Methodeutic examines how we should most *efficiently* participate in inquiry: it includes Peirce's attempts to construct a sort of cost benefit analysis of the economy of research – how limited resources should be allocated to maximum effect in a scientific community; and, as we shall see in chapter VIII, Peirce views the pragmatist principle as a methodological maxim.

The final philosophical science, metaphysics, provides the most abstract and general description of the general character of reality; it introduces cosmological assumptions that are common to all of the natural and human sciences. As we shall see in the final chapter of this volume, its philosophical character turns on the methods that it employs. Metaphysics discharges a number of regulative loans that are taken out at different stages during the investigation: it provides a specification of how reality must be if the various regulative hopes that are introduced at different stages of the investigations are all to be fulfilled. Rational autonomy depends upon those hopes: metaphysics tells us how reality is if they are absolutely true. Thus, it provides an account of reality which allows for our rational autonomy.

III

Categories

1 Categories and logic

We saw in the previous chapter that Peirce's theory of categories occupies a fundamental place in the development of his thought; the claims of the normative sciences to provide objective foundations for logic and epistemology depended upon their being able to make use of a set of objectively founded 'universal categories'. In this chapter, we shall examine the details of Peirce's theory, tracing the development of his claims from the 1860s to after 1900 and evaluating the different arguments he uses to support them. As a first, crude approximation, a theory of categories is a set of highly abstract conceptions which function as a complete system of *summa genera*; any object of thought or experience belongs to one or other of the categories. Suppose I classify a bird as a sparrow. This does not involve assigning it to a *summum genus*, for we view the class of sparrows as a subclassification of a sequence of more inclusive kinds – passerines, birds, living creatures, etc. It has been held that the most inclusive class in this sequence, one that does not result from the subclassification of.some wider class, is that of *substances*. Substance represents the ultimate kind to which sparrows belong. In that case, substance is a categorial concept. Philosophers have differed about what such concepts there are: Aristotle, for example, included quality, quantity, relation, location, etc., so that red fell under the category of quality, being large of quantity, and so on. If we have a set of categories, we have a system of classifications which has a place for anything we might experience or think about.

If a set of categories lists, in the most abstract terms, the sorts of things we think about or experience, then it is not surprising that it should provide the concepts to be used in providing a substantive characterization of truth or reality. Using the categories mentioned in the previous paragraph, we might describe reality as composed of substances, instantiating qualities, standing in relations, having location, and so on. However, it will be clear from the last chapter that, if Peirce is to use his list of categories in this way, it must not be an empirical matter, to be settled by inquiry in the natural or social sciences, as to what the categories are. Like other philosophers who rely upon a theory of categories, Peirce insists that we can know what the categories are *a priori*. They are doubly 'universal': first, they are grasped by, or available to, anyone capable of forming judgments about experience; and, secondly, they suffice to classify any possible object of thought or experience. We know that we could not encounter or imagine a world which did not conform to them. If the categories are used to construct a conception of what reality is like, in advance of any inquiries in the special sciences, we must be able to establish what the categories are without appealing to empirical beliefs or to the concept of reality itself.

Like Peirce himself, we shall approach his theory of categories through an examination of Kant's position. Kant thought that our knowledge was guided by a system of *a priori* categories, and Peirce's views were developed through a critical reflection upon these. If we begin this chapter with a sketch of the role of the categories in the *Critique of Pure Reason*, we shall be equipped to understand both the extent to which Peirce is a Kantian philosopher, and the features of his thought that are most original and distinctive.

The major difficulty in constructing a system of categories is epistemological: how can we justify the claim that we have discovered the fundamental components of reality? In particular, if we think of reality as objective, its character independent of what we take it to be, there seems to be a tension between two claims central to the theory of categories: that, first, the categories provide the most perspicuous fundamental classification of the elements of reality; and, second, that we have *a priori* knowledge of this classification. How can such knowledge of an independent objective reality be available which does not reflect the effect of the reality upon us through sensation and experiment? Kant employs an indirect strategy. First, he attempts to show that a certain set of categories must be acknowledged by anyone capable of making judgments; we cannot but use this system of categories in classifying our experience, and *a priori* reflection can reveal to us what they are. It is a further second stage to show that these categories are applicable to reality. Before considering this second stage, we must examine the argument of Kant's 'metaphysical deduction', in which he exploits a logical analysis of the kinds of judgments that rational beings can make to derive a list of the fundamental conceptions possessed by anyone capable of making such judgments.

We can easily imagine that a reasoner might lack the concepts of triangularity or humanity: he might lack any conception expressed by an ordinary predicate or relational expression. Thus, the list of fundamental conceptions must be derived without assuming that he has any particular 'material' concepts. Consequently, Kant takes into account only the formal or logical features of judgments. He turns to logic for a complete classification of the different forms that judgments can have, and holds that a concept is fundamental if it can be traced to an ability to make judgments of one or other of these forms. So he provides a table of judgments: he gives four triads of 'features' of judgments and claims that the form of a judgments can be specified by giving one feature from each triad. The table is:

Quantity	Quality	Relation	Modality
Universal	Affirmative	Categorical	Problematic
Particular	Negative	Hypothetical	Assertoric
Singular	Infinite	Disjunctive	Apodeictic

Thus, each judgment is either universal, particular, or singular, and so on. The key to the metaphysical deduction of the categories is that a distinct fundamental conception is involved in making judgments with each of these twelve features. In making hypothetical judgments, we manifest our grasp of the category of causation; in making categorical judgments, we manifest our grasp of the category of substance, and so on. Thus, Kant derives a table of twelve categories from his table of judgments, and claims to have grounded his categories in logic. The details of this second table need not concern us here. More important is the sort of argument used in deriving categories from the logical analyses of judgments. This seems to be that, for example, making hypothetical judgments about objects of experience simply requires a grasp of the concept of causation. The categories are 'original pure concepts of synthesis that the understanding contains within itself *a priori*' (A 80): simply by virtue of making judgments, we have available these categorial conceptions which can be used to make sense of the elements of experience.

The success of such a project depends both upon the adequacy of the original logical analysis of judgment and upon the right with which we move from features of judgments to categories. We need to justify both the claim that, for example, being conditional reflects a formal rather than a material feature of judgments, and the assertion that it is the category of causation that corresponds to this feature. In accordance with his rejection of psychologism, Peirce endorsed the attempt to give a system of categories a *logical* grounding. Remarking on the 'assurance against error afforded by Kant's method of investigating the categories', he notes that:

> Hegel thought there was no need of studying the categories through the medium of formal logic and professed to evoke them by means of their own organic connections. . . . But there is nothing in Hegel's method to guard against mistakes, confusions, misconceptions; and the list of categories given by him has the coherence of a dream. (R 895)

However, he was critical of Kant's views, noting that it was unsurprising that the merits of the Kantian method had not been appreciated 'because he himself applied it so ill' (R 895). He once accepted Kant's table of judgments, but he soon recognized that Kant's examination of the table was 'hasty, superficial, trivial and even trifling', marked by 'a most astounding ignorance of traditional logic' (1.560). Convinced that the theory of categories should be grounded in a more thorough treatment of the logical structure of arguments and propositions, he devoted much of his work in the 1860s to correcting the Kantian theory, and began to suspect that Kant's list 'might be part of a larger system of conceptions' (1.563), and as he worked on it, confessed that he seemed to be 'blindly groping among a deranged system of conceptions'.

Peirce's initial doubts about Kant's account rested upon finding relations of dependence between the different Kantian categories. At 1.563, he suggests that the category of causation can be seen as a mode of necessity: it is a modal notion, yet, by associating it with hypothetical judgments, Kant classifies it as a mode of relation. Attempts to remove such difficulties led to the belief that something was deeply wrong with Kant's logic and the table of judgments. For example, he came to believe that hypothetical and disjunctive judgments were interderivable, whereas Kant's table requires that they are irreducibly distinct forms of judgments. This interderivability claim, which prompted the thought – noted above – that Kant has no arguments for his table of judgments, is supported by the logical equivalence of the following two sorts of propositions:

If Socrates is a man, then he is mortal.
Either Socrates is not a man, or he is mortal.

(See NE iv 168.) Peirce's further investigations undermined his confidence in all of the details of Kant's table, but left him convinced that Kant's project of deriving a system of categories from a logical investigation of the structure of judgment and argument was of fundamental importance.

This first stage of the argument shows only that the categories can be seen as fundamental conceptions employed by those who make judgments. It is a further question whether they provide a classification of the elements of reality. Somebody might accept a version of the first argument, but draw a sceptical conclusion: if we can judge the world only in accordance with the categories, then, since we have no reason to think that reality incorporates the kinds of characters that the categories express, we have no reason to think that we can have knowledge of reality. A supplementary argument is required which will block such scepticism by justifying the claim that the categories present the fundamental features of reality. Since the argument should be philosophical, it must provide us with *a priori* knowledge that the objects of our experience conform to the categories.

The details of Kant's argument are difficult and controversial, so I shall treat it in a very sketchy fashion. It rests upon a complex analysis of experience which is supposed to show that it is only possible to experience something as a part of a world ordered according to the categories. The categories form a part of a definition of what it is to be an object of experience: we cannot experience a world other than as governed by the categories. In Kantian terminology, we can say that the categories are constitutive of the world of experience. Thus, we can know *a priori* that the objects of our experience are substances, subject to causal laws, and so on. If this is true, then our investigations of the world of experience are not threatened by the fact that our faculty of judgment operates in accordance with the categories of understanding. However, even ignoring the details of the argument, we are likely to be suspicious of anything which attempts to make ambitious *a priori* claims about the nature of reality – especially if these are grounded in premises about the nature of our faculty of judgment. What kind of link between reality and judgment does Kant have in mind?

We experience the world as objective: whether it is true that all swans are white is independent of whether any individual or group of individuals believe that it is true. Thus, there is scope for inquiries directed towards *discovering* what the fact of the matter is. We investigate what is, in a clear sense, an objective realm of facts. However, there is another respect in which reality is *dependent* on human thought: recall Peirce's remark that reality is independent of what any individual thinks but not independent of 'thought in general'. According to Kant, as well as the standpoint mentioned above from which we can inquire into what the facts are, there is another, in which we are 'occupied not so much with objects as with the mode of our knowledge of objects in so far as this mode of knowledge is to be possible *a priori*' (B 25). Knowledge gained from this standpoint is *transcendental*. When we adopt this standpoint, we realize that the empirical world does not correspond to things as they are in themselves.

Things as they are in themselves affect us, but their appearance is conditioned by their being brought under the categories. Crudely, we construct the empirical world by interpreting it as a world of substances obeying the requirements of the categories. This does not challenge the objectivity of inquiry, because the object of our investigations is normally the world of appearance, the empirical world, and not the world of things in themselves: we cannot pretend to knowledge of the latter. The important point is that reasoning from the categories of judgment to the nature of reality is mediated by a picture according to which empirical reality is shaped by the faculty of the understanding in accordance with the categories. Hence Kant's claim that although he is an empirical realist – we normally envisage ourselves as investigating an objective realm of facts – he is a transcendental idealist – from the transcendental standpoint, we can see that empirical reality reflects the constructive activity of the understanding.

We have now provided a framework that can be used to investigate Peirce's theory of categories. He hopes to follow Kant in deriving a system of categories from a careful study of logic.

> The method of Kant, properly carried out, would require, first, the invention of a perfectly exact, systematic and analytic language in which all reasoning could be expressed and be reduced to formal rules; and, second, the analysis of the signs of that language so as to make a table of all their varieties. The project [is] certainly difficult to carry out, and it will perhaps be impossible to be ever assured that it has been brought to completion. Still, we can easily satisfy ourselves by the making of the logical calculus, that the work done is right so far as it goes. (R 895)

It is well known that many of the central ideas of modern quantificational logic were developed independently by Frege in Germany and by Peirce and his pupils in the United States. Although there are many differences between their respective systems, there is enough in common for it to be useful to approach Peirce's doctrines by comparing them with Frege's. Frege, like Peirce, was working within a broadly Kantian framework (Kitcher, 1979), and, since his views are likely to be familiar to many readers, they enable us to present Peirce's categories in a way that makes them seem less odd than they are apt to. So, in the remainder of this section, I shall introduce the central move in Peirce's 'metaphysical deduction'; we can then turn to the arguments that he provides in defence of his position.

The sort of traditional logic employed by Kant analysed propositions into a single subject and a predicate. The two examples below both predicate mortality of different subjects, Socrates and all men respectively.

Socrates is mortal.
All men are mortal.

In spite of their rather different terminology, both Frege and Peirce
repudiate this kind of analysis. Frege begins by identifying a class of
proper names, expressions like 'Socrates', 'Caesar', 'the king of France',
which purport to refer to objects. The first sentence above also contains
the expression '. . . is mortal'. This is an 'incomplete' or 'unsaturated'
expression; it contains a gap to be filled by a proper name; it is a
linguistic function which yields a complete sentence when a name is
inserted as its argument. Given a different argument, this function yields

Caesar is mortal.

Some unsaturated expressions have two or more argument places, such
as '. . . killed . . .', '. . . likes . . .', '. . . gives . . . to . . .'. Completing
or saturating these expressions can yield sentences like

Brutus killed Caesar.
Caesar likes the king of France.

As is well known, Frege then offers an analysis of sentences like 'All
men are mortal' which denies that their form parallels that of 'Socrates is
mortal'. The universal quantifier 'All' is understood as a special kind of
unsaturated expression which takes an ordinary unsaturated expression
like '. . . is mortal' as its argument. The details of Frege's position do not
concern me here, and I shall just assume that the distinction between
names and incomplete expressions is reasonably clear. After 1885, Peirce
stressed much the same distinction: he stressed that any proposition that
can be used to make assertions must contain *indices* (which correspond
to Frege's proper names) and expressions that he called 'icons' which, he
asserted, were unsaturated (and which correspond to Frege's 'concept
expressions' – I shall generally refer to them as 'predicates').

It is not surprising that two scholars should arrive at these ideas
independently, or even that both should characterize predicates as
'unsaturated'. It was only a matter of time before the search for an
adequate notation for the logic of relations led to the recognition that, in
Peirce's phrase, a proposition can have several subjects. And, thinking of
functions as 'unsaturated' was already well established in non-logical
algebra. The development of the periodic table of elements in the first
half of the century provided a conceptual model which had been fruitful
in algebraic thought about functions, and the term 'unsaturated' was
taken over with this model. It was a further reflection of this model that
Peirce referred to the number of arguments in a predicate as its
'valency': thus '. . . killed . . .' has a valency of two, '. . . is mortal' a
valency of one, and so on. The chemical theory held that each element

86

had its valency – an atom of it had a certain number of unsaturated 'bonds', and the atoms could only actually occur in a stable molecule when these bonds were suitably saturated through combination with other atoms. For example, an atom of oxygen has two unsaturated bonds, and so it can combine with two hydrogen atoms (each of a valency of one) to form a molecule of water. Analogously, a predicate can occur in a proposition when its unsaturated places are filled by an appropriate number of names.

If we adopt this as our starting point, a programme for developing a non-Kantian metaphysical deduction suggests itself. Name (index) and predicate (concept expression, icon) provide the first two entries in a new table of judgments. We might then continue to classify predicates according to their valencies – monadic predicates, dyadic predicates, and so on – and then examine other sorts of expressions – connectives like 'and' and 'or', operators like 'it was the case that' and 'possibly', quantifiers, adverbs. As Peirce suggests, we could never be certain that we had completed the task. We then consider what fundamental conceptions are associated with these features. Frege's introduction of objects and concepts (functions) as the semantic values of names and predicates would represent the first stage of this inquiry; he might go on to classify concepts according to the number of argument places they have. Although Peirce follows this route too, the position that he reaches is importantly different. For, in deriving his categories, he pays greatest attention *not* to the distinction between indices and icons (names and predicates), but to the classification of incomplete expressions according to their valency. The analysis of his 'systematic and analytic language in which all reasoning could be expressed' yields two important discoveries. First, such a language would contain monadic, dyadic and triadic predicates – incomplete expressions of valencies one, two and three. Secondly, it would not contain any expressions of valency higher than three. There are three fundamental sorts of predicate expression; and Peirce labels the concepts manifested in the use of these sorts of expressions the concepts of firstness, secondness and thirdness respectively. These are his three universal categories.

The remainder of this chapter will be devoted to an examination of Peirce's arguments for these claims. In fact, their influence upon his work is so pervasive that they form the subject matter of most of the chapters that follow. This is especially true of the following chapter which explores some of the details of his theory of language, indicating how the categories are supposed to be used in understanding the functioning of expressions other than predicates. However, at this stage we must, at least, try to understand why Peirce denies that the use of indexical expressions requires mastery of a distinct additional category.

Why doesn't he follow Frege in recognizing the distinction between concept and object?

Peirce lacked Frege's subtle grasp of the logical character of our thought about objects; he did not develop a sophisticated logical treatment of identity, or examine other concepts that go together with objecthood. However, it would be a mistake to dismiss his metaphysical deduction on that account. He had a theory of the functioning of indices which justified his strategy. This theory will be discussed more fully in chapters IV and V. For the present we can note two features of it. First, paradigm instances of indices are demonstrative expressions like 'this' and 'that'. They do not function by introducing distinctive conceptual elements into propositions; rather, they denote existents directly. Hence, there is a clear sense in which *no* fundamental *conception* is manifested in the use of such expressions. But, second, this is not quite Peirce's position. Our mastery of the use of indices is displayed in our ability to use them in making assertions, and in our understanding them when they are used by others. This understanding must surely involve the exercise of concepts, so our ability to use indices must reflect some grasp of concepts. But, according to Peirce, this simply involves considering the relations between the index and its object, and between the index and various other signs. These relations are naturally expressed by predicate expressions of different valencies. The concepts exercised when we understand names or indices are already incorporated in the classification of predicates according to valency. Thus, Peirce often says that what is distinctive about the semantic functioning of indices is that they stand in brute *dyadic* existential relations to their objects. This makes clear that *part* of the defence of Peirce's theory must be systematic theory of language – discussed in the following chapter – which shows that the classification of predicates according to valency includes every conceptual element manifested in our use and understanding of any expression of the language.

The arguments that I shall discuss in the remainder of this chapter attempt to demonstrate the necessity of making provision for predicates with valencies one, two and three in a language adequate to represent the structure of reasoning, and to show that there is no necessity for expressions with a valency of four or higher. Two of them occur in early writings – one is in 'On a New List of Categories' from 1867, and the other appears constantly after 1870 – but Peirce continued to endorse both of them throughout his career. The third – an attempt to provide phenomenological foundations for the categories – appears for the first time around 1900, and reflects a development in Peirce's view about how the categories apply to reality: there is evidence that he moved away from transcendental idealism during the 1890s. Therefore, I shall begin by examining the two earlier arguments, and leave the phenomenological treatment until section three.

2 Logic, reduction and cognition

The thesis that an adequate logical language must provide for the use of monadic, dyadic and triadic predicates but need not allow for expressions with a valency higher than three faces counterexamples. The sentence

Birmingham is equidistant between London, Manchester and Bristol

contains the tetradic unsaturated expression

. . . is equidistant between . . . , . . . , and . . .

So reasoning that turns on the use of this predicate could not be represented in the Peircean logical language. However, the expressive power of our language would not be reduced if we lacked this tetradic relation. We might hold that, when properly analysed, this sentence is equivalent to one which lacks tetradic predicates:

Birmingham is equidistant between London and Manchester, and
Birmingham is equidistant between London and Bristol, and
Birmingham is equidistant between Bristol and Manchester.

At best, Peirce must hold that there is no need for *primitive* relations with a valency higher than three, and he must claim that when a sentence appears to involve a relation with a higher valency, this appearance can be removed through logical analysis. In addition, he must show that logical analysis will not suffice to remove the appearance that our language must contain triadic predicates: we cannot analyse all triadic relations into simpler terms. One of the two arguments that we shall consider here exploits an account of how complex conceptions can be constructed out of simpler ones, and claims that 'it is impossible to analyse a triadic relation, or a fact about three objects, into a dyadic relation. . . . On the other hand, every tetradic relation or fact about four objects can be analysed into a compound of triadic relations' (7.537). This 'remarkable theorem' (R 439) is stated many times from 1870 to 1910, and is central to Peirce's arguments for his categories.

The other argument can be understood as a response to the slightly different challenge that in reasoning about reality we simply have no call to make use of relations with a valency higher than (say) two. In 'On a New List of Categories' Peirce presents an account of how we are able to ascribe properties to elements of our experience which entails that our use of characters expressed by monadic predicates rests upon the use of conceptions of valency two and three – but no higher. If our conceptual framework is to answer to our need to find coherent order in our experience, it must contain monadic, dyadic and triadic predicates, but need contain none of a higher valency. Since this argument predates the other – if only by three years – we shall discuss it first. The reader should be warned that both of these arguments first appear before Peirce had fully developed his logic of relations and quantifiers. Indeed, in 1867, he still worked within the framework of traditional subject-predicate logic. This requires that they be handled with some care, but it is plain that Peirce thought that the central points retained their validity when the new logic was accepted.

(a) The 'New List'

The argument of 'On a New List of Categories' (1.545–559) is self-consciously Kantian. It attempts to derive some universal conceptions from a logical analysis of judgment and cognition: the categories are abstract conceptions that must be possessed by anyone capable of making judgments. Peirce starts from the assumption, borrowed from Kant, that the function of conceptual activity – of making judgments and of cognition generally – is to make sense of, or unify, the manifold deliverences of sense (1.545). He claims that the only way to show that a conception is valid is to demonstrate that it is impossible to reduce 'the content of consciousness to unity without introducing it'. In a reworking of the argument for a chapter of the 'Grand Logic' of 1893, he suggests that there are three aspects to the manifold character of sense: our experience displays 'a multitude of qualities of feeling', we experience a multitude of 'excitations of sense', and we find the world to contain a multitude of consciousnesses segregated into persons. Our conceptual activity enables us to find patterns in this variety, and we experience it as a single unified world. Peirce proposes to argue for a set of 'universal conceptions' by showing that they are required for the unification of experience; they are to be derived from a consideration of how it is possible to make sense of varied phenomena through conceptual activity. The argument is to rest upon a description of how the world can be brought under concepts – how it can be made sense of – but, in line with Peirce's general philosophical concerns, this must not be a psychological investigation of our cognitive faculties. What is required is a *non-psychological* account of cognition, which provides a logical account of judgment and mind. We saw some of the elements of Peirce's theory in the first chapter. Now we must examine one of the principal arguments he used in developing those views.

Both in the original paper and in the 1893 reworking, Peirce introduces his first two 'universal conceptions' without much argument; they are used to set up the terms of the argument and are not much discussed in his other writings. On each occasion, the first, substance, is presented as the conception 'nearest to sense', as the concept of 'the present in general, which represents the object of attention (see R 403 § 18; 1.547). It is a basically empty conception ('it has no connotation') which represents that which is to be unified. We seek to unify or make sense of substance by forming propositions about it: we judge that some substance – my typewriter, for example – is black or heavy. The second, equally empty, universal conception is being; this reflects the abstract sort of unification of our experience that we aspire to. The function of cognition is to unify substance and being; in less portentous language, the function of cognition is to form propositions that make sense of the many things we encounter in experience. So, what Peirce seeks to explain is how it is possible to find order in our various experiences by forming propositions about them.

Unsurprisingly, the account of cognition has three stages; it is developed in 1.551–554. The first claim is that when we form a proposition about something, we employ 'besides a term to express the substance, another to express the quality of that substance; and the function of the concept of being is to unite the quality to the substance' (1.551). The proposition attempts to make sense of a substance – say a stove – by ascribing to it some property or quality such as blackness. Hence, in the proposition

The stove is black.

there is an expression 'the stove' that denotes the particular substance, an expression that expresses the quality of blackness, and the proposition as a whole conveys that the quality belongs to the substance. (In this early paper, Peirce seems to claim that the copula 'is' performs this third role and thus expresses the category of being. Once he had developed his logic of relations, and came to describe the predicate '. . . is black' as an unsaturated expression, he ceased to claim that the copula performed a distinctive semantic task. Consequently, we should look for an interpretation of his argument which does not rest crucially on this early and abandoned claim.)

Central to Peirce's argument is the claim that our conception of a quality, such as black, is a 'more mediate conception', which is not simply given in our impression of the substance to which it is applied. Our grasp of what blackness is is independent of our knowledge that any particular object is black; it is because we understood the term 'black' before we had any acquaintance with the stove that we can use the quality to unify or make sense of the substance. Especially in the 'Grand Logic', Peirce allies this to the thought that our ascription of qualities to things is a kind of *theoretical* activity:

Upon watching a bee or ant, I exclaim, what sagacity, what strange instinct. The bee or ant which I judge to have that semiconscious mind is experientially known; but like everything experienced, it has something inscrutable about it which no description however elaborate can reveal. When I exclaim that I recognize a sort of mind in it, clearly I must already have some idea of mind. . . . For if this animal were the only object which suggested that idea, I should not be able to separate the idea from that particular animal; and if I had no separate idea I could not *attribute* or *assert*, or *judge* it of that animal . . . and that the idea brought from my previous reflections is applicable to this thing I see before me – *that* is not seen, but is rather a theory to account for what I see. (R 403)

I look at a black stove. There is a direct sensation of blackness. But if I judge the stove to be black, I am comparing this experience with previous experiences. I am comparing the sensation with a familiar idea derived from familiar black objects. When I say to myself that the stove *is* black, I am making a little theory to account for the look of it. (ibid.)

This permits us to see the route Peirce proposes to follow in deriving his categories. The answer to the question of how we are able to form propositions about things is that we ascribe qualities to them; in order to unify the manifold we need the concept of quality – the kind of thing typically expressed by a monadic predicate. However, Peirce insists that this only raises a further question: how are we able to ascribe qualities, our 'little theories', to substances? He hopes to argue for further categories by showing that they are required in order that the category of quality should be able to do its work of making sense of phenomena. Hence, in 1.546 he speaks of a 'gradation among those conceptions which are universal. For one such conception may unite the manifold of sense and yet another may be required to unite the conception and the manifold to which it is applied; and so on.'

This brings us to the second stage of Peirce's story. His claim is that our ability to discern qualities in things rests upon, or presupposes, an ability to make relational judgments: we could not have the concept of quality unless we had the concept of a (binary) relation. In the 'New List', the point is made both rapidly and cryptically.

Empirical psychology has established the fact that we can know a quality only by means of its contrast with or similarity to another. By contrast and agreement a thing is referred to a correlate, if this term be used in a wider sense than usual. The occasion of the introduction of reference to a ground (i.e. to a quality or property) is the reference to a correlate, and this is, therefore, the next conception in order. (1.552)

I think that light is cast upon this argument when we note two related facts. First, qualities provide characteristics that different things can share; things resemble because they share a quality and it can be a point of difference between them that one has a quality that the other lacks. This is just the familiar point that a quality is a universal, a one in many. Secondly, when we judge that two things are similar or that they differ, we can always be asked to specify the point of similarity or difference, the respect in which the things are alike or different. Two things can be alike in that both are red, or they may differ in that only one is round. If this is correct, then, unless we have the concept of quality, we shall not be able to make sensible judgments of similarity and difference. But, Peirce's point goes one step further than this: it is only because we have to account for similarities and differences that we *need* concepts of particular qualities. When he says that reference to a correlate provides the *occasion* of reference to a quality or ground, the picture that is suggested is that we, as it were, find ourselves making judgments of similarity and difference and only require the concepts of qualities in order to make sense of the similarities and differences that we notice. The concept of black is introduced as a part of a hypothesis to explain the similarities we notice among black things. This suggestion fits with his stress upon the mediate character of quality: the relational facts upon which ascriptions of quality depend are more immediate, more directly keyed to experience.

If our ability to ascribe qualities to things rest upon a more immediate capacity to make judgments of similarity and difference, we must now ask how *these* judgments can be made. What is the 'occasion' of these judgments? In fact, Peirce considers a more general question: how can we make relational judgments at all, not just judgments of similarity and difference. Peirce's claim – again tantalizingly and rapidly presented – is that 'the occasion of reference to a correlate is obviously by comparison' (1.553). We carry out comparisons and need to make relational judgments to make sense of what we are doing. An indication of his view of comparison is given by

> Suppose we wish to compare the letters 'p' and 'b'. We may imagine one of them to be turned over on the line of writing as an axis, then laid upon the other, and finally to become transparent so that the other can be seen through it. In this way we shall form a new image which mediates between the images of the two letters inasmuch as it represents one of them to be (when turned over) the likeness of the other. (1.553)

According to Peirce, what happens here is that we form

> *a mediating representation which represents the relate to be a*

representation of the same correlate which this mediating representation itself represents. (1.553. Peirce's italics)

We interpret one of the letters as a sign of the other. And the 'mediating representation' employs the triadic relation of representation in effecting its comparison. (Peirce's discussion considers cases where the representing function does not rest upon similarity, and relates this to dyadic relations other than those of similarity and difference. I shall not pursue this in this chapter.) I think we should understand this as follows. First, we find ourselves able to use things as signs of other things: we take one tree as a representative of other trees by using observations of one as a basis for predictions about the others; we use one square as a representation of another by forming expectations about the latter on the basis of constructions on the former; and so on. We can only make sense to ourselves of our ability to do this by claiming that the two trees (or the two squares) are similar. And of course, we make sense of this by positing a quality – of treehood or being square – which each instantiates. Thus, our ability to ascribe qualities to things rests upon an ability to use both dyadic and triadic relations. If only the theory of cognition here offered is true, Peirce has an argument for his set of categories.

The story is now ended. We might suppose that a further question now arises: how is it possible to use one element of our experience as a representation of another? But Peirce responds to this that all that is required is that there be a manifold of impressions, that we be confronted by things with points of similarity and points of difference. The concept of representation is the most immediate of the universal conceptions; it unifies the manifold directly. Sense can be made of this by noting that treating one thing as a sign of another is just something that we do: it is our ability to do this which suggests to us, according to Peirce, that some shared quality grounds this ability. But our ability to treat the thing as a sign does not have to rest upon a *prior* identification of a shared character. It was for this reason that, in describing Peirce's view, I spoke of our 'finding' ourselves using things as signs: the more mediate conceptions are introduced to enable us to make sense of our ability to do what we undeniably are able to do – although, until the concepts of relation and quality are introduced, we do not understand how we can do it.

This provides a chain of five universal conceptions, which Peirce lists thus.

Being
   quality
   relation
   representation

Substance (1.555)

Being is the most abstract and mediate, substance the most immediate, and the three 'accidents' (1.555) – the forerunners of firstness, secondness and thirdness – are ordered from the most mediate (quality) to the most immediate (representation). However, what ground does Peirce have for recommending acceptance of his view? His argument relies upon the use of a technique of analysis, with roots in scholastic philosophy and Aristotle, which he calls 'precision': the list of categories provides what I shall call a 'precisive chain'. Upon his claims for the technique of precision rests the non-psychological status of this theory of cognition; and as we shall see, the technique has an important role in his later phenomenological writings too.

The technique Peirce employs must satisfy a number of conditions: it must not rely upon the methods of psychology and the special sciences; it must show that his categories are genuinely and objectively distinct; it must also show that they are so intimately connected that we know that (say) relation *comes next* after quality. Precision is to yield a complete objectively valid ordering of distinct categories. In Aristotle's phrase, it is a device of separation, for distinguishing the different elements in cognition. But Peirce is anxious to distinguish it from two other forms of separation, which he calls 'dissociation' and 'discrimination'. The first of these is simply 'the consciousness of the one thing without the necessary simultaneous consciousness of the other' (1.549): it reveals facts about our psychological constitution, about what we can separate in imagination. Of course, this will not serve Peirce's purpose: there might be distinct fundamental conceptions although our imagination is unable to produce a state of affairs in which only one was instantiated. Discrimination is a purely semantic notion (1.549). According to Peirce, we can discriminate colour from space, and space from colour, but not red from colour: I think that this means that while there is an analytic entailment from something being red to its being coloured, there is no such entailment from it being spatial to it being coloured or vice versa. Discrimination will not answer to Peirce's purpose because he wants more than set of analytic truths. His explanations of precision are not very helpful. In a dictionary entry, written long after the original paper, he wrote that it is 'the act of supposing . . . something about one element of a percept upon which the thought dwells, without paying any regard to other elements' (1.548 n 1).

And, in the 'New List' itself, he claims:

> The terms 'abstraction' and 'precision', which were formerly applied to every kind of separation, are now limited, not merely to mental separation, but to that which arises from *attention to* one element and *neglect of* the other. Exclusive attention consists in a definite

conception or *supposition* of one part of an object, without any supposition of the other. (1.549)

Importantly, the relation of 'prescindability' is not symmetric: I can prescind space from colour, 'as is shown by the fact that I actually believe there is uncoloured space between my face and the wall', but I cannot prescind colour from space – I can conceive of there being space that is not coloured, but not of there being a colour patch which has no spatial extension.

There is a helpful illustration in the 'Grand Logic' (R 403):

I can *suppose* space has four dimensions. I do not myself believe it has four dimensions; and with all the habits of a lifetime of contemplating three dimensions, perhaps I cannot clearly *imagine* four dimensions. But I know perfectly well, in consequence of having diligently studied the subject, how things would look in four dimensions; that is, I can rather slowly and fancifully make out the successive appearances which would present themselves, if I had the power to walk about in such a space. Pictures of how such things would look have been made.

So space is prescindable from three dimensions. It seems that I can prescind A from B when I can judge that it is objectively possible that A might obtain but not B. The reason the relation is not symmetric is just that in such a case I may also judge that it is not possible that B without A. We can understand Peirce's argument by noting a modal structure involved in our conceptual framework. Suppose that a concept C is introduced because it is only by using this phenomenon that we can understand a class of phenomena P: the 'occasion' of the introduction of C is to explain P. Since we cannot form a coherent thought of the elements of P without unifying them under some conception, we cannot think of them except by reference to the concept C. The elements of P cannot be prescinded from C. However, as Peirce notes in 1.550, once a conception such as C has been introduced, there is 'no reason why the premisses which have occasioned it should not be neglected, and therefore the explaining conception may frequently be prescinded from the more immediate ones'. The 'explaining conception' may have applications that extend beyond those that occasioned its introduction.

Thus, to return to our table of categories, we might expect, if Peirce's claims were true, that being was prescindable from quality and not vice versa; that relation was prescindable from representation and not vice versa, and so on. And Peirce's argument rests crucially upon just these claims: the categories are ordered by the fact that successive members of the list are prescindable in one direction, and are not prescindable in the other direction. Unfortunately, in the 'New List' he provides virtually no argument for these claims, bluntly asserting them at the close of each stage in the argument. We might agree that, for example, the judgment that two things are similar cannot be prescinded from the thought that there is some quality which each has, whereas we can form the thought that something has a quality without supposing that it actually shares that quality with anything at all. But it would be useful to have the grounds of Peirce's claims about precision worked out more fully.

This argument is doubly Kantian. It exploits a Kantian view of the function of conceptual activity – to unify the manifold of sense. And it also links the categories to logic: in the final paragraphs of the 1867 paper, Peirce attempts to derive from his analysis of cognition a list of the different kinds of signs and uses this as a basis for classifying arguments. The categories are reflected in these tables of expressions and arguments; and Peirce goes beyond Kant in trying to ground his logical classifications in an analysis of judgment. The details of these classifications will be better discussed in subsequent chapters, and I shall concentrate on Peirce's direct arguments for his categories here.

(b) The remarkable theorem

We must now turn to the other argument, the one which rests upon a theorem of formal logic to the effect that while we can always analyse relations with a valency of four or more in terms of relations with a valency of at most three, there is no similar possibility of reducing triadic relations to combinations of dyadic ones. Why did he introduce this argument alongside the one found in the 'New List'? It is certainly simpler, and Peirce may have been more hopeful of winning assent to a mathematical theorem than to a complex analysis of experience. More important, however, is the fact that it is more general than the earlier argument. In 1868 Peirce had still not fully torn himself away from the assumptions of the traditional logic, while by 1870 his views on relations were developing. A minor manifestation of this is the fact that the earlier argument only establishes the necessity of a particular triadic relation, that of representation, while the 1870 argument is formulated more abstractly and more generally, in terms of triadic relations. It shows up better in the assumption, made in the 'New List', that the goal of cognition is to ascribe monadic characters to elements of experience. The paper is solely concerned with how we do this. When the logic of relations is taken more seriously, then the goal should be to discover monadic characters of and relations between elements of experience; and the argument would have to be supplemented to incorporate this. Although we do not need to use tetradic predicates in order to ascribe monadic characters to things, it could be argued that finding a four-term relationship would *itself* contribute towards unifying the manifold of sense. Hence, Peirce needs an additional argument that will block this: if he can show that tetradic relations are reducible to those of lower valency, he has the argument that he needs.

However, the best known systems of modern quantificational logic provide counterexamples to Peirce's 'theorem'. Within these logics, we can define triadic predicates in terms of dyadic ones using axioms of the form.

$$(x) (y) (z) (Rxyz \equiv (Ew) (Txw \text{ \& } Syw \text{ \& } Uzw)).$$

For example, we might define a relation R which a bears to b and c just in case there is someone of whom a is the aunt, b is the brother and c is the father. In spite of the existence of such counterexamples to Peirce's theorem, it would be a mistake to dismiss it as a simple mathematical error. Through the work of the English logician A. D. Kempe, Peirce was aware of the existence of logical systems which conflicted with his claim, and he attempted to respond to the challenge that they provided. Hans Herzberger has shown that Peirce's own formal logic did not contain all of the devices for constructing complex predicates out of simple ones that are available in most formulations of first order logic; and the theorem does actually hold for these rather unusual formal languages (Herzberger, 1981). Therefore, if a case can be made for restricting our attention to these languages, the remarkable theorem may retain its interest. So, we must attempt to see why Peirce wishes to disallow definitions of the sort described above.

The dyadic relation '. . . is a grandchild of . . .' can be defined in terms of the relation '. . . is a child of . . .': a is a grandchild of b just in case a is a child of someone who is a child of b. Thus,

$$(x) (y) (xGy \equiv (Ez) (xCz \text{ \& } zCy)).$$

Superficially this resembles the definition of the previous paragraph, but this one would be acceptable to Peirce. In order to see the difference, let us shift to a different symbolism, one used by Herzberger and suggested by Peirce's graphical logic. We represent the dyadic relation '. . . is a child of . . .' by a circle containing the label 'C', with two prongs representing the unsaturated 'bonds' or places.

We can form complex predicates or conceptions by linking these bonds, thus

When we do this we 'indefinitely identify' the two bonds that are linked: the complex relation holds between two things when the first

stands in the first relation to *something* which stands in the second relation to the second object. Hence, what is depicted corresponds to the kind of definition given in the axiom above. The notation permits us to display quite complex structures of predicates:

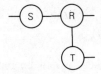

Now, suppose that we wished to display the structure of the definitional axiom of the previous paragraph in this notation. There we seemed to 'indefinitely identify' unsaturated bonds in three predicates, so the most natural way to represent it is

We can call this 'triple bonding'. We form a new conception by linking three simpler ones rather than by linking two. Now, Peirce insists that 'the combination of concepts is always two at a time' (1.294). He does not permit triple bonding.

If we model the formation of complex concepts from simple ones on the idea of 'indefinitely identifying' unsaturated bonds of the different conceptions, and if we accept Peirce's rejection of triple bonding, then his theorem holds.

The easiest way to show this employs an algebraic formula that Peirce himself relied upon. If we form a complex conception out of two conceptions of valancies μ and ν, by linking λ bonds of one with bonds of the other, the number of unsaturated bonds in the resulting complex conception is given by

$$(\mu + \nu - 2\lambda). \text{ (e.g. 3.484)}$$

In our definition of '. . . is a grandchild of . . .' we used one link to form a concept out of two dyads, so that the valency of the resulting conception is

$$(2 + 2 - 2.1) = 2.$$

The formula has its highest value when $\lambda = 1$, and it is a simple matter to verify that

$$(\mu + \nu - 2)$$

can equal three or more only when either μ or ν is equal to at least three. Hence, so long as all our devices for forming complex conceptions fit this rule, it is not possible to reduce triadic relations to dyadic ones. However, tetradic relations can be reduced to complexes of triadic ones, for

$$(3 + 3 - 2) = 4.$$

And in fact, all tetradic relations can be represented as constructed in this manner. As Herzberger records, Peirce devoted much energy to showing that mathematics has no need for techniques of definition which do not accord with this formula. As our example illustrates, familiar systems of first order logic do contain techniques for definition which fail to fit the rule.

Now we have two options. We can dismiss Peirce's result as a quirky feature of an eccentric logic which has no philosophical interest, or we can accept that the restrictions that he places upon acceptable definitions are natural and well motivated, in which case the familiar counter-examples to his theorem can be discounted. Of course, we could justify acceptance of Peirce's logic simply on the grounds that it reveals the structure of the categories so clearly. But, in that case, the theorem would be of no assistance in arguing for the categories. We should have to assume that they had already been vindicated using some other argument. So, can we construct an argument supporting the adoption of the Peircean logic which does not itself appeal to the categories? One possibility would be to argue that the reduction of triadic predicates to dyadic ones effected by using triple bonding is not genuine. If it could be shown that we could only reduce a triadic predicate to a combination of dyadic ones by *using* a conception which had to be thought of as triadic, or even tetradic, the reduction would be of little interest. For example, when we define the triadic relation R in terms of the three dyadic relations T, S, and U, we have to think of R standing in the tetradic relation of 'resulting-by-triple-bonding' from T, U and S. Hence, the definitional procedure does not show that tetradic relations are dispensable. On the other hand, if we think of a relation resulting by double bonding from two other relations we only have to use a triadic relation: the concepts we use in effecting the reduction are not at odds with the reductive claims that are made. Thus, the Peircean logic employs only those definitional resources that can be used in a genuine reduction of the valency of relations. This thought has some intuitive appeal, but it is difficult to find a clear sense in which (for example) a triadic or tetradic conception is exercised in the use of a statement like our axiom for the triadic relation R in the notation of familiar first order logic. Another possibility is to take from the sign theory of cognition materials for an argument that gives combining concepts two at a time a kind of legitimacy lacking in more complex forms of combination. When I form the complex relational expression

I acquire the means for interpreting an object that stands in the relation S to something as a sign of a pair of objects to which that something stands in the relation R. An interest in finding such significant relations, we might argue, is fully served by techniques for combining concepts two at a time.

Promising as I think both of these strategies are, I am not going to explore them further here. Although Peirce continued to attach great importance to both of the arguments that we have considered, after 1900 the third phenomenological approach emerges as the fundamental one, and we must now examine what that involves. Indeed, it might be possible to interpret this third argument as a response to the general problem, raised by our discussion of Peirce's theorem about reducibility, of how to justify our choice of a particular logic and formal language. However, when we examine why the development occurred, in section 4, it will emerge that it reflected a deeper shift in Peirce's position. Although it will be easiest to understand this shift when we have grasped what the phenomenological approach involves, it will be useful to begin our study of it by asking what Peirce could be looking for in an argument for the categories that goes beyond what was offered by the other two.

3 Phenomenology

The theorem of formal logic, as we remarked above, does not establish that science, for example, will actually have to make use of any expressions with a valency of three. It can only establish that if science does use triadic predicates, we cannot dismiss this as an appearance that will disappear under logical analysis. Although the argument of the 'New List' shows that at least one triadic relation must be employed in the theory of cognition, this relation describes a feature of our cognitive practice. Thus, neither of the arguments settles whether, for example, we need to use triadic predicates in describing the structure of physical reality. It is compatible with them that representation is the only genuine triadic relation. During the 1890s, Peirce came to believe that thirdness was operative in nature. Moreover, in ways that will be made clear below, the theory of reality that was developed in the normative sciences requires that a form of thirdness (mediation) is involved in reality. Hence, from the 1890s on, Peirce needs an argument for the categories that establishes more than the two earlier ones. It must justify the need to use predicates with valencies of one to three, and, in the process, it must provide us with the materials for constructing a substantive conception of truth.

To this end, Peirce moves towards what we can think of as an inductive confirmation of the thesis that there are relations of these three kinds. Indeed, in some writings from around 1890, his approach seems to be straightforwardly inductive: he looks at the sorts of conceptions employed in the different sciences (e.g. 1.354 ff). But, of course, this would not answer to his purpose. He cannot rely upon the results of the natural sciences, or use inductive techniques that require a logical justification, in an inquiry that is going to provide raw materials for logic and the other normative sciences. Yet, when he wrote 'The Logic of Mathematics' in 1896, the desire for something like an experiential justification is still evident. The question he raises there is 'what are the different systems of hypotheses from which mathematical deduction can set out, what are their general characters, why are not other hypotheses possible?' These issues about the 'necessary characteristics of mathematical hypotheses' do not differ from the issue about the structure of a language adequate to represent any course of reasoning that we have been considering. If there are interesting answers to these questions, genuine constraints upon possible hypotheses, these necessities 'must spring from some truth so broad as to hold not only for this universe we know but for every world that poet could create. And this truth like every truth must come to us from experience' (1.417). Peirce is looking for an experiential vindication of the categories, but the experience must inform us, not just of the character of reality, but of the character of all that can be imagined, conceived or invented. Hence it does not involve ordinary induction. As the following quotation from the 'Carnegie Application' makes clear, the phenomenological investigation, which by 1903 had been introduced to provide this special experiential knowledge, was not simply to analyse those conceptions which have a fundamental role in our current conceptual scheme. In accord with the aims of the normative sciences, it was to guide us in formulating the conceptual framework which best answers to the aims of inquiry.

> My aim . . . is far more ambitious than that of Kant, or even of Aristotle, or even in the more extended work of Hegel. All these philosophers contented themselves mainly with arranging conceptions which were already current. I, on the contrary, undertake to look directly upon the universal phenomenon, that is upon all that in any way appears, whether as fact or as fiction; to pick out the different kinds of elements which I detect in it, aided by a special art developed for the purpose; and to form clear conceptions of these kinds, of

which there are only three, aided by another special art developed for the purpose. (NE iv 51)

Phenomenology (after 1904, Peirce preferred 'phaneroscopy', a term which, he reasonably supposed, had fewer unfortunate connotations) is a pre-logical science which depends only upon mathematics. It uncovers the three categories – indeed, that is its sole role – but it makes no use of the concept of truth and there is no room for logical criticism of its methods and results. Although we must not, therefore, see it as issuing in claims which are assessable as true or false, still phenomenological results have a sort of objective validity. If they did not, they could not be used to ground our notion of an objective real world. Clearly, a central problem is to understand how there can be a discipline which answers to these strict demands. The dependence upon mathematics emerges in two ways. As chapter VI will make clear, Peirce assigns a broad meaning to 'mathematics': it extends beyond the boundaries of academic disciplines to cover all deductive or 'necessary' reasoning. Hence, the search for an adequate logical language simply is the search for a notation that can be used to articulate the structure of mathematical reasoning. Thus, phenomenology is used to confirm a thesis about the forms that mathematical reasoning – in this wide sense – can take. But, secondly, the methods to be used in phenomenology – for example, Peirce's two special arts – are themselves mathematical methods. It will be apparent that Peirce's belief that mathematics itself stands in no need of philosophical justification or logical criticism is of the first importance for the integrity of his philosophical system.

The 'universal phenomenon', or the 'phaneron', denotes 'the collective total of all that is in any way or in any sense present to the mind, quite regardless of whether it stands for any real thing or not' (1.284). In the Pragmatism lectures, Peirce says of phenomenology that

> I will not restrict it to the observation and analysis of experience but extend it to describing all the features that are common to whatever is experienced or might conceivably be experienced, or become an object of study in any way, direct or indirect. (5.37)

It is irrelevant to the phenomenologist whether the appearances that he contemplates are real, fictional, imagined, conceived as possible, or whatever. The phenomenological implications of an experience are the same, whether it is veridical or illusion; if this were not so, the discipline would not be pre-logical, since it would have to make use of the concept of truth. Phenomenology uses its two 'special arts' to analyse the phaneron, and produce a set of *summa genera* which will be adequate to classify any element of any phaneron. In order to see what these techniques are, we can begin by noting a passage, from the Pragmatism lectures, in which Peirce lists the three special capacities required by anyone who attempts a phenomenological investigation (see 5.42). The first of these is 'the faculty of seeing what stares one in the face, just as it presents itself, unreplaced by any interpretation, unsophisticated by any allowance for this or that supposedly modifying circumstance'. Supposedly, this skill is possessed by artists: those of us who think that snow is white in sunlight, grey in shadow allow interpretation and prejudice to distort our perception; an artist will tell us that it is yellow in sunlight and blue in shadow. We have to fight against distortion caused by such prejudice. Secondly, we require 'a resolute discrimination which fastens itself like a bulldog upon the particular feature that we are studying, follows it wherever it may lurk and detects it beneath all its disguises.' Finally, we need 'the generalizing power of the mathematician who produces the abstract formula that comprehends the very essence of the feature under examination purified from all admixture of extraneous and irrelevant accompaniments.'

These remarks do not inspire confidence. Our first reaction might be that they are vaguely inspirational maxims grounded in banal common-sense truisms about inquiry, or that they call for improbable capacities to have experiences wholly untainted with interpretation and to leap to broad and profound generalizations on the basis of small samples of instances. However, we can understand them by relating the second and third to the two 'special arts'. The first of these is already familiar from our discussion of the 'New List': the phenomenologist establishes what elements of the phaneron can be prescinded from each other. We attend to a particular element, and see from which aspects of its context it can be separated by precision. This technique – which bears a resemblance to Husserl's 'boundless free variation' – provides Peirce's fundamental phenomenological tool; it enables us to locate irreducible aspects of the phaneron, and permits us to focus on which features of these aspects are essential to them. Given the role of this technique in the 1867 discussion, it is not surprising that in later years, Peirce held that the 'New List' argument itself employed phenomenological methods. If this first art is possible at all, then it enables us to locate fundamental features of our thought and experience. It does not equip us to classify these features into general kinds, and thus to identify general categories. The second special art, an application of a common feature of mathematical practice, is supposed to help with this. As the reference to the generalizing power of the mathematician suggests, the mathematical techniques concerned involve the use of abstraction to obtain highly general mathematical models to account for phenomena. It will help us to understand this if we first illustrate some of the results of phenomenological investigation.

There is a difficulty about coming to grips with Peirce's phenomenological writings which reflects a fundamental feature of the discipline itself. He stresses that phenomenology does not issue in a body of accepted propositions; there is not a community of phenomenologists adding to the stock of shared knowledge, publishing reasoned conclusions, and so on. Each individual must be his own phenomenologist, must see for himself that there are three broad classes of phenomena (1.286–7, 2.197). In line with this, Peirce's own discussions are extremely allusive. He provides abstract characterizations of the categories, instances of them, instructions for coming to an acquaintance with them, metaphors and hints. In the end, the reader must decide for himself whether these hints enable him successfully to carry out a phenomenological inquiry and agree with Peirce's categorial doctrine.

The *Collected Papers* contain many illustrations of the phenomenological study of the categories, especially at 1.284–353 and 5.41–65. Both the study of signs in chapter IV and the examination of Peirce's theory of perception in chapter V will provide detailed examinations of some of these. My strategy here will be, first, to give the flavour of this approach to the categories by briefly looking at some examples and, then, to turn to an abstract characterization of what is going on which clarifies the techniques employed. We shall begin with one of Peirce's favourite examples of thirdness (see, for example, 1.345). Suppose that A gives B to C. We cannot analyse this into a sum of dyadic relations. We could start by listing

A put the object B down.
C picked B up.

But these two do not capture the idea that ownership of B was transferred from A to C: unless A intends to give B to C, and C realizes that A has this intention, no gift occurs. Try as we may to capture the content of the giving without using triadic notions, we fail and are forced to recognize that the phenomenon of giving is irreducible triadic. If it can be defined in terms of other notions, these will be psychological factors which are equally triadic: we cannot focus on the giving while banishing from our mind any thought of a giver, a recipient and a gift. (For useful discussion, see Rorty, 1961, pp. 200–1.) We cannot prescind giving from the three participants in the giving. So Peirce is claiming that we cannot use the technique of precision to help us form reductive analyses of notions like law, thought, intention, meaning, continuity: we are forced to recognize that these notions are *irreducibly* triadic.

At 1.24 Peirce considers the experience of 'putting your shoulder against a door and trying to force it open against an unseen, silent, and unknown resistance.' This involves 'a two-sided consciousness of effort and resistance . . .', it is a phenomenon that we are forced to think of in dyadic terms. Once I abandon the thought of my pushing against something, the character of the experience is lost. Similarly, when I perceive an existing object – my typewriter, for example – it is a part of the experience that the typewriter is experienced as other than myself – the experience has a dyadic element. As chapter V will explain, Peirce finds in this sort of phenomenon the clue to the analysis of individual existence; existing objects react against us and each other. Although, presumably, my interaction with the door can be explained as a law-governed process, still Peirce believes that I can prescind from this in dwelling on the experience of reaction. In order to experience the reaction I do not require any understanding of the laws that govern it, and I can even conceive that it may not conform to law at all. This experience of resistance or reaction is an instance of secondness: something irreducibly dyadic.

Firstness is the hardest of the three to focus on clearly, and it prompts some of Peirce's less helpful metaphors – it is a quality of feeling, and the 'flavour' of the phaneron, and it represents a 'positive qualitative possibility' (1.25). Suppose that I observe a red object – Peirce uses the example of the livery of a guardsman in London (SS 24). Now what I observe may involve elements drawn from all three categories – the guardsman is experienced as *other* than me, and as marching in a law-governed fashion. But, I can concentrate upon the colour of the uniform and prescind from the law-governed behaviour and even from the fact that the shade is decorating the uniform of an existing individual. Thinking just of the shade I think of it in abstraction from its setting: it is something which could be realized in an actual individual but need not be. I do not have to think of it as reacting with me or anything else: it is 'as it is independently of any other thing'. I don't think of it as part of the existing universe but as a qualitative character which could possibly be accompanied by the secondness that marks actual existence. I do not have to think of it as a relational phenomenon at all. It is monadic, firstness.

As the reader will have anticipated, the result of using the second of the special arts in reflecting upon these experiences is that we identify three fundamental classes of phenomena, and what distinguishes the members of the different classes is something analogous to valency: quality is, in some sense, monadic; struggle and surprise, and a host of other notions, are, in some sense, dyadic; and law, representation and so on are triadic. Whereas, in the first two arguments, we could see easily how the notion of valency had application, the problem here is to see what the precise force of these numerical characterizations is. Although Peirce never spells his doctrine out in just these terms, I think that we can express what he takes to be going on in a coherent and intelligible fashion.

First, whenever I think about something, attend to it or speculate about it, I form a representation of the object of my thought; subsequently, my knowledge of the object I am thinking about will be mediated via this representation. As we noted briefly above, and will consider in more detail in chapter VI, Peirce claims that this representation is a special kind of mathematical hypothesis. When I employ the first special art, I consider in what different contexts that representation can be placed without losing contact with its object. This representation will involve predicate expressions, or other signs which are analogous to predicates; and these predicate expressions will have a definite valency. The valency of the predicate sign will be reflected in the results I obtain when I carry out the operation of precision; and my contact with the object referred to will be mediated through a predicate sign with a definite valency. Hence the phenomenon referred to will be associated with a definite valency, namely the valency of the predicate sign used to think that phenomenon. Moreover, by carefully focusing on the phenomenon, seeing what it can be prescinded from, I achieve a representation of it which accurately reflects the nature of the phenomenon.

It is here that the second special art comes into effect. Hypostatic abstraction is an important aspect of mathematical practice. It enables us to transform predicate expressions into substantives and thus to introduce a new range of predicates to ascribe properties of abstract objects. For example, we may infer

The stove possesses blackness.

from

The stove is black.

and then introduce new predicates of abstract objects such as blackness. (For a fuller discussion of hypostatic abstraction see chapter VI.) The merits of this procedure are that it enables us to construct abstract second order mathematical theories which can then be applied to a wide variety of instances of less abstract reasoning. For example, given the not very interesting example provided above, we might be able to formulate generalizations about the possession of qualities and to bring these to bear upon ordinary ascriptions of qualities to individuals. Two steps of hypostatic abstraction are required in order to reach Peirce's theory of categories. First, by nominalizing on the sorts of predicates used in attending to ordinary features of our experience, we are able to fomulate claims about the valency of the phenomena. We move from

A gave B to C.

to

A's giving B to C is a triadic phenomenon.

We introduce numerical predicates of phenomena. Reflecting upon our phenomenological endeavours, we find that we are forced to acknowledge that there are monadic, dyadic and triadic phenomena, but we find nothing of a higher valency. This provides something analogous to inductive support for the conjecture that Peirce's logic provides a perspicuous language for representing anything we might think or reason about. A second step of hypostatic abstraction warrants a move from the sentence listed above to

A's giving B to C possesses thirdness.

Our experience instantiates firstness, secondness and thirdness. The generalizing genius of the mathematician is required to see where the use of hypostatic abstraction can enable us to formulate ever more general and abstract formulations.

Effectively, this provides an inductive demonstration of the adequacy of a certain formal language. As it were, we try it out, and find that it is ideally suited to expressing any possible chain of reasoning. As Peirce desired, we have an experiential grounding for the theory of categories and the choice of formal language. However, if it is inductive, we may wonder whether it can answer to Peirce's philosophical needs. Inductive results are fallible and provisional, but we saw in the previous chapter that Peirce requires foundations for his logic which do not risk empirical falsification. And, according to Peirce, we must look to logic to *justify* induction; in which case, it would be improper for logic itself to rest upon induction. As we shall see in chapter VI, this raises a general problem about Peirce's theory of mathematical reasoning. He thinks that all such reasoning is 'inductive', but that is has an *a priori* certainty which distinguishes it from induction in the natural sciences. His claim is that the fallibility of ordinary induction rests upon the fact that we are attempting to form generalizations about empirical reality, and thus must depend upon experience to provide us with instances in order to test generalizations. Since phenomenology is not restricted to a concern with the real, we can invent and construct our own instances. If a generalization is false, we do not have to wait for the world to provide us with a counterexample; we can construct one for ourselves *now*.

These claims appear to rest upon some questionable assumptions about the powers of the human imagination. Peirce wants us to be able to conclude from our phenomenological investigation that his three categories have universal application: they are binding on all people for all time; in endorsing the three categories, we speak with a universal voice. But our claims risk falsification from a number of directions. First, we may simply lack the ingenuity to conceive of the sorts of complex fictional cases required to show that additional fundamental conceptions are required. What we can invent may reflect the structure of the language we speak, and cognitive progress may require the development of new languages which admit of new and different possibilities. Peirce calls on us to contemplate the phaneron free of the influences of any interpretations and prejudices, but he provides no guarantee that this is possible. Secondly, we will be justified in drawing substantive philosophical conclusions from our phenomenological reflections only if we suppose that we can validly expect any rational agent to find the same general categories in his experience. Peirce remarks that it never occurs to us that others will not agree with our judgments; and so our judgments concern what is possible or thinkable rather than being biographical comments upon our own capacities. Yet, it is unclear how we are justified in this. We confidently claim to be able to speak with a universal voice in these matters, apparently requiring no justification that we can speak for others and seeking no support for our assurance that we can break through the veil of prejudice and interpretation. How can the technique yield anything more than fallible psychological data about our discriminative powers?

Although Peirce does not directly discuss this issue, I think we can see what his response would be. It was anticipated in our discussion of Peirce's phenomenological approach to the normative sciences in the previous chapter, and rests upon the observation that only if we are capable of discovering the categories in this fashion can we attain the autonomous self-control that we seek. I shall explain in the next section how the theory of categories grounds Peirce's work on the normative sciences. Since the discipline serves this foundational role, Peirce can claim that it is rational to adopt the ungrounded *hope* that phenomenology is possible. Subsequently, we must construct an account of mind which shows how we are able to acquire such knowledge, and a metaphysical model of reality which shows that the three categories genuinely function as *summa genera*. Part of the justification for these accounts of mind and reality will be that they explain how the regulative hopes that we employ in the philosophical sciences can be absolutely true. Thus a familiar Peircean argumentative strategy is used to ground the results of phenomenology. It is a regulative hope adopted when we undertake inquiries in the Normative Sciences, that we can accept the results of phenomenological reflection as having a form of objective validity.

There are marked similarities between Peirce's phenomenological approach to his categories and the practice of more recent philosophy. Indeed, although the numerological categories are 'so abstract and so far from the clichés of the history of philosophy', Rorty remarks that 'they are perhaps the best handles for grasping what one learns from [the later] Wittgenstein' (Rorty, 1961, p. 199 fn 5). Wittgenstein argues piecemeal for the irreducibility of a variety of notions, such as reason, meaning, intention, rule and so on; Peirce makes a similar point by asserting that thirdness is irreducible to secondness and firstness. The phenomena that Wittgenstein discusses in the *Philosophical Investigations* are mostly of the sort which Peirce describes as irreducibly triadic: this will be illustrated in subsequent chapters when we see Peirce's categories at work in accounting for the nature of a variety of phenomena. The similarity between Peirce and Wittgenstein is more marked than this, however. Cavell has noted, in his 'Aesthetic Problems of Modern Philosophy' (Cavell, 1976, pp. 73 ff), that when philosophers appeal to ordinary usage to justify a philosophical move – for example, the rejection of a reductionist proposal – they see no need to appeal to empirical facts about usage. Rather, they consult their own 'intuitions', report on what they find themselves wanting to say in certain circumstances, and claim to speak with a 'universal voice'. Unless the speaker could demand that others acknowledge what he says, his intuitions would be of no philosophical interest. For the Wittgensteinian, our ability to speak for all in mapping the grammar of our language is something we cannot justify, it marks a point where rational justification has come to an end. Yet, as Cavell notes, our ability to speak for all in this way is a necessary condition of our being able to continue to speak at all. Similarly, for Peirce, we demand the right to go by what we find ourselves wanting to say when we apply the special arts involved in phenomenological inquiry; we cannot justify our claim that our 'intuitions' have universal validity. But unless they could do so, common language and the rational control of deliberation would not be possible at all. Just as we have used Kant's doctrines in the *Critique of Judgment*, as an aid in presenting Peirce's conception of philosophical inquiry, Cavell stresses the analogies between what Kant calls the judgments of reflection and the claims made by philosophers who appeal to ordinary language.

Discussing the character of the sorts of investigations employed by Wittgenstein, Cavell remarks,

> the shortest way I might describe such a book as the *Philosophical Investigations* is to say that it attempts to undo the psychologizing of psychology, to show the necessity controlling our application of psychological and behavioural categories; even, one could say, show the necessities in human action and passion themselves. (Cavell, 1976, p. 91)

Note how appropriate this would be as a description of the theory of the mind that Peirce developed in the 1860s, and continued to defend throughout his life. He consciously described it as the 'logical conception of mind', attacking psychologism in logic on the grounds that logic is a science that is prior to psychology and used in making psychological ascriptions. What we must hope is that Peirce's logical conception of mind – his claim that all thoughts are signs – will enable us to explain how we have the capacities which phenomenology exploits. It will be several chapters before we are in a position to see whether this hope is satisfied.

Before turning, in the next section, to the bearing of the categories upon the nature of reality and the relations between Peirce's three approaches to the categories, I shall conclude this discussion of the general character of Peirce's phenomenology by trying to state more clearly why Peirce denies that phenomenology yields a body of truths. It seeems to result in the assertion of:

There are three categories, firstness, secondness and thirdness, and it is hard to see why we should not think of that as a truth. Furthermore, if this is asserted as a result of phenomenological investigation, it is unclear how Peirce can deny that phenomenology yields a system of propositions. While I am unsure what Peirce's response to this problem was, I can tentatively suggest two strategies that he might have adopted. One possibility would be to deny that phenomenology itself issues in this assertion. The culmination of phenomenological inquiry is the adoption of an adequate logical notation, which is a practical decision. Although the theory of categories can be derived from an inspection of this formal language – the language reveals or shows the structure of the categories – it is left to one of the normative sciences actually to carry out this derivation. A proper division of labour between the different philosophical sciences is required, in that case, before we see the force of Peirce's view. I doubt that Peirce's substantive point turns on such issues of demarcation. More important is the fact that, like all mathematical practice, phenomenology is concerned with *necessities*; firstness, secondness and thirdness are abstract mathematical entities. Peirce holds generally that mathematical claims do not represent assertions about reality; they are not assessable as true or false. In fact, as we shall see in chapter VI, he claims that such necessities are *prior* to the truth: they have a more fundamental kind of validity that we can acknowledge without having a clear grasp of the notion of truth. If we think of propositions as things that can be true or false – and this is a natural way to construe them – then sentences expressing mathematical necessities are not properly thought of as propositions. In that case, we acknowledge Peirce's point here when we admit that the theory of categories is not an attempt to describe the structure of reality: it purports to reveal necessary structures common to the real and the illusory, to all that can be thought or imagined.

4   The categories and reality

How do the phenomenological categories enter into the definitions of the beautiful, the good and the true provided by Peirce's normative sciences? Recall that Peirce seeks to support the objective validity of these definitions by showing that they are formulated in terms which reflect the universal categories that provide *summa genera* adequate for the classification of all possible experience. The upshot of aesthetics was:

> I should say that an object, to be esthetically good must have a multitude of parts so related to one another as to impart a positive simple immediate quality to their totality. (5.132)

First, there must be parts with their own distinctive character. These stand in a number of relations, but since there are many parts, these will include dyadic relations of (say) juxtaposition. Among these relations will be triadic ones which mediate between the different elements of the complex and unify them. Only triadic relations can serve this unifying role. The unification lends to the whole its own distinctive firstness, a 'positive simple immediate quality'. We have a structure of parts unified by a form of thirdness so that the whole has its own distinctive firstness. Thus is Peirce's claim formulated in terms of the categories. The three normative sciences differ in the nature of the elements which form the complex whole. Aesthetics assumes only that they have a distinctive qualitative character, their own firstness, and studies how 'firsts' can enter into an admirable totality. For ethics, the elements are volitions and consequent perceptions; both of these involve the element of 'reaction', the double consciousness of the agent of a world upon which he acts and which acts upon him which is characteristic of secondness. Thus ethics is concerned with how a structure of 'seconds' can be intrinsically admirable. Logic is concerned with how the deliberate adoption of rules of inference – which embody thirdness – can be absorbed into an admirable life. Reality itself is understood as involving all three elements: as we shall see in chapter V, Peirce believes that it involves observable facts – each with its qualitative firstness and the secondness that is distinctive of actual existence, forming an intelligible whole through the mediation of a form of thirdness, namely natural law. Thus, so long as we accept the results of Peirce's phenomenological analyses of concepts such as law and actual existence, we find a pattern in his accounts of truth and reality which reflect the structure of his categories.

In concluding this chapter, I want to return to the question why Peirce needed the phenomenological approach to the categories as well as the two earlier ones. We noticed in the previous section that he thought that this approach made fewer presuppositions, that it did not take for granted our current vocabulary or methods. Some further comparisons will enable us to formulate a question that is important for understanding the development of Peirce's thought. There are some *prima facie* tensions between things he says at different times that I shall not discuss here – for example, in 1867, quality is the most mediate of the categories, while after 1900, firstness is associated with immediate felt quality. In general, the arguments seem not to be in competition: the phenomenologist may use an argument from the logic of relations in the course of his inquiry – it may assure him that his failure to locate an example of fourthness does not reflect bad luck or an impoverished imagination. The argument of the 'New List' is itself, as we saw, phenomenological in spirit. As we noted, however, the later argument assigns an important role to forms of secondness and thirdness, which are not mentioned in the earlier discussion. From 1885, Peirce linked secondness with our experience of the world as external: an individual actually exists, he says, if we can stand in an irreducible dyadic relation to it. It seems here that secondness is being allowed to do the work that in 1867 called for the concept of substance; certainly, the argument of the 'New List' makes no reference to this particular dyadic relation. Secondly, from the mid-1890s, Peirce espoused an extreme realism about universals: reality, he holds, contains 'would bes', and we are directly aware of these forms of thirdness in experience. Phenomenological reflection reveals to us this essentially triadic feature of experience. Once again, the only form of thirdness introduced in 1867 was the relation of representation. As we have seen – and will see in more detail below – these newly introduced ideas enter importantly into Peirce's later conception of reality; reality is external and infused with law.

One set of questions that this raises concerns just what prompted these two changes in Peirce's views of existence and reality. However, in this chapter, I want to use them to formulate a problem about Peirce's attitude towards Kantian transcendental idealism. The 1867 position is wholly Kantian; the categories are derived from an analysis of the structure of thought, and reality is known to conform to the categories because reality is what will be know at the culmination of a process which necessarily employs the categories. In a straightforward sense, reality is shaped by the formal structure of the understanding, it is not independent of 'thought in general'. Hence, in his 1870 review of Berkeley's works, Peirce stresses that his 'realism' is a form of 'the phenomenalism of Kant', and Fisch reports that in a letter of 1886, written to F. E. Abbot, he describes himself as 'Not only phenomenalist but also idealist' (Fisch, 1967, p. 169). By 1890, Peirce's views had changed.

In 1885, Abbot, a Harvard classmate of Peirce who had attended some meetings of the Metaphysical Club in the early 1870s, published a fascinating book entitled *Scientific Theism*. The book grew out of lectures delivered at the Concord Philosophy School and purported to show that a proof of the existence of God was forthcoming if science was taken seriously. For our purposes, the most interesting part is the introduction in which Abbot produces some very modern sounding views about the nature of science. He first attacks Kant for being a nominalist. In Kant's work, he believes, the nominalist tradition was simply transformed into a vast philosophical system; it survived in the thought that generality reflected our activity of organizing the world of appearances, and was not present in the world of things in themselves. Abbot rejects nominalism, and claims that the practice of science is itself implicitly realistic: realism is science's philosophy of science. His realism – he sometimes called it relationism – is a complex doctrine, but we can capture its flavour by noting the three propositions he lists as presuppositions of all science, and as constituting 'the universal condition of the possibility of experience itself' (Abbot, 1885, p. 38). These are:

(1) An external universe exists *per se* – that is, in complete independence of human consciousness so far as its existence is concerned; and man is merely a part of it, and a very subordinate part at that.
(2) The universe *per se* is not only knowable, but known – known in part, though not in whole.
(3) The 'what is known' of the universe *per se* is the innumerable relations of things formulated in the propositions of which science consists; consequently, these relations objectively exist in the universe *per se*, as that in it which is knowable and known.

Abbot is a realist in double sense: he rejects transcendental idealism and believes that we have knowledge of *noumena*; and he rejects nominalism and thinks that among the constituents of this independent but knowable reality are relations, which are general phenomena, universals.

We can trace the change in Peirce's position in his altering responses to Abbot in the few years after *Scientific Theism* appeared. In the 1886 letter mentioned above, Peirce goes on to say that 'Being an Idealist of course, I cannot yet accept the objectivity of relations in the sense in which you mean it': Peirce's realism is still Kantian and opposed to Abbot's. In 1886, he reviewed Abbot's book in *The Nation* (CTN vol. 1, 71–4), and showed little sympathy for the claim that science presupposes realism.

But the physicist always talks and thinks of phenomena or appearances, and makes not the slightest pretention to have anywhere got down to the noumena, bottom facts, or ultimate subjects of appearances. He discovers, for instance, that air is viscous, and viscosity is a non-conservative force. It is a reality; but yet, according to the physicist, only a phenomenal reality. (p. 73)

Science, he stresses, need not hold that reality is 'independent of the final upshot of sufficient investigation' (p. 74); and he claims that the practice of science seemed to be metaphysically neutral.

In 1889, Peirce published a number of definitions of philosophical terms in the *Century Dictionary*. As Fisch notes, in these entries we find Kant classified as a nominalist, Abbot's relationism presented as the culmination of a discussion of realism and an endorsement of the claim that science is 'prevailingly realistic'. In the following years, he was to move closer and closer to the sort of view that Abbot defended. By 1903, in the Lowell Lectures, he announced that Abbot has shown that 'science has always been at heart realistic, and always must be so' (1.20, cf 4.1); and in 1905, he wrote that his position 'is distinguished by its strenuous insistence upon the truth of scholastic realism (or a close approximation to that, well stated by the late Dr Francis Ellingwood Abbot' (5.423). So, there is good evidence of a major shift in Peirce's position after 1886: we must be on the lookout for the manifestations of this change in his theory of perception and his account of the growth of knowledge, and, particularly, in his pragmatism. His stress upon the irreducible secondness of our experience of externality and his identification of law and generality as a prescindable form of thirdness are among these.

This change raises a number of problems, not least about the special problems that prompted it. What I want to focus on here is the relation between this abandonment of transcendental idealism and some familiar features of his later work. One of the advantages of transcendental idealism is epistemological. If we have *a priori* knowledge of principles that are constitutive of empirical reality, then the scope for scepticism is limited: there is no room for the Kantian to doubt whether empirical reality contains causally ordered substances. If reality is wholly independent of thought, then we may wonder whether cherished assumptions which guide the conduct of our inquiries rest upon a false conception of things in themselves. We might doubt whether there is any reality at all. If transcendental idealism is abandoned, then we need a different kind of support for our claim to be in touch with reality. One possibility would be to endorse a doctrine of immediate perception: in perception we are in direct cognitive contact with reality. As we shall see in chapter V, Peirce defended such a theory. However, what I am more concerned to stress here is the role he comes to assign, at just the time that he was moving to a more extreme kind of realism, to rationally adopted regulative hopes. If we have no transcendental guarantee that knowledge of reality is possible, then, Peirce thinks, at least we have the best of grounds for *hoping* that our cognitive strategies will put us into contact with the noumenal reality. Of course, this is not to be left as just a blind hope: metaphysics, the bridge between the normative sciences and the special sciences, has the task of contructing a plausible account of man and his place in nature which both accords with the discoveries of the special sciences and shows how the regulative hopes of the logician can be true. Peirce's metaphysics must show that it is not just a miracle that we have knowledge of the noumenal reality. As we shall see when we examine Peirce's metaphysical doctrines in chapter IX, the first publications to develop this metaphysical vision systematically appeared in 1892, and grew out of his work in the later 1880s. Peirce's realism, his metaphysics, and his attempts to ground the normative sciences with the aid of regulative hopes emerge together.

How does this development relate to the new phenomenological treatment of the categories? Is the phenomenological approach particularly appropriate if transcendental idealism is abandoned? According to Peirce's mature conception of logic, the logician reflects upon the results of a phenomenological confrontation with the phaneron, and, on that basis, develops an understanding of the concept of truth and discusses by what means the truth may be known. He has no occasion to think of reality as the result of our constructive activity; he can think of reality as an external law-governed realm with which he is immediately acquainted. Reality is an ideally coherent and admirable whole discerned in what is given in experience. The categories are not justified by being found implicit in a language that we must use in constituting empirical reality; rather, they are found in a language which is justified by a form of inductive testing – it is seen to be adequate to describe all that appears. Thus, so long as Peirce's theory of perception and metaphysics can be developed in ways that make sense on this extreme realism, there is nothing in the phenomenological treatment of the categories which forces Peirce to stay with transcendental idealism. On the other hand, if the argument from the logic of relations or the argument of the 'New List' provided the fundamental grounding for the categories, they could not be used in developing an Abbot-style realism. However, although it seems that the phenomenological treatment of the categories sits well with the abandonment of 'Kantian nominalism', it does not *compel* us to adopt realism. It is possible that our metaphysics might offer a form of transcendental idealism as the best explanation of how the regulative hopes which ground logic can be satisfied. We might subsequently decide that the phaneron is the result of unconscious processing employing standards of reasoning which ensure that appearances conform to the categories.

We must be careful in the way we handle Peirce's development from Kantian idealism to realism. The change he announces cannot be denied, and we have noted some of the doctrinal commitments that accompanied it. But, it would be a mistake to think of the opposition between idealism and realism in too simple-minded terms. There is a wide range of alternative positions available; and, given Peirce's continuing admiration of Kant, we should not be surprised to find that his final position is much closer to transcendental idealism than the discussion of the last few pages might suggest. A central question to be kept in mind throughout the following chapters is: just how extreme – how remote from the Kantian position – is the realism that Peirce defended in the years after 1890?

IV

Assertion and Interpretation: the Theory of Signs

1 Introduction

Know that from the day when at the age of 12 or 13 I took up, in my
elder brother's room a copy of Whately's 'Logic,' and asked him what
Logic was, and getting some simple answer, flung myself on the floor
and buried myself in it, it has never been in my power to study
anything, – mathematics, ethics, metaphysics, gravitation, thermo-
dynamics, optics, chemistry, comparative anatomy, astronomy,
psychology, phonetics, economics, the history of science, whist, men
and women, wine, meteorology, except as a study of semiotic. (SS
85–6)

This comment, written to Lady Welby late in his life, illustrates the
importance Peirce attached to his theory of signs – his semiotic. Many
of the central ideas were developed during the 1860s, but he continued
to write about signs throughout his life. Indeed, some of his most
systematic treatments of such topics are found in the correspondence
just alluded to, and were written well after 1900. There is no reason to
doubt Ransdell's claim that in excess of 90 per cent of his output is
directly about semiotic (Ransdell, 1977, p. 158). We have met a number
of doctrines about signs and representations in earlier chapters, and it is
now time to draw them into some systematic order. Since there is so
much material, it will be impossible to do justice to many of the details
of Peirce's claims, and I shall not say much about the development of
his views. Rather, I shall paint in the most important themes with broad
strokes, concentrating upon those which have a direct bearing upon the
logical and epistemological topics that we have been discussing.[1]

The Peircean inquirer is a member of a community of like-minded
persons who devote their lives to the disinterested pursuit of the truth.
When we ask the question how this is possible, two sorts of

considerations point us towards the need for an account of meaning and representation. First, the object of the life of science is to produce a true representation of reality. Until we know how thoughts and sentences can 'represent reality', our understanding of the life of science will be incomplete; indeed, our initial question could be reformulated as concerned with how it is possible for there to be, and for us to arrive at, true representations of reality. Secondly, we have to understand how collaborative activity among the members of a community of inquirers can take place. We advance towards the truth through conversation and dialogue with our fellows; the community is essentially one of dialogue and conversation. Thus, we also need an explanation of the linguistic acts which sustain the scientific community. Hence, as Brock has stressed, Peirce frequently identifies the objective of speculative grammar – the part of logic which develops the systematic theory of signs – as providing an analysis of the assertions made by 'scientific intelligences' (Brock, 1975). The theory includes a general explanation of what it is for something to have a meaning, to represent something other than itself; it accounts for the kinds of linguistic actions that are involved in 'scientific' (sc. 'cognitive') discourse; and it investigates what must be the character of a language usable as a vehicle for serious inquiry. So described, the concerns of the theory are clearly close to those of much work on the philosophy of language in the analytic tradition.[2]

This view of 'semiotic' as a general account of meaning and communication within a scientific community which provides the materials for explaining the soundness of inferences and methods fits Peirce's characterization of logic as

> only another name for *semiotic*, the quasi-necessary or formal
> doctrine of signs. By describing the doctrine as 'quasi-necessary' or
> formal, I mean we observe the character of such signs as we know,
> and from such observations, by a process which I will not object to
> naming Abstraction, we are led to statements, eminently fallible, and
> therefore in one sense by no means necessary, as to what *must be* the
> characters of all signs used by a 'scientific' intelligence, that is to say,
> by an intelligence capable of learning by experience. (2.227)

However, there are reasons for thinking that we have not yet described all that is central to Peirce's approach. A first cause for concern is that, while we here describe the theory of signs as an account of language and communication, it was introduced in chapter I as a theory of thought and inference. That this conflict is only apparent is clear from the fact that the semiotic theory of thought involved thinking of thoughts as analogous to publicly articulated assertions and arguments. The point is made in later work by stressing that 'thinking always proceeds in the

119

form of a dialogue – a dialogue between different phases of the ego' (4.6), a claim that is often repeated: an inner judgment is interpreted as like an assertion directed at a later stage of the self. Peirce often goes so far as to claim that the self is integrated by bonds of dialogue and conversation just like the scientific community: the theory of thought-signs involves viewing the thinking individual as a kind of sign using 'community'.

Many commentators give the impression that they find in Peirce's work on signs a distinctive contribution to the study of mind and language which is unlike what is found in the analytic tradition; and that semiotics provides a fundamental and illuminating academic discipline with a promise that was heralded by Peirce but lost to much of twentieth-century philosophy. The suggestion is that we find in Peirce's work not just the parallel development of themes found in the work of Frege, Russell or Wittgenstein, but also the framework for an integrated theory of culture. The quotation at the beginning of this section may reflect a similar ambition in Peirce himself – although it could be interpreted as claiming simply that any inquiry involves self-conscious reflection about how thoughts and arguments should be ordered in the pursuit of the truth. Where should we look to find this special character of Peirce's work? As we shall see, Peirce's theory makes use of a single primitive triadic relation, the sign-relation: the theory explains this relation and exploits the theory of categories to understand the various possibilities that are implicit within it. The first possibility, then, is that the sorts of explanation of semantic phenomena that result from this theoretical framework are unlike those developed by analytical philosophers. A second possibility relates more directly to the scope of the theory. Although Peirce's interest in the theory of signs is, initially, in its applications for the study of deliberation and methodology, the theory may have an explanatory power that outstrips what occasions its introduction. The theory of language is derived from a more general theory which, for example, also explains the functioning of natural, non-conventional, signs. The extended scope could be achieved either through producing a theory which also explained sign action among beings not concerned with learning from experience, or by finding new kinds of behaviour which are fruitfully described as 'learning from experience'. I shall say something more about Peirce's view of the range of semiotic phenomena at the end of this chapter.

In the following section, we shall discuss the general character of the sign relation and notice its connections with the theory of categories. We can then go on to consider some of Peirce's views about the semantics of the sorts of languages that must be used for serious inquiry, and raise some problems about reference and validity that will occupy us for the next few chapters. The final section will attempt to state what is distinctive, and what is valuable, in this work.

2 Thirdness and the sign relation

As the passage quoted above suggests, Peirce's method is to examine some central examples of sign action, to observe their features and use the method of precision to distinguish those which are essential to their being signs from those that are accidental, and to use this as a basis for generalization. His aim is not an analysis of the usage that the word 'sign' normally has. Just as the zoologist is not analysing the current meaning of 'fish' and rather asks what its meaning *ought* to be 'in order to make fishes one of the great classes of vertebrates' (SS 31), so Peirce is concerned with constructing a concept of sign that will be philosophically and theoretically valuable. Aware that he is stretching the notion beyond its normal use, Peirce sometimes proposes replacing 'sign' with the technical term 'representamen'; but he is not consistent in this, and we shall not follow him here. As noted above, I will not consider how far Peirce thinks the notion of a sign can be generalized until the end of the chapter – for the present, we shall concentrate upon thoughts, utterances, and familiar sorts of natural and conventional sign.

The point on which he is most insistent is that the sign relation is triadic: signs exemplify thirdness. Our first task is to see why he thinks this is so. There are abstract statements of the doctrine in many places, but the following quotations capture the flavour of them:

> In its genuine form, Thirdness is the triadic relation existing between a sign, its object, and the interpreting thought, itself a sign, considered as constituting the mode of being a sign. A sign mediates between the *interpretant* sign and its object. (SS 31)

(Notice here a hint of the more general claim that the sign relation provides the only true form of thirdness.)

> I define a Sign as anything which is so determined by something else, called its Object, and so determines an effect upon a person, which effect I call its interpretant, that the latter is thereby mediately determined by the former. (SS 81)

(Peirce admits that this formulation is less general than he would like. The claim that the interpretant is a state of a person is 'a sop to Cerberus because I despair of making my own broader conception understood' (ibid.).) The three terms of the relation are the sign itself, the object of the sign, and the interpretant, which is itself a sign and thus stands in the same triadic relation to a further interpretant! And Peirce insists that the sign *mediates* between the other two relata. As a first step towards understanding these notions, let us consider a very simple example of understanding a natural sign; we can then move on to consider linguistic examples.

We observe freshly stripped bark on a tree, and we treat it as a sign of the recent presence of deer. We observe the bark, and we learn of the presence of the deer from this observation; we claim that the stripped bark 'means' that deer have been in the area. The stripped bark, here, is the sign; as its object we can take the deer or the fact that there have been deer nearby; and the interpretant is our thought that there are deer nearby. We come to a thought about the deer, but our cognitive contact with the deer is mediated through the sign; indeed, we are even likely to think of the deer as those we have learned of through the sign. In a similar way, when someone tells me that, for example, it is raining and I allow this to influence my opinions about the weather, their utterance mediates between the weather and my opinions – and also between their beliefs and intentions and my beliefs about these. In all these examples, we find the pattern described in the definition from SS 81. The presence of the deer 'determines' the sign – it brings it about that the trees are stripped of bark – and the sign 'determines' us to have the beliefs about the deer; and thus, indirectly, the deer determine us to believe in their presence.

Although this example clarifies the three terms of the sign relation, it provides us with only a first approximation to Peirce's view. In particular, it leaves the notion of 'determination' very unclear; and does not really explain why sign action is triadic. In 5.472, Peirce explains a notion of 'dyadic action':

> An event A, may, by brute force, produce an event, B; and then the event, B, may in its turn produce a third event, C. The fact that the event, C, is about to be produced by B has no influence at all upon the production of B by A. It is impossible that it should, since the action of B in producing C is a contingent future event at the time B is produced. Such is dyadic action, which is so called because each step of it concerns a pair of objects.

The case provides simply a sequence of dyadic relationships. Given what was said in the previous paragraph, there is no reason to suppose that our deer example is not simply dyadic: the deer produce the stripped bark; and then, the stripped bark produces the belief. Nothing irreducibly triadic is going on at all. From 5.473, we learn that what is distinctive of *triadic* action is that 'an event A, produces a second event, B *as a means* to the production of a third event C'; in such a case, 'B will be produced if it will produce or is likely to produce C in its turn, but will not be produced if it will not produce C in its turn nor is likely to do so'. Triadicity here introduces something akin to purpose. The problem is to see how this can be applied to the example of the deer. It is not suggested, for example, that the deer strips the bark of trees in order that people should thereby come to the belief that deer have been around.

The bearing of these thoughts on Peirce's analysis emerges when we formulate what seems unsatisfactory about our initial description of the case. There seems to be a distinction between the following.

(1) Event E causes us to believe that P.
(2) We take E as evidence for, or as a sign of, the fact that P.

In case 2, our belief that P rests upon an assessment of E, upon our understanding of it; in case 1, there is no necessity that we have any opinion about E at all. 2 admits the possibility of our misunderstanding E, our misinterpreting it, while, in case 1, such talk is out of place. Nothing in our presentation of the simple example indicates how this distinction is to be drawn; we have not explained what is distinctive about case 2. In order to explain this distinction, we have to focus upon the way that the *interpretant* is produced – the process that Peirce christens 'semiosis'; effectively, the issue concerns what is involved in *understanding* a sign. It is semiosis that is irreducibly triadic; and therefore the production of the interpretant is, in a sense, purposive. In this case, a certain causal process leads from the stripped bark to our belief in the presence of deer. And we can certainly say of this process that if it did not in general lead us to have true beliefs, it is probable that the stripped bark would not after all have that effect upon our opinions. Alternatively, the stripped bark is interpreted as a sign of the presence of deer because that is a way for a scientific intelligence to learn about reality.

Sticking with our simple example, we can easily see how this works. If the stripped bark signifies the deer, this is because of some relation between the two; in this case, the deer produced the stripped bark – there is a brute dyadic causal relation between them. The statements

The deer produced the stripped bark on the tree.

and

The stripped bark is a sign of the presence of the deer.

are not equivalent. The former describes a dyadic fact, whereas the latter claims in addition that the bark has some sort of power to produce certain sorts of interpretations. However, the truth of the first of the statements can feature as part of the explanation of the truth of the second; it provides what Peirce sometimes called the *ground* of the significance of the tree. It is probably only because we know about what deer do to the bark of trees that we take the tree as a sign of deer; if we revised our beliefs about the habits of deer, then, since trees would no longer be a reliable indication of the presence of deer, we would no longer interpret them as having that significance. This provides a particularly clear example of the triadic production of interpretants; it is a case where our interpretation of the sign rests upon conscious reflection and upon beliefs about the relations between sign and signified which ground the sign's function.

These remarks need some further clarification, because in talking of an interpretation being required in order to learn from experience, or in order to discover the truth, we have lost track of the original three relata of sign, object and interpretant. Contact will be restored through a two-stage examination of the triadic character of the production of some signs. Suppose that I wish to communicate to someone that Peirce was an American philosopher; I wish to choose a sign that will lead him to believe the following things.

Peirce was an American philosopher.
C. H. believes that Peirce was an American philosopher.
C. H. wants me to believe that Peirce is an American philosopher.

I wish to produce something that he will interpret as a sign of Peirce's nationality, something that will lead him to have thoughts about Peirce. Therefore, I produce a sign that will produce further interpreting signs with the same object: if it did not produce signs with the same object, I would revise my practice and try a different sign. We have here the triadic production of a sign which will produce an interpretant in the same triadic fashion; and the example sticks close to the terms of Peirce's definition of the sign relation. The end in terms of which the sign is to be evaluated is that of producing another sign with the same object. The problem with the deer example was that the sign itself was not produced through triadic sign action, so we had to focus on the process of interpretation. What we should now notice is that interpretation itself involves producing a sign that will subsequently be interpreted in other thoughts and signs. I want to understand the natural sign in such a way that my interpreting thought can give rise to further thoughts about the object of the natural sign; I want to understand the natural sign correctly, because only then can its influence be transmitted *through* my interpreting thought. The point becomes clearer when we recall that a judgment is an assertion directed at later stages of oneself.

I have now said something about how a sign 'determines' its interpretant, and must add to this a remark about how the sign is 'determined' by its object. The *ground* of the sign functioning, we saw, is a relation between the sign and its object which is exploited in the interpretation of the sign: because the object stands in this relation to the sign, it is determined that it will be interpreted in a certain fashion.

A familiar feature of Peirce's theory of signs is a variety of complex and bewildering classifications of different sorts of signs. These will not be explained exhaustively in this volume, but I shall mention those that are relevant to the general argument. Mostly they work by bringing the theory of categories to bear upon the elements into which the notion of sign is analysed. For instance, Peirce distinguishes three kinds of grounds, and hence speaks of three kinds of signs which differ in the kinds of grounds they have. This introduces the most important of his many classifications, one that we shall return to on several occasions, so it will be useful to explain it now. In the example that we considered, the sign was fitted to signify the recent presence of deer because it stood in a dyadic existential relation to its object: if we come to believe that the deer did not strip the bark, then we shall revise our interpretation of the sign. When we use a floorplan to study the properties of a room, or a colour sample to decide upon a colour scheme, we exploit a property of the sign that it would have had even if its object had not existed. What fits these things for use as signs – the configuration of lines on the plan or the colour of the sample – are properties that they would have had even if the room or brand of paint had not existed; whereas, had the deer not existed, the trees would have lacked the property on which their semiotic functioning rests. We can use the plan or sample because of an isomorphism between them and their objects: there is a correspondence between properties that each could have had whatever the character of the other. The sign is suited to represent anything with the corresponding characters, and Peirce believes that anything has any number of properties that could be exploited for this sort of representation. Signs that exploit a dyadic relation between sign and object are called *indices*, and those which rest upon a shared character are *icons*. Icons are valuable because, since they share properties with what they represent, study of (e.g.) a floorplan can provide us with new information about what it plans; once we know the conventions of representation and the scale, then, measurements on the plan may provide us with new information about the dimensions of the room that it represents. Peirce believes that icons are central to the functioning both of natural language and of mathematical theories: these views will be the topic of chapter VI.

The third kind of ground leads to the class of *symbols*. A flag at the beach signifies that swimming is safe. The use of the flag does not exploit any resemblance between flags and states of the tide; nor is the flag the straightforward causal product of the tide or the current. What qualifies the flag for signifying the safety of the beach is the existence of a general practice of using flags for this purpose, the fact that flags are interpreted as having this meaning. The particular flag is an icon of many other flags which stand in the *triadic* signifying relation to the safety of the beach: it is a 'token' of the 'type', or a 'replica' of the 'symbol'. The symbol is a sort of abstraction definable in terms of the equivalence relation that suits all of its replicas to serve as icons of each other. Since this classification of signs rests upon the categories, Peirce would be able to claim that the classification is exhaustive; there can only be these three sorts of grounds. Most of his classifications involve the categories in just this way: Peirce is even able to establish what sorts of signs are *possible* before he has encountered examples of the different sorts. So long as the initial analysis of the sign relation is correct, the use of the categories to provide an exhaustive classification of signs is an *a priori* inquiry.

My introduction of the distinction between icons, indices and symbols has simplified Peirce's account in two ways; and removing both simplifications will introduce important themes which will be pursued further below. They both involve respects in which two or three of the sorts of grounds can be operative in one sign. In the kinds of sign systems that we shall be concerned with, there are no *pure* icons or indices; all the signs are, to some extent, symbolic. However, we can use the icon, index, symbol trichotomy to make a further subdivision of symbols. For example, it is arguable that it is only because there is a general practice of using them that we are able to apply colour samples; the colour chart is a sort of conventional symbol. However, what the convention requires us to do is to allow the shade of a colour patch to serve as a sign of the paint in (say) the tins labelled with the name under the shade. The convention instructs us in *how* to use the patch as an icon; we do not need a specific convention to determine the meaning of each patch, but a general convention which enables us to use the patch as an icon. Similarly, it is a familiar point that we require conventions to be able to interpret indices such as pointing fingers – we need to know what route to take from the end of the finger to find the object indicated. Once again, the convention is general and instructs us in how to interpret the pointing finger as an index. There is not a special convention determining the referent of every pointing finger. On the other hand, there may be highly conventional signs which involve no iconic or indexical elements: the convention completely specifies what the object is. Although Peirce is not wholly clear on the matter, there are passages that suggest that he thinks there are no pure icons or indices; and his normal usage of the three terms reflects the subclassification of symbols just alluded to. Thus, he holds that 'Any material image, as a painting, is largely conventional in its mode of representation; but in itself, without legend or label it may be called a *hypoicon*' (2.276): mostly, when Peirce stresses the importance of iconic representation, he means 'hypoicons' – see further discussion in chapter VI.

The second factor that complicates the issue can be introduced by reference to our example of the symbolic use of a flag to signify that a beach is safe for bathing. Somebody who correctly interprets this sign is required to grasp that it is safe to bathe on *this* beach *now*. The general convention holds that flying such a flag states that it is safe at the beach where the flag flies, during the time that it is flying. The convention does not uniquely determine the time and place of safe bathing; rather, in using the flag, we combine it with an indexical sign of the time and place: the location of the flag is an index of the place where bathing is safe. The flag can be understood as a sort of predicate that is claimed to be satisfied by the place that is indicated by the location of the flagpole. Any complex sign is likely to contain elements with different sorts of grounds.

Apart from introducing some of his terminology, my aim in this section has been to illustrate what lies behind Peirce's insistence on the triadic character of the sign relation. Two claims support this insistence, and both seem to be importantly true. The first is that a theory of meaning and signification is, at root, a theory of understanding: it must explain how we are able to understand or interpret the meanings of signs. We have not explained how expressions refer to particular objects unless we explain how, in use, they are understood to have that reference. In Peirce's thought, this emerges as the claim that for a sign to have a meaning or reference is for it to have a power to ensure that it is understood in accord with that meaning or reference, a power to produce an interpretant triadically. The second claim is that it is always possible to *misunderstand* a sign: there is a distinction between a correct interpretation of it, and one which is ungrounded. This emerges in the idea that interpretants are produced as a means to coming to a correct understanding of the object of the sign. Signs conduce to learning from experience by mediating between reality and our cognitions, and by storing learned material for subsequent interpretation and use. We can see here the justice of Peirce's remark that 'the essential function of a sign is to render inefficient relations efficient' (SS 31): through the stripped bark, the deer can act on me, although it cannot act on me directly. So far, much has been left vague, and we must now examine some specific claims about the nature of 'scientific assertions', in order to give them a more precise content.

3 The assertions of a scientific intelligence

In this section, we shall introduce some of Peirce's more specific claims about the properties that a language must have if it is to serve as a vehicle for scientific investigations. The task is to use the materials sketched above in order to produce an analysis of assertion; we can then ask what characteristics we should look for in a system of signs that can be used to articulate assertions. There are three Peircean doctrines that I want to explain.

(a) Assertive force and proposition

When we assert something, for example that Socrates is wise, what is asserted is a *proposition*. But,

> One and the same proposition may be affirmed, denied, judged, doubted, inwardly inquired into, put as a question, wished, asked for, effectively commanded, taught, or merely expressed and does not thereby become a different proposition. (NE iv 248)

The first move in Peirce's analysis of assertions, then, is to claim that making an assertion involves doing something with a proposition. We need both to explain what propositions are and account for their semantic properties, and to describe the distinctive character of the form of action on propositions described as *assertion*. I shall sketch Peirce's views on both of these matters.

Although he says little about the different sorts of things that we can do with propositions, we can find three characteristics that he finds in acts of assertion. First, an assertion is 'an act of an utterer of a proposition to an interpreter and consists, in the first place, in the deliberate exercise, in uttering the proposition, of a force tending to determine a belief in it in the mind of the interpreter' (NE iv 249). Thus,

(1) If U asserts that p to I, then U intends his utterance to be effective in bringing it about that I believes that p.

But, how can a mere utterance have this kind of force? Because, second, an assertion 'consists in the furnishing of evidence by the speaker to the listener that the speaker believes something, that is, finds a certain idea to be definitely compulsory on a certain occasion' (2.335).

(2) If U asserts that p to I, then U intends his utterance to show I that U believes that p and he intends I's recognition of this to provide I with a reason for believing that p.

However, since utterers can be insincere – they might assert that p when they do not believe that p – why should I take U's utterance as evidence of his belief? The answer lies in the third characteristic of assertions: when he asserts a proposition, the speaker takes responsibility for its truth. In a ritualized form, this is found when someone swears an oath before a 'notary public', thus incurring penalties if the affirmation is false. But, quite generally, an act of assertion supposes that, a proposition being formulated, a person performs an act which renders him liable to the penalties of the social law (or at any rate, those of the moral law) in case it should not be true, unless he has a definite and sufficient excuse. (2.315)

(3)   If U asserts that p, and U was not justified in believing that p, then, U incurs penalties. (It can be left vague what these penalties could involve.)

U intends I to see that U was prepared to risk censure if p is false, and to see that U intends him, on that basis, to believe that U believes that p, and to see that U intends him, on that basis, to believe that p himself. The act of assertion functions as a sign of all of this to its interpreter. Although, of course, it is a conventional matter that particular kinds of actions count as assertions, still the assertion serves as an index of these beliefs and intentions. The conventions merely guide us in how we may interpret and use such actions as indices. Their indexical character is evident from the fact that our understanding of the assertion rests on the belief that those beliefs and intentions produced the sign, the utterance would not have existed had the beliefs and intentions not been there. The conventions tell us what sorts of beliefs and intentions are expressed by assertions; we do not rely upon specific conventions to determine whose belief is in question, for example.

Peirce makes a few analogous remarks about linguistic actions other than assertions. When a proposition is articulated in a question, the speaker intends the interpreter to take responsibility for saying whether it is true or false; when it occurs in a command, he intends his interpreter to take responsibility for making the proposition true. (See Brock, 1981 and NE iv 39.) He also provides similar remarks about judgment.

[Even] in solitary meditation every judgment is an effort to press home, upon the self of the immediate future and of the general future, some truth. It is a genuine assertion . . .; and solitary dialectic is still of the nature of dialogue. Consequently, it must be equally true that here too there is contained an element of assuming responsibility, of 'taking the consequences'. (5.546)

He is not clear about the penalties we incur when we dissemble to future states of ourselves, or even about how far this is a possibility. I shall not delay over the details of Peirce's theory of assertion, beyond noting that it requires some reformulation to allow for how scientists may regard certain propositions as assertible although, as good scientists, they are careful not to *believe* their results.

Since a proposition can be the object of many different linguistic acts and mental attitudes, and since it can be expressed in any language (NE iv 248), we cannot identify a proposition with a particular linguistic form or sentence type. Moreover, since the indicative form is conventionally linked to the act of assertion, it should not be thought to reveal the structure of a proposition: 'the proposition in the sentence "Socrates est sapiens" strictly expressed, is "Socrates sapientum esse" ' (NE iv 248). Peirce sometimes claims that a proposition is not a complete sign but just a fragmentary part of assertions or judgments. I think his thought is that we can define a relation of '( ) expresses the same proposition as ( )' which holds between linguistic acts, mental acts and other complete signs. Reference to propositions as objects is obtained by hypostatic abstraction applied to this relation; reasoning is facilitated by introducing propositions corresponding to each equivalence class defined using the relation. For the present, we can take reference to propositions simply to point us towards the problem of accounting for how utterances can have a content, how they convey what truth the utterer has risked his reputation upon. This brings us to the second of the themes I want to raise.

(b)   Icon, index and symbol

In an 1885 paper, 'On the Algebra of Logic' (3.359 ff) Peirce introduces the thesis that an adequate language for articulating the content of assertions about reality must involve signs of all three kinds: symbols, icons and indices. This paper is fairly early, but Peirce held to this claim, although others of his views changed. At this stage, I shall just sketch the implications of this view, and Peirce's reason for defending it. It raises the issues that will occupy the two following chapters.

First, why must a language adequate for expressing serious assertions be symbolic? It seems so obvious that we are unsure where to look for an argument. In the 1885 paper, Peirce claims that without 'tokens' (i.e. replicas of symbols) 'there would be no generality in the statements, for they are the only general signs; and generality is essential to reasoning' (3.363). His illustration of this is unhelpful, but I can see two ways in which the point could be made out. First, reasoning involves evaluating one's inferences according to the standards that make up one's *logica utens*. These standards are *general* principles which declare that all inferences of a certain general class are valid. So, if such standards are to be used, signs and inferences must be presented as belonging to general classes: they must share properties, and thus all be replicas of general symbols. A rule of inference is then a statement about all the replicas of a symbolic representation of an argument. The second way of developing the point is rather different. Scientific inquiry takes it that things have general properties; when we assert that Socrates is wise, we ascribe to Socrates a property that other people may share. When I use a sign to ascribe such a general character to something, I mean to assert that that thing has a property that could be ascribed to anything else by using a similar sign. The sign can ascribe a general character to something because it is a replica of a symbol, other replicas of which could be used to ascribe the same character to other things. Both of these arguments link the need for symbols with generality, the first with the generality of rules of inference, the second with the generality of the predicate.

More important for understanding the structure of Peirce's thought, however, are the other two claims: among the symbols employed in such a language must be some whose meaning fits them to function as indices and some that work like icons. It is primarily singular terms and quantifiers that are indices, and predicates that are icons; but recall that the functioning of all of these expressions has a symbolic aspect. The argument for the need for indices in the 1885 paper runs:

> But tokens (i.e. replicas of symbols) do not state what is the object of discourse; and this can, in fact, not be described in general terms; it can only be indicated. The actual world cannot be distinguished from a world of imagination by any description. Hence the need of pronouns and indices . . . (3.363)

Roughly, the argument is that, in order to say something with a predicate such as '( ) is red' or '( ) loves ( )', I must be able to identify existing objects to which I apply those predicates; and, it is not possible to refer to existing objects simply by providing general descriptions of them. The simplest kind of indexical that is used to pick out existing objects is a demonstrative, and so the simplest kind of sentence which reflects the functioning of indexical signs would be something like

this loves that or (perhaps) he loves her.
this is red.

Peirce's reasons for denying that reference can be secured in wholly descriptive terms are linked with his insistence upon the brute secondness of the notion of actual existence. They will be discussed in detail in the next chapter, and I will not elaborate them here. Nor will I deal fully with how his claim informs his views about all the other kinds of referring expressions. Even after developing his logic of relations, Peirce spoke of the structure of sentences in terms of 'subject' and 'predicate'. In connection with a sentence such as

Brutus killed Caesar.

he was happy to say any one of

131

(1) The subjects are 'Brutus' and 'Caesar' and the predicate is '( ) killed
    ( )'.
(2) The subject is 'Brutus' and the predicate is '( ) killed Caesar'.
(3) The subject is 'Caesar' and the predicate is 'Brutus killed ( )'.

Now, we can formulate his claim about indices thus: subject expressions
must pick out their objects indexically.

It will link this doctrine with the claims about assertion, if I explain
the central idea behind Peirce's treatment of quantifiers. (For a fuller
discussion, see Hilpinen, 1982.) Peirce sometimes remarks that because
the utterer risks all upon the truth of the proposition he asserts, he can
be seen as its 'defender' and has an interest in its truth. The interpreter
has a more hostile attitude, since he does not want to adopt a belief and
assert it himself without first assessing the risk he takes of his own
assertions being successfully challenged (R 9). So, Peirce often speaks of
the interpreter as the 'opponent' of the utterance (R 515). The defender
tries to substantiate the assertion, the opponent to refute it. When a
singular proposition is asserted, then it is fixed what state of affairs
confirms or disconfirms the utterance; it is a straightforward matter
what we should do to determine whether the utterer should incur the
penalty. When a sentence contains quantifiers, the indices do not
determine precisely which objects the relational expression or predicate
is asserted to be true of. The indices are 'indefinite'. Suppose that U
asserts

Some warrior is brave.

He reserves to himself the right to determine the individual it is to be
evaluated with respect to. He is only subject to sanction if he selects a
warrior as the one in question and it turns out that that warrior is not
brave, or if it can be shown that it would be impossible for him to select
a warrior with respect to whom his assertion is defensible. If he asserts,

All warriors are brave.

then he allows the interpreter the right to nominate the value of the
index: he faces sanction if any non-brave warrior can be produced by
the interpreter (R 515). In fact, the account is not restricted in its
applications to assertions. If it is reformulated in terms of *defender* and
opponent, then it can be applied to other sorts of speech acts involving
quantifiers too. Our understanding of quantifiers involves a grasp of
procedures for producing propositions in which the quantifiers in a
sentence are replaced by ordinary indices; and these propositions are to
be evaluated in the course of evaluating the quantified sentence.

Why, finally, should we think of predicates as icons? This topic will
be discussed in great detail in chapter VI, so I shall content myself here

with sketching the main line of thought. He assumes that an adequate language must facilitate *reasoning*, discovering new facts about what we know by deductive or mathematical reasoning. And he thinks that only iconic representations can be used to discover new facts about their objects – recall our discussion of floor plans and colour charts in the previous section. If we have a diagram of a state of affairs, inspection of the diagram can reveal unnoticed facts about the state of affairs that it diagrams. Hence, in the 1885 paper, we find

> All deductive reasoning, even simple syllogism, involves an element of observation; namely, deduction consists in constructing an icon or diagram the relations of whose parts shall present a complete analogy with those of the parts of the object of reasoning, or experimenting upon this diagram in the imagination, and of observing the result so as to discover unnoticed and hidden relations among the parts. For instance, take the syllogistic formula

> All M is P
> S is M
> _____
> So, S is P

> This is really a diagram of the relations of S, M and P. The fact that the middle term occurs in the two premisses is actually exhibited, and this must be done or the notation will be of no value. (3.363)

This example might indicate that a formal logic must exploit iconic representations of the structures of arguments, although more argument is needed if the point is to carry full conviction. Although that would suffice to make Peirce's point that an adequate logical and scientific language must use icons, it does not yet establish Peirce's frequent claim that predicates are typically icons.

I shall note just two features of predicates, reflected in their role in reasoning, which make this claim appropriate. First, predicates are unsaturated expressions with a definite valency. This valency has a bearing on the kinds of arguments involving the predicate that are valid, and in an adequate notation the valancy of the predicate is shown in its expression. For example, we might write,

( ) is red
( ) loves ( )

and so on. The predicate expression is an iconic sign because its unsaturated bonds correspond to the valency of the relation that it expresses: the notation 'diagrams' a feature of the relation expressed. We assert that a dyadic relation holds between two objects by using a representation in which a dyadic relation holds between indices for the two objects – they saturate the two bonds of a relational expression. Secondly, when I use a predicate to ascribe a property to an object, the expression I use will occur in many other statements that I accept. For example, I shall accept that

Whatever is red is coloured.
Whatever is red reflects light of wavelength φ.

The fact that the expression occurs in all these contexts is exploited when I reason about the object I take to be red. My understanding of the predicate expression involves a grasp of the relations to other predicates and relational expressions articulated in other statements that I accept. The set of statements involving the predicate that I accept provides a sort of 'diagram' of the corresponding property and its relations to other properties. Hence, the typical notation for predicates functions iconically and thus facilitates reasoning. More needs to be said about the iconic character of reasoning and predicate expressions. I have not yet explained just how deductive reasoning is observational or indicated just what the objects of predicates are so that we can understand how there can be the sort of isomorphism between icon and its object that Peirce insists upon. However, I hope that it is now clear why Peirce thinks it important to stress the role of icons in a logical and scientific language.

(c) Conditionals and predication

We can now understand how Peirce's categories are reflected in the structure of language: they appear not just in the valencies of unsaturated expression, but also in the sorts of grounds possessed by other signs. We explained the act of assertion and the role of singular terms in terms of their indexical function – the ground of their semantic functioning is a dyadic relation. So long as all of the expressions employed are icons, indices or symbols, the three numerological categories are implicit in their use. However, even if all of the expressions used in building up propositions reflect the categories, it is possible that further categorial conceptions are manifested in our ability to form and understand complete propositions that involve them. What is the semantic functioning of the different ways of combining indices and icons into complete propositions? Does this manifest an additional category?

I shall approach the question indirectly, by way of a description of Peirce's opinion on one of the philosophical issues that most divided logicians in the nineteenth century. It concerns the relation between categorical and hypothetical propositions, for example,

All seals are mammals.
If all seals are mammals then seals give birth to live young.

You will recall from our examination of Kant's table of judgments in the previous chapter, that he thought that these represented fundamentally different forms of judgments. Just as Peirce questioned the claim that the distinction between hypothetical and disjunctive propositions reflected an irreducible logical difference, so many logicians had debated whether categorical could be reduced to hypothetical or vice versa. A view on this issue had clear implications for the form that one's formal logic should take. If hypotheticals were reducible to categoricals, then a formal treatment of the categorical syllogism would not require supplementation by a separate treatment of arguments involving hypotheticals. Peirce often discusses this issue, and the following remarks reflect the views he expresses in some later texts (e.g. NE iv 169 ff; NE iii 414 and see Dipert, 1981 for a helpful fuller discussion). In effect, he claims to discern a common form in both of the propositions above. The presence of a conditional in the categorial claim is a familiar theme from the formalization of such propositions using the predicate calculus. Roughly, we can paraphrase the example above as,

Anything is such that, if it is a seal then it is a mammal.

The sentence is represented as involving a conditional open sentence within the scope of a universal quantifier. Peirce holds that a similar form can be discerned in the hypothetical sentence. This is because he believes that ordinary conditionals involve an implicit quantification over 'cases'. We can paraphrase the example above,

All cases are such that, if they are cases of all seals being mammals, then they are cases of seals giving birth to live young.

In each case, we find a 'boolean' (a conditional open sentence) within the scope of a quantifier. In each case, the quantifier indexically signifies what universe of discourse we should use in evaluating the proposition. Peirce supposes that, in ordinary usage, we understand the quantification as ranging over *possible* cases: the sentence would be true if the consequent was true in any possible state of affairs in which the antecedent was true. However, contextual indicators can suggest that we have a different universe of discourse in mind; and for purposes of formal logic, it often simplifies things to restrict attention to the actual case, so that the conditional expresses the familiar material conditional (e.g. 3.374–5). Each sentence has a form which Peirce could express thus:

$$(x) \ (Ax \mathbin{>\!\!\!-\!\!} Bx).$$

The expression ' $\succ$— ' represents a connective that lies at the heart of both forms of sentence construction; its significance is close to that of the horseshoe in more familiar notations. Since he has a negation sign available, our problem of accounting for the semantic force of combining terms into a proposition can be approached by considering the meaning of ' $\succ$— '. The only propositions that are excluded are wholly singular ones, such as:

That is a seal.

Such propositions only occur properly in perceptual judgments, and will be examined in the next chapter.

Although Peirce sometimes explains the meaning of ' $\succ$— ' by saying, in effect, that a conditional is false only if the antecedent is true and the consequent false, we should look more closely at explanations that use the sign theory more explicitly. Roughly, Peirce's thought seems to be that 'A $\succ$— B' means that A's being the case is a sign that B is the case. An assertion of 'A $\succ$— B' is defensible only in this circumstance, so that the utterer faces censure if A is the case and B is not. Hence, as Peirce often puts it, the subject of a categorical proposition is a sign of the predicate, and the antecedent of a conditional is a sign of the consequent; we have to allow him some looseness about use and mention here. Thus, the sign relation provides an analysis of the structure of propositions; and thirdness is revealed in the form of the proposition.

What we have found in this section is a sketch of how the theory of signs can be used to provide a general account of how language works. This general account of language would fall into two parts. First, there would be a systematic explanation of the procedures involved in defending and opposing (verifying and falsifying) propositions of different kinds. The second component accounts for the different things that we do with propositions – using them to perform communicative actions, adopting cognitive stances towards them, or making them the objects of our mental acts – by relating these actions, attitudes and acts to the procedures of defence and opposition. However, there is a notion central to the whole theory – we have used it constantly in these pages – which has been left very obscure. This is the *object* of a sign. What sorts of objects do signs have? What are the 'objects' diagrammed by predicates? Taking up this issue in the next section will provide us with an opportunity to examine the relations between the theory of signs and the substantive account of truth provided within the normative sciences. I mentioned above that Peirce's central concern could be formulated in semiotic terms: how can representations be veridical, and how can we conduct our inquiries to ensure that we obtain veridical representations of reality? We have to trace the connections between representations and truth which will enable us to give those questions some content.

4 Objects and interpretants

The question from which we shall begin is: what is the *object* of a sign like an indicative sentence that expresses a proposition? Peirce often refers to such signs as *dicisigns*, or *dicent* signs; they can be used to say something that can be assessed as true or false (2.309 ff). It is hard to find a settled statement of Peirce's response to this question, and I shall concentrate upon one text, a 'Syllabus' published in the *Collected Papers* at 2.309 ff. Since we have discussed their functioning already, I shall ignore dicent signs that contain quantifiers and conditionals and, assuming that ordinary proper names are indices, examine examples like

Tully has a wart on the end of his nose. (2.315)
Cain kills Abel. (2.316)

As will be clear from earlier remarks, Peirce takes both to be of subject-predicate form, the second sentence having two subjects or having the ordered pair of Cain and Abel as subject (2.316). 'Tully', 'Cain', and 'Abel' are assumed to be indices, and '( ) has a wart on the end of his nose' and '( ) kills ( )' are unsaturated expressions – predicates, 'rhemes' or 'sumisigns'. (I shall resist the temptation to quote most of Peirce's technical terminology, which is extensive and somewhat barbarous. For the views of the ethics of terminology which support these coinings, see Oehler, 1981 and Ketner, 1981.)

The indices denote actually existing things, secondnesses to which they stand in a dyadic relation. Thus, 'Tully' denotes the man Tully, 'Cain' denotes Cain and so on. The predicate expression is an icon of a firstness of quality, something whose identity does not turn on its relations to other things. However, what concerns us here is the object of the dicisign as a whole. Now Peirce claims that the dicisign must contain two parts – a subject and a predicate – and is itself an index of an object which 'involves something corresponding to those parts' (2.311). The existing objects denoted by the indices must be so connected to the firstness represented iconically by the predicate, that the dicisign as a whole can indexically represent an object that incorporates both.

Hence the Dicisign must exhibit a connection between these parts of itself, and must represent this connection to correspond to a connection in the object between the (objects denoted by the indices) and the Firstness . . . (2.311)

> [If] the Dicisign has any object, it must be an index of a Secondness subsisting between the Real Object represented in one represented part of the Dicisign to be indicated and a Firstness represented in the other represented part of the Dicisign to be Iconized. (2.312)

Simplifying a bit, the idea seems to be that the object of the dicisign is the inherence of the quality expressed by the icon in the existing thing(s) indicated by the indices. The object, in that case, would be something similar to what is often referred to as a *state of affairs*. These rather vague formulations point us towards rather important questions which will be taken up in the next chapter. They concern both why we should think of the dicisign as an *index* of this state of affairs, and, more important, how we are to make sense of this relation between a firstness or a quality, and an existing thing – what sort of 'subsisting' 'connection' is this? Does it introduce an additional category?

Next, I want to note some of the logical features of the thoughts and other signs that serve as interpretants. First, an interpretant of a particular sign refers to a particular object, and represents that object *as* the object of the sign interpreted. For example, when I interpret the name 'Tully' I think of that name as serving as an index of the individual Tully; and when I interpret the dicisign 'Tully has a wart on the end of his nose' I think of that sign as containing a part that is an index of Tully, a part that is an icon of having a wart on the end of one's nose, and as being an index of the state of affairs of Tully having that quality. (In 2.310, Peirce suggests that since the original sign determines its interpretant, the sign itself represents itself as having all of these properties. But, this is a complication that we can ignore here.) If I have a lot of additional knowledge about the objects of the sign, there is no reason why this should not be reflected in the interpreting thought. Fuller descriptions of the objects of the signs may be employed. Thus, I can interpret the sentence we are considering as containing a part that is an index of the famous orator Cicero who . . . , and as containing a part that is an icon of the quality of having a small hardish excrescence on the end of the organ that is used for smelling and breathing . . . etc. One effect of the growth of scientific knowledge is that our interpretations of assertions can become ever richer and, in Peirce's phrase, more developed. We come to a fuller knowledge of what the object of the sign is. It is consonant with this that drawing an inference from a proposition we hear asserted can be an important part of coming to an interpretation of it. Having heard and understood an assertion, I may set myself the task of obtaining a more developed interpretation of it. These more developed interpretations will convey far more about the objects than was conveyed by the original assertion.

Peirce contrasts three kinds of interpretant, the immediate, dynamic and final interpretant. The immediate interpretant is the interpreting thought that is, so to speak, called for by the sign itself. Someone who did not see that our sentence meant that Tully had a wart on the end of his nose would, simply, not have understood the sentence. Someone might exploit his knowledge of Roman history to go beyond the immediate interpretant, treating the utterance as a sign that *Cicero* had a wart on his nose. This, the interpreting thought that is actually produced on some occasion, is the dynamical interpretant. The final interpretant is difficult to describe clearly, but the idea is that it is the interpretant which would be reached if a process of enriching the interpretant through scientific inquiry were to proceed indefinitely. It incorporates a complete and true conception of the objects of the sign; it is the interpretant we should all agree on in the long run, were we to inquire for long enough. When Peirce describes science as a process of sign interpretation, we can now see what he means: learning from experience involves moving ever closer to the final interpretants of assertions that have been made in the scientific community.

Relatedly, but more mysteriously, there is a distinction between real and immediate object; Peirce distinguished the real and immediate object of any sign. I think it is misleading to see this as calling for two distinct actual existents referred to by an index, for example. The contrast is between the object as it seems to be at the time at which the sign is first used and interpreted, and the object as it is known to be in the final interpretant. It is better expressed by contrasting two answers to the question: what object does this sign refer to? One is the answer that could have been given when the sign was used; and the other is the one we could give when our scientific knowledge is complete. Of course, since on many questions we have already reached the answer that will be the object of the ultimate consensus, the immediate and real object may be the same. The thought that underlies the distinction is that we have to wait on scientific inquiry to discover the real character of the object of our assertion or other sign. Then, we can again redescribe the character of science: it attempts to discover the real objects of our assertions. And we can also see that our original question of how it is possible to discover the nature of reality can be recast as the question how there can be a process of sign interpretation which will account for the fact that our assertions have discoverable real objects.

The final issue to be considered in this section is: how are these claims about the nature of assertion, the structure of propositions, and the sorts of objects possessed by dicisigns to be brought into harmony with the theory of truth developed in the normative sciences? In a sense, that raises the principle question for the remainder of this volume. But, we can briefly bring to bear some of the points that have just been made to indicate a route towards the solution of it. A dicisign, we saw, represents a quality (a first) and an existing thing (a second) to stand in a brute dyadic relation. The sign interpretation employs rational procedures to find order (thirdness) in the juxtaposition of existence and quality reported in the dicisign. We discover the real object by finding law in the world of our experience. The end of inquiry laid down by the normative sciences is an end to be followed in developing our understanding of our assertions, and filling out our knowledge of their objects. Our task now is to tackle in detail the question how we should act when we resolve to seek the truth.

How far have we got in our examination of Peirce's theories about signs? As I mentioned at the beginning of this chapter, my concern has been to indicate the broad themes and approaches which characterize his work; the details will receive more treatment subsequently. However, we have uncovered what is involved in his insistence upon the triadic character of sign action and we have a broad outline of the concepts he uses in analysing assertions and propositions. In the course of doing this, we have been able to trace a further thread in Peirce's defence of his categories; there is no indication so far that the mastery of a natural or scientific language betrays the use of categorial conceptions other than those elaborated in chapter III. If our understanding of the assertive force of utterances, of the significance of the propositional tie, and of the use of singular terms or indices can be accounted for in terms of our grasp of the triadic sign relation and our ability to think about the different sorts of grounds that different signs have, then there is no need to supplement the three categories, firstness, secondness and thirdness. Finally, through noting some of Peirce's classifications of objects and interpretants, we are able to see the force of his claiming that science is a form of sign interpretation.

Readers who are familiar with the development of analytic philosophy of language in this century will recognize many of these Peircean themes. In the previous chapter, we noted that Frege and Peirce share the doctrine that predicates are unsaturated expressions, and the distinction between assertoric force and propositional content is also found in both. The claim that predicates are icons has clear affinities with Wittgenstein's picture theory of the proposition – although Peirce has no sympathy for the doctrine of logical atomism. And the insistence that a theory of assertion and understanding has a fundamental role in philosophy is more common ground between Peirce and the analytic tradition. This prompts the question whether the many differences in terminology, focus and style do not conceal a broadly similar approach. Does a Peircean semiotics promise anything distinctively new or different from a philosophical account of language of the familiar kind? Since there are so many differences of detail, it is hard to offer a clear answer to this question. Peirce's Kantian orientation and theory of categories lend a flavour to his work which is absent from Frege, Russell or the early Wittgenstein; and his lack of sympathy for anything like the logicist programme of grounding mathematics in logic, together with his interest in problems in the logic of science, led his thought to develop in somewhat different directions. And he places a stress upon the irreducibility of semantic notions, and upon the ways in which our practices create the possibility of understanding and interpretation which have more in common with the *Philosophical Investigations* than with the writings of 1900–20. Finally, as we shall see immediately below, Peirce dreamed of a theory with a broader application in logic and metaphysics than Frege or Wittgenstein. But, in spite of these differences, I think it is best to approach Peirce assuming that he sought something very similar to an analytical philosophy of language. He desired a systematic theory of assertion or understanding, and planned to use this to explain the validity of forms of deductive inference and of our mathematical practice; and he proposed to use this systematic theory of meaning to justify the adoption of methods of ampliative inquiry. Although differences of interest and philosophical temperament led him into the task of producing complex *a priori* classifications of signs which may have no ready application, this should not prevent our seeing that his underlying motivation and basic ideas have much in common with what has fuelled the more familiar developments of the twentieth century.

5   *The scope of semiotics*

I have concentrated, in this chapter, on the bearing of Peirce's claims about signs on questions about assertions made in the course of serious inquiry. And this is consonant with the view that the theory of signs is primarily concerned with the sorts of assertions made by a scientific intelligence, someone capable of learning from experience. Inquiry is to be thought of as a triadic process of sign interpretation, guided by the goal of coming to know the real character of the objects of our signs. In concluding the discussion, I shall offer some comments on the ways in which the general theory of signs – semiotics – could be thought to have broader and more ambitious aims. How extensive is the class of sign phenomena? Is it limited to utterances and thoughts employed in cognitive discourse, or has it a wider extension?

Many suppose that the theory should have application to a much wider range of human 'representations', and hold that it could be used to illuminate our understanding of painting, music, literature, customs and traditions, myths and symbols, and aspects of our conversational linguistic practice that are not directed towards the discovery of the truth. Understanding, in such cases, is linked to interpretation, and, it can be argued, has the appropriate triadic structure. It is not necessary to view such representations as assertions, and the goal according to which our practices of interpretation are judged need not be that of seeking the truth. Rather, we are pointed towards a general theory of the triadic interpretation of signs as a means of securing some end or goal; and the theory of scientific assertions would be a special determination of this theory. What is crucial is the triadic character of the process of interpretation; it is a teleological process guided by a (perhaps not consciously formulated) 'goal of interpretation'. Although he was not primarily interested in such applications of the theory, Peirce would have been sympathetic to generalizing it in this way. Some scholars find useful materials for doing so in the many classifications of signs that Peirce provided in the years after 1900. They result from applying the categories to the abstract analysis of sign action to establish *a priori* what sorts of signs are possible. Many of the signs that emerge from the classification would have no real role in scientific discourse. Since it would be impossible to do them justice except at great length, and since they have little direct bearing on the central themes of this book, I am not going to discuss these complex classifications.

Two other examples discussed by Peirce suggest that the theory can be generalized still further. The first involves seeing triadic action in the animal world, and describing this in semiotic terms. Remembering that inference is a process of sign interpretation, notice this passage, from 'A Theory of Probable Inference' published in 1883.

> In point of fact, a syllogism in *Barbara* virtually takes place when we irritate the foot of a decapitated frog. The connection between the afferent and efferent nerve, whatever it may be, constitutes a nervous habit, a rule of action, which is the physiological analogue of the major premiss. The disturbance of the ganglionic equilibrium, owing to the irritation, is the physiological form of that which, psycho-logically considered, is a sensation; and logically considered, is the occurrence of a case. The explosion through the efferent nerve is the physiological form of that which psychologically is a volition, and logically the inference of a result. (2.711. cf 6.286 and elsewhere)

Other passages suggest that his view of this example is ambivalent. In the absence of some flexibility of response which would enable the frog to respond to new situations and learn new responses, the example – like one he discusses of an ordinary thermostat – could be described as involving only dyadic action (see 5.473 and generally, Ransdell, 1977, p. 160 and Short, 1981). However, the example illustrates that where we find 'triadic action' in nature, phenomena that we find it useful to describe in teleological terms as involving adoption of means towards an end or processes that involve final causation, Peirce would be ready to describe what we find in terms drawn from the theory of signs. As Short notes (1981, pp. 375–6), Peirce takes 'being governed by a purpose or other final cause' to be 'the very essence of the psychic phenomenon in general' (1.269), and links this with his semiotics in the assertion that 'The mind works by final causation, and final causation is logical causation' (1.250).

> In effect, Peirce generalized the concept of the mental to bring out the continuity between the human mind and other types of teleological process: in scores of passages he spoke of the behaviour of microörganisms, biological evolution, and even the growth of crystals as exhibiting mentality. (Short, 1981, p. 375)

What we find in this work, I think, is an attempt to generalize the analysis of signs so that sign action is coextensive with 'triadic action' and incorporates all forms of thirdness. Ordinary assertions provide our main exemplars of a process formulated in much more general terms, of which they are a special determination.

This tendency culminates in the objective idealism that Peirce defends after 1890. Matter, he tells us, is effete mind; it is just mind become hidebound with habits. Persuaded that a form of monism must be true and convinced that materialism cannot account for mental phenomena, Peirce claims that physical phenomena are fundamentally mental. The importance of this doctrine for his system, and the arguments he provides in its support, will be discussed with the rest of his metaphysics in chapter IX. At this stage, I want to point out how it permits a generalization of the sign theory so that it accounts for all thirdness. As we shall see, Peirce identifies natural law as a form of thirdness. Thus, he claims that it operates according to the general pattern of 'triadic action', by final causation, and thus assimilates it to sign activity. He needs to explain how the law is related to the actual existent events that conform to it, and exploits an analogy with the relation between the law of the land and acts that conform to it. In a famous passage, he writes that 'a law, by itself without the addition of a living reaction to carry it out on each separate occasion, is as impotent as a judge without a sheriff' (7.532), and insists that no sense can be made of efficient causation without final causation (1.220). The picture that emerges is that the actual reactions occur 'in order that' the law be realized; and the derivation of the reactions from the law can be conceptualized as analogous to inference, a process of sign interpretation. The 'cosmic sheriff' is required to ensure that the actual world interprets the natural laws correctly!

I am not going to comment upon these bizarre doctrines here, beyond pointing out that the notions of final causation and sign interpretation obviously become very attenuated as the theory becomes more abstract and its applications of a greater variety. The applications of the theory in logic would not be threatened if these generalizations of it turned out to be unsatisfactory; and the generalizations stand or fall with Peirce's objective idealism. It is not even fruitful at this stage to speculate about how much explanatory force a theory of such generality can have, or about how much content remains for notions like sign and triadic action at the limit. However, I hope this brief discussion has conveyed something of the importance that Peirce's semiotics had for him: it provided the philosophical foundation of what he thought was the principal mode of operation of the cosmos – final causation.

Conclusion to Part One

We have now arrived at a general understanding of Peirce's philosophical project. He seeks a first philosophy prior to all of the natural and human sciences, and is, throughout, sensitive to problems about just how there can be such a discipline. Using techniques drawn from mathematics and phenomenology, he attempts to construct a substantive conception of truth or reality, and he argues that it is rational to devote our lives to the scientific search for an accurate representation of that reality. By contributing to the growth of knowledge we can become fulfilled, autonomous and happy rational beings; we adopt an ultimate aim which we can continue to revere whatever misfortunes we may meet. Our task now is to examine more closely Peirce's account of how we can act in accordance with this overriding aim, and his attempted proof that, when we seek the truth, we adopt an aim which is, in fact, attainable. He has to convince us that procedures are available to us that will reveal the nature of reality. We have already examined, in general terms, the fundamental notions that he employs, his system of categories and the theory of representation that he derives from his study of signs. We must now look more closely at the details of these theories by seeing how they are put to work in an account of how knowledge is possible. Thus, in chapter V we examine the role of perception in grounding claims to knowledge, in chapter VI we consider the validity of deductive reasoning and our mathematical practices, and in chapter VII we discover how the inductive methods of the sciences exploit perceptual information, mathematics and deductive reasoning to guide us towards the truth.

As we have developed the general framework of Peirce's philosophical thought, we have had to pass over many of the details with a forward reference to later discussion. We shall now begin to discharge many of the promissory notes issued along the way. For example, chapter V will contain a more detailed explanation of how Peirce's three categories are encountered in experience, and of the relation between the abstract characterization of reality provided in the normative sciences and the familiar world of our experience. And both chapter V and chapter VI will deepen our understanding of Peirce's theory of signs, through detailed discussions of the role of indices in perceptual judgments and icons in mathematical reasoning. In chapter VI, on mathematical reasoning, we at last get down to the true foundations of Peirce's system, considering why he thinks that mathematics needs no foundations and can thus provide a vehicle for investigations in first philosophy. Finally, we shall study the metaphysical view that Peirce defends in order to vindicate his right to adopt the many regulative hopes that are required to keep his investigation going.

At several points we have presented Peirce's doctrines as inspired by, or responding to, ideas which are found in Kant. Although the relations between Peirce and Kant will be less on the surface from now on, they are none the less importantly present. To a considerable extent, Peirce is eager to show that certain Kantian doctrines are dispensable. Kant thought it necessary to supplement his theory of categories with other doctrines in order to provide a comprehensive theory of knowledge; Peirce denies that the supplementation is required. According to Kant, empirical knowledge requires the cooperation of two distinct faculties. The understanding employs general concepts to formulate thoughts about objects which are presented to us through 'sensibility': sensibility yields 'intuitions' which, roughly, are the representations of material things which provide materials for thought (A 19, B 34). Just as the understanding is constrained to conceptualize experience in accordance with the categories, so sensibility can only present objects to us ordered in space and time. Space and time, the 'forms' of sensibility, reflect how things appear to us, but not how they are in themselves. Just as the categories reflect how our understanding constitutes empirical reality, so space and time reflect the fact that empirical reality is conditioned by the forms of our sensibility; they are empirically real but transcendentally ideal. Hence, an important part of the Kantian programme will involve linking these different *a priori* elements, showing how the categories are applied to things in space and time. Moreover, Kant believes that mathematical knowledge is obtained by mapping the structure of these forms: geometry studies the structure of space, pure mechanics the structure of time, and arithmetic the structure of some rather abstract combinatorial possibilities which reflect the structures of both space and time. There are many similarities between the claims about perception and about mathematical knowledge to be found in the works of Peirce and Kant. Both reject representational theories of perception and claim that we have direct knowledge of the empirical world; and both hold that the mathematician studies a structure by constructing an instance of it and examining its properties. But Peirce does not adopt the Kantian thesis that space and time are the forms of our sensibility. He thinks that he can use his categories to perform the tasks that prompted Kant to supplement his with *a priori* forms of intuition. In both chapters V and VI we see Peirce showing that he can construct adequate theories of perception and mathematics using simply his theory of categories and the theory of signs.

As well as observing things and bringing them under general laws, we seek to embed these discoveries in a 'system' of knowledge (B 673). We construct abstract and wide-ranging theories which bring explanatory order to the many regularities that we observe: empirical laws are seen as derivable from more abstract laws, sciences are reduced to more abstract sciences, and a systematic unity is sought in the whole of our knowledge. Kant's categories neither prescribe the form that this unity should take, nor guarantee that it can be found. Yet we plainly have criteria, standards of plausibility and explanatory completeness, which guide us in developing and evaluating theories. Thus, the categories and forms of intuition have to be supplemented by further concepts which guide theory choice. These derive from reason. This faculty is primarily exercised in moral or practical decision, and metaphysical excess results if we think that its guiding principles, the *ideas*, are readily applicable to the empirical world. However, the ideas do have a limited *regulative* role in theoretical inquiry: using them to evaluate theories we hope that the world can be displayed as meaningful and intelligible; we approach the world as if it were constructed by a benevolent deity in order to be knowable and comprehensible to us. But we do not *know* that their use will provide knowlege. We just hope that higher genera can be found which will unify all the variety that we find in experience, that further inquiry will help us to subdivide the kinds that empirical inquiry has uncovered; and that our experience displays continuity rather than discontinuity (B 670 ff).

These claims will remind us of several Peircean themes. Science aims for a unification of experience which goes beyond the unification that is involved in simply having perceptual beliefs; this additional unification is described as something which it is rational to pursue although we have no guarantee that it can be achieved. Moreover, it links the maxims that guide inquiry with the standards applied in ethical and aesthetic judgment: both aesthetic judgment and the employment of the ideas in science involve understanding phenomena as exhibiting structures to be understood in teleological terms, as being particularly appropriate for appreciation by our cognitive apparatus. However, once again, Peirce is eager to distance himself from Kant. In chapters VII and VIII we shall find that he hopes to account for all aspects of theory choice without making use of any concepts which are not subject to the categories, which are not rules for the ordering of possible experience. At one point, he specifically glosses pragmatism as the rejection of the Kantian doctrine – which he is tempted to call 'practicalism' – that the ideas of practical reason have a role in science. All concepts that are used in science can occur in what Kant called pragmatic beliefs, by which he meant beliefs that are relevant to anticipating the future run of experience (5.412). But, we must now turn to the details of Peirce's theory.

PART TWO

Knowledge and Reality

V

Perception and the
Outward Clash

1   Introduction

In 1885, Peirce quoted Hegel, 'We must be in contact with our subject
matter, whether it be by means of our external senses, *or what is better*,
by our profounder mind and our innermost self consciousness' (8.41 n),
and he commented:

> The capital error of Hegel which permeates his whole system in every
> part of it is that he almost altogether ignores the Outward Clash.
> . . . [This] direct consciousness of hitting and getting hit enters into all
> cognition and serves to make it mean something real. (8.41)

While Peirce and Hegel agree that the 'outward clash' of the external
senses *can* put us into contact with our subject matter, or enable our
cognition to 'mean something real', Hegel views this as a second-rate
sort of contact with reality and aspires to something better. Peirce, on
the other hand, holds that this form of secondness is our only means of
access to reality; the real world which is the object of our inquiries is,
we might say, only *encountered* through perception. The theory of
perception obviously occupies a fundamental role in Peirce's epistemology, and we must now turn to an examination of his account of how
our beliefs can be answerable to perception. First, we must clarify what
is at stake in the discussion of how we are in contact with our subject
matter, of what the problem is about how cognition can 'mean
something real'.

In 'Sense and Certainty', Goodman argues that 'we cannot suppose
that statements derive their credibility from other statements without
ever bringing this string of statements down to earth.' Although some of
our opinions may be supported by their deductive and probabilistic
links with other statements, he insists that 'credibility does not spring

151

from these connections by spontaneous generation. Somewhere along the line some statements must have initial credibility' (Goodman, 1952, pp. 162–3). The growth of knowledge requires that some beliefs represent new inputs, and these can constrain other opinions because of the deductive and other links that they have to them. It is natural to suppose that it is perceptual beliefs which have this 'initial credibility'; although, as Goodman notes, this is far from being the only possibility. If we do adopt this natural supposition, we should have an explanation of the importance of perception for the growth of knowledge: the rational support possessed by any opinion would be traced, eventually, to the 'initial credibility' possessed by perceptual beliefs, this credibility having been transmitted through the deductive and probabilistic links between statements. If we agree that it is through the statements with initial credibility that we 'make contact with' reality, we might conclude that some argument like Goodman's is what Peirce alludes to in his 1885 discussion. He is eager to block a regress that threatens if we hold that every opinion is the product of a conscious inference from other opinions.

However, we can easily see that more is going on than this. As I noted above, a defence would be required of the claim that it is perceptual beliefs that have this grounding role. One form this defence could take would be a demonstration that, as a matter of psychological fact, people do attach an initial credibility to beliefs that result from perception. But, if that were all the defence that was offered, it could remain an open question whether serious investigators should attach much importance to these beliefs in their deliberations. We need an explanation of why investigators should make their theories answerable to the products of perceptual experience; and it is not enough to say that, as a matter of psychological fact, people are very sure of their non-inferential perceptual reports. Our sense of this issue will be sharpened when we consider the implications of Peirce's fallibilism. Common sense, as well as reflection upon scientific practice, assures us that although perceptual reports may have 'initial credibility', they are at best a fallible guide to the nature of reality. While we test our theories against perceptual reports, we also appeal to our theories and hypotheses in deciding whether a surprising observation deserves credence. Unless we have a principled explanation of when and how theory can be allowed to override experience – and it is not enough to refer simply to the psychological fact that we are very sure of some observations and some theories – we are likely to lose track both of a special role for perception in enabling our cognitions to 'mean something real' and of the idea of an objective reality whose character is not determined by our psychological constitution.

As the quotation with which we began suggests, the point that Peirce

152

wants to stress is *semantic*; he is not simply trying to block a regress of justification. Of course, the pragmatist principle itself indicates that meaning and perceptual experience are related: we clarify the meaning of a general term by describing the *experiential* consequences of acting upon something to which the term applies. However, if we explain Peirce's point in this way we shall once again miss his fundamental concern. As has been explained above, one of Peirce's goals is to find a non-question-begging proof of his pragmatism. Especially after 1900, we can see his stress upon the importance of the 'outward clash' as an attempt to forge a link between perception and cognition that can be used as a premiss for the argument for pragmatism: it is *because* we encounter reality through perception that the application of the principle will clarify the whole meaning of a term. In the 1885 manuscript, it is claimed that the importance of the outward clash is a consequence of a result in formal logic. We shall see below that this result concerns the nature of reference. However, before elaborating how Peirce's doctrine can be viewed as a thesis about reference, I shall introduce some of the themes involved by linking it to some of his later theories of truth.

We saw in chapter II that Peirce's substantive conception of truth or reality incorporates the idea that reality is encountered through perception. His position was caricatured as involving the claim that a statement was true if it formed part of a coherent body of theory none of whose deductive consequences clashed with experience. This rested upon the assumption that reality could be shown to be a sort of aesthetic unity, involving qualitative characters standing in brute dyadic relations, which were mediated by law. Perception provided the raw material, so to speak, for this harmonious structure. The coherence of Peirce's position depended upon our finding solutions to two distinct problems about perception. The first has not been discussed above. It is that we must be able to describe perceptual experience using the philosophical categories in a fashion that makes clear how the substantive conception of truth can be understood as the right sort of structure of firstness, secondness and thirdness. One of the themes of this chapter will be the phenomenological analysis of perceptual experience which is intended to provide a response to this problem.

The second problem arises out of this and leads us into the issues concerning perception and reference. The substantive definition of truth risked circularity. Staying with our caricature of the position, we can see that the account would be circular if we had to use the notion of truth in explaining what was involved in having consequences that *clash* with experience – as would be the case if, for example, we unpacked this as having consequences which are inconsistent with a true perceptual report. If perceptual judgments were infallible, then the circularity would not arise; we could simply say that the true theory will have no consequences which conflict with perceptual judgments. But Peirce is a fallibilist and cannot escape the problem in this fashion.

The second problem about truth was simply that of avoiding this circularity. Fallibilism raises further problems about just how perceptual judgments are revised, and how their corrigibility is compatible with the fundamental character of the outward clash. Central to Peirce's response to these difficulties is the claim that the fundamental form of reference to existing objects involves the use of demonstrative expressions, indices, in perceptual judgments. Subsequent inquiry may lead us to revise our conception of the object of a given perceptual judgment, but this subsequent inquiry is still anchored to reality through that perception. When I correct a perceptual report, deciding that what seemed to be a grazing cow was really a rock on the distant hillside, what I am thinking about is still the thing encountered in the original misleading perception. I discover the real object of my perceptual judgment. And, it is only because of this link traced back through the original perception that the subsequent thought means (i.e. refers to) anything real at all. These points will be familiar from the discussion of immediate and real objects in chapter IV. They are also, as Peirce acknowledges in 8.41, of Kantian pedigree. For Kant, space and time are the forms of outer and inner sense and constitutive of empirical reality. Importantly, they provide a framework for the identification and re-identification of material objects; material objects can be referred to on the basis of their spatio-temporal location. For Peirce too, the theory of perception has at its core a theory of reference.

We can distinguish four elements in the view of perception Peirce defends. First, perceptual judgments are certain and 'acritical': they do not result from controlled deliberation and we cannot but find them compelling when we form them. They have 'initial credibility' but, and this is the second point, we can come to regard them as conveying false information about the world – they are fallible. Thirdly, he holds to a form of immediate perception. Like Kant, he thinks that we are directly acquainted with elements of empirical reality, and not with states of ourselves which represent or intervene between ourselves and empirical reality. Finally, the primary form of reference to existing objects involves the use of demonstrative expressions in perceptual judgments. The third element demonstrates the links between Peirce's thought about perception and his account of reality; and the fourth brings reference to centre stage. All these themes will be discussed in this chapter. Part Two provides a description of Peirce's views about the phenomenological structure of perceptual experience, and introduces his views about the logic of perceptual reports or perceptual judgments. In the following section, there is a fuller examination of his account of reference, and his views about how perceptual judgments are revised. The final section provides a fuller discussion of thirdness and generality. In accordance with his later extreme realism, and wanting to retain the idea that the elements of reality are all present in perceptual experience, Peirce wanted to show that generality or thirdness is perceived. Hence, this seemed an appropriate place to offer some explanation of his many murky claims about the reality of universals.

2 Percepts and perceptual judgments: the elements of perception

There are, in our cognitive experience, two elements; the immediate data, such as those of sense which are present or given to the mind, and a form, construction, or interpretation, which represents the activity of thought. Recognition of this fact is one of the oldest and most universal of philosophic insights. However, the manner in which these elements, and their relation to one another, are conceived, varies in the widest possible manner, and divergence on this point marks a principal distinction amongst theories of knowledge. (Lewis, 1929, p. 38)

Through perception we acquire information about our environment, and the judgments we form are occasioned by a sensory contact with their objects. A theory of perception has to explain the connection between these two elements – the sensory confrontation and the conceptual interpretation of what is seen – in a way that is phenomenologically plausible and yet provides suitable foundations for an explanation of how knowledge is possible. Both Kant's distinction between sensibility and understanding, and the empiricist's discussion of the relation between the sense data of which we are immediately aware and the opinions we form on their basis, are versions of the dichotomy that Lewis – attempting to reconcile Kant and empiricism in a form of 'conceptual pragmatism' – refers to in *Mind and the World Order*. In Peirce's mature writings about perception – I shall concentrate here upon two texts from about 1903, the Pragmatism lectures and a draft entitled 'Telepathy' (5.14 ff, 7.597–688) – Lewis's two elements appear in a distinction between 'percepts' and 'perceptual judgments'. Perceptual judgments comprise the first premises for reasoning, prompted by our sensory experience. 'All our other judgments are so many theories whose only justification is that they have been and will be borne out by perceptual judgments' (5.116). The percept is a form of sensory given; it is the sensory awareness of reality which prompts, and is described by, the perceptual judgment. 5.115 suggests that Peirce would separate the elements in time: *after* the percept has been formed, we go on to judge what it is that we perceive.

Peirce's theory probably owes a lot to the similar views developed by James in his *Principles of Psychology*. Although he is not cited in Firth's article 'Sense-Data and the Percept Theory' (1949–50), the explanation and defence of the 'percept theory' given by Firth provides a useful guide to the sort of position Peirce defends, as also does the defence of similar views in Anscombe's paper on the intentionality of sensation (Anscombe, 1981, ch. 1). In the paper nominally about telepathy, Peirce is uneasy about distinguishing percept from perceptual judgment very sharply and concludes that both are abstracted from the 'percipuum' which incorporates both sensory and conceptual elements. However, to simplify the explanation of his views, I shall here follow the strategy that he employed himself, first providing a simplified account of perception which sharply distinguishes percept and perceptual judgment, and only when that has been accomplished introducing the important factors which made him favour the more sophisticated theory.

In a 1905 manuscript, Peirce wrote that 'a percept is much like a moving picture accompanied with sounds and other sensations' (R 939); and in the Pragmatism lectures, we learn that it is 'an image or moving picture or other exhibition' (5.115). This might lead us to suppose that by 'percept' he means something like what other philosophers have meant by a 'sense datum'. The sense datum theory distinguishes different kinds of sensory awareness, usually immediate (or direct) and mediate. The 'sense data' of which we are immediately aware are not physical objects, but are either sensory states of ourselves or abstract objects such as 'surfaces'. Our sensory contact with the familiar physical world is mediated through our more direct awareness of these sense data. There is scope for different views about the nature of this mediation, and about the range of properties that we may directly sense in our sense data. Many would follow the familiar line that in order to describe what is immediately perceived, without conceptual elaboration, we make use of a very limited vocabulary; our visual sense data being described as a two-dimensional arrangement of coloured patches, and so on. One motivation for views of this kind rests upon the thought that it is impossible that we should be mistaken about those things of which we are immediately aware. Since the possibility of illusion and hallucination shows that we may be mistaken in any of our perceptual beliefs about material objects, it follows that we are not immediately aware of them. The quotations above suggest that Peirce accepts this kind of position: we are immediately aware of 'pictures' or images and thus only mediately aware of the material things which these depictions represent.

However, this would be a misrepresentation. At 7.619, we find the claim that, when he sits writing in his room, the yellow chair with a green cushion that he sees on the other side of his table *is* the percept. And he insists that describing percepts as 'images' should not be taken to commit him to the view that they represent things other than themselves.

> The chair I appear to see makes no professions of any kind, essentially embodies no intentions of any kind, does not stand for anything. It obtrudes itself upon my gaze; but not as deputy for anything else, nor 'as' anything. (7.619)

Firth characterizes the percept theory in a negative way: it rejects the sense datum theorists' distinction between different sorts of awareness (immediate and mediate); and it rejects the denial that we can be sensorily aware of ordinary material objects. Peirce's view accords with this: his sensory awareness of the chair and cushion is not indirect or mediate. The chair is part of the total percept that he is aware of at some time (Firth, 1949–50, pp. 446 ff).

Although we must thus grant that a material object can be perceived as immediately as anything can, it would be a mistake to conclude that a percept is simply some portion of the physical world. Rather, it is an intentional object; and when Peirce describes it as the immediate object of the perceptual judgment, the term is used in the technical sense discussed in the previous chapter. First of all, it is allowed by Peirce that the percept may turn out to be a hallucination. The chair he appears to see might not exist at all, hence the appropriateness of Firth's characterization of the percept as an 'ostensible physical object': the percept purports to be an independent material object, but may not be so (p. 449). Secondly, the physical object perceived, where the perception is veridical, will have characters that it does not share with the percept. For example, although Peirce's chair is the heaviest piece of furniture in his room, it is consistent with the chair being a part of his percept that the heaviest piece of furniture in the room is not part of it. Roughly, the percept is described in a sort of answer to the question 'What did you see?' And when the question is answered in this fashion, the fact that someone saw an F does not entail that there is a real F that he saw; and from the fact that someone saw the G, and the truth that the G is H, it does not follow that he saw an H. (Cf. Anscombe, 1981, for further discussion.) Although the object Peirce saw happened to be the heaviest object in his room, this property of it was not present in his sensory experience.

When he discusses percepts, Peirce stresses three characteristics of them which are evident to phenomenological reflection. First, they embody qualitative characters, 'qualities of feeling', each of them is 'something positive and *sui generis*, being how it is quite regardless of how or what anything else is' (7.626). 'A visual percept of a yellow chair with a green cushion, that is quite different from being green with a yellow cushion.' Differences in the subject matter of the percept are thus reflected in systematic differences in its qualitative character. The stress upon the *firstness* of these 'qualities of feeling' suggests that we can prescind any of the qualities instantiated in the percept from any of the others; we can conceive of a percept which contains any one of the qualities, while not containing any of the other qualities that occur with it in this percept – although, of course, we do not have to be able to conceive of it being instantiated in complete isolation from all other qualities at all. This suggests that all of the qualities instantiated in the percept are logically independent, a position reminiscent of the logical atomism of Russell and Wittgenstein. It also suggests that only a very limited range of qualities can be genuinely instantiated in a percept, leading to the conjecture that Peirce may not be far from a sense datum theory which holds that only simple colour and shape predicates are applicable to percepts. An illustration will clarify the problem that worries me here. Is 'being a chair' one of the qualities of feeling that the percept may instantiate? If not, then it seems likely that our cognitive contact with the chair is mediated through a contact with a percept describable in simpler terms and Peirce's claim that the chair is the percept and is immediately perceived looks questionable. On the other hand, if this *is* a quality of feeling found in the percept, we may reasonably doubt whether it is prescindable from all the other qualities of feeling located there. For example, it is hard to see how we can conceive a chair without a back or seat. The initial impression that this provides a knockdown argument against Peirce's formulation of the percept theory is mistaken, however, and looking at the example in more detail will help us to grasp the extension of his notion of firstness.

Suppose that we are examining a chair. We can see pieces of wood connected to each other, lengths of fabric attached to the wood, and so on. We see that the structure is rigid and has a definite shape. But, for some reason, we cannot make out what it is that we are looking at. Suddenly we see that it is a chair: all falls into place and our percept clearly becomes one of a chair. It is compatible with this change occurring that there is no change in our view of what parts the object has, or of the physical relations they stand in. Rather, the familiar structure of parts falls into place as a familiar and intelligible whole. It would be natural to say that we sense or feel a unity in the thing, and we might gesture towards this feeling in an attempt to explain how our percept has changed. It would be natural for Peirce to say that the pleasure we feel when this occurs is aesthetic pleasure; we become aware of the chair as a structured unity. As we noticed in chapter II, Peirce claims that we can take pleasure in things which involve a structure of parts so unified as to impart a simple firstness to the whole. The feeling of unity is not a logical product of the properties of the parts, or something which itself contains features of the parts as parts: rather, it emerges from the structure as a simple feeling. Peirce must hold, I think, that any experience of something as a unified whole finds a firstness in what is perceived of the sort that he describes in his writings on aesthetics. The problem now raised is of explaining how that *can* be prescinded from the other features of the object. The discussion of the chair example shows that Peirce requires an answer to this problem if he is to reconcile his claims about percepts with the doctrine of immediate perception of physical objects.

That what we can call 'being an ostensible chair' is a form of firstness cannot require that our seeing something as a chair does not depend upon the object having a kind of structured complexity: only things with certain sorts of parts in certain sorts of relations can be ostensible chairs. What then can be the force of the claim that ostensible chairhood is prescindable, that we can attend to this property while ignoring the properties of the structure and its elements? We have already argued for the converse claim; we may have a complete awareness of the elements and their relations without yet seeing the object as a chair, and our coming to see the object as a chair does not have to rest upon some change in our beliefs about the parts and their relations. But what could show that we can attend to the fact that the whole structure is a chair while ignoring the properties of the parts? There are a number of psychological phenomena which suggest that although something is a chair only in virtue of its parts having certain structural properties, still, when we perceive something as a chair, this does not involve our *attending* to those parts and their relations. For example, when we see something as a chair, we are likely to miss changes in its properties, even important structural ones such as, say, the removal of a leg. Many perceptual illusions rest upon the fact that once we see an object as of a certain kind, our awareness of the details of parts and structure is likely to be reduced. This would be enough to establish Peirce's point, I believe, but it can also be argued for in a different way. Chairs can vary in many ways: they can differ in shape, colour, size, design; not all have legs or arms; perhaps not all even have backs. In spite of such changes, Peirce would claim that the sense of 'ostensible chairness' remains constant, so we can prescind this property from any one of the other properties of the parts or structure. He must hold that phenomenological reflection will force us to accept this, that it will force us to acknowledge that the sense of chairhood is a form of firstness.

I hope that this discussion has made plausible the idea that we can have a notion of being ostensibly a chair. This notion is applicable to elements of the percept, and indeed, the percept presents things to us as ostensibly chairs. When we apply this notion to something, we do not do so on the basis of an inference from information about the simpler parts of the object. Rather it is applied directly, and ostensible chairhood is a form of firstness, prescindable from the other characters of the percept. We can now move on to the other two features of percepts that Peirce remarks upon. The percept, he claims, *compels* the acknowledgment of the perceiver, 'the perceiver is aware of being compelled to perceive what he perceives' (4.541, 1906). One clue to the fact that something is a percept rather than a vivid imagining is that the latter is sometimes subject to the will, whereas the former never is: I can choose whether to look or not, but if I choose to look, I cannot choose what I see. Finally, the percept

> neither offers any reason for such acknowledgment or makes any pretence to reasonableness. . . . It acts upon us, it forces itself upon us; but it does not address the reason, nor *appeal* to anything for support. (7.622)

Percepts are thus brute, compulsive experiences, composed of qualities of feeling. Just as the first consideration found firstness in the percept, so the second and third point towards the secondness of outer experience. Peirce hopes to connect this brute irrational character to the 'double consciousness' involved in perception, the fact that I experience the percept as *other* than myself. However, we should leave trying to understand this connection until we have introduced his views about perceptual judgments.

Perceptual judgments, our first premises for the assessment of other judgments, describe percepts. The outward clash issues in perceptual judgments. They are forced upon us by processes that we are powerless to control or criticize, yet they are propositional in form and describe the character of the percept. The typical form of such a judgment is

That is f.

where the demonstrative picks out either the percept or some part of it. For example,

That is a green chair with a yellow cushion.

The question that naturally arises is: how do we know when a judgment of this kind accurately describes the percept? Why are we justified in taking these claims about the nature of our percepts seriously? It is important to distinguish two different kinds of criticism of perceptual judgments. Suppose that, having made the judgment given above, I look back at the chair and judge,

That is a blue chair with a yellow cushion.

I may then conclude that my former judgment misrepresented the

160

colour of the chair, and I shall then abandon it. It does not follow that I misdescribed my percept. The chair may, simply, have looked green to me at the time. However, we might suppose that there is another possibility; my percept was the same on the two occasions, and I misdescribed it at first. If there are these two possibilities, then the perceptual judgment can misdescribe the percept that occasions it. The question that concerns me here is how we can establish when this is so.

Peirce claims that when we make perceptual judgments, we are aware of no reason for judging as we do. The perceptual judgment does not 'in any degree resemble a percept. It is as unlike it as the printed letters in a book, where a Madonna of Murillo is described, are unlike the picture itself' (5.54). Nor are there discernible logical relations between them; a percept is not a proposition and cannot stand in *logical* relations with anything (7.628). Hence, Peirce concludes that the perceptual judgment is an *index* of the percept: it results from it by a form of dyadic action which phenomenological reflection can neither understand nor criticize. I blindly accept the perceptual judgment without any ground or reason to do so. This suggests that we cannot find a point of view from which we can compare percept with perceptual judgment and establish whether the latter correctly describes the former. Passages like the following support this view.

> We know nothing about the percept otherwise than by the testimony of the perceptual judgment, excepting that we feel the blow of it, the reaction against us, and we see the contents of it arranged into an object in its totality, – excepting of course what the psychologists are able to make out inferentially. But the moment we fix our minds upon it and *think* the least thing about the percept, it is the perceptual judgment that tells us what we perceive. (7.643)

> There is no warrant for saying that the perceptual judgment actually *is* such an index of the percept other than the *ipse dixit* of the perceptual judgment itself. (7.628)

What appears to follow from this is that the perceptual judgment yields infallible knowledge of the nature of our percepts.

Peirce accepts this consequence (5.186); only verbal slips can lead our perceptual judgments to misrepresent our percepts, we cannot misdescribe them. Peirce would have agreed with Anscombe's assertion that we could never intelligibly assert something like,

> It strikes me now as having the colour it struck me as having before, and it now strikes me as yellow, therefore I was wrong in thinking before that it struck me as blue. (Anscombe, 1981, p. 44)

It does not follow from this, however, that our perceptual judgments are incorrigible. Although the perceptual judgment is an index of the percept, it presents itself as an assertion about reality. Compare these three assertions.

That is a green chair.
There appears to me to be a green chair.
I have a percept of a green chair.

My finding myself making a perceptual judgment expressed in the first of these assertions provides me with conclusive, incorrigible, reason for accepting the second and third of the three claims. But, the perceptual judgment itself makes a fallible judgment about reality: if I am the victim of a hallucination or visual illusion, the judgment is false. The percept 'presents itself' as an external reality, and this is shown in the logical character of the perceptual judgment, which contains a demonstrative expression referring to an external existent. The immediate object of the perceptual judgment is a green chair: the judgment is true only if its real object is a green chair too. The real objects of the second and third assertions are the immediate object of the first.

The fallibility of perceptual judgments requires the truth of a proposition that Peirce stresses, that perceptual judgments involve generality: we ascribe to the percept the general characters of being a chair and being green, for example (5.151 ff, 5.181). It is enough to point to the presence of predicates in perceptual judgments – expressions like '. . . is a green chair' – to show that this is so. Its connection with the fallibility of perceptual judgments is also obvious: because of the other characters connected in a lawlike way with the property of being a chair, we can test the perceptual judgment by deriving predictions from it. We predict that the object will not change its shape or location without explanation, that if we look back in the same place we shall still see a green chair, that it will support our weight, and so on. If these predictions are disappointed, then we reject the perceptual judgment that occasioned them, or revise the theories we used in deriving them. Peirce endorses the claim that this makes perceptual judgments look rather like hypotheses or products of abductive inference, and says that

abductive inference shades into perceptual judgment without any sharp line of demarcation between them; or, in other words, our first premisses, the perceptual judgments, are to be regarded as an extreme case of abductive inferences, from which they differ in being absolutely beyond criticism. The abductive suggestion comes to us in a flash. It is an act of *insight*, although of extremely fallible insight. It is true that the different elements of the hypothesis were in our minds before; but it is the idea of putting together what we had never before dreamed of putting together which flashes the new suggestion before our contemplation. (5.181)

This claim is important, and immediately raises several questions. It recalls the argument of the 'New List': the perceptual judgment provides a 'little theory' about what is perceived. But, given the obvious difference between first premisses and the conclusions of abductive inferences, and given that we are not to draw on psychological evidence about the unconscious information processing that leads to the formation of percepts and perceptual judgments, there is a problem about how its truth can be revealed to phenomenological reflection. What reason have we for thinking this strange claim true? What are the premisses of these inferences? A second difficulty is not easily formulated clearly. If the perceptual judgment is a hypothesis about the percept, which assigns it to a certain general kind, then it is unclear why the perceptual judgment should be an infallible guide to the nature of the percept. It might be a bad hypothesis, or a bold one whose content extends far beyond what is perceptually given. Unless the generality expressed in the perceptual judgment is also present in the percept, there seems to be an unbridgeable epistemological gap between them. Although he does not formulate this second difficulty in these terms, I think that we can take the more sophisticated view mentioned at the beginning of this section as a response to these and related difficulties.

First, what phenomenological evidence is there for the claim that perceptual judgments are 'acritical abductions', the limiting case of abductive inference? Peirce's strategy is to find intermediate cases between acritical perceptual judgments and abductions that are subject to full self-controlled monitoring. The claim that we have *no* control over our perceptual experience proves to be an oversimplification. One of Peirce's examples of the brute irrational compulsiveness of perceptual experience was a description of sitting in a stationary train, knowing that another train was slowly moving by, irritated by the unreasonableness of its perceptually seeming to be one's own train that was moving. We might reason with the experience, dwell upon its illusory character and speculate about the causes of the illusion, but we are powerless to control the experience (7.643). Yet, 'if one only looks down and watches the wheels turn, in a very few seconds [the other train] will seem to start up'. In this case, we rely upon tricks to achieve a sort of control over our perceptual experiences, but these are unnecessary, for you can change an uncontrollable perceptual experience 'into a controllable imagination by a brief process of education' (7.646). Peirce uses a number of examples to illustrate this, the most familiar being the Schroeder stair (7.647, 5.183).

When you look at it you seem to be looking at the stairs from above.

163

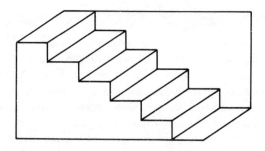

You cannot conceive it otherwise. Continue to gaze at it, and after two or three minutes the back wall of the stairs will jump forward and you will now be looking at the under side of them from below, and again cannot see the figure otherwise. After a shorter interval, the upper wall, which is now nearer to you, will spring back, and you will again be looking from above. These changes will take place more and more rapidly, the aspect from above always lasting longer, until at length, you will find you can at will make it look either way. (7.647)

'The perceptive judgment, and the percept itself, seems to keep shifting from one general aspect to the other and back again' (5.183). These phenomena, Peirce claims, function as the 'true connecting links between abductions and perceptions' (5.183). The fact that the difference is reflected in how things look is taken to show that a classification of the object 'is contained in the perceptual judgment': it is not a conceptual extrapolation based upon perceptual judgments which are neutral about which of the general aspects is seen. 'If the percept or perceptual judgment were of a nature entirely unrelated to abduction, one would expect that the percept would be entirely free from any characters that are proper to *interpretations*' (5.184). Peirce further argues for the presence of 'interpretation' in perception in a fashion reminiscent of his 1868 discussion: he points out how our expectations and interests lead us to see things other than as they really are – it takes a very special skill for a proof reader actually to see the letters written on the page, and most of us see the letters we think ought to be there (5.184).

The second problem that we raised concerned how, if the perceptual judgment functions as a hypothesis, we can continue to claim that it provides incorrigible evidence of the percept. The fact that the *look* of the stair changes as we shift from one general aspect to another suggests that somehow generality is present in the percept itself – it is not only the perceptual judgment that changes. In 7.643, Peirce introduces the 'percipuum' as 'the percept as it is immediately interpreted in the perceptual judgment' and claims,

The percipuum, then, is what forces itself upon your acknowledgment without any why or wherefore, so that if anybody asks you why you should regard it as appearing so and so, all you can say is, 'I can't help it, That is how I see it.' (7.643)

There is, of course, no problem about how the perceptual judgment informs us of the nature of the percipuum, but as a solution to our problem, that is a fudge. We need to understand how the classification found in the judgment is reflected in the sensory character of the experience itself. In the light of an earlier discussion, we can claim that each general aspect has its own distinctive firstness. But that does not settle the question because we see a change in the apparent relations of the elements of what we see. The response that is suggested by Peirce's 1903 discussions involves the claim, important to Peirce as we shall see subsequently, that perceptual experience is *continuous*. We do not confront a discrete series of distinct percepts (or percipua) but we are aware of a continuous flow of experience. Hence, perception involves a 'continuous series of what discretely and consciously performed, would be abductions' (5.184) – I think that we should understand this puzzling remark as claiming that, for all the time that I perceive the chair, I am keeping contact with it and judging that it is (still) a chair. The consequence of this that Peirce brings to bear on the issues we are examining here is that any length of experience, no matter how short, will contain elements of memory and anticipation. Although the 'confrontial' is pouring in on us all the time, there is really nothing – no experience – that is purely confrontial, untainted by memory and imaginative anticipation (7.653). In that case, the classifications involved in our perceptual judgments can influence the construction of our experience. According to how we classify the stairs or the train, we place our experience in a context which anticipates a different future run of experience. Our expectations influence what we see.

Peirce's introduction of the percipuum raises real problems of interpretation, and represents one stage of his wrestling with issues of genuine difficulty. Bernstein has called attention to several passages from the years 1901–3 in which Peirce emphasizes that percepts contain no generality. For example, 'A percept contains only two kinds of elements, those of firstness and those of secondness' (7.630. cf 1.253, 2.146, 2.603). Our own discussion of percepts has reflected this. Since generality is involved in perceptual judgments, the epistemological gap between the two that we have been discussing opens up at once. Furthermore, if our confrontation with external reality through having percepts does not involve generality, the way is opened for the nominalist conclusion that general concepts merely reflect our conceptual activity in making sense of our experience. Thirdness is not part of the empirical world. Other passages – especially from slightly later –

declare that 'our very percepts are the results of cognitive elaboration' (5.146). We have seen that Peirce finds generality in the very sensory character of our experience. Talk of the percipuum – fusing the percept and perceptual judgment into a single whole – is an attempt, I suggest, to prevent those problems arising by rejecting an oversimple dichotomy of cognitive processes. If we can prescind the firstness of our perceptual experience from the rest (or prescind its secondness), it does not follow that we can find distinct cognitive processes: the percept-perceptual judgment distinction reflects imposing a crude cognitive model on the phenomenologically rich complex of the sensory and the conceptual which is the 'given' of perceptual experience. Thirdness is given in the percipuum, it is perceptually experienced. Our acritical judgments report what we see; they involve general classifications; and our reports of shifts in general aspect show that there are sensory manifestations of thirdness in the percipuum. However, although these remarks are phenomenologically rich and exciting, it is hard to be sure that Peirce was ever happy with the form they received. In the following two sections, we shall take up further issues about the role of secondness and thirdness in perception, and about the role of perceptual reports in obtaining knowledge of reality.

In this section we have sketched the main lines of thought involved in Peirce's mature doctrines about perception, and we have deepened our understanding of his account of firstness. The following sections develop, in turn, our grasp of the role of secondness and thirdness in perception. We turn first to a study of Peirce's theory of indexical reference and the nature of actual existing things; and, secondly, we take up some of the questions we have just raised about generality and perceptual experience, looking at how Peirce attempts to relate generality and continuity.

3 Indexical reference and individual existence

We can now begin to see how Peirce avoids the circularity that threatened the account of truth he developed through his work in the normative sciences. Perceptual judgments are compelling, accepted as certain and, most important, acritical. Since they do not result from controlled deliberation, there is no scope for logical criticism of our practice of making them. So long as we think of 'clash with experience' in terms of clashing with perceptual judgments, no circularity is involved when logic sets as its aim to obtain rules which will yield judgments that do not clash with experience. However, as we have seen, Peirce thinks that perceptual judgments are fallible; subsequently, we might reject an opinion that originated in an indubitable perceptual judgment. So we must not define truth by saying that a true opinion does not conflict with any perceptual judgments that are actually true. For, reasoning is involved in establishing whether such a judgment is true. A question then arises about just how fallible perceptual judgments can constrain inquiry at all. How can we correct a perceptual judgment and discover the nature of its real object? We can now make a start upon understanding Peirce's answer to this question, but we shall not settle the issue until we have discussed Peirce's theory of ampliative inference more fully in chapter VII.

The question is primarily one about the reference of the demonstrative index which picks out the subject of a perceptual judgment. Anscombe reports,

> I once opened my eyes and saw the black striking surface of a
> matchbox which was standing on its end; the other sides of the box
> were not visible. This was a few inches from my eye and I gazed at it
> in amazement. Asked to describe the impression as I remember it, I
> say: 'Something black and rectangular, on end, some feet away, and
> some feet high.' I took it for three or four feet distant and it looked, if
> anything, like a thick post, but I knew there could be no such thing in
> my bedroom. (Anscombe, 1981, p. 16)

The immediate object of the perceptual judgment is a large black post, some distance away (let us suppose), and the real object is a nearby matchbox, standing on end. How do we find out that this is the case? How was reference to the matchbox secured in a judgment which displays such a total misconception of its character?

We must approach this question indirectly through a more general discussion of demonstratives. The general term that Peirce uses for the referent of the demonstrative is an *individual*. All perceptual judgments are singular judgments which make reference to individuals (3.611–3); and it is a mark of individuals that reference to them must be indexical. Thus we must look at one of the most difficult and complex areas of Peirce's thought, his theory of individuals. In the course of this, I hope we shall come to a better understanding of the category of secondness. Indexical reference, secondness and individuality go together for Peirce. Indeed, in the years before he admitted the need for quantifiers and other indices – before the mid-1880s – he defended an extreme form of realism; he denied that any true individuals existed, claimed that there were no singular propositions, and asserted that 'being at all is being in general' (5.349; 3.93 n). I am just going to examine his later views here.

The distinction between particulars or individuals, on the one hand, and universals or 'generals' on the other, is a familiar one, and provides the context for the discussion of Peirce's views. I lack the space for a detailed examination of the mediaeval disputes that he often refers to in putting his position forward, but it will be useful to look briefly at some of the problems about universals that lie in the background. We must distinguish two problems about universals. One concerns just what general characters like redness or rapidity are. It is related to issues about what is involved in understanding general terms like predicates, and can be formulated: what are the objects of signs for predicates or relations? The second problem is about what is involved in such general characters being instantiated in concrete particulars: how can particular things be red? We can sharpen our understanding of this second issue by noticing that we could have a complete grasp of all the general terms and laws required to describe and explain the course of events while being ignorant of the character of the actual world. We may not know what individuals exist in the world, what properties these individuals actually have, or which individuals participate in interactions instantiating which of the laws. The properties and laws may suffice to restrict the range of worlds which are possible, but they do not determine which world is actual. To characterize the actual world, we must specify what things it contains and which of the properties they have. What we encounter in perception, then, is the instantiation of qualities by particular existing things. The perceptual judgment refers to an individual, a quality, and asserts that the former instantiates the latter. It is natural, then, to admit two kinds of entity to our ontology, universals or generals and particulars or individuals and to claim that they have different 'modes of being'. The theory of individuals is concerned with describing the particulars or individuals which exist and instantiate general characters: what mode of being do they have? and, how do they instantiate these general characters or universals? Peirce goes along with a strict distinction between two 'modes of being' – as a realist, he allows that universals and laws are 'real', but individuals, he claims, 'exist' (3.613; 5.503). What are existing individuals and how is indexical reference to them possible?

Peirce first insisted that reference to individuals must be indexical as a consequence of a 'theorem in formal logic', in the 1885 review of Royce's *The Religious Aspect of Philosophy* that we have already referred to on several occasions. Royce argues from the existence of error to a form of absolute idealism, relying upon some claims about reference. Peirce paraphrases the argument thus,

> The subject of an erroneous proposition could not be identified with
> the subject of the corresponding true proposition, except by being
> completely known, and in that knowledge no error would be
> possible. The truth must, therefore, be present to the actual
> consciousness of a living being. (8.41)

The argument is very obscure, but Peirce finds in it a *reductio ad absurdum* of an assumption that he ascribes to Royce. This is the assumption that:

> The real subject of a proposition can be denoted by a general term of
> the proposition; that is, that precisely what you are talking about can
> be distinguished from other things by giving a general description of
> it. (8.41)

The assumption seems to be that we find out what object a singular
proposition is about by establishing what uniquely satisfies some
description provided in the proposition. Suppose we make an assertion
of the form (1) shortly followed by one of the form (2).

(1) A is B.
(2) A is not B.

'A' is a general description of the subject of the proposition. There are
two possibilities here. Either, the second assertion *corrects* the first, or
the general description is true of more than one thing, and the things of
which it is true include both things which are B and things which are
not B. Peirce's claim seems to be that unless reference has an indexical
component, we could never be justified in endorsing the first of these
alternatives and recognizing that an error was made. And this must rest
upon some assumption like:

> Unless a description of an individual entails every property of the
> individual – unless it is like a Leibnizian individual concept – there is
> no assurance that the description is true of only one individual.

If this assumption were true, then we can see that there is a difficulty
about how we could both refer to something, knowing what we were
referring to, and hold a mistaken belief about it. Since we should need to
know what we were referring to in order to decide that an error had
been made, then there would clearly be a problem about making sense
of error. But, why should we not have a description of an individual
which sufficed to pick out uniquely, without meeting this stringent
condition?

For example, we could identify an object by giving its spatial location
at some fixed time. Granted that no two things can be in the same place
at the same time, this could suffice to identify it uniquely. Perhaps
Peirce could use an example such as Anscombe's to claim that we may
even be mistaken about the spatial location of an object. In the 1885
discussion, he offers a different response: Kant has shown that non-
descriptive reference is required for knowledge of points in space and
time.

> One instant of time is, in itself, exactly like any other instant, one
> point of space like any other point; nevertheless dates and positions

can be approximately distinguished. And how are they so distinguish-ed? By *intuition* says Kant; perhaps not in so many words; but it is because of this property that he distinguishes Space and Time from the general conceptions of the understanding.

Reference to locations in space and time must, according to Peirce, be indexical. His claims about such reference point us towards his connection of existence and secondness. Distancing himself obscurely from Kant's position, he insists that 'it is by volitional acts that dates and positions are distinguished' (8.41).

The definition of an individual that Peirce favoured in his later work is stated clearly in Baldwin's *Dictionary*.

[An] individual is something which reacts. That is to say, it does react against some things, and is of such a nature that it might react, or have reacted, against my will. (3.613)

It is a familiar thought that existing concrete individuals enter into causal interactions. They act on us through perception, and we act on them through our actions. Since our control of existents is limited, they can cause us perceptual surprise and can lead our plans and projects to be disappointed. Peirce takes this to be brute dyadic action: although it normally accords with law, and is susceptible of an explanation in terms of laws, we can prescind from conformity of law in attending to the element of brute confrontation involved in our experience of existing things. Peirce may try to support this claim about prescindability by insisting that we can conceive that there could be chance interactions which do not accord with law at all – indeed, he thinks that there are such. This reaction, he claims, introduces a brute unintelligible element into our experience: our percept gives us no reason for its acknowledg-ment, and there may be no reason why this possible world was created rather than some other one which instantiates the same laws.

In experience we react with an existent individual. The dyadic character of this element of experience emerges in its being a confrontation between us and some existent with which we react. As well as 'feeling' its impact, the presence of brute reaction in perception, and the dyadic character of this reaction, is shown by the presence of an indexical in the perceptual judgment, an expression the ground of whose function is this brute dyadic interaction. So, to return to the example we took from Anscombe, what seems to the perceiver to be an interaction with a large pillar some distance off is in fact an interaction with a nearby matchbox. Our question remains: how can we establish that this is so?

Saying that individuals react does not tell us much about the nature of objects like matchboxes. What are these things with which we react? In the *Dictionary* entry, we are told that 'everything whose identity consists in a continuity of reactions will be a single logical individual. Thus, any portion of space, so far as it can be regarded as reacting, is for logic a single individual; its spatial extension is no objection' (3.613). Individuals are spread out in space and time continuously. Indeed, space and time are general notions which are introduced to render intelligible these continuities of reaction (see Thompson, 1981, pp. 145 f). Thus, if I make a perceptual judgment

That is a matchbox.

my judgment is true if my perceptual experience is a part of the continuous spread of reactions which constitutes a particular matchbox. So, the question about how Anscombe corrects her misidentification of what she sees can now be put: how can someone having a percept of a large pillar some way off be part of the continuity of reactions which comprises the matchbox? Peirce's own remarks upon how we identify and re-identify perceived individuals are unhelpful. In the 1885 paper, he said,

It might be asked *how* two different men can know they are speaking of the same thing. Suppose, for instance, one man should say a flash of lightning was followed by thunder and another should deny it. How would they know they meant the same flash? The answer is that they would compare notes somewhat as follows. One would say 'I mean that very brilliant flash which was preceded by three slight flashes, you know.' The second man would recognize the mark, and thus by a probable and appoximate inference they would conclude they meant the same flash. (8.42)

This seems to suggest that the identification is a fallible hypothesis, tested empirically against certain 'marks'. Given the shared property, it is more likely that there was one individual than two, and that both reacted with it. How can this vague picture help us with the matchbox example?

A general term such as '. . . is a three feet high pillar' or '. . . is a matchbox' ascribes a general character to any continuity of reactions to which it is applied. Our understanding of such terms invokes systems of laws which we expect the individual to conform to. Pillars don't mysteriously disappear, or change into matchboxes, but are stable entities whose appearance does not change very rapidly. Matchboxes contain matches which can be used to produce fire, they have a characteristic appearance and feel, their look will change in a systematic way as we move relative to them. And so on. The fact that once it gets light, or we cease to be drowsy, or we move, we cease to have percepts characteristic of an impact with a pillar, makes it unlikely that our original percept was part of a 'pillar-series' of reactions. Given the direction in which we were looking, the future run of our experience, and the accepted fact that, in a drowsy state, a matchbox might look like a pillar, we are ready to accept the hypothesis that the pillar percept was part of the continuity of reactions that makes up the matchbox. Accepting this hypothesis reduces further perceptual surprise. It is only because the hypothesis that we saw a pillar produces expectations which are disappointed that we are able to doubt it at all; it is because the hypothesis that we saw a matchbox produces intelligible order in our experience – we have to accept no unintelligible surprises – that the hypothesis is acceptable. We build up a store of common-sense knowledge about how things look, about what sorts of perceptual interactions we can have with things, and we exploit this in trying to identify the real objects of our perceptual judgments. We shall see in chapter VII how far such judgments can constrain the growth of knowledge.

A special case of revising perceptual claims occurs when we decide that our percept is not a reaction with an existing individual at all: the ostensible physical object is rejected as an hallucination or illusion. A useful discussion of what guides us in establishing whether we are seeing a real individual is found in 8.144. Whether a percept is 'experience of the real world or only experience of a dream, is a question which I have no means of answering with absolute certainty. I have, however, three tests which, though none of them is infallible, answer very well in ordinary cases.' The first is to try to 'dismiss the percepts'. Commonly, although not always, a 'fancy or daydream' can be dismissed by an act of will, while a percept never can. A second test is to consult one's fellows; although shared hallucinations occur, the fact that others share my percept provides good reason to think it veridical. Finally, and this links up with the remarks of the last few paragraphs, 'I make use of my knowledge of the laws of nature (very fallible knowledge confessedly) to predict that if my percept has its cause in the real world, a certain experiment must have a certain result which in the absence of that cause would be a little surprising.' Hence, he says, if we all think we have seen a ghost, we can 'try what an imaginative kodak would say to it. So Macbeth made the experiment of trying to clutch the dagger.' Real things resist the will, are available to all, and conform to discoverable laws. This fits suggestively with the claim that we are all forced to acknowledge them, no matter how rigorously we subject our beliefs to experimental test.

4 Generality: thirdness and continuity

To conclude this discussion of Peirce's views on perception and individual existence, we must look more closely at some of his claims about generality, his realism about universals. This realism is expressed in a number of ways. In a famous passage in the Pragmatism lectures, he claims that '*Thirdness* is operative in nature' (5.93), that there are active general principles (5.101), and elsewhere he emphasizes the objectivity or reality of 'would-bes' (5.467). The irreducibility and objective validity of claims such as

If I were to clutch this dagger, it would resist the pressure of my hand.
If I were to measure that pillar with a ruler, it would prove to be three feet high.

reflects this metaphysical realism. The connection between such claims and the general characters referred to by predicates will be discussed further in chapter VIII – Peirce emphasizes that no one who did not accept this form of metaphysical realism could possibly find the kind of verificationism that is implicit in his pragmatism at all plausible (5.503). However, we can see from the discussion of the previous section that Peirce believes that our understanding of a general term provides us with a battery of 'would-be' claims that can be used in evaluating perceptual beliefs. In the 1903 lecture, he makes the prediction that a stone he is holding will fall if he lets go of it, and offers to test this experimentally by dropping the stone. He recognizes that his audience will think this a very silly and pointless experiment and attributes this to the fact that they *know* what will happen when he lets go of the stone. However, he claims, it is only if general principles are operative in nature, if they know that if he were to drop the stone it would fall because they know that such objects fall when dropped, that we can explain the audience's knowledge of the result of his 'experiment'. The generalization covers all possible cases, and is not simply a report of a regularity among those cases that have actually occurred. If this is accepted, then the connection between the realism and thirdness can be seen; the general active principle is a third which mediates between letting go of the stone and the stone's falling. It is because all such stones fall that letting go of this stone is followed by its falling.

Leaving aside the assessment of these arguments, we can note a *prima facie* conflict between the claim that predicates express generals, predicates being analysed as expressing bodies of laws and 'general active principles' and the claim that the object of the predicate of a dicisign is a quality or a first. We are inclined to see the qualitative character of our experience as introducing a general character to it, yet its classification in terms of the categories prevents our doing this. How are these apparent conflicts to be resolved? In part, this is an issue we have discussed before, but we can now present the matter in a clearer way. There are lawlike connections between the qualities that are instantiated in the continuous reactions that make up observable reality. Associated with a notion like chair is a body of laws and generalizations which indicate what patterns of reaction are compatible with our identification of something as a chair. These laws mediate the reactions, enabling us to see them as a unified whole. With this is associated a distinctive firstness, prescindable from those laws in thought. A grasp of the concept of a chair will involve both an ability to identify chairs on the basis of how they look, on the basis of this firstness, and an ability to assess propositions about chairs employing the various laws and general principles that enter the full conception of a chair. Reference to Peirce's claims about aesthetic value are again to the point: we can experience something as an aesthetic unity without intellectually grasping how its elements are mediated in the whole; but, an intellectual understanding of the whole will require a grasp of these mediating relations. It is suggestive, if obscure, to describe the felt quality as the 'firstness of a thirdness'.

Peirce often links his realism with views about continuity: he says that the question whether generals are real is the same as the question whether there are true continua (6.172–3; NE iii 925). This introduces one of the darkest areas of his philosophy, the doctrine which he calls the 'keystone of the arch' of his system, namely 'synechism', defined in Baldwin's dictionary as 'that tendency of philosophical thought which insists upon the idea of continuity as of prime importance in philosophy and, in particular, upon the necessity of hypotheses involving true continuity' (6.169). At first glance, the link between the reality of generals and the existence of continua is wholly obscure; and Peirce's discussions of these topics contain many false starts and are very complex. However, in view of the importance that he attached to these themes, we must try to make some sense of them. We must hope too that we shall gain some insight into the sources of the new extreme realism of the 1890s, for that seems to be connected with a development in Peirce's understanding of continuity. It will not be possible to avoid some discussion of Peirce's mathematical writings about continuity, but, to prepare the way for this, we can begin by noticing some connections between realism and continuity which give his claims as least a modicum of plausibility.

Two of these will repay our attention. First, for the realist, we respond to some shared nature or general principle when we classify things together by bringing them under the same general term; for example, we classify things as red, as oak trees, or as made of zinc. In one of the *Popular Science Monthly* papers of 1878, Peirce considers the position of a naturalist who has collected a number of specimens which display marked similarities, and who wonders whether they should be classified together. Let us suppose that they are moths, and his attention is drawn to their wing markings. Although none of these are exactly the same, many take the form of a rather similar S-shape, and others have a shape closer to a C. Is there one species, two, or more than two? Without intending to offer a general theory of classification, Peirce suggests that we will be justified in classifying those with S markings together if we believe that we could find forms intermediate between any of those which we have; and, if intermediate forms could be found which connect the C-shape to the S-shape, then we might conclude that there is just one form. The suggestion is that if the specimens form a kind or natural class, they will vary continuously along some dimension. In the same way, the range of shades that we classify as red exhibits continuous gradation between certain (vague) limits. In this early paper, the stress is upon whether we can actually find a continuous spread of cases, but in later work, the claim would receive a realist formulation: are the specimens that we have and the cases that can be encountered in the course of experience to be seen as 'drawn from' a continuous range of possible cases – not all of which are actual? So, at least in some cases, our understanding of a general term takes it to collect together things that can vary continuously, within certain limits, along various dimensions.

Secondly, we might connect continuity to causal processes. When we speculate about whether one event is the cause of another, we may be guided by whether we can find a continuous route whereby the influence of the first is transmitted to the second: if we cannot find such a path, then we will be sceptical of the causal hypothesis that we are considering (see Salmon, 1979). Both in this case of causal explanation, and in the example of classification, we make sense of the relation between distinct events (the cause and effect, the moth with the S marking and the moth with the C marking) by embedding them in a more complex structure (a continuous process, a continuous array of possibilities): the continuous structure 'mediates' between the distinct things and makes them intelligible to us. And for the realist Peirce, *triadic* action is involved in each case – the possibility of instantiating the continuous process, or fitting the continuous array explains why the effect occurred as it did, and why the specimens are as they are. Hence, we find some plausibility in what at first seemed a strange association of ideas, and we can admit continuity as one of the forms of thirdness.

But, Peirce's synechism involves themes which are both deeper and considerably more murky than the points that have been made so far, and it rests upon a distinctive view about the nature of continuity. The observations that we have made do not show that it is a necessary condition of adopting realism that we view these processes, and arrays of cases, as continuous. Nor does it indicate how these continuities somehow reveal to us the nature of generality. Indeed, given the discussion so far, we could view a general as a special sort of abstract particular – a class containing further abstract particulars, namely possible objects. Since Peirce casts such scorn upon the nominalism of Platonists who view universals as special *objects*, this cannot be his position. How does synechism enable him to avoid it? And, in view of the verificationism implicit in Peirce's pragmatism, how are we able to form a clear understanding of the arrays of unactualized possibles which this realism involves? I am far from sure that I understand all that is involved in Peirce's doctrines here. They are difficult; and although he attached very great importance to them, he does not spell them out fully and clearly anywhere. The suspicion that he never succeeded in working them out fully is very tempting; but lacking a full scholarly treatment of the manuscripts which deal of these matters, it is sensible to be cautious. In the remainder of this section I shall sketch some of the themes that emerge more clearly from the texts.

First, it is one of Peirce's objections to nominalism that it blocks the road of inquiry (for Peirce, the greatest of sins): it denies that any *explanation* can be offered of why objects are classified as they are. Our classificatory practice has to be accepted as a brute fact. We saw above that Peirce's realist explains the facts of our classificatory practice by, for example, showing that the individuals that we classify are drawn from a more inclusive range of possible cases. The discontinuities in the actual cases are explained away when we use possible cases to mediate between them. Of course, a question then arises about why we classify those possible cases together: is that to be accepted as just a brute fact? If the array of possible cases that we used in the first explanation itself contained gaps or discontinuities, then we should ask for an explanation of those gaps. But, if the set of possible cases that formed the explanans contains no discontinuities, it, somehow, *exhausts* the range of possibilities along the appropriate dimension; then no further explanation is called for. (This is not quite correct, and will be qualified in chapter IX: for present purposes, it will serve.) If there are no discontinuities, we have what Peirce calls 'ultimate mediation': there is no need for further explanation of the relations between the elements. Peirce appears to hold that it is only continuous arrays of possibilities, only continuous processes, that stand in no further need of explanatory mediation (see 6.173; and generally, Dauben, 1982).

The second theme, which supplements this discussion, is provided by Peirce's logical analysis of continuity. It is important to bear in mind that, unlike Cantor and Dedekind, Peirce's interest in the mathematics of continuity – and transfinite set theory generally – was not primarily motivated by an interest in the foundations of analysis. Although, famously, he anticipated more recent developments in non-standard analysis by defending the consistency and intelligibility of infinitesimals

(Dauben, 1982), philosophical concerns were to the fore; Peirce wanted to analyse the structures involved in our ordinary experience of continuity (Dauben, 1982). It is tempting to think of a continuum as a particular kind of ordered set of points, and to direct philosophical analysis towards establishing just how many points a continuum contains and how they are ordered. Our worry that Peirce was viewing a general as an abstract object reflected just this temptation. However, the development in Peirce's mathematical thought which prompted his synechism and his 'extreme realism' was what he took to be a refutation of that plausible assumption. The argument runs as follows. Peirce independently produced an argument to the effect that there is an infinity of distinct infinite cardinal numbers: it rests on the claim that for any n, whether finite or infinite, 2^n is always larger than n. He claimed, again independently of Cantor, that, if N is the number of natural numbers, 2^N, 'the first abnumerable multitude', represents the number of real numbers that there are. We obtain a set with 2^{2^N} members when we add the infinitesimals, and so on. One way to understand the process whereby the hierarchy of infinite sets is generated is that we can 'move up a level' by replacing each member of an infinite set by a sequence of members with as many members as that infinite set. Peirce appears to argue from the possibility of generating ever more numerous sets that any infinite set or sequence, however its members are ordered, involves features which can be recognized as discontinuities, and hence does not represent the structure of the continuum – we can always make sense of replacing a member by an infinite sequence of which it is a member, for example. Hence, we cannot think of the continuum as a complex sequence of points – for any such sequence displays discontinuities.

What then can we say about the continuum? First, the attempt to specify its structure never ends: we think of it as an infinite sequence of infinite sequences of infinite sequences of infinite sequences. . . . As we move up the hierarchy of infinite sequences, we get closer to the continuum, but no one of these sequences captures its character. Our grasp of continuity reflects this structure, however: we think of it as 'generating itself' through this 'never ending process', its description never being completed. We grasp that any description of its structure that we produce *could* be replaced by a fuller, more accurate, but still incomplete one.

> The result is, that we have altogether eliminated points. We have a series of series of series, *ad infinitum*. Every part, however closely designated, is still a series and divisible into further series. There are no points in such a line. There is no exact boundary between any parts. (NE iii 126)

The continuum is somehow 'cemented together', and is not composed of points.

> Such supermultitudinous collections stick together by logical necessity. Its constituent individuals are no longer distinct or independent. They are not subjects but phases expressive of the properties of the continuum. (NE iii 95)

What is the connection between these ideas and generality? Peirce claims that the continuum *is* a general; why should that be? In particular, why should continuity be what generality comes to when we take seriously the logic of relations (R 439)? I *think* that the way to look at it is as follows. When we reason about a continuum – about time or a continuous process – we use existential quantifiers to pick out parts of the continuum and we reason about the relational properties of the elements that we refer to. So to speak, we find a relational structure in the continuum and that provides a focus of our reasoning. However, no one relational structure captures the nature of the continuum, and we cannot quantify over all of the elements of the continuum. The relational structures we reason about are, in a sense, determined by the nature of the continuum we are reasoning about, but they do not exhaust its character. Just as we think of a law as something which determines a number of different interactions, so we think of the continuum as determining an infinite number of different, albeit related, relational structures. We can think of the continuum as general, then, in the sense that it determines an infinite set of relational structures as its 'extension': if we think of a process as continuous, then we believe that it will always be possible for us to produce more complex characterizations of relational structures which 'fit' or 'are determined by' that continuous process. Peirce often speaks as though a continuum involves real unactualized possibles, and this may only mean that we have to acknowledge that there are ways of characterizing the relational structures involved in the continuum which it would be possible for us to recognize, but which we never shall articulate. Peirce may have in mind a further thought, that a continuum contains the possibility of endless sorts of relational patterns of *reaction*, not all of which will actually occur. Hence, when we encounter a finite sample of moths, related in various ways, we can understand this relational structure as one of those that is determined by the complex range of continuities that determine what it is to be a moth. We view the specimens we encounter not as a fragment of a more complex continuous relational structure (for there is no such structure) but as one of the relational structures determined by a system of continua.

But, why should we acknowledge the reality of these continua of unactualized possibles? They seem to go beyond anything that is encountered in experience. Once again Peirce's thought is difficult to discern, but he appears to reason thus. Although we do not experience the continuum of possible moths, still continuity is present in experience. We are aware of the continuous passage of time (7.649), and of processes in time. Earlier in this chapter, we noticed Peirce's stress upon the continuity involved in perception. Hence we have the concept of continuity, and the related concept of real possibility; indeed, at times Peirce claims that we perceive possibilities being realized as we observe reality progressively determined in time. Thus equipped with the concepts of possibility and continuity, a bridge is required to justify us in recognizing unobservable continuities. This bridge is provided by the methodological principle that we should never rest upon the conclusion that some regularity is inexplicable: we saw in our brief discussion of nominalism above that Peirce believes that interpreting the specimens as drawn from a continuous range of possible cases provides a kind of ╷ 'ultimate explanation' of their properties: continuity involves 'ultimate mediation'.

Many of the issues that are raised by these doctrines will become clearer when they can be placed in a context provided by Peirce's views of scientific method, his pragmatism and his metaphysical views. It is probably no accident that the doctrines emerged at a time when his metaphysical views were well developed. Moreover, although these logical doctrines are original and unusual, stress upon the logical importance of continuity is something that Peirce had learned from Kant and Hegel. I discussed them at this stage in the book because they cast some light both upon Peirce's insistence on the continuous character of the percipuum, and because they illustrate how he thought that thirdness was immediately perceived. Although the obscurity and difficulty of much of the material makes it hard to reach a critical assessment of it, we can make a few preliminary comments. One is that, so far as I can tell, Peirce nowhere makes it very clear just how the experience of a spatial or temporal continuum commits us to the reality of unactualized possibles, and, it is clear, this is important for the overall structure of his argument. Secondly, he relies upon the claim that we perceive true continua; something in the perceptual experience makes it clear that we confront something that is genuinely continuous and not a 'pseudo-continuum', a relational structure made up of points which has, say, 2^{2^N} members. It is difficult to see how we discriminate these in ordinary perception, and to understand how our experience would differ if it only contained pseudo-continua. Apart from an occasional suggestion that we should lack the concept of the past in such circumstances, and an even rarer one that unless we confront real continua Zeno's paradoxes of motion would raise insuperable difficulties, Peirce offers little assistance with these difficulties. However, even if we cannot accept the uses Peirce makes of the notion of continuity, his realism responds to an important strain in ordinary thought, and many of his theses about continuity are plausible, challenging and interesting.

VI

Mathematical Reasoning and the *a priori*

1 Introduction

The five large volumes that make up the *New Elements of Mathematics* amply illustrate both the breadth of Peirce's mathematical concerns and the proportion of his time that was devoted to mathematical topics. Alongside studies in mathematical logic and foundational issues, we find discussions of a wide range of topics: drafts of textbooks employing novel ideas of how the subject should be taught; mathematical studies of map projection deriving from his work for the United States Coastal Survey; discussions of linear algebra, probability, the four-colour problem, the theory of measurement, non-Euclidean geometry. Since he grew up in a family of mathematicians, and had so much close knowledge of the subject, his views on the nature of mathematics could hardly fail to be important for an overall assessment of his philosophical achievement. But, if that were the only reason for examining them the need to be selective in a volume that is to be of manageable and moderate length might lead us to mention these views in passing or discuss them in a cursory fashion. In fact, for at least two reasons, Peirce's writings about mathematics are closely integrated with his work on the issues that concern us directly here; his doctrines about how mathematical knowledge is possible are presupposed by his accounts of knowledge and reality, and by his accounts of philosophical method.[1]

Peirce's conception of the scientific method of settling belief is experimental. We advance towards the truth by a carefully monitored sequence of interactions with the objects and events that we investigate, acting upon them and observing the consequences of our actions. While this stress upon experiment seems appropriate when we think of the sorts of knowledge provided by the natural sciences, it can leave us puzzled about the investigations carried out by mathematicians. Investigations in number theory or set theory do not seem to involve experiment or observation. In that case, his account of the life of inquiry, of the nature and importance of truth, would have only limited application, and would fail to account for those areas of our knowledge which seem most certain and secure. Consequently, an explanation of the nature of mathematical knowledge must be provided in order to block a potential counterexample to Peirce's account of truth and inquiry.

But, this does not exhaust the reasons for looking closely at Peirce's philosophy of mathematics. It has a key role in providing the foundations for his entire system, as is shown by the position of mathematics in the classification of the sciences. Mathematics is the one discipline that depends upon no other: phenomenology and the normative sciences employ mathematical techniques and mathematical results to establish the validity of the categories and arrive at a specification of the aim of inquiry. If this is not to seem crazy, we should note that, for Peirce, 'mathematics' does not refer to a particular academic discipline, or the study of a particular subject matter such as 'quantities'. Rather, all *a priori* reasoning, all of the thinking that we do on paper or in our heads, counts as part of mathematics. He wants to offer a uniform account of mathematical practice which incorporates both our everyday practice of 'necessary reasoning' and the more rigorous practice of professional mathematicians. Any proposition, he thinks, can be looked upon as a mathematical theory and used as a starting point for mathematical reasoning. Philosophy is mathematical in two ways. First, it relies upon *a priori* reasoning, or mathematical reasoning to reach its conclusions. Secondly, this being the case, the use of sophisticated mathematical techniques can bring new rigour and exactness to philosophical reasoning. Hence,

> philosophy requires exact thought, and all exact thought is mathematical thought. . . . I can only say that I have been bred in the lap of the exact sciences and if I know what mathematical exactitude is, that is as far as I can see the character of my philosophical reasoning. (R 438)

> My special business is to bring mathematical exactitude, I mean *modern* mathematical exactitude, into philosophy, and to apply the ideas of mathematics in philosophy. (Quoted in Eisele, 1982, p. 337)

Most notably, this involves refining mathematical logic, using mathematics to study the nature of arguments and the structure of propositions more exactly.

If mathematics is to fill this demanding foundational role, then, as Peirce notes in the 'Minute Logic', it stands 'in no need of Ethics', and 'has no need of any appeal to logic' (4.241, 242). Whereas disputes can arise in the special sciences that can be settled only by a logical reflection, mathematics can never turn to logic for guidance. While the natural scientist may attempt to evaluate his methods by seeing whether they are calculated to provide knowledge of reality, the mathematician has no such need to evaluate his methods. Mathematics never throws up logical questions, and logical investigations can never prompt us to revise our mathematical practice. Considering the obvious objection that mathematicians have often committed logical errors, Peirce responds,

> [In] mathematics errors of reasoning have occurred, nay, have passed unchallenged for thousands of years. This however, was simply because they escaped notice. Never, in the whole history of the science, has a question whether a conclusion followed *mathematically* from given premises, when once started, failed to receive a speedy and unanimous reply. (4.243)

Mathematical reasoning, he thinks, is so much more secure than any result in logic proper, that an appeal to logic by a mathematician could never be warranted. So, as is required by Peirce's view of the role of mathematics, we shall find Peirce claiming that mathematical practice is acritical, that it stands in no need of justification and foundation, that it gives rise to no problems requiring a logical solution. Whereas logic has to *justify* adoption of particular methods of ampliative inference, all that it can do for mathematical practices is *describe* and *explain* their validity.

This relates directly to a problem that has been outstanding since chapter II. We noticed there that Peirce had to take for granted certain notions of logical consistency in developing his account of truth, and remarked that his theory would be circular if it were necessary to explain consistency in terms of truth – saying, for example, that propositions are inconsistent if they cannot all be true. It is mathematical reasoning that reveals these consistencies and inconsistencies, and the special foundational role of mathematics means that we are free to rely upon its techniques in advance of developing the substantive notion of truth in the normative sciences. In ways that will become clearer below, Peirce would have happily endorsed Wittgenstein's dictum that mathematics is antecedent to truth (Wittgenstein, 1967, p. 45). Our explanation of the validity of mathematical reasoning must not consist simply in showing that it is a means to discovering truths: rather, our understanding of truth and reality reflects a prior grasp of mathematical necessities.

On a number of occasions, Peirce describes familiar features of mathematics and its products which are to be used to test a philosophical account of its nature. The account must explain how, in these respects, mathematics differs from the special sciences. First, its conclusions have a kind of necessity not found in the special sciences; they relate not merely to what is actually the case but 'to a whole general range of possibility' (4.232). As well as this modal status, mathematical results have distinctive epistemological properties. We can achieve a certainty which seems to go beyond what is found in the natural sciences (4.237). Our knowledge is *a priori* and requires no observation of external objects; and it is uncontroversial – we are practically infallible for 'only blundering can introduce error into mathematics' (NE iv xv). Consensus on the correct answer to a problem will be held up only by stupidity, a slip, or a failure to understand the terms of a problem. There is no reason here to talk of the long run. We also find widespread reference to abstract objects – sets, numbers, structures – which are not existing individuals: we know about them although we do not encounter them in perception and they do not react with other things. And, while in the special sciences great certainty is available only if we are prepared to accept results that are exceedingly vague, mathematics combines great certainty with an exactness that exceeds anything found elsewhere (4.237). Finally, there are a number of characteristics which give mathematics its value for us. First, its results can be applied in thinking about problems that arise in other areas of inquiry: we can *use* mathematics to help with difficulties in physics, psychology or philosophy. Secondly, it can be a source of surprises – mathematical reasoning can yield novel facts which can be exploited when we try to tackle practical problems. Our task is to explain how there can be a discipline which provides certain, exact, necessary, surprising, and above all, useful, results.

Peirce's denial that mathematics depends upon logic forces him to reject some familiar kinds of Platonism. I have in mind the doctrine, defended by Frege, that mathematics studies a body of truths, that there is an independent body of objects and truths which form the subject matter of mathematics. According to this picture, the task of the mathematician is one of *discovery*; and the question can surely arise whether the methods currently used by mathematicians are adequate for discovering those truths. We must then admit the possibility that logical reflection upon the nature of mathematical facts could show that mathematicians have relied upon methods which cannot be guaranteed to reveal those facts to us. By assigning mathematics a foundational role in his canon of sciences, Peirce repudiates the possibility of such criticism, and thus repudiates any account of mathematical truth that would permit it. Mathematics does not attempt to discover a special range of facts or truths, or to reveal to us a particular segment of reality. Once we abandon the picture of mathematics helping us to discover a special range of facts, however, its status becomes very problematic. As the last paragraph suggested, mathematical results display something like 'objective validity': Peirce thinks that we can know with certainty, uncontroversially, that they hold in all possible worlds, not just in the actual one. It is natural to try to reconcile this with the rejection of Platonism by attributing the uncontroversial character of mathematical results to the fact that they lack content. They simply reflect arbitrary conventions, and are tautologous or analytic propositions, true in virtue of the meanings of expressions contained in them. However, even if this position can be formulated intelligibly and the formidable objections it faces met, there is the problem of reconciling it with the fact that mathematics 'presents as rich and apparently unending a series of surprising discoveries as any observational science' (3.363). If mathematics does not study a range of distinctive facts, how can it provide useful and surprising results?

2 *Iconic representation and mathematical practice*

Over the next two sections, we shall discuss the fundamental ideas involved in Peirce's treatment of mathematics. Leaving the questions of how mathematics can provide us with surprising new information, and of the nature of the mathematicians' reference to abstract objects, to section 3, we can begin by reviving an issue raised in the chapter about signs – the role of iconic representation in the thoughts and assertions of those engaged in the pursuit of knowledge. This will enable us to uncover what we can think of as the Grundgedanke of Peirce's philosophy of mathematics and to assess his attempts to explain the modal and epistemological character of the discipline, how it produces results which purport to hold in all conceivable circumstances and which are presented as known with an almost infallible certainty. We can then understand how mathematics can occupy its foundational role in Peirce's classification of the sciences.

We must begin by considering the applications of mathematics. While, as we have seen, Peirce believed that thinking of the applications of science will prevent our grasping the real nature and point of scientific activity, he thought that the point of mathematical activity lies in its applications. But even here, his main concern is with applications in pure science and philosophy rather than with those directed towards solving practical or 'vital' problems. In one description of mathematical activity, Peirce writes,

> A practical problem arises, and the physicist endeavours to find a
> soluble mathematical problem that resembles the practical one as
> closely as it may. This involves a logical analysis of the problem, a
> putting of it into equations. The mathematics begins when the
> equations or other purely ideal conditions are given. (NE iv xv)

Although the quotation is not very explicit, it suggests several relevant points. Suppose that we are studying a physical system, and want to predict what will happen to it under certain circumstances. By attaching numerical values to certain magnitudes, and using a system of equations, we *replace* our initial physical question by a purely mathematical one of (say) solving for certain unknowns, given the values and the functional relationships described in the equations. Distinguishing these two questions reveals that a division of labour can operate. The mathematician who solves the mathematical problem will understand the problem even if he lacks all knowledge of, and interest in, the physical problem that it derives from. However, just as the terms of the mathematical problem were derived from the physical one, so its solution provides the basis for a solution to the problem that prompted the mathematical work. Although, 'when a mathematician deals with facts, they become for him "mere hypotheses", for with their truth he ceases to concern himself' (3.428), someone whose interest is more directly in the facts may profit from observing what the mathematician discovers about these 'mere hypotheses'. An illustration of some of these points is provided by the use of a logical calculus to assess an argument. Uncertain about the validity of a complex argument, we might translate the premisses into the notation of (say) the predicate calculus. We then pose a purely mathematical problem: is it possible to construct a proof, within a given system, of an expression which can function as a translation of the conclusion of the argument, using only the rules of the calculus and the translations of the premisses as undischarged premisses? Someone could tackle this problem although he had no grasp of what the calculus was being used for; he need not even understand that it is a logic. In spite of this, if he solved the mathematical problem by finding a proof of the translation of the conclusion, we should take this as showing that the original argument was valid.

This description of mathematical activity prompts many questions. There are many branches of mathematics which do not seem to have any applications in the special sciences – for example, investigations of large cardinal axioms in set theory. Is it possible to understand these studies within the sort of framework here suggested? For the present, however, I shall postpone discussion of these, and concentrate upon just three questions. First, what relation must obtain between a mathematical problem and a non-mathematical one, for the solution to the former to be applicable to the solution to the former? What is involved in (in Peirce's phrase) a mathematical problem 'resembling' a practical one? In the framework of Peirce's thought, it is natural to say that the physicist interprets the set of equations (for example), as a *sign* of the physical system that he is studying – and the logician interprets the formal translations as signs of the premisses of the argument. In that case, our question concerns *how* the equations signify the physical state of affairs: what is the *ground* of the physicist's interpretation of the mathematical formalism? If the equations were introduced as an arbitrary index for the problem – like a proper name – there would be no reason to suppose that the solution to the mathematical problem would have application to the physical one. So, what sort of ground must underlie the interpretation of a mathematical theory involved in applied mathematics if mathematics is to be useful?

The mathematician himself does not think of his problems and equations as signs of practical problems and physical states of affairs: he need have no knowledge of or interest in the applications that his work can receive. However, it seems obvious that his equations are signs, and that he understands and interprets them as such. It would be perverse to deny that mathematical results can be asserted, for example, although these would not be assertions about reality. The second question concerns just what the *objects* of mathematical representations are. The physicist takes the objects to be physical states of affairs; but the pure mathematician must take them to be something else. The applicability of mathematics must require some systematic relation between these objects: it must be because the signs have the objects that the pure mathematician takes them to have that they can have the application that the physicist takes them to have. So we need an account of the pure mathematician's understanding of his theories.

This second issue is related to the third. Presented with a mathematical problem, the mathematician uses certain techniques to solve it; he reasons and calculates, constructs proofs and demonstrations and so on. There must be constraints upon what can count as an acceptable proof or calculation: if the mathematician could do anything that came into his head, then mathematics would display no kind of objectivity at all, and there would be no reason to suppose that the results of proofs and calculations could be applied to solve practical problems. The third issue, then, concerns the objectivity of proof and calculation: how do we make sense of the fact that there is often a unique 'correct answer' to a mathematical problem? Since we should expect someone's grasp of what is a permissible step in a proof or calculation to reflect their understanding of the mathematical propositions that they are working with, the relation to the second question is clear: how does a mathematician's understanding of the objects of his representations determine his sense of what is a permissible step in a proof or calculation?

According to Peirce, mathematical theories are *icons*. Applied mathematicians use mathematical formalisms as icons of physical states of affairs; hence the claim in the quotation from (NE iv xv) that the physicist looks for a mathematical problem that 'resembles' his practical one. As we saw in chapter IV, a sign is an icon when the ground in virtue of which it is interpreted as a sign of its object is a property it shares with the object, a property that it could have even if the object did not exist. What suited a patch to serve as a colour sample was its shade: it could conceivably have had that shade even had its object not existed; and, although the use of iconic signs always rests upon a framework of conventions, the sample could conceivably have had that shade if these conventions had not obtained. Conventions guide us in identifying and exploiting similarities for purposes of thought and communication. We saw that Peirce thought that a sign system must be iconic if it is to be used for reasoning (4.544); in his philosophy of mathematics, this thought is developed more fully. At first sight, the idea is unpromising: algebras and systems of equations do not appear to resemble the physical states of affairs studied with their aid. What kinds of shared properties could account for their role as icons?

I shall approach this question through a consideration of some more plausible examples. The first is the familiar one of the colour sample. Suppose that our 'practical problem' is of planning a colour scheme for a room. Without trying each out, and having to repaint the room many times, we wish to establish which colour combinations are pleasing to the eye. Therefore, we produce samples of the different colours we are considering and raise the question: which combinations of these samples are pleasing to the eye? The question 'resembles' the question which arrangements of colours on the walls of the room will be acceptable; but it is much easier to solve. Hence, we manipulate the samples, observe the results of our manipulations, and use the acceptability of an arrangement of samples as a guide to the merits of different ways of painting the room. We are able to do so because the samples display the colours that the room would have if it were painted according to the different schemes. Although this does not look like an excercise in mathematics, it shares some of the characters of Peirce's description of applying mathematics. For example, someone could approach the 'sample' problem with no knowledge of, or interest in, the practical problem which prompted it. We could imagine there being an academic discipline concerned with providing general solutions to problems of colour matching; exponents would be interested only in samples, but their results would have general application. We must consider below whether the products of sampling theory would have the modal and epistemological character of mathematical theorems.

In a 1906 paper, 'Prolegomena to an Apology for Pragmaticism', Peirce uses a different example to illustrate the role of icons in the growth of knowledge. He considers the use of maps and plans by military strategists, and remarks that they are valued even by those familiar with the terrain of the battleground. The maps are diagrammatic or iconic representations, because, relative to the general conventions used by the map-maker, the shape and arrangement of the lines, and the size and distribution of coloured areas, reflect the shape and character of coastlines, rivers, woods, etc. A strategist might 'desire the maps to stick pins into, so as to mark each anticipated day's change in the situations of the two armies'. Peirce glosses this by saying that 'one can make uniform experiments upon diagrams; and when one does so, one must keep a bright lookout for unintended and unexpected changes thereby brought about in the relations of different significant parts of the diagram to each other' (4.530). If we cannot experiment with the battlefield itself, we can experiment upon adequate icons of its key features.

Neither of these examples looks properly mathematical, but they illustrate some of Peirce's views about mathematical practice. Iconic reasoning is valuable because we can experiment upon manipulable icons when we cannot experiment upon reality. Experiment upon and observation of icons replaces experiment upon and observation of reality (4.530). So far, the differences between the special sciences and mathematics are small. Just as a chemist observes a particular sample of a substance and uses this as a basis for generalization to a conclusion about anything with the same chemical structure, so a mathematician uses investigation of a diagram as a basis for similar generalization. It is important to see just how seriously Peirce takes this comparison. He considers an objection to it. The chemist is not properly described as investigating a particular sample; rather, he examines a 'molecular structure' which is equally present in all samples, which 'in all his samples has as complete an identity as it is in the nature of molecular structure ever to possess' (4.530). Supposedly, the chemist studies the 'very object' of his investigation (the structure) directly, and not mediately *via* particular samples. The objection which Peirce wants to refute claims that it is otherwise with iconic reasoning: the icon or diagram holds us at one remove from the true object of our investigation. In contrast, Peirce claims that the 'very object' of the inquiry is just as much present in the diagram which functions as our sample. With the colour sample illustration, we can see how this can be so: the samples are just as truly coloured as the walls of the room can be. Intuitively, we can agree that we study the colours and their relations directly, just as the chemist studies the structure of the substance directly. It is less plausible with the map example: it seems that the map holds us at one remove from the object of our inquiry, which is the nature of the terrain. If we see how Peirce's point holds for this example, we shall understand its applicability to mathematics generally.

When we use something as a map of an area, we interpret each point on the map as an index of some point on the area mapped. Then, we can learn about the properties of, and relations between, points on the ground, by noting the properties of, and relations between, their indices. If an index falls in a blue area, for example, its object is a place in the sea or in a lake or river; if two indices are two inches apart on the map, then their objects are two miles apart on the ground; if one index is between two others, then its object is between those of the others; and so on. There is a correspondence or isomorphism between the map and the ground that it maps. The extension of the relation '. . . is two inches from . . .', used in describing the map, will be a set of pairs of indices – all those pairs of indices that are two inches apart. The extension of the relation '. . . is two miles from . . .' used in describing the terrain, will be a set of pairs of points – all those pairs of points that are two miles apart. If we use '$f(i_i)$' to refer to the object of the index i_i, then we shall find that, whenever the first set of pairs contains the pair $<i_n, i_m>$, the second set will contain $<f(i_n), f(i_m)>$ and vice versa. Similarly for the extensions of monadic predicates and triadic relations. If we know that there is this kind of correspondence between the map and what it represents, then, any information we have about the properties of the parts of the map will be a source of information about the relations of the objects of those parts of the map. Peirce describes this correspondence between the relationships found in the sign and those found in what it represents by saying that sign and signified display the same 'form of relation': the map is an icon of the terrain because both embody relational structures of the same form.

It will be apparent from the abstractness of these formulations that the 'spatial' character of the map is inessential to its iconic functioning. By 'spatial character' here I mean what grounds the feeling that the map, somehow, *looks* as the terrain would if looked at from sufficiently far off. The spatial relation of being two miles distant was signified by another spatial relation between the indices, that of being two inches apart. So long as the correspondence mentioned above is maintained, the relation between indices corresponding to being two miles apart could be that of saturating the first and second bonds of tokens of '. . . R . . .' in asserted propositions of the mathematical theory. A description of the terrain using indices and ordinary predicate expressions provides a formal theory which displays the same form of relation as the terrain described. Although it might be less easy to use than a familiar sort of map, a verbal description of a terrain is just as much an iconic representation of it. The object on which the mathematician experiments, then, is a mathematical diagram – something very pictorial like a map or geometric figure, or something more abstract like a set of axioms and rules. We describe the diagram by specifying relations that hold between indices occurring in the diagram. When we apply the diagram to a practical problem, we interpret the indices – assign them parts of the physical state of affairs as objects – so that the extensions of the relations that interest us between elements of the physical state of affairs correspond to the extensions of syntactic relations between the indices. In modern parlance, we treat the state of affairs as a model of the mathematical theory.

The challenge to his view that Peirce drew out of the comparison with chemistry was that the mathematical diagram holds us at one remove from the 'very object' of mathematical inquiry, while the molecular structure he studies is wholly present in the sample that the chemist examines. His response is given in 4.530. What is the 'object' of mathematical reasoning?

> It is *the form of a relation*. Now this form of relation is the very form of the relation between the two corresponding parts of the diagram. For example, let f_1 and f_2 be the two distances of the two foci of a lens from the lens. Then

$$\frac{1}{f_1} \quad + \quad \frac{1}{f_2} \quad = \quad \frac{1}{f_o}$$

> This equation is a diagram of the form of the relation between the two focal distances and the principal focal distance; and the conventions of algebra (and all diagrams, nay all pictures, depend upon conventions) in conjunction with the writing of the equation, establish a relation between the very *letters f_1, f_2, f_o* regardless of their significance, the form of which relation is the *Very Same* as the form of relation between the three focal distances that these letters denote.

Just as the molecular structure is present in the sample, so the form of relation is found in the mathematical diagram. The parallel with chemistry seems complete. So in this case, there is a correspondence between the extensions of two relations: the relation between the three physical magnitudes concerning focal distance, and the relation between numerals such that their substitution for f_1, f_2, and f_o in the equation above provides an assertible sentence of arithmetic.

We can now see Peirce's answers to the first two of the three questions that we raised about his account of mathematics. The ground of interpretation of a mathematical theory when it is applied is iconic: the theory itself is a relational structure the elements of which are indices; and the theory is applicable to states of affairs containing elements involved in a relational structure of the same form. There is an isomorphism between the mathematical theory and the reality to which it is applied. The second question asked what, for the pure mathematician, was the *object* of a mathematical diagram. The answer, plainly, is a form of relation (4.531); the mathematician is concerned with the forms of different relational structures, and his theories instantiate them. However, we shall not be able to assess this claim until we have examined Peirce's views about the nature of abstract objects, such as forms, in the next section. For the present, we shall accept this as a vague but plausible view. The Kantian roots of Peirce's position should be obvious. Kant thought that mathematics involved forming constructions in pure intuition; reflection upon such constructions acquainted us with the formal structure of appearance. Peirce, of course, rejects Kant's notion of intuition, and thus denies that mathematics is concerned with the form of sense. But, he agrees that mathematicians must use constructions – diagrams constructed on paper or in the imagination – which instantiate the formal structures that they investigate. The objects of mathematics are present in perceptible objects: they can be displayed to sensible intuition, and thus investigated by means of the senses and through experiment.

3 Mathematical discovery and mathematical necessity

When we construct an instance of a form of relation, we do not specify all of its properties. Although the structure we produce is our own construction and shares many of the logical characters of fictions – it is likely to be indeterminate in many respects so that many questions about it have no determinate answer (NE iv xiii) – still it will have properties other than those we mention in constructing it. We may set up a list of axioms and rules of inference and thus specify a structure, while not having complete knowledge of all the theorems that can be derived from the axioms using those rules. Some of the unnoticed features of our construction may be very surprising; a proof may shake an earlier assurance that some proposition was not a theorem of the system. If this were not so, if mathematics did not yield surprises, there would be little point in mathematical activity. The activity of proving some unnoticed feature of the mathematical icon involves, according to Peirce, 'observation and experiment'. We must now look more closely at Peirce's theory of proof. We have to make sense, first, of how a series of specifications which set up a mathematical theory may determine the truth of certain propositions which are not mentioned in them. How can a theorem be a logical consequence of a set of axioms and rules? Secondly, how can proof, 'experiment and observation', uncover these unnoticed consequences of our constructions? Finally, how can our constructions have discoverable but surprising consequences?

Peirce was aware that the surprisingness of mathematical results had seemed problematic to many philosophers. He was scathing about Mill's vague empiricism about mathematical truth, and attributed it to his having supposed that to claim that a proposition is logically necessary committed one to the view that it was trivially verbal. This rests, he says, upon the prejudice that 'the operations of demonstrative reasoning are nothing but applications of plain rules to plain cases'; such thinkers assume that 'Barbara in all its simplicity represents all there is to necessary reasoning' (4.91). Something similar is involved in Kant's doctrine that mathematical results are synthetic. The analytic-synthetic distinction is important, for we all have 'occasion to ask whether something is consistent with (our) own or somebody's meaning' and we distinguish this from 'a question of how experience, past or possible, is qualified' (4.86). The former concerns what is 'involved in' a hypothesis: and Kant, perhaps supposing that 'in our thoughts we made logical definitions of things we reason about', spoke of the predicate of an analytic judgment being 'confusedly thought in' the subject. This psychological formulation is unnecessary, however. The first kind of question concerns what is 'logically compossible' with a hypothesis: an analytic consequence of a hypothesis is 'involved in' it in the sense that it can be 'evolved from it'. Formulated in this way, there is no reason why we should not find that unobvious and surprising consequences can be evolved from a hypothesis.

According to Peirce, his 'first real discovery about mathematical procedure' (NE iv 49) was the distinction between two kinds of deduction or proof: corollarial and theorematic deduction. The 'philosophers', like Mill and Kant, take only the former seriously. The terms derive from the structure of proofs in Euclid.

> [While] all the 'philosophers' have followed Aristotle in holding no demonstration to be thoroughly satisfactory except what they call a 'direct' demonstration, or a 'demonstration why' – by which they mean a demonstration which employs only general concepts and concludes nothing but what would be an item of a definition if all its terms were themselves distinctly defined – the mathematicians on the contrary, entertain a contempt for that style of reasoning, and glory in what the philosophers stigmatize as 'mere' indirect demonstrations or 'demonstrations that'. Those propositions which can be deduced from others by reasoning of the kind the philosophers extol are set down by mathematicians as 'corollaries'. That is to say they are like the geometric truths which Euclid did not deem worthy of particular mention, and which his editors inserted with a garland or corolla, against each in the margin, implying perhaps that it was to them that such honor as might attach to these insignificant remarks was due. In the theorems, or at least in all major theorems, a different kind of reasoning is demanded. (4.233)

Corollarial deduction does not yield surprises: 'it is only necessary to imagine any case in which the premisses are true in order to perceive that the conclusion holds in that case' (NE iv 38); the corollary is 'deduced directly from propositions already established without the use of any other construction than one necessarily suggested in apprehending the enunciation of the proposition' (NE iv 288). It is theorematic deduction that enables us to 'evolve' surprising consequences from our hypotheses: 'it is necessary to experiment in imagination upon the image of the premiss in order from the result of such experiment to make corollarial deductions to the truth of the conclusion' (NE iv 38); the theorem can only be demonstrated from previously established propositions if we 'imagine something more than what the condition (indicated in the premisses) suppose to exist' (NE iv 288). Theorematic deduction calls for imagination, for invention in experimenting upon the icon, and for placing our hypotheses in a wider context by supposing something more to exist than they strictly require.

As the reader will have anticipated, the distinction has its roots in the structure of proofs in Euclid. He describes such proofs thus:

> A theorem regularly begins with 1st a *precept* for a diagram, in which letters are employed. There follows, 2nd, the general enunciation. Then comes 3rd, the *ecthesis*, which states that it will be sufficient to show (what) must, in every case, be true of the diagram. The 4th article is the *subsidiary construction* by which the diagram is modified in some manner already shown to be possible. The 5th article is *demonstration*, which traces out the reasons why a certain relation must always subsist between the parts of the diagram. Finally, and 6thly, it is pointed out . . . that it was all that it was required to show. (NE iv 238)

The proof establishes a general conclusion by study of a particular diagram of the structure being investigated; the mark of *theorem* proving is stage 4 – a subsidiary construction modifies the diagram in some permissible way. We can prove the theorem only by modifying, or adding to the diagram, and then studying the properties of the transformed diagram. We may be reminded of the additional lines that are drawn on a diagram in the course of proving, say, Pythagoras's theorem. However, the geometric example may not help us to understand the general point. In the nineteenth century, it was often supposed that the diagram produced in the course of a proof was essential for establishing a geometric theorem. A purely algebraic proof was impossible, because reference to the diagram and to constructions upon it was required at certain stages of the proof. This belief was an error: axiomatizations of geometry are possible which enable us to prove theorems without constructing diagrams. If the diagrams are of only heuristic assistance in proving theorems, we cannot advance from observations of the use of the diagrams to general conclusions about the logic of proof. But this does not refute Peirce's general position. A proof within an axiomatic system is, for him, just as much the use of icons or diagrams as was the standard Euclidean presentation of the proof of a geometric theorem. He thinks that something *analogous* to a subsidiary construction is involved even in these cases: the focus of mathematical ingenuity is upon something analogous to the drawing of additional lines upon a diagram in the course of a geometric proof. Can anything systematic be said to give sense to this analogy?

It will make Peirce's thought clearer, I think, if we begin by examining the nature of corollarial deduction. We shall use a simple example, a syllogism in Barbara.

> All sparrows are passerines.
> All passerines are birds.

So, All sparrows are birds.

The inference is obvious in the intuitive sense that no one who understood both of the premisses and who brought them together could reasonably doubt that the conclusion followed from them. Borrowing Peirce's symbol, we can characterize the form of the inference thus:

> 1 $(x) (Sx \succ\!\!-- Px)$
> 2 $(x) (Px \succ\!\!-- Bx)$
>
> 3 $(x) (Sx \succ\!\!-- Bx)$

or, more simply,

> 1' S are P.
> 2' P are B.

So, 3' S are B.

1' functions as a diagram of the first premiss of the original inference, and 2' diagrams the second premiss. As Peirce notes, the diagrammatic character of this representation is evident in the fact that the same letter 'P' occurs to express '. . . is a passerine' in each diagram. The second premiss is understood as providing a rule for transforming the diagram representing the first premiss: it permits us to transform 1' into 3' by substituting 'B' for 'P' in 1'. Relying upon 2', we experiment in a permissible way upon 1' and obtain 3': observing the result of our experiment, we return to the original inference and conclude from our mathematical reasoning that the conclusion 'All sparrows are birds' follows from the premisses. The elements of experiment upon a diagram – imaginatively transforming it – and observing the consequences of our experiment are present in a simple case of corollarial reasoning. It is of a piece with the view that mathematical reasoning is

195

iconic that inference proceeds by substitution. However, if experiment upon a diagram is involved even in a simple corollarial deduction, we shall be puzzled about how the presence of subsidiary constructions upon a diagram can be the mark of theorematic deduction: what special obvious or trivial character have the constructions involved in these simple corollarial inferences?

The answer to this question must lie in Peirce's suggestion that corollarial reasoning uses only constructions 'suggested in' the premisses (NE iv 258). If somebody asserted the two premisses of our inference, and colligated them – brought them together and wondered what followed from them – then, if it did not occur to him that he could use the second premiss to make the substitution in the first that yields the conclusion, this would show conclusively that he failed to understand one of the premisses. To understand a universal proposition involves grasping that it can be used to warrant such substitutions; a semantic account of the universal proposition explains the validity of such obvious reasonings in Barbara. Part of what is involved in accepting a universal proposition simply is having a habit of using it as a rule in deriving conclusions by Barbara. In line with this, we can see how the argument can be generalized. For example, our understanding of the word 'and' licenses the 'experiment' of deletion that warrants the inference.

Peirce was American and Kant was German.

So, Peirce was American.

Similarly for other logical constants; our understanding of such expressions involves grasp of a rule for manipulating diagrams, and the experimental component of a train of corollarial reasoning involves only manipulations which are explicitly licensed by the rules governing the use of logical constants present in the premisses. A system of natural deduction rules for the predicate calculus, then, would provide a list of substitution experiments that may be used in corollarial reasoning using propositions containing quantifiers and truth-functional connectives. Peirce's own system of 'existential graphs' provides a formulation of first order logic in which the rules are explicitly formulated as instructions for the manipulation of iconic representations of propositions.

Although it is correct that such a generalization is possible, we should miss a fundamental feature of Peirce's thought if we did not notice his claim that 'all reasoning is in an excessively general sense of the form of *Barbara*' (NE iv 176). This suggests that the validity of Barbara has a different, more fundamental character than that of inferences whose validity turns on the meaning of 'and' or 'or'. As a first step towards understanding this, notice that we can always supply inferences with additional premisses which articulate the rules used in getting from premisses to conclusion. For example, if we reason,

> Socrates is a man.
> _____
So, Socrates is mortal.

we can formulate the 'leading principle' we use as the additional premiss

> If Socrates is a man, then Socrates is mortal.

or

> Anyone who is a man is mortal.

In the same way, we could suplement the inference we discussed above with the premiss

> If Peirce was American and Kant was German, then Peirce was American.

We then obtain the conclusion of the original inference by *modus ponens* from two premisses, rather than by and-elimination from one. Obviously, there is no limit to the process of adding to our list of premisses by articulating the leading principle relied upon in the inference. Secondly, it will always be possible to add premisses to an inference so that it relies upon *modus ponens*. When the inference is one that we currently think is logically valid, like our example of an inference in and-elimination, this will involve adding a premiss that is analytic; the conditional premiss above could not be denied by anyone who understood the word 'and'. Altering Peirce's discussion slightly, we can say that when an argument has been filled out so that it relies only upon *modus ponens*, it is maximally 'complete'. Once this is done, the inference is presented in a particularly perspicuous fashion, and is, 'in an excessively general sense', an inference in the form of Barbara. How could this be so?

The validity of the inference in and-elimination turned on the particular meaning assigned to the word 'and'. 'And' is a logical constant because it can be understood by anyone who has a grasp of the notion of truth, by anyone who accepts the presupposition of logic. The validity of *modus ponens*, like the validity of Barbara, depends solely upon the transitivity of the fundamental logical relation ' >— '. Recall that we saw in chapter III that this relation provides the common logical structure of categorical and hypothetical propositions. Furthermore, ' >— ' is explained in terms of the sign relation itself: both *modus ponens* and Barbara reflect the transitivity of the sign relation. Whereas we could envisage an adequate language that lacked the means to form conjunctive sentences, we could not imagine a language which did not present one thing as a representation of another, which lacked the means to express the notion of interpretation. An inference is in Barbara in Peirce's general sense if its validity is traced to the fact that

If A is a sign of B and B is a sign of C then A is a sign of C.

So understood, 'Barbara' captures a very wide range of inferences. These include *modus ponens*, Barbara in its more familiar narrow sense, but also include others, such as

Cain killed Abel.
All who kill Abel should be punished.

So,   Cain should be punished.

John insulted Jane.
Whenever one person insults another, the first should apologize to the second.

So,   John should apologize to Jane.

and so on. The transitivity of deducibility, formulable as a metalogical rule,

If A $\vdash$ B and B $\vdash$ C then A $\vdash$ C.

equally rests for its validity upon the same principle. When the subject-predicate distinction is generalized to allow for multiple subjects in one sentence, then some complex patterns in the logic of relations are seen to instantiate Barbara in this general sense.

On some occasions, Peirce argues for the validity of this pattern in a more abstract fashion. Suppose that we draw the inference that

S is P.

Since this represents a conclusion about S, it must rest upon a premiss that is itself about S. Let this be

S is M.

This inference is warranted only if we are justified in substituting 'P' for 'M' in this premiss: we follow a rule which permits us to predicate P of anything that we predicate M of; it expresses the truth that anything M is P. This is the only way in which we could get from our premiss to the conclusion. Once this rule is transformed into a proposition and introduced into the inference as an additional premiss, we find that the form of the argument can be diagrammed,

S is M.
M is P.

So,   S is P.

which is familiar from texts in traditional logic as the pattern of inferences in Barbara. (See, for example NE iv 175.)

A train of corollarial reasoning, then, can be presented as a chain of inferences each in 'Barbara in a general sense'. The premisses of each inference in the chain will be either the conclusion of an earlier inference in the chain, a premiss of the overall argument, or a statement which spells out our understanding of a logical constant. What additional elements are involved in theorematic deduction? What is the general character of the constructions or experiments which are *not* specifically allowed for in our understanding of logical expressions? The connection between Peirce's distinction and modern discussions of decidability is obvious. If an effective procedure were available for finding the solution of any mathematical problem, it could hardly be the case that 'mathematics calls for the profoundest invention, the most athletic imagination, and for a power of generalisation in comparison to whose everyday performances the most vaunted performances of metaphysical, biological, and cosmological philosophers in this line seem simply puny' (4.611). Moreover, just as modern logicians stress that it is the presence of relational predicates that renders elementary logic undecidable, so Peirce insists that it is only with the development of the logic of relations that the character of theorematic reasoning becomes readily discernible (NE iv 58). Given Peirce's interest in whether the future work of necessary reasoning could be left to machines, it is tempting to construe Peirce's doctrine as an early dim anticipation of the undecidability of the logic of relations. Thus Hintikka has seized upon the Peircean distinction as an anticipation of his own distinction between depth and surface tautologies. This too, involves generalizing from the role of auxiliary constructions in Euclidean proofs to indicate a general feature of proofs, and links the capacity of proofs to provide surprising results to the fact that, in the logic of relations, intermediate stages in a proof may consider complexes of individuals with more constituents that are referred to in either premisses or conclusions. Thus, we imagine something which 'goes beyond what was given in a full articulation of the problem' (NE iv 38, 288, and Hintikka, 1980). While such comparisons are clearly relevant to developing Peircean themes in this area, I doubt that they help us to get to the heart of his thought. The metalogical notions employed were not ones that he used, and tying his doctrine closely to claims in modern metalogic requires ignoring claims that Peirce attached importance to. For example, he conjectures at one point that the need for theorematic reasoning reflects the current state of mathematical ignorance; in time, he supposes, it may be possible to reach a point where only corollarial reasoning is required in mathematics. (NE iv 289). Moreover, at several places, he takes the use of abstract reference as crucial to the most important and widespread forms of theorematic reasoning; Hintikka has to ignore or play down these claims. Finally, he is somewhat ambivalent about the relation between the logic of relations and issues of decidability. At 4.611 we find the claim that 'even the logic of relations fails to eradicate [the notion that necessary reasoning could be left to a machine] completely' and the suggestion that relational logic tends to 'insinuate' the view that in necessary reasoning 'one is always limited to a narrow choice between quasi-mechanical processes; so that little room is left for the exercise of invention' (but cf 3.641).

The need for invention and imagination in mathematics is seen from observation of what mathematicians do. I think we may understand Peirce's picture thus. Faced with a mathematical problem that cannot be solved by corollarial reasoning, mathematicians are often able to interpret their problem as a special case of another more tractable mathematical problem. In what can be seen as an application of mathematics within mathematics, they see that if some other problem is soluble, then a solution to their initial problem can be obtained. This may lead to a refining of mathematical concepts, enriching mathematical theories, which will make it possible to solve the initial problem through corollarial reasoning in future. An illustration of this pattern can be taken from Lakatos's discussion of Euler's theorem in *Proofs and Refutations*. The issue concerns whether there is a constant relationship between the number of faces, vertices and sides on a regular polyhedron; the task is to prove that there is such a relationship, that the number of vertices is two greater than the sum of the number of faces and the number of edges,

$$V - E + F = 2$$

Cauchy proposed that the result be proved by transforming the problem as follows: we imagine the polyhedron to be hollow with a surface made of thin rubber, and having removed one face, we stretch the remaining surfaces flat upon a board without damaging them. Since we have removed a face without removing an edge or a vertex, we can see that if we can prove

$$V - E + F = 1$$

for this two-dimensional figure, we shall have a proof of the result for regular polyhedra. The result of the construction is that we have replaced our original problem by another drawn from another area. The two-dimensional figure provides an icon of the original polyhedron, and reasoning about it will provide knowledge about the problem that concerns us. When we originally raised the problem about regular polyhedra, it was no part of our concept of a regular polyhedron that such figures can be stretched out in this manner. Inventive imagination was required before this could even be seen as a possibility. Hence, the experiment upon the figure differs from that found in corollarial reasoning. Lakatos's discussion helps us to see what Peirce might have meant when he talked of transforming theorematic deductions into corollarial ones. We might allow the proof to help us to sharpen our concept of a polyhedron, replacing a vague everyday notion with a more precisely defined one. One way to exclude certain bizarre counter-examples and preserve the adequacy of the proof is to build into our definition of a regular polyhedron that it is a figure that can be stretched out flat when a face has been removed. If such a definition is adopted, then the construction carried out in the course of the proof becomes one that that is explicitly allowed for in the premisses; the reasoning becomes corollarial. Proofs guide us towards improved definitions of key mathematical concepts. (I shall not discuss how far this would be a sound methodological ploy. For a fuller discussion, see Lakatos, 1976; Wittgenstein, 1967.)

A second illustration will enable us to introduce some of Peirce's views on the ontology of mathematics. In the *Carnegie Application*, he writes that abstraction is

> so essential to the greater strides of mathematical demonstration that it is proper to divide all theorematic reasoning into the Non-abstractional and the abstractional. I am able to prove that the practically most important results of the mathematical method could not in any way be attained without this operation of abstraction.
> (NE iv 49)

Abstraction leads to reference to individuals such as numbers, classes (see NE iv 49–50), relations, forms, expression types. They have no secondness, do not react with observers or each other, and so are not *existing* individuals. Yet, for all that, they are real objects. Since 'an abstraction is something denoted by a noun substantive, something having a name', 'it belongs to the category of *substance*'. Moreover, they are real substances because 'On pragmatistic principles *reality* can mean nothing except the *truth* of statements in which the real thing is asserted' (NE iv 161–2). Since there are true statements containing numerals, numbers have reality, but their mode of being is distinct from that of *existent* individuals. In what does the truth of a statement containing an abstract singular term consist? What sort of being do classes and numbers have?

Abstract singular terms are introduced through a form of reasoning which Peirce calls *hypostatic abstraction*.

201

Honey is sweet.

So, Honey possesses sweetness.

The abstract singular term is derived from an expression which, in the premiss, occurs predicatively (see e.g. 4.234). Similarly, reference to numbers rests upon statements in which numerical expressions are used 'adjectivally' in describing classes (4.155; cf Murphey, 1961, ch. XII). For example,

The class of books on this shelf has eleven members.

Reference to classes is similarly derivative from statements in which individuals are grouped according to a shared property or listed. Once we introduce abstract singular terms, we need a vocabulary of predicates to use in making assertions about them. Since we may then introduce abstract singular terms by hypostatic abstraction from these predicates, Peirce envisages a hierarchy of objects ordered according to their degree of abstractness: the lowest grade results from hypostatic abstraction applied to predicates of existents, the next grade from applying it to predicates of abstractions of the lowest grade, and so on (NE iv 162). Mathematical progress involves moving to ever higher levels of abstraction.

It is in line with this that Peirce claims that 'an abstraction is a substance whose being consists in the truth of some proposition concerning a more primary (i.e. less abstract) substance' (NE iv 162). 'Sweetness has a mode of being that merely consists in the truth of propositions of which the corresponding predicate term is the predicate' (4.234). Statements about abstraction of one level are true in virtue of statements about less abstract objects; abstractions have a second grade kind of being, they are *ens rationis* (4.464). But, in that case, how can abstraction serve mathematical discovery? If any proposition containing abstract singular terms could be *translated* into one that contained only the corresponding predicate, then surely abstract reference is eliminable and cannot be essential for mathematical progress. Peirce's answer is suggested by the entry on relatives in Baldwin's *Dictionary*. Once we have introduced abstract individuals, 'it becomes possible to study their relations, and to apply to these relations discoveries already made respecting analogous relations' (3.642). Through hypostatic abstraction, we discern relational complexity in things that may not be evident from our normal means for describing them. For example,

Honey possesses sweetness.

sees a dyadic relationship in something which is presented in

Honey is sweet.

as involving only monadic predicates. By finding new more complex forms of relation in phenomena, we are able to bring to bear our general theories of those forms to the study of the phenomena. Through hypostatic abstraction, we reformulate our hypotheses in ways that enable us to apply the insights of other mathematical theories to their solution. Successive steps of abstraction enable us to see our problem as analogous to one in set theory or number theory, just as stretching the polyhedron enables us to see analogies between one problem and another. So long as we bear in mind that abstractions are only *entia rationis*, this procedure enables us to use new, more abstract techniques in solving mathematical problems without introducing error.

4 Certainty and necessity

Having explored some of Peirce's claims about the representations used in mathematics, we can return to the characteristics of mathematics that we discussed in the first section. As the discipline that grounds the hierarchy of the sciences, mathematics, we saw, had to be acritical; there must be no scope for logical criticsm of the practices of mathematicians. In addition, mathematics has a distinctive epistemological status. Its products are certain, obtained by *a priori* methods that are 'practically infallible'. Finally, mathematical results describe features not just of reality but of any possible or conceivable world: unlike the products of the natural sciences, mathematical results are necessary truths. Yet we saw in section 2 that the mathematical method is inductive and observational. Just as a chemist provides a theory of a molecular structure by observing a sample which instantiates it, so a mathematician studies a form by observing and experimenting upon a 'diagram' which instantiates it. Given this parallel, the contrasts between mathematics and the sciences seem hard to sustain. Therefore, we must now ask how Peirce reconciles his picture of what mathematicians do with his claims about the special characteristics of mathematics. However, we have also seen that the integrity of Peirce's system requires that mathematics have this special character: the 'mathematical' approach to philosophy and logic can only be carried through if mathematics is not vulnerable to philosophical criticism. Haack's suggestion that only confusions prevented Peirce seeing that his general fallibilism can be extended to mathematics ignores the importance of these claims for the structure of his philosophy as a whole (Haack, 1979). The importance of these issues for the evaluation of his philosophical system is, thus, clear.

Peirce uses two definitions of mathematics. One, obtained from his mathematician father in 1870, is that it is 'the science which draws necessary conclusions' (e.g. 4.229); the other is that 'Mathematics is the study of what is true of hypothetical states of things' (4.233, and see 4.238 where the two are discussed together). The clue to both is provided by Peirce's remarks about applied mathematics, which we have discussed. It is only when a mathematical problem has been found that 'resembles' a physical one that mathematical activity begins; mathematical activity *per se* loses sight of the practical problem that prompted it. 'When a mathematician deals with facts, they become for him mere "hypotheses", for with their truth he ceases to concern himself' (3.428); mathematics is wholly hypothetical and asserts no matter of fact (4.232). The objects of mathematics are forms, *entia rationis*; from a mathematical result, it will follow that *if* the hypothesis of the mathematical investigation corresponds to anything real, then the product of the investigation will also have application. But, the mathematician has no interest in the applicability of his work. Indeed, at 4.238 Peirce considers whether we should include in mathematical activity both the framing of mathematical hypotheses and the investigation of their properties, or whether (as the first definition seems to suggest) the framing of a hypothesis is extra-mathematical. He notes that 'immense genius has been exercised in the mere framing of such general hypotheses as the field of imaginary quantity and the allied idea of Reimann's surface, in imagining non-Euclidean measurement, ideal numbers, the perfect liquid', but conjectures that work specifically tied to the *application* of mathematics should be excluded from mathematics proper. Constructing hypotheses requires 'poetic genius' but not scientific work. It is not a mathematical matter which sets of axioms, which relational structures, are worthy of investigation; mathematical activity is restricted to elaborating the consequences of systems of diagrams or axioms. Mathematicians construct proofs of theorems (T) from hypotheses (H); their results are reported most explicitly in statements of the form:

H entails T

or

If H diagrams a state of affairs, then T diagrams that state of affairs.

It is such claims that when true are necessarily true; such statements which are knowable, *a priori* and with certainty, by experimenting upon, and observing diagrams.

We can test a chemical hypothesis only if we are able to find concrete samples of the molecular structure that we are interested in. Even if we can find samples, they may prove to be unrepresentative – perhaps containing impurities – so experiment upon a sample does not uncontroversially provide certain knowledge of the structure. Peirce stresses that in mathematics, on the other hand, 'experiment can be multiplied *ad libitum* at no more cost than a summons before the imagination' (4.531). 'I can glut myself with experiments in the one case, while I find it most troublesome to obtain any that are satisfactory in the other' (4.87). His point seems to be not merely that we can construct our own samples of forms of relation, whereas we must find samples of molecular structures in the environment, but that we can do so in the imagination: and 'over the Inward, I have considerable control, over the Outward very little' (4.87). However, this last flourish must be inessential: the crucial point is that we can construct instances of mathematical structures 'at will'. If correct, this might explain the *a priori* character of mathematics: we do not depend upon experience to provide our samples, but rather construct them ourselves, either in our heads or on paper. It is less clear that it explains mathematical certainty: surely limitations of imagination and mathematical facility could lead us to construct an unrepresentative sample of the structure we seek to investigate. Furthermore, in general, we find one presentation of a proof absolutely compelling, more so than we ever find an ordinary induction based upon a sample of one. We do not use this prized control over our constructions to test our proofs by producing lots of samples, varying, perhaps in incidental respects like size, colour and so on. If mathematical proof is to have the features that Peirce desires, we must have an effective way of establishing that our sample is totally representative: if we experiment correctly with our sample, then we can know with certainty that what we discover holds of any instantiation of the same form of relation.

But, even if we can explain how we are justified in thinking our samples representative, the inductive model cannot be the whole story. The analogy between ordinary scientific induction and method in mathematics seems to provide room for a notion of mathematical truth, and for the logical evaluation of mathematical methods; Peirce's insistence that mathematics is *pre-logical* undermines the value of this analogy. If our ability to construct instances is all that is distinctive about mathematical 'inductions', then Peirce's account of mathematics fails to answer to the needs of his system. If mathematics is genuinely 'acritical', then mathematical certainty and necessity must be grounded in a demonstration that (somehow) we cannot fail to reason correctly in this area. This will remind us of the doctrine discussed in chapter I, that mental action – thought generally – conforms to the patterns of *valid* inference. Can Peirce argue that we cannot be ignorant of the real objects of our mathematical representations, and that our mathematical reasoning cannot fail to conform to Barbara (in a very general sense)? Although I am not aware that he discusses this explicitly, I think we can see, from materials already discussed, that Peirce can produce such an argument.

Mathematical activity could lead to error if our diagram was either not a representative replica of its symbol, or if that symbol was not a representative instance of the form of relation which it denotes. Of course, one sort of mathematical error arises when we *misunderstand* the public meaning of a representation, but that cannot be what is at issue here. Logical criticism would have a role if we could correctly understand the representation, but still come to a false mathematical belief with its aid. We understand the premisses, but draw conclusions from them which do not genuinely follow. But, this requires that a distinction can be drawn between understanding a representation, and using it as a premiss in inferences. For Peirce, understanding a representation involves interpreting it in thought – taking it to be a representation of some object. Thus, this distinction can be drawn only if interpreting a representation and using it as a premiss in inferences are distinct. If all that shows how I interpret

> All men are mortal.

is the fact that I deduce

> Socrates is mortal.

from

> Socrates is a man.

then it is clear that my reasoning cannot fail to conform to Barbara. The fact that the validity of Barbara is traced to fundamental properties of the sign relation lends support to the idea that this is an important feature of Peirce's thought. Treating A as a sign of B simply is treating A as a sign of whatever B is a sign of (e.g. 5.320): accepting a proposition involves adopting a certain habit of inference.

This is only part of the story, however. In the last chapter, we saw that we can be deeply deceived about the real objects of our perceptual judgments. Peirce must believe that we cannot be similarly deceived about the objects of our mathematical representations. The explanation must lie in the fact that mathematical objects, forms of relation, are abstract objects, *entia rationis*. Since they do not react with us, or with other things, we have no access to them that can be used to override what is provided by our beliefs about them. The reality of the form of relation simply consists in what is discovered about it through mathematical reasoning. It might be helpful to say that we refer to the form of relation primarily as 'the object of this mathematical theory': the theory could not fail to be a representative instance of it. Hence, when our application of a mathematical theory leads to a bridge falling down or our bank account becoming overdrawn, we are less likely to question our mathematical reasoning (especially if it survives careful checking) than to question its applicability to this particular problem. The mathematician, remember, forgets about the practical problem that prompted the investigation and just studies the purely mathematical problem that is presented. What the fact that we can construct instances of mathematical structures should be used to stress is *not* the fact that it makes induction particularly easy, but the fact that it reveals that mathematical objects lack secondness, that they are abstractions with only a second grade kind of reality.

We have now described the main elements of Peirce's philosophy of mathematics, and we can understand the distinctive epistemological and modal character that mathematical assertions are supposed to have. In consequence, we have surveyed the contents of all of the pre-logical sciences in Peirce's pantheon, as well as discussing a number of topics from logic such as the analysis of the sign relation and the analysis of truth. So, we are now ready to turn to the logic of ampliative inference, Peirce's proof that, if we conduct our inquiries properly, the truth is available to us, his vindication of induction.

VII

The Growth of Knowledge: Induction and Abduction

1 Introduction

We have now examined Peirce's theories of truth and representation and surveyed the products of the 'pre-logical' sciences. We have considered his views about the logic of acritical perceptual judgments and his account of *a priori* necessary reasoning. It is now time to raise the fundamental question: what leading principles, what methods and patterns of inference, should make up the *logica utens* of the earnest seeker after truth? We have to justify forms of ampliative reasoning by showing that their adoption would answer to the needs of someone who has adopted the single-minded pursuit of truth as his overriding aim. Thus, if he is to carry out his project successfully, Peirce must provide a description of the methods and arguments used in scientific research and demonstrate their validity, derive their adequacy from 'the presumption from which science starts out'. Peirce was confident that he did have a justification of induction and the other components of the scientific method, and believed that, sooner or later, everyone would have to endorse his view (NE iii 211). He discussed these topics on many occasions, and there is considerable consistency in the things he says at different times. I shall concentrate here upon elaborating the main themes in his mature position, and shall not say much about the respects in which his views did develop.[1]

The elements of Peirce's view of science are familiar. The scientist produces hypotheses, and then tests them against experience. Scientific progress requires both that we have a reliable source of hypotheses for testing and efficient means for testing them. Discovery of the truth would be impeded if the correct hypothesis simply failed to occur to us as worth testing, or if our methods of testing hypotheses forced us to reject the correct one or to endorse one that was mistaken. If I am to devote my life to the pursuit of truth, then I require at least some assurance that progress will not be held up in one of these ways. In his mature work, Peirce used the term 'induction' to refer to the patterns of inference employed in empirically *testing* hypotheses; and the process whereby we decide which hypotheses are worth critical attention, he calls 'abduction'. So, in this chapter, we shall examine Peirce's attempts to justify induction and abduction.

As Laudan has explained, the strategy of defending science by showing that it is self-correcting was widely adopted in the nineteenth century: even if science leads us into error in the short run, it will eventually uncover the error and guide us forward to the truth (Laudan, 1981, ch. 14). Peirce's own contribution to the logic of induction remains within this tradition.

> The true guarantee of the validity of induction is that it is a method of reaching conclusions which, if persisted in long enough, will assuredly correct any error concerning future experience into which it may temporarily lead us. (2.769)

The point can be illustrated even with what Peirce calls 'Crude Induction'. Crude induction derives a universal generalization from the observation of a few instances. In a 1901 paper, Peirce illustrated this through an example, derived from Quetelet, of a Greek who, having spent his life in the Mediterranean, comes to the Bay of Biscay and observes the tide's regular rise and fall. He concludes, tentatively and provisionally, that the tide will rise, without exception, every half-day forever. The inference has the form

All observed As are B.

So, All As are B.

Peirce claims that such an inference is not better or worse grounded according to the number of As that are observed. Rather, its justification consists simply in the fact that

> it was the result of a method which, if it be persisted in, must correct its result if it were wrong. For if the tide was going to skip a half day, he must discover it, if he continued his observations long enough. (7.215)

If we rely upon crude induction, we tentatively adopt universal generalizations and keep a lookout for falsifying instances. Peirce finds this a weak and unsatisfactory form of inference, and claims that it has little or no role in science. First, its self-correcting character is conditional upon all of the observations being actually made – if we miss a few observations, we can have no assurance that we have not missed the unique counterexample, in which case we should hold on to a false belief till the end of inquiry. Secondly, there is 'no probable indication in advance, if its conclusion is to break down; so long as it does not break down, there is nothing to be said but that no reason appears as yet for giving up the hypothesis' (7.215). I take this complaint to be that we can make no judgments of the forms: this hypothesis seems to be well confirmed by experience; or, in the light of our experience, this hypothesis does not look very promising and should be tested more thoroughly.

The two forms of induction that are used in science are quantitative and qualitative induction. These two are self-correcting, but not in the crude falsificationist way of crude induction. We employ quantitative induction when we infer, tentatively and provisionally, the relative frequency of events in a population from information about their frequency in a sample drawn from the population. If half the beans in a handful drawn from a sack are white, I conclude that probably about half of the beans in the entire sack are white. We use qualitative induction when we test theoretical hypotheses by deriving predictions from them which can be tested against experience: for example, we test the hypothesis that a substance is acid by observing whether it turns blue litmus paper red. As Peirce admits at NE iii 204–5, in earlier writings, qualitative induction is often referred to as 'hypothesis' or 'induction in depth'. As we shall see in subsequent sections, Peirce claims that sampling is involved in both kinds of induction; in qualitative induction we sample the testable predictions that can be derived from the hypothesis. Sampling, he thinks, provides the key to ampliative inference (2.726; 6.40): the character of sampling is responsible for the self-correcting character of induction generally. In the following two sections, we shall examine the logic of abduction and the two varieties of scientific induction more fully.

As will be evident from this discussion, Peirce thinks he has a solution to a problem of induction: without relying upon inductive reasoning, he aims to show that the use of induction will provide us with knowledge of reality. The strategy is to employ the substantive conception of truth developed through the normative sciences, and, using mathematical reasoning, demonstrate that inductive reasoning will reveal to us the nature of that reality. Since there are many 'problems of induction', and since there is much dispute about just what has to be shown if we are to provide objective foundations for inductive logic, it will be useful to remind ourselves of some of the things that Peirce does not undertake to establish. He does not offer a justification of the use of induction in obtaining information that can be applied in solving vital practical problems in the short run. There is no logical guarantee that induction will be of any practical or short run value at all. We saw in chapter II, that his task is to show the goodness of induction in the context of the project of cooperative pure inquiry: it will contribute to the eventual discovery of the truth. It accords with this that Peirce has no sympathy for the kind of inductive logic which holds that a body of evidence warrants attaching a particular probability (say, a justified degree of belief) to a conclusion: an inductive inference is not valid because, whenever the premisses are true, the conclusion is probable. The next section will indicate some of the reasons for this belief. Finally, the problem of induction, for Peirce, does not rest upon scepticism about whether there are laws or natural necessities. Within the nominalist tradition, from Hume to Reichenbach, any method which seems to uncover general laws is suspect: how can we be justified in using induction when there may be no laws or constant regularities to be discovered. Peirce lacks these nominalist scruples. Phenomenology has taught us that thirdness is an element of reality: the question concerns whether induction can reveal its character to us.

It should be clear that the adequacy of induction is not a trivially analytic matter. Although he may have defended this view in the 1860s, and although it is possible to find later passages that suggest it, Peirce does not want to rely upon the argument that, since the truth is whatever we believe in the long run, then, whatever results from the continued use of induction will be the truth (see Lenz, 1964; Madden, 1981). We saw in chapter II that he relies upon a substantive notion of truth, cast in terms of the categories and developed in the normative sciences. On the other hand, the adequacy of the scientific method is not an empirical matter (cf Skagestad, 1981). Reflection upon the history of science may illustrate the details of how science grows, and it may enable us to decide why it grows so fast. It may help us to decide whether it grows gradually or in sudden large leaps (1.107 ff; Sharpe, 1970). But, the justification of our methods of ampliative inference is to be in an *a priori* investigation which does not use the products of the special sciences.[2]

2 *Quantitative induction and probability*

When we carry out a quantitative induction, we move from a premiss which describes the character of a sample drawn from a population (about the handful of beans drawn from the sack) to a conclusion about the population as a whole (about the beans in the sack). Rather than examine this kind of inference directly, we shall begin by looking at some inferences that move in the opposite direction: we know the character of the population as a whole, and we use this information to estimate the nature of a sample drawn from that population. Peirce looks on these as a form of *deductive* reasoning, and the following examples illustrate some of its forms.

1   Most people wounded in the liver die.
     A was wounded in the liver.

So,   probably, A will die.

1′   75% of those wounded in the liver die.
     A was wounded in the liver.

So,   with a probability of .75, A will die.

2   75% of the beans in that bag are white.
     This large handful of beans was taken at random from that bag.

So,   probably, the proportion of white beans in this handful is close to 75%.

1 and 1′ are forms of *simple probable deduction* (2.695); and 2 is a *statistical deduction* (2.700). In each case, the first premiss provides the 'rule' which is applied to a 'case' to yield the result given in the conclusion. The first premiss could, in each case, be reformulated as a probability statement:

> The probability of someone wounded in the liver dying is high.
> The probability of someone wounded in the liver dying is .75.
> The probability of a bean drawn from that bag being white is .75.

Furthermore, there is a temptation to say that the conclusion is a probability statement too. For example, in case 1′

> It is .75 probable that A will die.

Then, in order to explain the validity of these inferences, we should have to explain the meanings of the probability statements that function as premiss and conclusion.

It is very important to see that Peirce resists this way of understanding these inferences. Compare the following 'necessary deduction'.

3   Anyone wounded in the liver dies.
     A was wounded in the liver.

So,   necessarily, A will die.

It is not the conclusion of this valid argument that it is a necessary truth that A will die; rather the adverb 'necessarily' indicates that the conclusion follows necessarily from the premisses – it is not possible that the premisses be true and the conclusion false. The conclusion is simply

A will die.

This is also the conclusion of 1; the adverb 'probably' indicates, once again, how the conclusion follows from the premisses. In this case we only know that most of the arguments of this form that have true premisses also have true conclusions. If we made a practice of reasoning in this way, then, so long as we are not mistaken about our premisses, we shall usually be led to a true conclusion. Similarly, when, in case 1', I infer 'So, with a probability of .75, A will die' I indicate that my conclusion, 'A will die' issued from a sort of argument which leads from true premisses to a true conclusion 75% of the time. (For a general discussion of this, see Hacking, 1980.)

> So long as there are exceptions to the rule that all men wounded in the
> liver die, it does not necessarily follow that because a given man is
> wounded in the liver he cannot recover. Still we know that if we were
> to reason in that way, we should be following a mode of inference
> which would only lead us wrong, in the long run, once in fifty times;
> and this is what we mean when we say that the probability is one out
> of fifty that the man will recover. (2.697)

The probability primarily attaches not to the conclusion of the argument, but to the genus of arguments to which the argument belongs: 'it is the ratio of the number of arguments of a certain genus which carry truth with them to the total number of arguments of that genus' (2.657 – presumably, the total number with true premisses).

This provides an explanation of the meaning of genuine probability statements, such as

The probability of someone wounded in the liver dying is .75.

We have already seen, on several occasions, that Peirce links universal propositions with the leading principles of arguments. If I believe that All F are G, then I shall expect that any argument of the form

a is F.
_____
So, a is G.

has a true conclusion if its premiss is true. Similarly, if I accept the probability statement given above, I shall expect that 75% of arguments of the form

A is wounded in the liver.
_____
So, A will die.

have true conclusions, if their premisses are true. The general proposition defines a genus of arguments. This explains the meaning of probability statements in accordance with the pragmatist principle: it explains the meaning of the probability statement by drawing out what we expect to be the consequences of our inferential activity if it is true. Thus, we anticipate that

> [as] we go on drawing inference after inference of the given kind, during the first ten or hundred cases the ratio of successes may be expected to show considerable fluctuations; but when we come into the thousands and millions, these fluctuations become less and less; and if we continue long enough, the ratio will approximate towards a fixed limit. (2.650)

Peirce defends a version of the frequency theory of probability. his formulation in terms of arguments – which he claims to have got from Locke (2.696) – is equivalent to more familiar formulations in terms of the relative frequencies of *events*. He prefers not to use this notion because 'Some of the worst and most persistent errors in the use of the doctrine of chances have arisen from this vicious mode of expression' (2.651). In later work, his view is reformulated in accordance with his realism. For example in 1910, considering the claim that the possibility is one third that a die thrown from a dice box will turn up a number divisible by three, he comments that this statement tells us how the die *would* behave in appropriate circumstances; it does not simply report the frequency of 3s and 6s in actual throws. The probability, or propensity in modern terminology, is an underlying trait which *explains* the frequencies that are actually observed. Even with this modification, we can see that Peirce wants to combine two elements in this theory. The first is that probabilities are *objective*; whether the probability that someone with liver damage will die is .75 or .98 is a matter of real physical fact (2.697, 2.650). Peirce will not accept the subjectivism of those who, like de Morgan, construe probabilities as degrees of belief. And second, probabilities are empirically accessible through observable frequencies. (See Skagestad, 1981, pp. 216 ff for a useful discussion of this.)

There are many details of Peirce's writings about probability that I shall not pursue, such as his demonstrations that the mathematical calculus of probabilities can be used to diagram these limiting frequencies. However, before we turn to the real topic of this chapter, induction, there are two issues I want to raise. As we noted above, Peirce's theory does not allow him to assign probabilities to singular propositions; a singular proposition does not define a genus of arguments. When I assert that, probably, A will die, then I convey that my inference that A will die belongs to a general kind with the property that were I to adopt the general policy of relying upon such inferences, most of them would issue in true beliefs. This raises a problem which

214

Peirce acknowledges. He considers a pack of cards, twenty-five red and one black. He can be sure that if he were to make a very large number of drawings from this pack, the vast majority would be red; if he predicted that he would draw red on each occasion, he would be almost always correct. So long as many such drawings are to be made, we can understand how probability can be a guide to life. The problem arises when only one choice, only one inference, is to be made. Suppose that someone is to make just one drawing of a card, and he has a choice whether to choose from this pack or from one containing twenty-five black cards and one red. 'If the drawing of a red card were destined to transport him to everlasting felicity, and that of a black one to consign him to everlasting woe, it would be folly to deny that he ought to prefer the pack containing the larger proportion of red cards, although, from the risk, it could not be repeated' (2.652). As Peirce notes, it is hard to account for this on his analysis of chance: if he chooses the red pack and draws the black card, it will be little consolation that this would not often happen if he made a lot of choices. 'He might say that he had acted in accord with reason, but that would only show that his reason was absolutely worthless. And if he should choose the right card, how could he regard it as anything but a happy accident?' (ibid.). We want to say that the choice is rational; but we cannot account for its rationality, if we adopt Peirce's analysis of statements of probability.

Some philosophers find in this difficulty a refutation of the frequency view of probability, but it is not clear that any of the alternatives provide a satisfactory answer to it. In his 1878 paper, Peirce responds to it in an odd fashion; he takes it to support a view which, we have seen, he defends elsewhere, that rationality requires altruism. Even if I draw only one inference of the genus in question, similar inferences may be drawn by others: in the long run, infinitely many inferences of the form may be drawn. My consolation, as I consign myself to everlasting woe, is that I have done my bit towards ensuring that as many people as possible obtain everlasting felicity. More generally, if we hope that intellectual inquiry will continue indefinitely, and we have an altruistic concern for the good of the wider community of inquirers, then we are justified in going by probabilities: even if we do not benefit from doing so, we can be assured that, in the long run, most of the inferences drawn within the community will have true conclusions. The 'social sentiment' is presupposed in reasoning, and the validity of probabilistic inference depends upon the altruistic sentiments of 'Charity, Faith and Hope' (2.655). That something is wrong with this is evident when we consider the plain irrationality of the misanthropic response, 'I have no interest in the welfare of my fellow man, so I may as well choose the black pack.' A response to this is implicit in the later doctrines that we discussed at the end of chapter II. When we participate in scientific activity, we do subordinate ourselves to the wider community. Our inferences are evaluated in terms of what they contribute to science, not how far they satisfy our selfish interests. These altruistic concerns are lacking only in connection with the 'vital' concerns of practice: the example we are considering is one of vital rather than scientific importance. Peirce denies that our use of inference in practical decision should, or could, be provided with a logical foundation. We respond to instinct and tradition, and it would be impertinent, 'treasonous', to try to subject these to logical self-control. Thus, Peirce can feel assured that his odd approach to the difficulty does have application in the area which is his real concern; and it indicates all the more clearly the limits of logical self-control. His treatment of probability accounts for the role of the notion in science.

The second of the issues to be raised as a preliminary to the discussion of induction concerns the special features of statistical deduction, of inferences like 2 above. If we know that exactly 75% of the beans in the bag were white, we should still be somewhat surprised if *exactly* 75% of those in our handful were. However, so long as the handful was large and the bag well shaken, we could be very sure that the proportion of white beans in the handful would be between, say, 70% and 80%. It is possible to calculate the probability that the proportion of white beans in the handful will fall between 74% and 76%, 70% and 80%, 50% and 100%, and so on. The details of these calculations are not important. So, the conclusion of the inference is that the proportion of white beans in the handful falls within a certain interval – although, as 2 indicates, the boundaries of the interval will not always be precisely specified.

This has a direct relevance to the logic of quantitative induction, in which we move from a premiss such as

75% of the beans in this handful are white.

to a conclusion like

Close to 75% of the beans in the bag from which the handful is drawn are white.

Both inferences, the statistical deduction and the quantitative induction suppose that the proportion of white beans will be about the same in the bag as in the handful (cf 6.40); and we can see the appeal of Peirce's remark that the induction is good only if the corresponding deduction is (2.715). There are other points of resemblance between induction and the kinds of deduction we have examined in this section.

[In] demonstrative reasoning the conclusion follows from the existence of the objective facts laid down in the premisses; while in probable reasoning these facts in themselves do not even render the conclusion probable, but account has to be taken of various subjective circumstances – of the manner in which the premises have been obtained, of there being no countervailing considerations, etc. (2.696)

These inferences have no value unless the premiss about the population has been obtained by reliable means and the sample is genuinely fair and random. Moreover, in each case, the conclusion is acceptable only if we are aware of no further information which undermines the evidence: for instance, we may know that no bag has more white than black beans, or we may been told that this handful is unrepresentative. The inferences can be carried out more or less well. There is scope for self-control, for trying to carry them out correctly.

The bare claim that quantitative induction is self-correcting is vague. It is necessary to find a more precise formulation of the notion of 'validity' that applies to such inferences. It will be helpful to look at two competing candidates, both of which scholars have claimed to find in Peirce's writing. The first is suggested by, among other passages, a discussion of the inferences

> Minos, Sarpedon, Rhadamanthus, Deuclion, and Epimenides are all the Cretans I can think of.
> But these are all atrocious liars.

So, Pretty much all Cretans must have been liars.

Although we cannot assign a probability to this particular inference, Peirce claims, we do know that the proportion of Cretans who were liars 'can be probably approximated to by an induction from five or six instances'. At worst, he thinks, 'the ratio so obtained would probably not be in error by more than 1/6' (2.689). This rests upon familiar mathematical results, which exploit the properties of the binomial distribution – Peirce considers no other distributions. Suppose that we attempt to estimate the proportion of the members of a population that are F by taking samples with n members each: r/n gives the proportion of a sample that is F. We can do this by using a function which maps r and n on to an interval around r/n: we tentatively conclude that the proportion of the entire population which is F falls within this interval. We can calculate the probability that the true proportion will fall within this interval; and we can adopt a rule with the property that, with a high probability, the conclusion of the inference will be true. If we adopt such a rule and use it consistently, we can know that, in the long run, most of our quantitative inductions – most of our interval estimations – will have true conclusions. (I assume throughout that the premises are true.) The probability of a true conclusion will be higher if we are content to conclude that the true value falls within a wide interval, and will fall if we aim to pinpoint it more exactly. Again, I shall not go into the details of the mathematics. The important point is that probabilities can be attached to these rules for sampling, so that we can demonstrate that some of them meet this criterion of validity.

C1   A rule for quantitative induction is valid if, and only if, in the long run, most of these inferences with true premisses that accord with the rule would have true conclusions.

There is evidence that, from the 1860s Peirce was drawn to C1 and there can be no doubt that these considerations reflect much that is central to his account of inductive behaviour.

As Levi points out, on this understanding, there is a clear sense in which quantitative induction is self-correcting, and Peirce's view resembles modern developments in the theory of confidence interval estimation due to thinkers like Neyman and Pearson (Levi, 1980; see also Hacking, 1980). Relying upon a passage from the 1882 article, 'A Theory of Probable Inference', Levi claims that when Peirce says induction is self-correcting, he does not mean that 'following an inductive rule will, in the messianic long run, reveal the true value (for the proportion of Fs in the population). His thesis can be put this way: Either the conclusion reached *via* an inductive rule is correct or, if wrong, the revised estimate emerging from a new attempt at estimation based on a different sample will [with high probability] be correct' (1980, p. 138).

However, important as these doctrines are for Peirce, he attached most importance to a different justification of quantitative induction, one that did promise to reveal the truth in the 'messianic' long run. This emerges most clearly in the important 1892 paper 'The Doctrine of Necessity Examined'. Having presented his defence of induction, he imagines that someone might object to him that more can be said for induction that he allows. The example is one of estimating the proportion of grains of wheat of quality A in a ship by drawing handfuls from different parts of the hold. The objector points out that 'if the true ratio of grains of quality A were 0.80 and the handful contained a thousand grains, nine such handfuls out of every ten would contain from 780 to 820 grains of the quality A', and reminds Peirce that it is very probably that any handful he draws will be a reliable guide to the character of the population (6.42). Peirce's reply is that such figures are relevant only if the sampling is properly random and independent. If we do not know that the sampling has these properties, we cannot rely upon the results of such calculations. Peirce wants a justification of induction which shows that the inference has value even if we have no knowledge of how the samples were produced. 'When we cannot ascertain how the sampling has been done or the sample character selected, induction still has the essential validity which my present

218

account of it shows it to have' (6.42).

We can easily see why this should be. First, we have no effective criterion for establishing that a system of sampling is random. Indeed, randomness is itself a statistical notion: to say that the sampling is random is to say that any member of the population has an equal chance of being selected. Although we can try for randomness, we often have no grounds for assurance that we have succeeded. For example, people sampled swans in the fifteenth century, not realizing that their geographical location meant that a proportion of the population had little chance of being selected; and this led to the false conclusion that all swans were white. Secondly, we can imagine inquirers stuck in an odd corner of the universe where – due to its unrepresentative character – none of their inductions rests upon properly drawn samples. If their inductions were of no value, they could make no contribution to science. If this is a real possibility, then it is unclear that the life of science could be sustained as an ultimate aim. Peirce's project requires him to show that, even in this position, someone's inductions are of value and that they can contribute to the growth of knowledge. Hence, although the doctrines about confidence interval estimation have a place in our everyday assessment of the value of induction, Peirce wants a justification of this kind of inference which does not rest upon such strong assumptions about the character of the sample used.

Sampling the wheat from the hold of the ship, we conclude, 'experimentally and provisionally', that close to 80% of the grain in the cargo is of quality A.

> By saying that we draw the inference provisionally, I mean that we do not hold that we have reached any assigned degree of approximation as yet, but only hold that if our experience be indefinitely extended, and if every fact of whatever nature, as fast as it presents itself, be duly applied, according to the inductive method, in correcting the inferred ratio, then our approximation will become indefinitely close in the long run . . . so that if experience in general is to fluctuate irregularly to and fro, in a manner to deprive the ratio sought of all definite value, we shall be able to find out approximately within what limits it fluctuates, and if, after having one definite value, it changes and assumes another, we shall be able to find that out, and in short, whatever may be the variations of this ratio in experience, experience indifinitely extended will enable us to detect them, so as to predict rightly, at last, what its ultimate value may be. . . . (6.40)

Peirce is nowhere very clear about exactly what he has in mind, but many scholars see an anticipation of the views which Reichenbach defends in *Experience and Prediction* and elsewhere.

According to Reichenbach, our ability to guess the nature of populations from samples rests upon what he calls the *principle of induction* (Reichenbach, 1938, p. 340). Suppose that we have drawn n grains from the hold, inspected them and then replaced them. If m of these were of quality A, we shall use h_n to stand for the ratio m/n, the proportion of A grains in the first n drawn. The principle of induction (the 'straight rule') counsels us to expect that, were we to extend the drawings beyond n, say to s, the value of h_s would lie in a small interval around h_n. With each additional drawing, we may be led to modify our expectations: if h_s is not close to h_n, then, henceforth, we expect the proportion of A grains to be close to h_s. In fact, we have no real reason, at any point, to believe that the observed frequency will be maintained, this is a 'blind posit'. But, in a passage reminiscent of Peirce, 'in choosing h_n as our posit, we anticipate the case where n is the "place of convergence." It may be that by this anticipation we obtain a false value; we know, however, that a continued anticipation must lead to the true value, if there is a limit at all' (p. 353). The argument rests upon the claim that, the aim of induction is 'to find series of events whose frequency of occurrence converges towards a limit' (p. 350). This is a straightforward consequence of the frequency theory of probabilities: if m/n is the proportion of A grains in the hold, then, if we keep on drawing grains and replacing them, the proportion of A grains among the grains we draw will become arbitrarily close to m/n. For any small ϵ, there will be a point in the sequence of drawings after which the observed ratio does not differ from m/n by more than ϵ. Thus, if there is a statistical regularity to be discovered, obeying Reichenbach's principle and constantly revising our 'posits' would ensure that at some stage we acquired a settled and correct assessment of the regularity. Of course, we can never be sure that we *have* reached this point; we can only know that we cannot fail to reach it if we continue sampling for long enough. In accepting such an argument, Peirce would need to make only minor revisions. The main one would result from the fact that he thinks that laws of nature are never *exactly* true (1.402 f): at best, he would expect the sequence of observations to converge on a point where the observed frequency stays close to m/n – there may be values of ϵ, such that the series never reaches a point after which the observed ratio always falls within ϵ of m/n. And the argument seems to fit the claims of the passage from 6.40.

The obvious complaint about this interpretation is that it relies just as heavily upon the assumption that sampling is fair and random as did the view we examined above. If we do not stir the grains, and always draw the next grain from the spot that we replaced the previous one, there may be no limiting frequency in the observations at all, or the series may converge on a value other than the proportion of A grains in the hold. Peirce considers this objection in the 1892 paper. Considering the possibility that some grains might never occur in a sample or do so rarely, he responds that 'the instances excluded from being subjects of reasoning would not be experienced in the full sense of the word, but would be among those *latent* individuals of which our conclusion does not pretend to speak' (6.42). I think we should understand this as claiming that if there is a limiting frequency of A grains in the observations, then we have discovered a genuine statistical regularity. We may, however, be mistaken about the significance of this regularity. For instance, if the limiting frequency is m/n, we have established that the probability of a grain drawn *by that method* being of quality A is m/n: we have *not* established that the probability of a grain drawn from the hold by fair methods being of quality A is m/n. The sampling procedure is allowed to determine which are the individuals of which our conclusions *does* pretend to speak. If there is a limiting frequency in the observations, we have uncovered a genuine form of law of thirdness in our experience.

The criterion of inductive validity employed here is

C2 A rule for quantitative induction is valid if, and only if, its continued use in investigating the proportion of Xs that are Y will eventually reach a point where every further application of the rule would have a true conclusion.

There is ample evidence that Peirce employed such a criterion, although doubt is possible about whether the rule he had in mind was Reichenbach's. If the problem of randomness is handled in the way suggested by the passage from 6.42, one might easily stay with the earlier version of how quantitative induction proceeds, and rest upon the fact that, if there is a limiting frequency in the observations, then, in the long run, the distribution of A grains in samples will reveal this. We can rely upon the method of confidence-interval estimation justified by our knowledge of what the method can produce in the 'messianic long run'. (C2 would then require slight modification.) I am not aware of any text which makes Peirce's position explicit.

Before raising general questions about the adequacy of such a response to problems about induction, we should examine Peirce's views about the validity of qualitative induction. A standard objection to this position is that although he claims that all forms of induction are self-corrective, he only offers an argument in defence of this claim for the easy case of quantitative induction. Von Wright's complaint that '[the] Peircean idea of induction as a self-correcting approximation to the truth has no immediate significance . . . for other types of inductive reasoning than statistical generalization' (Von Wright, 1965, p. 226) can stand for many similar quotations that could have been taken from a wide variety of commentators. Therefore, in the following section, we shall examine what Peirce can say in defence of the self-corrective character of qualitative induction.

3 Qualitative induction and abduction

Peirce gives a subtle and complex account of how qualitative induction proceeds, but we can grasp its character if we assimilate it to the kind of hypothesis testing known as the hypothetico-deductive method. We test a hypothesis by deriving predictions from it, and by evaluating those predictions. Thus, we test the hypothesis that some individual is a Catholic priest by seeing whether his dress, utterances and activities are those of a Catholic priest; we test a general scientific theory such as the kinetic theory of gases by observing whether observed regularities are those that we should expect were this hypothesis about unobserved reactions correct. 'This kind of reasoning may be described . . . by saying that it tests a hypothesis by sampling the possible predictions that may be based upon it' (7.216). However, the inference differs from that other kind of sampling – quantitative induction – because these predictions do not function as *units*: there is no sense to be attached to the claim that, for example, 4/5 of the predictions based upon a certain hypothesis are true. To see this, note that we could predict that our Catholic priest will wear black clothes, that he will wear black trousers and will wear a black shirt. How many predictions is this? One, two or three? A purely conventional solution to this difficulty will not do, for the answer we give will influence how these predictions are weighted against, say, the prediction that he will carry a rosary, or conduct masses. We have a large number of different predictions to make use of, but no ready way to quantify or compare them. We have to weigh the importance of the different predictions, but the calculus of probabilities will not help us in this (see 7.216, 2.759).

We shall not understand Peirce's claims about qualitative induction unless we are careful to specify just what question such inferences set out to answer. Confusion about this is responsible for the scepticism about Peirce's theory that I alluded to. If we understand quantitative induction according to Reichenbach's theory, then its self-correcting character is rather complex, having three elements. Suppose that, at a certain stage of inquiry, we adopt a particular posit about the proportion of Fs that are G. Then,

(i) If our posit is false, it will be rejected by continued application of the straight rule.

(ii) 'Reject' is perhaps not the best word to use, for, in fact, the posit is *modified*; it is replaced by another hypothesis.

(iii) Even if the new hypothesis is not *better* than the one that it replaced, we know that positing it is a means to securing the further modifications that will lead us to the truth.

When we raise the question

What proportion of Fs are G?

the techniques of quantitative induction provide us with a *recipe* for, eventually, reaching the correct answer to the question. It is reasonable to insist that, if induction is self-correcting in any interesting sense, then it provides a recipe for answering the questions that prompt its use. Suppose, then that we raise the question:

What does X do for a liviing?

and we expect to answer this by qualitative induction, then we must expect that if testing our predictions forces us to reject the hypothesis that he is a Catholic priest, then the induction will suggest an alternative hypothesis and is eventually bound to come up with the correct answer. Since this is absurd, it seems to follow that qualitative induction is not self-corrective: it does not offer a recipe for discovering the truth.

If, on the other hand, we think that qualitative induction is used to answer 'yes–no' questions like,

Is X a Catholic priest?

this difficulty evaporates. As inquiry proceeds, induction can tentatively recommend 'yes', reject that and suggest 'no' and so on; we can hope that it can be shown that if one of these answers is correct, then induction will lead us to settle on it stably in the long run. While narrowing the scope of induction in this fashion might rescue the self-correcting character of qualitative induction, it does so only by prompting scepticism about science. If induction does not guarantee to answer all of the why questions that prompt scientific endeavour, what reason have we for thinking that science will discover the truth about reality in the long run. Induction only tests hypotheses that have been proposed, but science needs a supply of fruitful hypotheses or reality might forever elude our understanding. We have to understand how induction combines with other things in the activity of science in order to grasp clearly what the question for qualitative induction is, and how science can provide us with knowledge. Therefore, before examining the details of Peirce's account of qualitative induction, we must examine the part of the scientific method which yields fruitful hypotheses, abduction.

Two distinct issues arise in Peirce's treatment of abduction. Abduction provides hypotheses for inductive testing: we test theories with a 'high place in the list of theories . . . which call for further examination' (2.776). In other words, we might think of a number of theories of the phenomena that puzzle us and we order them, testing first those that rank higher in this ordering. The progress of science would be held up, first, if the true theory did not appear on the list at all; our imagination might fail us so that the true explanation of the phenomena does not occur to us. Secondly, if the correct theory received a very low ranking, we might never get around to testing it. Therefore, we have to explain how we have a reliable source of hypotheses, and why we are good at making guesses about the nature of phenomena; and we have to clarify the rules we follow in ranking explanations as more or less plausible. The *logic* of abduction is concerned with the second of these issues: in what circumstances are we justified in the opinion that a particular hypothesis is worthy of inductive testing?

> Science presupposes that we have a capacity for 'guessing' right. We shall do better to abandon the whole attempt to learn the truth however urgent may be our need of ascertaining it, unless we can trust to the human mind's having such a power of guessing right that before very many hypotheses shall have been tried, intelligent guessing may be expected to lead us to the one which will support all tests, leaving the vast majority of possible hypotheses unexamined. (6.530)

Peirce relates this 'mysterious guessing power' (6.530) to what he calls the 'primary abduction' underlying all scientific research: that 'the human mind is akin to truth in the sense that in a finite number of guesses it will light upon the correct hypothesis' (7.220); that 'the facts in hand admit of rationalization, and of rationalization by us' (7.219). Although supported by the history of science – 'it has seldom been necessary to try more than two or three hypotheses made by clear genius before the right one was found' (7.220) – this is a hypothesis which would have to be 'embraced at the outset, however destitute of evidentiary support it may be' (7.219). The reason we have to make this bold assumption will have been anticipated by the reader. It is 'for the same reason that a general who has to capture a position or see his country ruined, must go on the hypothesis that there is some way in which he can and shall capture it': we meet one more of the regulative hopes on which science rests, the whist player transformed into a military strategist. The necessity for the assumption is argued both on the grounds that we have to be sure that the correct theory will occur to us, and on the grounds that we need a reliable ordering of the possible explanations of our facts which 'may be strictly innumerable'.

Whatever its basis, the assumption is that we have a 'natural instinct for truth' (7.220). We cannot provide any reason for our best guesses, and they do not result from self-controlled logic. In the Pragmatism lectures, Peirce is happiest to say that

> man has a certain Insight, not strong enough to be oftener right than wrong, but strong enough not to be overwhelmingly more often wrong than right, into the Thirdnesses, the general elements, of Nature. An Insight, I call it, because it is to be referred to the same general class of operations to which Perceptive Judgments belong. This Faculty is at the same time of the general nature of instinct. (5.173)

It was a mark of the great men of science that their guesses were particularly inspired; there are endless passages where he describes the abductive skills of Kepler and other heroes. There is also a curious paper, published as 'Guessing' (Peirce, 1929), in which Peirce tries to indicate the role of blind guessing, unguided by conscious reason, in a far-fetched autobiographical detective story (for discussion, see Sebeok and Umiker-Sebeok, 1980). I shall say something more about this instinct in the following section, which will look generally at the role Peirce assigns to instinct and common sense in the growth of scientific knowledge. We shall see there that he hints at an evolutionary explanation of the faculty: we should expect the instinct conducive to obtaining food and shelter to put us into harmony with the laws of the universe; and, since we have developed in accordance with natural laws, we should expect to find those very laws natural or simple. For the present, the scientific and metaphysical defence of this regulative hope is irrelevant to its logical functioning, and Peirce's claim is that unless it is warranted science is impossible.

As I suggested above, Peirce does provide rules we should follow in deciding which hypotheses are worth subjecting to inductive test. First, of course, the hypothesis to be tested must explain the phenomena that prompted the search for a hypothesis in the first instance; we must be able to see that if the hypothesis is true, the surprising phenomena to be explained are to be expected (7.220). Moreover, it must be empirically testable; we must be able to derive conditional predictions from it and subject it to experimental test (7.220; 5.197). This amounts simply to the claim that it must satisfy the pragmatist principle (see the following chapter). Peirce argues for this by claiming that rules for the selection of hypotheses should be framed in the light of what is to be done with them. Since what we do with a hypothesis is to 'trace out its consequences by deduction, to compare them with the results of experience by induction, and to discard the hypothesis, and try another as soon as the first has been refuted' (7.220), the requirement of inductive testing means that the hypothesis 'must consist of experiential consequences with only so much logical cement as is needed to render them rational' (7.220). We should favour theories that seem simple and natural to us (6.477), and those that appeal to our sense of plausibility; we should prefer them to cohere with our most fundamental metaphysical views, hence preferring theories which do not propose inexplicable discontinuities and rejecting theories which claim that anything is absolutely inexplicable (e.g. 6.158); we should prefer theories that explain a wide range of phenomena to those with limited scope (7.221); we should be mindful of the kinds of theories that have been successful in related areas, and prefer hypotheses which employ similar kinds of explanations; and so on. Peirce appears to want us to try those hypotheses that seem most plausible and probable in the light of information available, but he is tempted also by considerations which count against this. At 5.599, for example, he warns against attaching too much importance to 'antecedent likelihoods' in testing theories; they are 'mostly merely subjective' and are likely to lead us to miss 'remarkable opportunities'. In part, this passage just warns against relying upon the *a priori* method (see chapter II), and adopting theories which seem right without concern for whether they have verifiable predictive content. But, for example at 2.780, he urges us to test theories that 'would throw a great deal of light upon many things' if they were true, and comments that more suprising and unexpected theories are likely to cast more of this sort of enlightenment. But, the 'leading consideration in Abduction' is 'the question of Economy – Economy of money, time, thought, and energy' (5.600).

I have already mentioned the importance of economic considerations in Peirce's methodology (chapter II, section 6). Their relevance here is that we should prefer hypotheses that can be tested cheaply, and quickly. If it seems that a few experiments can settle the matter, this provides a reason for preferring the hypothesis, especially if current experimental techniques will be sufficient for this testing. If a theory makes a few very surprising predictions, it is in its favour that we are likely to be able to falsify it with just one experiment (7.220). If the experimental work involved in testing a hypothesis would be likely to be done anyway in testing other theories, that provides a further reason for taking it seriously (7.230). (See Rescher, 1978, ch. 4 for a fuller discussion.)

Guided by these varied criteria, we decide to test hypotheses inductively. Qualitative induction is occupied only with testing hypotheses, and not with providing replacements for hypotheses that have been abandoned. The replacements issue from further 'abductive suggestions'. We can now return to the problem of qualitative induction itself: what sorts of verdicts does it give on the hypotheses that it tests? And, how are the verdicts justified? As is evident from passages quoted above, one result of qualitative induction can be the rejection of a hypothesis. If the predictions derived from the hypothesis are disappointed, then the hypothesis is false. Such rejection, however, will be provisional and fallible. First, we may make a mistake in testing the prediction. Sticking with our non-scientific example of establishing whether X is a Catholic priest, our claim that he does not wear black may rest upon a trick of the light, or upon our having mistaken someone else for X. Secondly, we may be mistaken in thinking that Catholic priests do wear black – the prediction may not follow from the hypothesis. Thirdly, most of the predictions we use will be vague: for the most part, Catholic priests wear black most of the time; most Catholic priests believe in God; and so on. As Peirce stresses, when one of our predictions is disappointed, we have to assess its importance and decide how much weight should be attached to it. He thinks that no precise rules can guide us in this; we must rely upon tact and instinctive common sense. As Skagestad has stressed, Peirce was aware of the problem of the underdetermination of theory by evidence: given a perceptual surprise, there may be a variety of ways of revising our corpus of asserted propositions which restore order to our opinions. (See 1.450, Skagestad, 1981, p. 182.) So falsification is not an unproblematic concept. The next chapter will discuss in much more detail the relations between hypotheses and the predictions that are derived from them, and we shall return to these issues then.

When induction decides in favour of a hypothesis, its verdict is all the more fallible since it relies only upon a small number of successful predictions: the man in black clothes whom we observe celebrate Mass may be a confidence trickster or an actor on a film set. When the proposition is 'accepted', it is not looked upon as conclusively established, nor is it accepted as a reliable basis for action. It is best to see the acceptance in economic terms: having survived rigorous severe testing, it is rational to divert resources to other hypotheses, regarding this one as assertible at this stage of the growth of science, knowing full well that, if it is false, this will emerge when our future reliance upon it leads us into surprise. This is especially easy because the hypothesis is one that both appeals to our instinctive sense of plausibility and has survived severe test.

There is a further complication. The initial abduction only supports the claim that the hypothesis is *approximately* true: we should be very surprised if it escaped all falsification at its first testing, Hence, we look to the results of inductive testing to suggest to us how the hypothesis should be polished and revised. Of course, we should not make *ad hoc* adjustments to rescue the theory against any falsification, and the adjustments are likely to be gradual (7.216).

The familiar history of the kinetical theory of gases well illustrates this. It began with a number of spheres almost infinitesimally small occasionally colliding. It was afterward so far modified that the forces between the spheres, instead of merely separating them, were mainly attractive, that the molecules were not spheres, but systems, and that the parts of space within which their motions are free is appreciably less than the entire volume of the gas. There was no new hypothetical element in these modifications. They were partly quantitative, and partly such as to make the formal hypothesis represent better what was really supposed to be the case. (7.216)

Peirce insists that it was anticipated when the hypothesis was first introduced that such modifications would be required to bring it into true harmony with the facts. This raises the serious question of how we recognize that a change in our theory introduces 'no new hypothetical element'. The theory Peirce defends resembles what we find in the more recent writings of Kuhn (1962) and Lakatos (1970), but it is natural to suspect that he cannot give these interesting but vague ideas a precise content.

There is a *prima facie* tension between two elements in the theory of science that has emerged from our study of Peirce's writings. We have noticed in earlier chapters that Peirce defends quite a strong thesis about the convergence of human knowledge. If different inquirers begin to investigate the same problem, then, even if they have no contact with each other, they will eventually be led to the same solution. There is an answer to the problem which all serious inquirers are fated to reach if they investigate with enough diligence and integrity. But, now, to set against that, we find that qualitative induction calls for tact and instinctive weighting of competing considerations by investigators. Judgments of plausibility and relative importance must be made which cannot be seen as the mechanical application of methodological rules which are objectively defensible. There was evidence that Peirce acknowledged that observations do not *determine* how we should adjust our hypotheses and commitments in response to perceptual surprise. The tension is simply that if theory choice rests upon such messy instinctive factors, there is no reason to think that it is sufficiently constrained to ensure that different inquirers will eventually agree upon the same theories. This is a familiar problem from discussions in the philosophy of science, and we must begin to look at whether Peirce has any response to it. This discussion will pursue two themes. One has been mentioned already, and is the topic of the next chapter. This is the body of doctrines about meaning and understanding that make up Peirce's pragmatism. It confronts the issue just what is involved in the different inquirers settling on the *same* hypotheses. The second will be discussed immediately, and introduces Peirce's use of the motion of common sense.

4 Critical commonsensism

In the years after 1900, Peirce came increasingly to describe his epistemological position as a development out of the Scottish philosophy of common sense of Reid and Hamilton which provided the background assumption of most of the philosophical work at Harvard in the mid-nineteenth century. We can see from 5.505 that he saw three elements in the insight of this philosophical school. First, justification 'will have to come to a halt somewhere' and rest upon some opinions which are accepted without grounds or justification. Second, the beliefs which provide 'the bedrock of truth' are indubitable, and beyond rational support and criticism. Third, 'they must be regarded as the very truth', so that our reliance upon them does not leave our knowledge without secure foundations. In this spirit, Peirce wrote that 'if you absolutely cannot doubt a proposition . . . it is plain that there is no room to desire anything more' (6.498). As Peirce himself admits, there had been a common-sense strain in Peirce's thinking since before 1870. We saw it, in chapter I, in the rejection of Cartesian assumptions about method. The Cartesian, hunting for rational justification for 'first principles', claims to doubt what is, in reality, indubitable, and Peirce encouraged philosophers to have no truck with 'spurious' or 'paper' doubt. After 1900, the target is Kant as much as it is Descartes. The critical philosopher demands to know with what right we employ first principles, and transcendental idealism provides a response to this demand – we know the principles to be true of empirical reality because they are constitutive. In previous chapters, we have seen Peirce stress the role of indubitable acritical perceptual beliefs and mathematical inferences in the growth of knowledge, We must now look at a further application of this theme.

Both in 'Issues of Pragmatism' (5.438 – the best published source of Peirce's late views on common sense) and in a manuscript of similar date published in the *Collected Papers* (5.502–537), Peirce reports a development in his understanding of common-sense certainties which has moved him closer to the position of Reid and the other Scottish philosophers (5.444, 5.509). In earlier writings, he had held that 'there is no definite and fixed collection of opinions that are indubitable, but criticism gradually pushes back each individual's indubitables, modifying the list, yet still leaving him beliefs indubitable for the time being' (5.509). By 1905, he thought that there was 'a fixed list, the same for all men' (5.509): the changes are so slow that, for ordinary purposes, we can ignore them. Plainly, these common-sense beliefs do not reflect perceptual judgments, but also include general theoretical and moral principles. Peirce speaks of unquestioned assumptions about space and time, the assumption of the criminality of incest, the proposition that fire burns; he would probably include our assurance that induction will be a reliable basis for action in the short run. They provide a bedrock of shared certainties which enable us to cope with vital questions and everyday matters, and which have a role in the growth of science.

It is easy to see that this role could have a bearing on the problems discussed at the end of the last section. These indubitable propositions will tend to be maintained when our theories are adjusted to accommodate perceptual surprise: in Quine's phrase, they lie near the core of our scheme of beliefs and are revised only in extreme circumstances (Quine, 1953, ch. 2). Thus, they function as constraints limiting us in how we order our opinions in response to experience. If they occupy this role, we can see the importance of the development in Peirce's views just described. If they represent that core of our conceptual scheme that is much the same for all men (cf Strawson, 1959, p. 10), then we can expect them to constrain all theorists in a similar way, and thus we have reason to expect different investigators to converge upon similar opinions. If they vary, from person to person and from time to time, then, since different inquirers employ different constraints, such convergence would be very surprising. So, ideally, they provide a bedrock of shared certainties which offer foundations for shared standards of theory selection. Peirce acknowledges the resemblance beween his common-sense principles and Kant's constitutive principles. His position is 'but a modification of Kantism'.

> The Kantist has only to abjure from the bottom of his heart the
> position that a thing-in-itself can, however indirectly, be conceived;
> and then correct the details of Kant's doctrine accordingly, and he
> will find himself to have become a Critical Commonsensist. (5.452)

It is because of his nominalistic grip upon the idea of a thing in itself that the Kantian still demands that the principles which he cannot really doubt be given epistemological credentials through transcendental logic. This raises once more the issue of the relation between Peirce's position and Kantian idealism, an issue better discussed in the context of Peirce's pragmatism below.

The name 'critical commonsensism' is meant to suggest a fusion of themes from the seemingly incompatible traditions of commonsense philosophy and critical philosophy (see 5.505). How is the common-sense doctrine transformed when it becomes 'critical'? First, in another very Quinean claim, Peirce allows that common-sense certainties are fallible: there are circumstances in which we could be brought to reject them. But this would be a slow process, and before they were rejected they would cease to be indubitable and become proper targets for rational criticism. Indeed, criticism and doubt have a role in the use of common-sense beliefs generally. First, even if a belief seems to be indubitable, we should try to doubt it. The Cartesian thought experiment of seeing what can be doubted is intellectually respectable. Error lies in thinking that success can be achieved more easily than it is. Thus, serious attempts to doubt propositions enable us to locate those which are genuinely indubitable (5.451). Second, and more important, the use of common-sense certainties in scientific inquiry involves the use of critical self-control. Science invokes instinctive common-sense beliefs, but also uses the normative sciences to control its activities. Thus, the question arises how someone controlling his reasonings in accordance with an ultimate ideal can use his common sense.

In part, we have seen, Peirce's view is that he cannot but trust it. In addition, he hopes that this trust will take him to the truth; he hopes that his instincts put him in harmony with reality (see the discussion of the previous section). Critical commonsensism draws attention, also, to two further features of commonsense beliefs. First, they are excessively *vague* (see 5.446–450 and Brock, 1979). At 4.237, we find the claim that 'It is . . . easy to be certain. One has only to be sufficiently vague' (4.237). The vaguer a proposition is, the fewer precise predictions can be derived from it, and the easier it is to rescue it from falsification. Take the proposition that fire burns (5.498). So long as we do not specify just what is burned by fire, in what circumstances, little will show that this claim is false. Once we attempt to replace this vague proposition by a more precise one, one from which we can derive clear predictions, then it becomes easy to doubt its truth. Hence we can see something on the way that these shared bedrock certainties are supposed to constrain scientific activity. We have a stock of vague indubitable beliefs, and one function of science is to give them precise form. If a scientific theory is refuted, this does not refute common-sense certainties but simply calls on us to provide new precise formulations of them. This relates directly to our discussion of qualitative induction. The instinctive commonsense embodied in our abductive sense, our sense of plausibility, recommends a vaguely formulated hypothesis. It is this vaguely formulated hypothesis which retains its integrity, remains constant, as we test, refute and revise, more precisely formulated articulations of the core theory. Our hypothesis is that a theory of a certain very generally formulated kind is true, and this constrains the development of our thought. Since the hypothesis rests upon our common-sense conceptions of plausibility, it is embedded in our theoretical grasp of the world and only with difficulty dislodged.

Just as its vagueness enables an acritical certainty to fit into the self-controlled activity of science, so other features require the scientist to treat it with caution. Peirce obviously assumes that our capacity for common-sense beliefs, and these cognitive instincts themselves, can receive evolutionary explanations. In a passage from 1883 in 'A Theory of Probable Inference', we find that natural selection leads man, as well as the animals, to have two sorts of adaptively useful ideas.

> In the first place, they all have from birth some notions, however crude and concrete, of force, matter, space, and time; and in the next place, they all have some notion of what sort of objects their fellow beings are, and of how they will act on given occasions. Our innate mechanical ideas were so nearly correct that they needed little correction. . . . The other physical sciences are the results of inquiry based on guesses suggested by the ideas of mechanics. The moral sciences, so far as they can be called sciences, are equally developed out of our instinctive ideas about human nature. (2.753)

Although an early paper, it is clear that this reflects a view that Peirce retained after 1900. The ideas are developed in response to the needs of 'a primitive mode of life'. In normal circumstances we can be sure that they will serve us well. But, once we move beyond the sorts of cases involved in their normal natural application, we must be careful of using them. These common-sense beliefs only remain indubitable in their application to affairs that resemble those of a primitive mode of life. 'It is, for example, quite open to reasonable doubt whether the motions of electrons are restricted to three dimensions, although it is good methodeutic to presume that they are until some evidence to the contrary is forthcoming' (5.445). Since our intuitive physical beliefs developed to help us to cope with ordinary macroscopic physical objects, it is unsurprising that they provide us with useful tools in constructing physical theories which describe and explain such things. Once science loses contact with the objects of everyday experience, we can only *hope* that our instinctive abductive sense will prove a reliable guide. Hence, as in the kinetic theory of gases, we find ourselves thinking about unobservable phenomena in terms of hypotheses which display our assumptions about ordinary physical objects – we think of gases as like ordinary objects bouncing off one another – and, although it is natural for us to think of things in these terms, we must be wary of the fact that the picture seems to be the only one available, and seems indubitably correct. In our thinking about gases, we rely upon instinctive beliefs in areas beyond those of their original application: we can only hope that they will lead us to the truth.

There are two elements to the position we now find Peirce defending. First, science rests upon broad vague indubitable propositions. These determine what is a possible or plausible theory, and they enable us to respond rationally to perceptual experience. In particular, vaguely formulated hypotheses, whose plausibility is a matter of instinct, provide the background to most scientific activity which is concerned with formulating and testing more precise theories which sharpen up the vague ones. Secondly, the indubitable common-sense foundations on which science rests are not historically conditioned. They manifest a shared heritage common to all traditions and all inquirers, and reflect fundamental facets of human nature. In the light of this, their application to advanced science is somewhat problematic. For

> Modern science, with its microscopes and telescopes, with its chemistry and electricity, and with its entirely new appliances of life, has put us into quite another world; almost so much so as if it had transported our race to another planet. (5.513)

Once science escapes from the down-to-earth areas where our common-sense standards of plausibility are reliable, it is far from clear that we have shared standards that can be used to provide a convergence of opinion among inquirers who do not communicate or collaborate. The hoped-for convergence must there be based upon the thought that we can only approach the truth if we assume that familiar models will guide us to it. And we assume that everyone will share the same familiar models. Whether this is enough to secure convergence is far from clear. Moreover, many philosophers of science have drawn on studies in the history of science to support a view which embraces just the first of the two elements of the Peircean position. The acritical standards of plausibility which guide theory choice are historically conditioned. (See e.g. Kuhn, 1962; Lakatos, 1970.) Once this is accepted, then Peirce's anticipated convergence seems to be on very shaky ground. However, we cannot come to a final verdict upon Peirce's claims until we have looked at the semantic theses linked with his pragmatism.

VIII

Pragmatism

1 Introduction: the pragmatist principle

Peirce's writings on his pragmatism, the doctrine for which he is most famous, fall into two groups. Although he did not use the term in print, his writings of the 1870s introduce the doctrine and provide arguments for it and illustrations of its applications. This early discussion culminates on 'How to Make our Ideas Clear', which was discussed in chapter II. When William James publicly defended his own pragmatism for the first time in 1898, he attributed the doctrine to Peirce and referred to this 1878 paper. Peirce himself discussed the doctrine again after 1900. As well as the Pragmatism lectures, delivered at Harvard in 1903 (5.14–212), and three articles representing an unfinished attempt to prove the doctrine in *The Monist* in 1905 – namely 'What Pragmatism Is' (5.411–437), 'Issues of Pragmaticism' (5.438–463), 'Prolegomena to an Apology for Pragmaticism' (4.411–463) – there is an enormous amount of manuscript material, some published in volume five of the *Collected Papers*. This return to the doctrine was partly a response to the notoriety that James had won for pragmatism through his 1898 lecture and subsequent publications. (For some of the chronology, see Fisch, 1977.) Peirce was both anxious to exploit his new fame as the originator of pragmatism to obtain more recognition of his own views, and annoyed at the pale copy of his own position that was popularly associated with the term 'pragmatism'. He constantly stressed that his position was distinct from that of James or Schiller; he denounced their nominalism; and he claimed that his doctrine alone was susceptible of a rigorous philosophical proof. Irritated that his term was used to refer to an alien doctrine, he proposed to use the term 'pragmaticism' to refer to his particular version of pragmatism, claiming that this term at least was 'ugly enough to be safe from kidnappers' (5.414). As we noted in

234

chapter II, he claimed to have long doubted the truth of pragmatism because he thought that, in his 1878 paper, he erected it upon psychologistic foundations. The non-psychologistic proof that he continually promised was the culmination of the attempt to provide new objective foundations for logic and the normative sciences which was introduced in chapter II, and which has been discussed at length.

The pragmatist principle is a logical principle, and is developed in the third branch of logic, methodeutic (Fisch, 1981, fn 9). This discipline investigates what rules we should follow if we want to conduct our inquiries as efficiently as possible – it includes the economic investigations into scientific research that we mentioned in the previous chapter. The principle provides a rule for obtaining a clear understanding of the concepts we use in science and the hypotheses that we investigate: it tells us what we should do in order to obtain a clarity of understanding of these conceptions which will enable us to control our inquiries as effectively as possible. However, the interest of the principle does not hinge upon a concern with useful methodological advice. Rather, the fact that this is good advice – if Peirce is correct – reveals important truths about meaning and reality. An illustration will make this clear. Suppose we consider a hypothesis, perhaps the one we discussed above, that

X is a Catholic priest.

We have an ordinary understanding of this propositon, we can use it, assert it, and so on. But, we want the sort of self-conscious understanding of it that is required to subject our testing of the hypothesis to logical self-control. We notice that we would derive from this proposition the conditional claim

If I were to examine the colour of X's clothes, I would probably find that they were black.

There can be no doubt that noticing this would enhance the clarity of our self-conscious grasp of the hypothesis; and we could enhance it further by finding yet further such conditionals that could be derived from the proposition. And, having such knowledge would enable us to test the hypothesis inductively. This clarification would involve deriving from the hypothesis conditionals of the form

If action A were performed, the observational consequence O would (probably) be observed.

The crux of the pragmatist principle involves the assertion that, in seeking a self-conscious grasp of our understanding of the hypothesis, we need *only* to examine what conditionals of this sort can be derived from it. Nothing else is relevant. Hence the formulations

Consider what effects, which might conceivably have practical bearings, we conceive the object of our conception to have. Then, our conception of these effects is the whole of our conception of the object. (1878, 5.402)

In order to ascertain the meaning of an intellectual conception one should consider what practical consequences might conceivably result by necessity from the truth of that conception; and the sum of these consequences will constitute the entire meaning of the conception. (1903, 5.9)

The *whole* meaning of an intellectual predicate is that certain kinds of events would happen, once in so often, in the course of experience, under certain sorts of existential conditions. (c 1906, 5.468)

And, in the Pragmatism lectures, Peirce glosses his doctrine in the claim that a theoretical judgment expressed in the indicative mood provides a 'confused' expression of a thought whose sole content 'lies in its tendency to enforce a corresponding practical maxim expressible as a conditional sentence having its apodosis in the imperative mode' (5.18).

Some of the illustrations that he provides in the different discussions will make the doctrine clearer. One was discussed at length in the previous chapter. Applying the doctrine to the concept of probability yields the doctrine that the meaning of the judgment

The probability of the coin landing heads when tossed is one half.

can be expressed,

If you were to keep tossing the coin, the limiting frequency of heads among the tosses would be one half.

We have also noticed how Peirce applies the theory to the analysis of reality.

It is really the case that p.

means

If anyone were to inquire diligently into the question whether p, he would eventually, after some finite time, come to an affirmative answer that would not be shaken by further inquiry.

(This was the 1878 version of the theory of reality.) In 'How to Make our Ideas Clear', he offers analyses of weight, and hardness, and sketches a general account of force that will repay examination. We are aware of many sorts of forces – accelerations, velocities, gravity, and so on – and we can think of the concept of force as introduced to bring unity to them, perhaps through hypostatic abstraction. Our interest in forces, he claims, rests upon the fact that they enable us to account for changes in motion. The parallelogram of forces is introduced as a mathematical rule which enables us to resolve forces into their components, and to calculate the results of compounding a number of different forces. We can use it, for example, to diagram the relations between accelerations. Now, our concept of force embodies a 'grand fact' (5.404) – and only one grand fact (ibid.).

> This fact is that if the actual changes of motion which the different particles of bodies experience are each resolved in its appropriate way, each component acceleration is precisely such as is prescribed by a certain law of Nature, according to which bodies, in the relative positions which the bodies in question actually have at the moment [fn. Possibly the velocities also have to be taken into account], always receive certain accelerations which, being compounded by geometrical addition, give the acceleration which the body actually experiences. (5.404)

Roughly, all there is to having the concept of force is believing that a mathematical theory such as the parallelogram of forces can be used to predict the relations between empirically observed accelerations. Thus, Peirce criticizes those who speak of force as a 'mysterious entity', and those who claim that although they know all of the *effects* of force, they do not understand what force is.

Other applications include an interesting paper of 1897, a review of Schroeder's *Algebra und Logik der Relative*, in which a logic of relations is developed as a way of applying the pragmatist principle to clarify the concept of relation (4.456 ff). Also, it is a result of the experimental character that Peirce ascribes to mathematics that the principle can be used to elucidate mathematical conceptions: my understanding of such a concept is shown in the predictions I should make about the perceptible consequences of experimenting upon diagrams. It must also be applicable to the vague propositions which, we have seen, are important for science. It will be helpful for later discussion if we elaborate this a little. The relations between the pragmatist principle and Peirce's theory of assertion will be obvious; the principle indicates the publicly ascertainable circumstances in which an assertion can be criticized – the speaker commits himself to the truth of those predictions. One style of argument that Peirce uses in supporting the doctrine involves reflecting upon what features of a hypothesis or proposition are relevant to assessing scientific assertions of it. The assertion of a vague proposition is like the assertion of an existentially quantified proposition: the speaker reserves the right to specify more precisely just what will show that his assertion was unwarranted. (Peirce frequently links the semantics of vague sentences to those of existentially quantified ones (e.g. 5.505).) When I assert a vague proposition I commit myself to the claim that some precisification of the proposition is defensible. This can be cast in the conditional form required by the pragmatist principle along some such lines as,

> If I were to conduct my inquiries with sufficient diligence, then I should produce a precisification of the proposition that p, which has the property that anyone who inquired into it would come to a stable acceptance of it in some finite time.

I become liable to the penalties that follow wrong assertion only when it is established that no such precisification of the vague proposition is available.

It will be apparent that Peirce's position resembles a number of verificationist theories that have been defended over the last century. He describes his position as a species of 'properpositivism', and often uses the principle, as did the logical positivists their similar conception, to expose the emptiness of the claims of metaphysics. In 'How to Make our Ideas Clear', for example, he applies the doctrine to show that the Catholic doctrine of transubstantiation had no meaning. He does not object to the Protestants claiming that the elements of the sacrament are flesh and blood 'only in a tropical sense'. Indeed, he often stresses that the principle does not elucidate all of the meaning that a proposition has: it is 'merely' a device for clarifying 'intellectual concepts', which are those on which 'arguments concerning objective fact may hinge' (5.467). What he objects to is the claim that something may be *really* blood while having all the sensible characteristics of wine (5.401). In 'What Pragmatism Is', he attacks those who would bring similar metaphysical element into science itself, scorning Balfour's claim that 'the physicist . . . seeks for something deeper than the laws connecting possible objects of experience', namely 'physical reality' itself, unrevealed in experiments. As we saw in the last chapter, Peirce thinks that a hypothesis should bring together a mass of lawlike patterns in phenomena with 'a minimum of logical glue'. This may suggest a view of science similar to the operationalism of Bridgeman, of the instrumentalism defended by other members of the positivist movement. However, I do not want to prejudge this issue, and we shall develop our understanding of Peirce's position through the rest of this chapter.

As I mentioned above, after 1900 Peirce set himself to find a proof of pragmatism. Whether he actually found one that satisfied him is a topic we shall discuss in a later section. In a manuscript – in which he announced that he had a proof only it was very complicated – there is a telling passage which indicates what a proof has to achieve. How is pragmatism to be proved, he asks, 'in the teeth of Messrs. Bradley, Taylor, and other high metaphysicians, on the one hand, and of the entire nominalistic nation, with its Wundts, its Haekels, its Karl Pearsons, and many other regiments, in their divers uniforms, on the other' (5.468). As this suggests, he saw the challenge to his doctrine as coming from two distinct directions: an adequate proof should convince both a metaphysician like Bradley and a nominalist like William James of the correctness of Peirce's formulation of pragmatism. Peirce thought that pragmatism could only be plausible if a form of metaphysical realism was adopted: it was incompatible with the nominalist assumptions of most of the positivists who held similar doctrines, and of most of those who welcomed the philosophical movements of pragmatism. Therefore, a proof of pragmatism must contain a proof of realism and a vindication of the sort of purified philosophy Peirce believed in. The next section takes up the connections between pragmatism and realism.

The challenge of the 'high metaphysicians' was different. We can imagine it taking several different forms. Somebody could complain that in order to do logic and philosophy, it was necessary to make use of concepts the importance of which could not be elucidated through the application of the principle. Philosophy is an *a priori* discipline, and the principle only unpacks the empirical component of the meaning of a concept. Thus, intellectual activity requires *a priori* concepts, and the pragmatist principle has only a limited application. Alternatively, the complaint might be that depriving all but empirical concepts of 'intellectual significance' deprives ethics and the other sciences of value of objective foundations. Among the logical positivists, verificationism frequently led to a form of ethical non-cognitivism, and we can imagine the metaphysician viewing this as a *reductio ad absurdum* of the claims about meaning which grounded the denial of objective value. This last comment indicates the force of the high metaphysician's challenge. Insofar as the pragmatist criticizes the practices of the metaphysician, the latter can take the fact that these criticisms follow from his position as demonstrating the falsity of pragmatism. Peirce's proof has to be good enough to block this response. A third form which the attack can take involves asserting that science itself makes use of concepts whose meaning cannot be clarified using the pragmatist principle. It was Kant's claim that ideas, whose meaning could not be spelled out in empirical terms, had an essential regulative role in the development of theory. They articulated our conception of what was involved in a body of laws being unified in a theory so as to form a 'system of knowledge'; they underlie our understanding of what it is for a theory to have explanatory power.

We can see straightaway that many of the doctrines we have discussed in earlier chapters have a role in Peirce's response to these problems. The experimental conception of mathematics together with the claim that the methods of philosophy are mathematical are supposed to make room for a conception of an *a priori* philosophy which is consistent with the pragmatist principle. Peirce's frequent insistence that philosophy relies upon observation, but appeals to no facts that are not immediately available to everyone, equally attempts to account for the distinctive character of the discipline without playing into the hands of the despised Bradley and his cohorts. In chapter II, we saw Peirce attempt to provide for objective values without compromising this conception of philosophy, without having to use conceptions that could not be completely clarified using the pragmatist principle. Finally, in the last chapter we saw Peirce try to account for our sense of plausibility and our instincts about explanatory power without requiring us to use special non-empirical conceptions. Our finding a theory plausible did not rest upon testing it against a criterion framed in non-empirical terms: it was an acritical, non-conceptual response. In 'A Neglected Argument for the Reality of God', a paper to be discussed in the final chapter, Peirce attempts to make sense of his religious beliefs without compromising his pragmatism. Thus, he makes a thorough attempt to provide a consistent defence of his pragmatist views.

We shall evaluate Peirce's support of his pragmatism in section 4. In the two sections preceding that one, we shall try to come to a better understanding of just what the doctrine involves, disccussing, in section 2, the relations between pragmatism and realism, and, in section 3, the bearing of pragmatism upon the issues about the convergence of opinion upon the truth that were discussed at the close of the previous chapter.

2   Pragmatism and realism

As Peirce often affirms, the intellectual meaning of a conception or proposition always lies in the future (5.481–3). It spells out how acceptance of the proposition would affect conduct, and indicates what circumstances are relevant to evaluating an assertion of the proposition. The pragmatist principle unpacks the meaning of a proposition as a set of *conditional expectations*. This feature of the position can seem to have odd consequences. For example, when the principle is applied to a proposition about the past, it will apparently reveal that the proposition is really about future evidence for the past event. Consider

It rained yesterday morning.

What conditional predictions does acceptance of this proposition commit us to? Presumably that, if we inspect the records, we shall find evidence of rain yesterday, or that, if we ask around, we shall find many people with memories of rain yesterday, and so on. While we would agree that it is these matters that are relevant to evaluating an assertion that it rained yesterday morning, still the proposition is not *about* the future evidence (cf. Lewis, 1929, p. 150 f; Ayer, 1946, pp. 101–2 for similar views).

As well as raising a question about what is involved in thinking of something as *past* – what does the pragmatist principle tell us about the concept of pastness? – these examples raise a problem about Peirce's claim that any truth is, in principle, discoverable. It is a natural thought that much of the past is just lost to us: there is a fact of the matter about whether at least on inch of rain fell on a certain area of Britain exactly thirty thousand days ago, even if we should never have any reason to believe that it did or that it did not. But, what conditional expectations show that we think that this is so? Peirce's theory of reality seems to imply that if some proposition would never be settled either way, then reality is indeterminate with respect to whether it is true. Can Peirce make sense of the realist assumption that there are truths which we could never discover however long we investigated them? He can insist that we can never know for certain that evidence may not emerge that confirms the proposition in question; but we generally make the stronger assumption that the proposition would have a determinate truth value even if we could not find out what it was.

In 'How to Make our Ideas Clear', Peirce discussed a related example; thirty years later, in 'Issues of Pragmatism', he returned to this earlier discussion with some embarrassment and revised his response to it. As he described it in 1905, the case concerns a 'diamond which, having been crystallized upon a cushion of jeweller's cotton, was accidentally consumed by fire before the crystal of corundum that had been sent for had had time to arrive, and indeed without being subjected to any pressure than that of the atmosphere and its own weight' (5.457, cf. 5.403). The question to be settled is: was that diamond hard? In 5.403, the application of the pragmatist principle to the concept of hardness had yielded the result that if something is hard, then, if we were to scratch it with something else, we should be unlikely to damage it. The challenge posed by the diamond example is that the stone was destroyed before being tested for hardness. Peirce's response was that there would be 'no falsity' in saying that *this* diamond was soft: it is a purely verbal matter what we say, and does not make any difference to the content of our assertions or the facts as we represent them. There is no possibility that we shall be led into perceptual surprise if we adopt one of the formulations rather than the other. This case provides a case where we would normally feel that we knew that the diamond was hard, and Peirce is suggesting that our inclination to say this does not represent knowledge but simply reflects our taste for the simpler formulation. We can consider a variant of the example which poses the problem about there being facts which will never be discovered. Suppose that a diver was sent to test the diamond. Unfortunately, he died before completing the operation, and when we recovered his body, still clutching the corundum, it was unclear whether he had been attacked by sharks before or after trying to scratch the diamond. We become convinced that evidence will not settle this one way or the other. Yet, we believe that either he did rub the corundum against the diamond or he didn't – although we are sure that a stable consensus will never be reached on either of the disjuncts. Peirce's discussion suggests that he would say that there is no fact of the matter here; it is a purely verbal matter whether we say he did reach the diamond or that the sharks caught him before he had time to do so. Can a pragmatist avoid these counterintuitive claims?

When Peirce returned to the diamond example in 'Issues of Pragmatism', he deplored the 'nominalism' of his earlier discussion and insisted that, as a pragmatist, he could know that the diamond *was* hard. We know that if we had tried to scratch it with corundum, no impression would have been made. The claim that the diamond was hard can be understood as an inference from the two premisses,

This object is a diamond.
All diamonds are hard.

When the object was identified as a diamond, we can suppose that this was a perceptual judgment based upon the brilliance and shape of the stone. Although acritical, the judgment was akin to an abduction presenting a hypothesis about the object; the hypothesis would be rejected if the object turned out not to satisfy the laws that are true of all diamonds. The claim that all diamonds are hard is, we may suppose, a law which has been inductively well confirmed. Were something that looked like a diamond to turn out to be soft, this would refute the identification of it as a diamond and not the generalization that all diamonds are hard. The generalization does not summarize what has been observed to be true of each diamond. As Thompson nicely puts it, the law represents one truth, a general principle true of all diamonds, actual and possible (Thompson, 1978). It is one of the general principles which, Peirce thinks, is operative in nature. Hence, he wrote of this example, that the diamond was 'a mass of pure carbon, in the form of a more or less transparent crystal . . .'; it was 'insoluble, very highly refractive, showing under radium rays . . . a peculiar bluish phosphorence, having as high a specific gravity as realgac or orpiment, and giving off during its combustion less heat than any other form of carbon would have done' (5.457). Many of these qualities are 'inseparable' from being hard, and, like hardness, they are believed to result from the 'high polemerization of the molecule'. Scientific progress teaches us the laws that determine what it is to be a diamond: and we cannot make sense of something being a diamond but not instantiating the laws which, science teaches, are true of all diamonds. The response of 1905 was possible because of the development in Peirce's views of modality during the 1890s. His early view of modality was of a kind that he later called 'subjective'. 'It is possible that p' could always be paraphrased 'It is not known that not-p' and was an expression of human ignorance (see 3.514; cf 3.527). Similarly, to say that something must happen is to say that it is known that it will happen. Later, he contrasts objective modality with these, and claims that pragmatism requires that there be real objective modalities, and links this with metaphysical realism.

There are two respects in which his position calls for such 'real' possibilities and necessities, and they are linked to two ways in which 'generals' influence the course of events. First, Peirce believes in an 'open future': the future is 'objectively vague' (5.461). If someone says 'I can go to the seashore if I like', he expresses not just ignorance about his future behaviour, but also that 'the complete determination of conduct in the *act* not yet having taken place, the further determination of it belongs to the subject of the action regardless of external circumstances' (5.455). His conception of logic and the normative sciences rests upon the supposition – or hope – that reasoning can increase our control over how we determine our conduct and the future course of events. Although he does not discuss the matter in much detail, it is plain that Peirce does not endorse the kind of compatibilism which claims that such rational self-control is compatible with the truth of physical determinism. Through self-control and deliberation, general ideas and principles have an influence upon the course of events: in the first paper in the *Monist* series, Peirce stressed his allegiance to the 'great fact' that 'the ideas "justice" and "truth" are, notwithstanding the iniquity of the world, the mightiest of the forces that move it' (5.431). Certainly, Peirce thinks that unless we had the freedom to decide upon which of a range of possible futures were realized, there would be no point in developing the sort of logic of which pragmatism forms a part. If our decisions do not shape the world, if we cannot control it, we do not need a methodological maxim designed to increase our rational self-control.

But this is only part of the story. For, again, the pragmatist principle supposes that our power to determine the future course of the world is limited. Sometimes, determination of events is dependent upon external circumstances. The pragmatist principle tells me that if I exercise my freedom to drop a fragile object, or to toss a fair coin a large number of times, then I cannot but expect that the object will break, or that about one half of the tosses will yield heads. It tells me what would, and must, be the consequence of my conduct. This supposes that there are necessities governing things, necessities covering any possible course of events I may initiate. In fact, what the pragmatist principle does is to articulate just how law mediates the succession of events that occurs.

Thus, both laws and thoughts can mediate the relations between events that occur; both provide the element of thirdness which, we saw in chapter two, provides an aesthetic unity both in external reality and in the activity of the scientific inquirer. In fact, we can see the influence of all three categories in the pragmatic maxim. Recall that the form of the conditionals we obtain from applying the principle is

If we perform action A, then we shall have perceptual experience P.

Both volition and perception involve the shock of reaction, of secondness. And we have already discussed the fusion of firstness and secondness in perception. The conditionals provide the element of thirdness, of mediation, which binds together the firstness and secondness into the intelligible world.

Subsequent forms of verificationism avoided subjunctive formulations. Notoriously, they failed to provide analyses of statements about the external world, in part, because they could provide no adequate analysis of subjunctive idioms, such as statements about dispositions. (For the whole story, see Hempel, 1950 and Skagestad, 1981, ch. 3.) If Peirce's realism is justified and consistent with his pragmatism, his position would be more defensible than that of the positivists. However, most philosophers sympathetic with what they take to be the general thrust of Peirce's thought would be uneasy about this realism. How can we know that a generalization applies to possible cases as well as actual ones? The question with priority is plainly: what sense can Peirce, the pragmatist, make of the claim that a generalization applies not only to the cases that will actually occur, but also to all possible cases? His response is already implicit in the discussion in the last section of chapter VI. His mathematical work during the 1890s made him believe that he had provided an adequate logical analysis of continuity, and he declared that the question of the truth of realism was the same as the question whether there are real continua. I do not want to pursue these thorny issues any further at this point. We shall return to these issues in the next chapter when we consider how far his metaphysical views enable him to explain the truth of realism. For the present, I want simply to indicate how Peirce took his pragmatism to be inextricably linked to his realism, to his theory of categories, and to the conception of logic described in chapter II.

Let us now return to some of the other questions about the past that were raised at the beginning of this section. Recall that we had two worries. First, the claim that past-tense statements are really about future evidence seemed to be called for by Peirce's pragmatism, yet is very counterintuitive. Secondly, there is an evident tension between Peirce's theorem about truth – that if a statement is true, then it would be the subject of a stable consensus of opinion among those who inquired into it for long enough – and the common-sense truth that many facts have left no discernible trace and are lost for ever. In 'Issues of Pragmatism', Peirce undertakes to apply the pragmatist principle to the clarification of the distinction between past, present and future. He rests heavily upon the claim that it is only events in the future that we can control, and the assertion that it is only things in the past that can act upon us. The past acts upon us 'not at all in the way in which a law or principle influences us, but precisely as an Existent object acts' (5.459). The past is 'the existential mode of time' (5.460): our relation to the past exemplifies secondness. The future has no secondness but is general or 'objectively vague'. He divides past-tense beliefs into two classes. One class – we can call them historical hypotheses – refer to the part of the past that lies 'beyond memory'. The belief that Christopher Columbus discovered America 'really refers to the future' (5.461): when I defend such a claim, I make a guess about how the evidence will turn out. For the other beliefs, however, Peirce seems to deny this. He writes,

> How, then does the Past bear upon conduct? The answer is self evident: whenever we set out to do anything, we 'go upon', we base our conduct on facts already known, and for these we can draw only upon our memory. . . . In short, the Past is the storehouse of all our knowledge.
>
> When we say that we know that some state of affairs exists, we mean that it used to exist, whether just long enough for the news to reach the brain and be retransmitted to tongue or pen, or longer ago. (5.460)

There is evidence here of a familiar kind of account of knowledge: it is a necessary condition for 'A knows that p' that A's belief that p result from the action (direct or indirect) of the fact that p. He may suggest that utterances of past-tense sentences are normally taken as expressions of knowledge; and it is the imputation that the assertion in some way reflects the action of the event described which is missing from a straightforward future-tense paraphrase. In that case, the assertion would be unwarranted if it did not represent 'knowledge', even if what it described actually occurred. As Peirce allows, when we receive information, it makes a difference to us whether it represents knowledge or a conjecture. But, the thought is not worked out in any detail and, although Peirce takes these remarks to illustrate a pragmatist construal of the past tense, he nowhere spells out the results in the conditional form that pragmatism requires.

Finally, what can be said about facts that have vanished in the mists of time? Peirce does not discuss these explicitly, but I think that some points can be made in defence of his position. Well, can Peirce make sense of the fact that:

> The diver either tested the diamond or he didn't, although no one will ever know which.

First, we can see that the strategy he uses to cope with the original version of the diamond example seems to be applicable here. Although we can grant him that the law of the excluded middle is not in general true – reality is indeterminate in many respects, and mathematical entities, in particular do not always satisfy it – it could well be a well-confirmed generalization about human behaviour that indeterminacies do not arise in this sort of case. Equally, it could be well confirmed that evidence rarely emerges at a later date about actions performed under water by people now dead. In that case, each conjunct of the claim could be assertible, although neither disjunct of the first conjunct is now, or is ever likely to be, assertible. Moreover, this much could be a matter of general consensus. But, in that case, we have a truth which will never be discovered however long inquiry continues for. If we persist in saying that it is indeterminate whether the test was carried out or not, we are committed to the thesis that a disjunction may be true, although neither disjunct is true. Having made some progress with this issue, and having, I hope, sharpened up some issues with a clear bearing upon Peirce's attitude towards idealism and realism, I want to leave this issue until we turn to the idealism issue for a fuller discussion below.[1]

3 Pragmatism and reality

Although Peirce's pragmatism is supposed to explain how an independent reality can constrain our opinions through perception, the reader is likely to sense certain tensions between claims Peirce makes about reality and the verificationist flavour of his pragmatism. For example, Peirce insists that if a proposition accurately describes reality, then any rational agent who investigates its truth would, after a finite time, come to a stable belief in it. He allows that the fated consensus upon a true proposition is not restricted to human inquirers, but would include any rational agent, even Martians. When we participate in physics, we assume that any physical truth is accessible to us, or to any rational agent. Since we allow that different rational beings might have different sorts of sensory apparatus – Martians may lack the sense of sight but have a sense analogous to the sonar of bats or dolphins – it seems to follow that the description of the world that we seek should make use of no terms for secondary qualities, no terms like 'red' or 'loud' which are relative to particular modes of sensory awareness. Red is how things can look, loud is how they can sound: such expressions occur primarily in perceptual judgments. Since our Martians lack a grasp of what it is for something to look red, they cannot grasp the concept of redness; and so a concept like redness cannot occur in the correct physical description of the world. We might suppose that the theoretical terms of science, expressions like 'electron', 'gene' or 'protein', have the desired independence of concepts parochial to a particular form of sensory awareness. But, as Peirce writes in 'Issues of Pragmatism', the view of the pragmatist is that all that is meant by saying that a substance has, for example, a certain inner structure is that 'if a substance of a certain kind should be exposed to an agency of a particular kind, a certain sort of sensible result *would* ensue. . .' (5.457). When we explain the meaning of a term by using the pragmatist principle, it seems that we must use terms that occur in perceptual judgments, terms for secondary qualities. In that case, we could not expect the Martians to attach the same meaning to theoretical expressions as ourselves, and the convergence of opinion which Peirce talks about is impossible.

Although he does not discuss this problem in these terms, I think that Peirce should be able to accommodate it. First of all, he insists that secondary qualities *are* real. The fact that *red* is relative to sight does not make redness subjective; 'the fact that this or that is in that relation to vision that we call being red is not *itself* relative to sight; it is a real fact' (5.430). Although the Martian may not know the distinctive *firstness* associated with red, still he may use the notion with the same cognitive or conceptual content as ourselves. As with any concept, we clarify our concept of red by using the pragmatist maxim: we should probably find that it contained such conditionals as,

x is red only if,   if a competent perceiver were to examine x in a good light, he would judge x to be red.

if he examined x and a green object, he would be able to discriminate between them.

if we measure the wavelength of the light reflected by x, we find that it is . . . etc.

These could be grasped and used by the Martian. What he could not do is use himself as a competent perceiver in carrying out the experiments mentioned in the first two of these conditionals; he must defer to an 'expert' perceiver, or use a seeing person as a measuring instrument.

But, even if we accept this and agree that the Martian could share the concept of red, still there is little reason to think that he would develop it himself if he had no contact with human beings. We still face the problem that he would be unlikely to invent a hypothesis whose meaning is spelled out – by us – in perceptual terms. However, when we bear in mind Peirce's stress upon the vagueness of hypotheses it is possible to see how the Peircean position could be maintained by loosening our understanding of what is required for the fated convergence of opinion to occur. Supposing that both we and the Martians develop a term that refers to Holm oaks, both communities could construct the vague hypothesis

Holm oaks form a species.

This leads both to expect to find laws governing the behaviour of Holm oaks, and, searching for a more precise understanding of 'Holm oak' each develops more determinate hypotheses which can be clarified using the pragmatist principle. Although these hypotheses will have different meanings – because our vocabulary of terms for secondary qualities differs from that of the Martians – still it can be recognized that both are precisifications of the same vague hypothesis. When we meet the Martians, and learn their vocabulary, we can enrich our conception by adding to it the elements which the Martians can contribute. As an alternative way of making much the same point, we an say that we enrich our conception by explaining the reactions of Holm oaks and Martians, or by explaining how the Martians' conception differs from ours. Thus, in such a case, where different conceptions can be seen as precisifications of one vague hypothesis, we can make sense of a weaker kind of convergence which does not require a shared vocabulary of terms for secondary qualitities.

Unfortunately, this appears to deal with only one of a range of possible cases, for could not the different traditions develop radically different hypotheses which satisfactorily accounted for all their observations? If that were possible – and, if their abductive senses differ, it seems it should be – then, once more, it seems that there is no reason to anticipate a long-run consensus of opinion. Discussing such possibilities depends upon our having a clear grasp of what is involved in two hypotheses being the same or different. Now it seems clear that Peirce wants the pragmatist maxim to function as a criterion of identity for hypotheses: it is a sufficient condition of two sentences expressing the same hypothesis that, when we clarify them using the pragmatist principle, we find that they make the same conditional predictions. For example, there is no empirical difference between the two hypotheses,

All rabbits have two ears.
Every undetached part of a rabbit is a part of a creature with two ears.

Applying the principle could show us that there was no real disagreement between people who disputed about which of these was properly true: whichever we accept, we shall form the same conditional expectations. If two competing hypotheses could both survive as much empirical testing as could be provided, this would be a sufficient condition of their representing the same theory. Hence, the pragmatist principle provides an account of theoretical equivalence which rescues Peirce's convergence thesis from the difficulties we discussed at the end of the previous chapter. We can usefully distinguish two convergence theses that Peirce defends. Since we rely upon a shared body of common sense, and use similar secondary qualities, we can reasonably hope that the hypotheses we produce will be noticeably similar to those produced by other human inquirers. This facilitates inquiry and helps us to feel confident that we are on the right track. The thesis we are now considering is more abstract: application of the pragmatist principle can show that theories which appear to be very different, using different ontologies and different sorts of explanatory principles are truly equivalent.

However, this use of the principle appears to run into familiar difficulties. We talk freely of hypotheses competing and of them making the same conditional predictions; and it is plausible to gloss this by saying that they attempt to explain the same perceptual judgments, and predict that the same perceptual judgments will be made. However, we saw in chapter VI that perceptual judgments contain general terms and are themselves similar to hypotheses. If theoretical innovation can influence the terms we use in reporting the character of our percepts, then exponents of competing theories may characterize their predictions differently: both make only successful predictions, but there is no shared vocabulary in which these predictions can be described. If, as Peirce says, defenders of different theories inhabit different worlds (1.99), then it is plausible that they see different things. Each theory is confirmed by a set of perceptual judgments which only its exponents can make. In that case, it is not easy to see how the Peircean criterion of theoretical equivalence is to be applied: how do we establish that theories are either competing or equivalent?

Various responses to these difficulties suggest themselves. We could distinguish the vocabulary of our 'common sense' theory from the terms introduced in theoretical science, and claim that theories are tested against predictions cast in common-sense terms. However, while this may be a factor in the development of human science, it cannot answer to the general difficulty here. First, although common sense is remarkably stable, it does evolve through time, and, given its evolutionary origin, is not likely to be constant among all rational beings – Martians included. Secondly, Peirce grants that theory may lead us to revise our common-sense claims and perceptual judgments: two theories may both avoid perceptual surprise although they do not agree upon the common-sense claims that are true, because they are allied to different techniques for explaining away common-sense perceptual judgments. Alternatively, we may distinguish relatively theoretical from relatively observational terms. Using an example suggested by the discussion of the concealed diamond, we can claim that all that is involved in being brilliant is (say) looking brilliant to normal observers in normal circumstances: someone who failed to grasp that this was a predicate that related to how things *looked* would misunderstand it. However, we know that looking like a diamond and being a diamond are distinct; the predicate ', . . . is a diamond' is 'more theoretical'. Perhaps, when we apply the pragmatist principle we are to restrict attention to predictions cast in these relatively 'observational' terms. Notoriously, this is a difficult distinction to draw and there is little evidence that Peirce wanted to make anything of it. We would do better to look elsewhere for a Peircean solution to these problems.

The function of theory is to explain our percepts, to account for them by showing that they enter into a harmonious intelligible whole. Since perceptual judgments provide only fallible descriptions of reality, a successful theory is not required to endorse them all. Rather, theory attempts, as we have seen, to identify the real objects of these perceptual judgments; it seeks to interpret perceptual judgments, and in the process, to produce a more developed description of the objects of the demonstrative or indexical expressions that they contain. In characterizing the real object or referent of this index, it is not required that the theorist should employ classifications that are available to – or salient for – the person who made the judgment. He classifies the object by finding a continuous spread of reactions of which the making of the judgment is a part; he attempts to specify what the perceiver was perceiving, but does not restrict himself to using terms that the perceiver would recognize as describing his perception. So, the problems that we are now concerned with stem from the apparent possibility that theories which use different systems of classification might each, to their own satisfaction, be able to account for the real objects of all the perceptual judgments made by all subjects of experience. The dilemma that this apparent possibility raises can be brought out as follows. If at most one of these theories can be true, then it is difficult to see how we have any reason to expect consensus upon the one true theory in the long run. On the other hand, if the theories are equivalent, so that there is no objective fact of the matter which is correct, then it is hard to see how application of the pragmatist principle can bring this equivalence to light. Moreover, if this second horn is accepted, we are forced to conclude that there is no unique correct system of classification; and this seems to clash with Peirce's rejection of nominalism. It is natural to suppose that if universals are real, then there is an objectively correct system of classifications which reflects the nature of these universals.

As suggested above, however, it is this second position that Peirce defends, and we must now see how he can do so. In chapter VI, we stressed that in identifying the real object of a perceptual judgment, we are guided by our knowledge of how it appeared in the percept. We can only understand why the judgment was made when, guided by an interpretation of the predicate employed in the perceptual judgment, we can explain why the object appeared as it did. It would go against Peirce's most deeply held philosophical principles to think that this could not be explained. It would follow from this that although the defender of one theory may reject the classifications employed by the other theory, he will produce an interpretation of the predicates that express these classifications that would make it possible, in principle, to predict in what circumstances they would be applied in perceptual judgments. It can thus enter into his understanding of many of his own predicates that a defender of the other theory would apply one of *his* terms to an object to which the predicate applied in certain specifiable circumstances. Hence, both theorists can agree upon what perceptual judgments the defender of each theory can make. They will make predictions of the form:

> if an object is F, then, if we present it to a defender of the other
> theory in circumstances C, then that person will probably form the
> perceptual judgment 'That is a G'.

And, they can allow that if the defender of the other theory does express this judgment, then he has made a 'correct assertion', and should not be open to sanction or criticism.

It follows from this that there may be different systems of classification which differ in salience, one being much more natural or useful to us than the other, both of which accurately reflect the necessities to be found in reality. This raises questions about just what Peirce's conception of reality is: it begins to have a somewhat amorphous character. It is as if cognitive activity inevitably reads into reality a sort of articulated structure, a system of classifications, which enables us to bring our experience under control, but which does not itself correspond to anything real. Indeed, Peirce's picture of reality is close to this. He sees it as a continuous spread of reaction and feeling; where we draw boundaries in thinking of it as containing individual objects, or how we classify the continuous ranges of possibilities which underlie general laws and characters is up to us. Generality is real, but dividing things into classes reflects our interests and conventional decisions. It accords with this that Peirce thinks that the theoretical entities introduced by scientific entities result from hypostatic abstraction and hence enjoy only a second-grade of reality (see chapter VII). He even speculates that bringing together elements of perception into discernible *things* may involve similar hypostatic abstraction (4.235 and fn). The present discussion makes it clear that Peirce would take a similar anti-realist view of our choice of a particular set of classifications in constructing scientific theories.

Before going on to consider what reason there is for thinking Peirce's pragmatism true, we should note that Quine has objected that Peirce's theory fails to accommodate the holistic character of scientific change. Peirce assumes that conditional predictions can be derived from any given hypothesis, and these specify what the meaning of that hypothesis is. Quine's objection is that no hypothesis has a set of empirical consequences to call its own. We derive predictions from a body of theoretical beliefs and other opinions, and if the predictions are surprised, we may accommodate the surprise by adjusting any of the beliefs in the set. If the litmus fails to turn red, then, rather than deciding that the substance we are testing is not acid, we may conclude that the litmus was poorly constructed, that the theory underlying the use of litmus tests should be questioned, that our senses deceived us, and so on. So, how can we take the conditional about the behaviour of litmus to elucidate the meaning of 'acid', rather than as reflecting the implications of a large body of theory? (See Quine, 1953, ch. 2.) This raises an interesting challenge for Peirce's position because he makes many of the same observations himself. (For remarks of a broadly Quinean character, see 1.332; 1.74; R 290 and Almeder, 1980, pp. 38–9.) So, unless Peirce is inconsistent here, we should look for an interpretation of his position which escapes the objection from the holistic account of the link between theory and observation.

It is helpful to begin by dropping controversial philosophical terms such as 'meaning'; Peirce uses the pragmatist principle as a rule for clarifying our *conceptions* of hardness, force, the past and so on. Our conception of hardness, for example, is elucidated by listing laws governing the behaviour of hard things that we take to be true. We might discover that one or more of these laws are false, but we can adjust our conception of hardness without ceasing to use that term with a constant or intelligible meaning. This is because a vague concept of hardness lies in the background, controlling our attempts to provide it with a more precise formulation. Moreover, although we use the conditionals extracted through the use of the pragmatist principle in testing our hypotheses, it is clear that they are not of equal importance; we saw in the last chapter that Peirce thought we relied upon instinctive judgments of the relative importance of different experiential consequences of a hypothesis in carrying out qualitative inductions. Thus, although we may currently believe that if our hypothesis is true, then a certain experiment will have certain consequences, it is by no means certain that if our prediction is disappointed, we should abandon the hypothesis. On several occasions, Peirce counsels us to be flexible and ready to rescue our hypotheses by making compensating adjustments elsewhere in our corpus of beliefs in certain circumstances (5.376;

Almeder, 1980, pp. 38–9).

In applying the principle, we are to use mathematical reasoning – theorematic and corollarial deduction – in deriving conditionals from the hypothesis. The crucial question for understanding Peirce's position is: what other premisses may we make use of in carrying out these derivations? While he does not explicitly discuss this question, the answer seems clear. Although, as Peirce insists, scientists do not actually *believe* their current results, it is clear from our discussion of Peirce's treatment of induction, that the community of inquirers can sort propositions into a number of classes. First, there are those that we cannot doubt, however hard we try; we cannot conceive of it being necessary to subject them to further experimental test. As well as these common-sense claims, there are propositions which have been tested and, after a few experiments, it has been decided that further investigation is unnecessary – uneconomic – at this stage, and they are certified as assertible at this stage of scientific progress. Finally, there are propositions which are still being tested, or have not yet been subjected to investigation. Peirce must hold that any proposition from one of the first two of these classes can be used in deriving conditional predictions from hypotheses. In that case, we can understand why they are of varying degrees of importance – the most important being those that are also derivable from the vague background hypothesis that governs our theorizing, and the least important being those that depend upon the precise form of background accepted beliefs which, we admit, are at best approximately correct. Moreover, if this is correct, we should expect our hypotheses to become steadily richer as scientific knowledge grows. (Although, as I mentioned above, Peirce does not explicitly defend these views, they fit the sort of remarks he makes about the semantics of predicates, from early papers like 'Upon Logical Comprehension and Extension' (1867) (2.391 ff) – the principle elucidates the 'informed depth' of a concept – to much later writings. And see 5.196, from the Pragmatism lectures, which makes it fairly clear that this is what Peirce has in mind.)

4 Seductive persuasions, scientific proofs and the philosophical proof of pragmatism

As we noticed above, Peirce devoted much of his energy after 1900 to constructing a philosophical proof of pragmatism. Although he had 'seductive persuasions' and 'scientific proofs' of the doctrine (5.468), he needed the watertight construction which would convince those of all philosophical temperaments. In 1905, he claimed to have a proof which left 'no reasonable doubt on the subject', and many papers and manuscripts aim to set down a proof which Peirce thinks he has available. (See, for example, R330, in which the argument is 'anachazanenally or recessively stated' or R 297 which claims that there are three arguments, or ways of presenting the argument, but peters out as it begins to elaborate them.) There is much room for doubt whether Peirce did have an argument that met his severe standards – as late as 1911, he admits that he lacks a proof of one of the premisses of his arguments, the claim that there are just three forms of reasoning (NE iii 1778). However, that does not deprive his arguments of interest; we may doubt whether a philosophical argument can ever have the cast-iron character that he sought.

Two arguments can be identified without difficulty. First, when he articulated the doctrine in print in 1878, Peirce presented a supportive argument in 'How to Make our Ideas Clear'. He later repudiated this argument, referring to it as a 'merely rhetorical defense' (R 279). The argument that persuaded him that the doctrine was correct around 1900 was presented in the Harvard lectures on pragmatism in 1903 (R 279) – but this argument was 'far from simple' and 'still left too many difficulties' (ibid.). The general strategy of this argument is clear enough, however, and it provides the core of most of the arguments he used in the following years. Since I lack the space to examine all of these later discussions in detail, I shall first describe and compare the strategies employed in the arguments of 1878 and 1903, and then attempt to explain what were the gaps in the later argument that Peirce saw a need to fill. This will enable us to understand the sorts of moves he was making in his later philosophical work.

The first argument depends upon a theory of belief which the members of the Cambridge Metaphysical Club obtained from their reading of the Scottish philosopher and psychologist, Alexander Bain (see Fisch, 1954). As Peirce expressed the view in his paper, 'The essence of belief is the establishment of a habit; and different beliefs are distinguished by the different modes of action to which they give rise' (5.398). So, a belief is a kind of behavioural disposition, and the identity of such a habit depends on when and how it causes us to act (5.401). Since the sole aim of inquiry is to obtain settled belief, its goal is to obtain settled habits of action. In order to clarify our understanding of a proposition, we have only to discover what behavioural disposition we should acquire if we were to believe it. Hence, we have only to determine when and how accepting that proposition would lead us to act. 'As for the *when*, every stimulus to action is derived from perception; as for the *how*, every purpose of action is to produce some sensible result.' From this, Peirce concludes,

Thus, we come down to what is tangible and practical, as the root of every real distinction of thought, no matter how subtle it may be;

254

and there is no distinction of meaning so fine as to consist in anything but a possible difference of practice. (5.400)

Beliefs determine actions because they can be expressed as conditional expectations; we expect that a certain sensible result will follow particular actions, and can thus know how to act if we want that sensible result. The pragmatist principle enjoins us to clarify our understanding of a proposition by determining what habits of expectation it involves, how it can guide action.

The behavioural theory of belief which Peirce is using here is not developed in much detail, and I shall not discuss it critically here. Of more immediate concern are Peirce's own grounds for dissatisfaction with this position. The discussion of the development of Peirce's views on truth and reality provides the clue to some of these. Is Bain's theory of belief a theoretical proposition of psychology? And is there anything other than empirical grounding for the claim that all that human beings *want* is a sensible result? The 1878 discussion says little to allay worries of this kind. Peirce's own later remarks focus on the tendency of the paper to subordinate theory to practice.

> Some are turned against pragmaticism because they think it comes too near to making action, – mere brute force – the *summum bonum* – I know of the existence of this objection from having, not very long ago, myself entertained a suspicion that such was the character of pragmaticism and from having almost abandoned the principle, on that account. (R 284)

And in R 296, he claims that the 1878 argument was question-begging because it assumed that a human belief consists in a behavioural disposition. As is evident from a letter to Calderoni (see 8.211), Peirce was convinced that the human agent could raise himself to higher ideal purposes, and in R 284 is at pains both to enlist the idealist Royce as representing the 'genuine upshot' of pragmatism and claiming that the doctrine identifies 'the development of the idea' as the *summum bonum*. He requires a proof of pragmatism that will accommodate these truths. More to the immediate point, the proof will only convince the 'high metaphysicians' if it prevents them inferring from the 'evident falsity' of the anti-metaphysical doctrine to the falsity of assumptions about belief and human goals upon which it rests. Bain's theory of belief will only appeal to those who are predisposed against metaphysics in the first place. Hence, Peirce needs either a proof of pragmatism which bypasses Bain's theory of belief, or a proof of Bain's theory strong enough to convince Bradley and his friends.

Reflecting upon his 1903 argument two years later, Peirce commented that it 'was far from being a simple one; for its presentation occupied seven carefully written lectures in Harvard University, and yet still left too many difficulties' (R 279). However, we should not be put off by this complexity. The argument for pragmatism involves defences of Peirce's accounts of self-control and the normative sciences, his theory of categories and semiotics, and his treatments of deductive reasoning, induction and abduction. Without being aware of the fact, we have already examined many of the details of the proof. The task is to show that investigators dedicated to the self-control of their reasonings in pursuit of the truth should adopt the pragmatist maxim as their only methodological rule for the clarification of conceptions and hypotheses. The use of the maxim will bring to the surface all those features of the meaning of a hypothesis which are relevant to the control and monitoring of inquiry. Plainly, the argument must rest upon an understanding of the aims of inquiry and of the kinds of arguments and methods that inquiry involves. Thus, as Peirce acknowledges to Calderoni, his argument rests upon the assumption that only three kinds of reasoning are involved in science, abduction, induction and deduction. Pragmatism is 'simply the doctrine that the Inductive method is the only essential to the ascertainment of the intellectual purport of any symbol' (8.209).

At 5.196, in the Pragmatism lectures, we find the assertion that 'the question of pragmatism' is simply 'the question of the logic of abduction'. All that the principle 'really pretends to do' is to provide a rule which governs 'the admissibility of hypotheses to rank as hypotheses, that is to say, as explanations of phenomena held as hopeful suggestions': it enables us to see that a proposition genuinely expresses a hypothesis and to clarify the content of the hypothesis, and it also enables us to see when two propositions express distinct hypotheses. We establish such a rule by reflecting upon 'the end of an explanatory hypothesis', which is 'through subjection to the test of experiment, to lead to the avoidance of all surprise and to the establishment of a habit of positive expectation that shall not be disappointed' (5.197). We seek to find mediation and law in the world of our experience. If that were true, then any hypothesis would be admissible that set up such a habit of expectation and was inductively testable. 'This is approximately the doctrine of Pragmatism'. In order to test hypotheses and to use them to find order in our experience, we need to know only what conditional expectations can be derived from them through deductive or mathematical reasoning. As Peirce insists, there is likely to be little disagreement with the claim that applying the pragmatist principle contributes to the clarification of hypotheses.

Why didn't Peirce rest content with this proof? In the light of his theory of science, it seems that all one risks in asserting a proposition is that experimental results or other empirical evidence will show it to be mistaken. Only in those circumstances will an assertion be criticized or rejected, so Peirce's theory of science appears to support the 'experimentalist's view' that the content of an assertion is to be spelled out in accordance with the pragmatist principle. Yet Peirce devoted enormous energy to constructing a proof which seemed always to be just beyond his grasp. In the letter to the Italian pragmatist Calderoni, already referred to, Peirce says that the argument for pragmatism from the nature of the scientific method 'goes to show that the practical consequences are *much*, but not that they are *all* the meaning of a concept' (8.211). This can only mean, I think, that the argument always risks meeting a counterexample. Someone may point to two hypotheses, for example, which are plainly equivalent according to the pragmatist maxim, but with the property that science evidently finds one a preferable hypothesis. Such a counterexample would simultaneously show that Peirce's account omits part of the method of science, and that the principle does not reveal the entire meaning of a conception. Such concern is present in the remarks on continuity in the final Pragmatism lecture. He worries about whether hypotheses involving real continuity have a distinctive pragmatic meaning that distinguishes them from hypotheses which talk only of complex indenumerable sequences. If not, then his pragmatism would lack foundations because he uses real continuity to explain the realism about generals which underlies pragmatism. Also, he was convinced that hypotheses which invoked real continuity did provide better, more complete explanations than those which did not (cf Kant B 670 ff). In the 1903 lecture, he announced that these phenomena could only be accommodated if we grant that we have direct perceptual awareness of real continuity. In order to protect the doctrine from refutation it is necessary to provide a proof of Peirce's 'synechism' – the 'tendency of philosophical thought which insists upon the idea of continuity and, in particular, upon the necessity of hypotheses involving true continuity' (6.169) – and to link it appropriately to perception. A related worry appears in the letter to Calderoni.

Man seems to himself to have some glimmer of co-understanding with God, or with Nature. The fact that he has been able in some degree to predict how nature will act, to formulate general 'laws' to which future events conform, seem to furnish inductive proof that man really penetrates in some measure the ideas that govern creation. Now man cannot believe that creation has not some ideal purpose. If so, it is not mere action, but the development of an idea which is the purpose of thought. (8.211)

We have seen the origins of a response to this in Peirce's treatment of his categories and the dependence of logic upon ethics and aesthetics:

we shall take the story further when we look at his metaphysics in the following chapter. The passage suggests, once again, that ideas might govern theory choice which cannot be fully elucidated using the pragmatist maxim. We can see the same thought in operation in some of Peirce's remarks about common sense. Somebody might object that when we choose hypotheses for testing we make use of a notion of plausibility, preferring some hypotheses to others on grounds that do not involve comparing their empirical consequences. If this is so, then pragmatism does not provide all that there is to the logic of abduction. By attributing these preferences to acritical, instinctive, common sense, Peirce evades the difficulty. They do not result from deliberate controlled choice based upon an analysis of the hypotheses under consideration; they do not reflect conceptual activity at all. Hence there is no reason to suppose that in making such choices we have to exercise concepts which cannot be accounted for in pragmatist terms.

Plainly, what Peirce would like is a demonstration that any such doubts about his doctrine are unwarranted; he wants an argument which shows that no concepts whose meaning cannot be fully explained by applying the pragmatist principle *could* have a role in science. This provides the context for his various attempts to provide a proof of pragmatism after 1903. I lack the space to provide a detailed examination of the arguments that he used; so I shall comment on some of the strategies that emerge in the writings of this time. These writings have two related features. First, they contain an enormous amount of work explicitly concerned with the theory of signs. This was the period of Peirce's correspondence with Lady Welby, and the period which saw the development of his most complex and detailed classifications of signs. Secondly, many of the manuscripts are devoted to the development of Peirce's 'Existential Graphs'.[2] These are part of a system of formal logic which, Peirce hoped, was adequate to express any course of mathematical reasoning, and which was supposed to make the diagrammatic character of such reasoning particularly obvious. The system has some similarity to modern natural deduction systems, and falls into three subsystems. The alpha-graphs correspond roughly to the propositional calculus, the beta-graphs to the predicate calculus. The third subsystem, the gamma-graphs, contain the rudiments of a possible world treatment of modal inference and attempts to account for the logic of abstraction. The gamma-graphs are clearly intended to contain the most important forms of theorematic reasoning. Many of the manuscripts from the period under discussion make attempts to construct a satisfactory version of the gamma-graphs: there is little reason to think that this task was completed. The fullest published treatment of the graphs was in 'Prolegomena for an Apology for Pragmatism', and it is a reasonable conjecture that both the work on signs and the development of the graphs had a role in the proof that Peirce sought. So, I shall finish this chapter by trying to explain why Peirce's search for a proof took these directions.

Since pragmatism is a doctrine about the meanings of intellectual concepts, it should, ideally, be established as a theorem of semiotics, the theory of signs. When we apply the pragmatist principle to clarify a concept or hypothesis, we interpret it; and the interpretant that we produce is one that makes the content of the original sign as explicit as it can possibly be made. So, the plausible strategy is to undertake a general investigation of the sorts of interpretants that general signs or concepts can have, identify some interpretant as the most explicit or 'ultimate' one, and then show that applying the pragmatist principle provides *that* interpretant. Hence, Peirce claims that pragmatism is a thesis about the 'ultimate logical interpretant' of a concept or hypothesis. We can follow the argument without exploring all Peirce's classifications of inter-pretants. An argument familiar among empiricists runs thus: we can show that we understand an expression by providing a synonym or by giving a verbal definition of it, and we can use synonyms and definitions to teach the meanings of expressions. However, these represent indirect ways of explaining the meaning of an expression; they simply point out that it is the same as the meaning of some other expression. In order to break out of the web of words, we must have a way of explaining or teaching meanings which does not consist in providing definitions or synonyms, such as ostensive teaching or explaining the meaning by showing what the expression applies to. Peirce uses a similar argument. A logical interpretant of a sign is one that displays the cognitive or conceptual contents of the sign. If the interpretant is itself an assertion or judgment, then how it interprets the sign depends upon how it, in its turn, is interpreted. An 'ultimate interpretant' is required which displays the meaning of the sign but does not itself require interpretation. This interpretant must be a mental state or event, and it must itself be general – or else it cannot interpret the general or conceptual content of the sign. But, how it interprets the sign must not depend upon how it in its turn is interpreted: it must not be a general sign (5.476). Hence, from the 1903 Pragmatism lectures onwards, we find Peirce asking what is the ultimate logical interpretant of a concept or hypothesis. And he claims to be able to prove that the only possible answer is 'a change of habit of conduct'. I understand the ultimate meaning of a concept when I know how I would modify my conduct – given my desires and other beliefs – if I came to accept it as true: accepting it would make a difference to what I would do, in certain circumstances, to achieve my goals (5.476). The pragmatist principle advises us to clarify our hypotheses by indicating how accepting them would modify our understanding of the consequences of our actions. Hence it reveals the ultimate logical interpretants of concepts and hypotheses.

If the proof that habits are the only candidate for the status of ultimate logical interpretants were readily identified, this argument would have some force. Being 'would-bes', habits are suitably general, although there may be grounds for doubt about whether their identity is really independent of how they are interpreted. It is hard to be sure how far the holistic character of Peirce's pragmatism, discussed in the previous section, enables this view to escape traditional objections to behaviourism. We can only specify the would-bes by indicating what the agent would do, given all his other beliefs, and given the relative strengths of all of his desires. We can specify these beliefs and desires, it seems, only by using general concepts. However, if all of these beliefs are held constant when the pragmatist principle is applied, the difficulty might be avoided. The problem then is that the agent's 'tendencies towards action' depend not only on whether the truth of a proposition makes an action conducive to the satisfaction of a desire that he has. They also depend upon the relative strength of that and other desires, and upon his judgment as to the best or most efficient means to satisfying that desire. It may be possible to get round these difficulties by speaking of the habit as a tendency to be surprised if certain volitions don't have anticipated upshots, and then to account for surprise in terms of firstness and secondness, without any conceptual element. But, the details of that are problematic, and since there is no satisfactory proof that only habits can serve as the ultimate interpretant, we shall not pursue this further.

The role of the existential graphs is more complex. First, if they were completed, they would show that all mathematical reasoning can be construed as experimentation upon diagrams, and hence block one source of counterexamples to pragmatism. In fact, Peirce sometimes claims that working through abstract mathematical examples provides the clearest way of seeing that the thesis is correct. However, their role is more central than this. The graphs are supposed to provide 'moving pictures' of thought; they enable us to study the logical character of all deliberation or reasoning. If there were aspects of meaning which were not revealed through the application of the pragmatist maxim, then they would be reflected in the use of hypotheses in deliberation – for they certainly do not emerge in ordinary inductive testing. Hence, if the existential graphs could be completed, we could use them to find out whether such non-pragmatic intellectual meaning was to be found.

A sufficient study of the graphs should show what nature is truly common to all significations of concepts; whereupon a comparison will show whether that nature be or be not of the very ilk that Pragmaticism (by the definition of it) avows that it is. . . . (S)hould the theory of Pragmaticism be erroneous, the student would only have to compare concept after concept, each one, first in the light of the Existential Graphs, and then as Pragmaticism would interpret it, and it could not be that before long he would come upon a concept whose analyses from these two widely separated points of view unmistakably conflicted. (4.534 n – from a projected later paper for the *Monist* series of 1905–6)

If all that there is to deliberation is induction, deduction and abduction, then pragmatism is safe. The crucial issue concerns whether in completing the system of graphs it would prove necessary to acknowledge further kinds of reasoning; and to grant that further aspects of intellectual meaning are required to explain how these further kinds of intellectual activity operate with concepts. It is my conjecture that Peirce never constructed the proof that he was looking for. In 1911 he wrote,

I am unable yet quite to *prove* that the three kinds of reasoning I mean are the *only* kinds of sound reasoning; although I can show reason to think that it can be proved, and *very strong* probable reasons for thinking that there is no fourth kind. (NE iii 1778)

I doubt that he solved this problem in the few manuscripts that date from later than this.

IX

Evolutionary Cosmology
and Objective Idealism

1 Introduction: logic and metaphysics

In his 1905 paper 'What Pragmatism Is', Peirce affirmed that pragmatism shows that 'almost every proposition of ontological metaphysics is either meaningless gibberish . . . or else is absurd' (5.423). Once all this nonsense is dismissed, philosophy can get down to the serious business of studying 'problems capable of investigation by the observational methods of the true sciences'. However, from the 1890s, in a series of papers in *The Monist* and elsewhere, we find Peirce developing a metaphysical theory of his own. Acknowledging a resemblance between his own views and those of Schelling, he defends a form of objective idealism which claims that matter is 'effete mind' and involves a complex evolutionary cosmology. In a passage which looks to be the product of armchair ontological metaphysics, he writes,

> In the beginning – infinitely remote – there was a chaos of unperson-
> alized feeling, which being without connection or regularity would
> properly be without existence. This feeling, sporting here and there in
> pure arbitrariness, would have started the germ of a generalizing
> tendency. Its other sportings would be evanescent, but this would
> have a growing virtue. Thus the tendency to habit would be started;
> and from this, with the other principles of evolution, all the
> regularities of the universe would be evolved. At any time, however,
> an element of pure chance survives and will remain until the world
> becomes an absolutely perfect, rational and symmetrical system, in
> which mind is at last crystallized in the infinitely distant future. (6.33)

Although Peirce claims that pragmatism has the advantage over other forms of 'prope-positivism' in that it allows for a 'purified' scientific metaphysics (5.423), it is easy to sympathize with admirers of Peirce's work in logic and epistemology who are horrified about what Gallie calls 'the black sheep or white elephant of his philosophy' (Gallie, 1952, p. 216). Many commentators suggest that these metaphysical writings are simply inconsistent with central themes in his logic (Wiener, 1949, pp. 84–5; Gallie, 1952, ch. 9; Almeder, 1980, ch. IV). Others simply ignore it (Ayer, 1968). Looking back to the metaphysical writings of his youth (CW1 passim; Esposito, 1980; Murphey, 1961; Wiener, 1949), and bearing in mind his religious views and antipathy to the mechanical philosophy and Darwinism, it is easy to conclude that Peirce's interests drew him in two conflicting directions. He was blinded to the incompatibility of these metaphysical excesses with his work in logic.

However, I think that this would be a mistake. Peirce certainly linked his metaphysical writings to his pragmatism and logic, and, even if we reject the metaphysical views that he actually defended, we can see that some form of metaphysics was actually called for by the doctrines that we have been examining. In the remainder of this introductory section, I shall introduce three points of contact between metaphysics and the Peircean logic. First, the task of metaphysics is to examine 'the most general features of reality and real objects' (6.6 – this paragraph gives a list of topics that metaphysics, so characterized, studies). The scientific method is to be employed in this investigation, and metaphysics counts as a part of philosophy – and not a special science – because it does not rest upon 'special' observations or use experimental techniques. Hypotheses are tested against everyday observations, ones that are open to all and ignored only because their very obviousness prevents our noticing them (1.34; 6.3). In the light of this, Peirce predicts that metaphysics should be very easy – harder than mathematics, but much more straightforward than any science that has to use experimental techniques to obtain relevant observations. He speculates in a fragment from 1898 that the unsatisfactory state of the discipline results from its having been left in the hands of scholars whose primary interests were practical, namely theologians. He seems to think that somebody with a passion for the truth and a free afternoon ought to be able to clear up most of the outstanding metaphysical issues (6.1–5).

We shall discuss later whether Peirce consistently uses the method of science in his own metaphysical inquiries. At least we can see that he attempts to reconcile these aspects of his work. A second point of contact is the logic of abduction. In chapter VII, we saw that our choice of which theory to test reflects instinctive common-sense judgments of plausibility. We also saw that, once we move beyond the realm where these instincts had their original application, there is little reason to suppose that they will be reliable. Hence, as science becomes more abstruse, more abstract, we need an alternative basis for evaluating hypotheses – instincts that evolve to help us pursue our food are of little assistance when we consider theories that explain how physical systems behave at very low temperatures. Peirce believes that if we have an adequate metaphysics, we can turn to this for guidance about the sorts of hypotheses that should be taken seriously. The metaphysics tells us what reality is like, and this must be reflected in our theories. So long as the scientific method genuinely is employed in metaphysics, this will not mean that abduction must make use of concepts which cannot be fully clarified using the pragmatist principle (1.408). Peirce's synechism, the claim that we should favour hypotheses that involve real continuity, exemplifies this sort of use of the metaphysics.

Finally, there is a species of argument which makes much clearer than the other claims do the fact that metaphysics is a part of philosophy rather than a very abstract science: the metaphysical doctrines have a crucial role in the full development of the doctrines and arguments discussed in the previous eight chapters. Peirce's investigations belong to a familiar tradition which tries to determine how reality *must* be given so that it is intelligible to us. Crudely, there are certain gaps in the arguments we have discussed, and the metaphysical cosmology is supposed to fill those gaps. Two of these gaps are of major importance. In specifying the end of inquiry, as well as at later stages in the argument, Peirce has to allow that phenomenological reflection shows that the three categories have universal application, and he had to assume that no fourth category will ever be found. Unless we assume that the results of phenomenology have universal and objective validity, the Peircean enterprise never gets off the ground. But, our right to speak with universal voice on these topics is not grounded in reason: we have no reason to think that we can do so. Secondly, at several stages in the argument, assumptions were introduced with the status of regulative hopes: we had no reason to think them true, but we adopted them because their truth was a necessary condition of our attaining the goals of inquiry. There were several of these, but the most important of them can be summarized in the claim that there is a reality which is knowable by us. If there is no law to be discovered, or if our abductive sense is so ill-attuned to reality that there is no reason to think that we could find the answer to any empirical question in a finite time, then our adoption of the life of science committed us to goals that cannot be achieved. Peirce writes that one function of metaphysics is to explain how reality must be if the regulative hopes of logic are absolutely true. It must provide a description of the most general features of reality which shows that the three categories are universal, that there are real laws, and that there is that affinity between us and reality which accounts for our ability to know its character. We are to repay the regulative loans taken out in our logical investigations (1.487). Peirce's claim is that his evolutionary objective idealism is the only theory which answers to

264

these demands: it provides an account of reality, of mind, and of experience, which entails that the categories are universally present in experience and that reality is fully intelligible to us (cf Murphey, 1961, pp. 17–18). The analogy with Kantian strategies of justification is obvious. Both Kant and Peirce claim that inquiry rests upon principles which we grant objective validity, but which we cannot justify our adoption of without circularity. In each case, it is necessary subsequently to explain the right with which we do this. In each of the three critiques Kant offers a transcendental deduction of the principles that are employed. And Peirce's metaphysics occupies a similar role. In the light of the scientifically confirmed metaphysics, we can understand that it is not a miracle that our search for self-realization through the self-control of our reasoning could succeed.

These metaphysical writings mostly date from after 1885. Although he discussed related topics fairly constantly from that time to the end of his life, the most useful and complete treatment of issues in metaphysics is in a series of five papers which appeared in *The Monist* during 1891–3. These are:

'The Architecture of Theories' (6.7–34)
'The Doctrine of Necessity Examined' (6.35–65)
'The Law of Mind' (6.102–63)
'Man's Glassy Essence' (6.238–71)
'Evolutionary Love' (6.287–317)

Since they date from the early 1890s, they are not as clear as subsequent writings are about the relation between metaphysics and the normative sciences. However, they do provide the most accessible and intelligible treatment of these puzzling doctrines and provide a useful statement of Peirce's metaphysics.[1]

2   Law and explanation

My aim in this section is to formulate the problems which led Peirce to endorse his evolutionary cosmology. I shall concentrate upon problems that arise out of his work in logic, so the question that concerns us is: what problems arise out of the regulative hopes adopted in the course of scientific inquiry which demand that we adopt a Peircean evolutionary metaphysics? In the course of this discussion, we shall discuss some theses about explanation and law which are of independent interest apart from their role in supporting the metaphysical vision. I have already hinted that other considerations predisposed Peirce in favour of the evolutionary view. These will be discussed when we turn to the details of the story in the following section.

We must start from an assumption which Peirce makes much of.

Nothing is inexplicable; any intelligible 'why' question has an answer. This derives from the regulative hopes upon which inquiry rests, for it is a consequence of the claim that reality is fully intelligible to us, and that any question we raise can be answered. It is only a regulative hope, but it imposes considerable constraints upon theory choice: any hypothesis which accounts for one set of puzzling phenomena by positing facts, laws and processes which are themselves inexplicable is to be rejected. There are no brute regularities or laws which must be accepted as providing ultimate truths which cannot be explained in their turn. It is evident that Peirce supposes that nominalists and empiricists cannot meet this condition. Employing a Humean analysis of law, they will take it as a brute fact about reality that it instantiates certain regularities, and do not think of this as something that itself requires an explanation. To accept that a hypothesis posits ultimate regularities is to commit the cardinal sin in the eyes of the logician, it is to block the road of inquiry; it prevents us raising why-questions which could fruitfully push inquiry forward, and forces us to acknowledge limits to our ability to comprehend reality (6.60).

Before looking at an illustration which may make Peirce's claims clearer, we must see how he understood 'explanation'. Explanations

> supply a proposition which, if it had been known to be true before the phenomenon presented itself, would have rendered that phenomenon predictable, if not with certainty, at least as something very likely to occur. It thus renders that phenomenon rational, – that is, it makes it a logical consequence, necessary or probable. (7.192)

His view is similar to that of the logical empiricists: we explain an event by invoking a law, in the light of which the event was likely to happen. Although he makes further remarks about the pragmatics of explanation, this is the core of his position (see 7.201). We look for an explanation whenever we fail to find a regularity which we accept or we encounter an unexpected regularity (7.194). Hence, we do seek an explanation of why a die turns up ace: this is not surprising and cannot be made 'rational'. In general, as Peirce insisted in the course of a dispute with Paul Carus, it is regularity that needs to be explained. Most irregularities do not puzzle us at all.

> In what state of amazement would I pass my life, if I were to wonder why there is no regularity connecting days upon which I receive an even number of letters by mail and nights on which I notice an even number of shooting stars. (7.189)

But, whenever we become aware of a regularity in our experience, it is natural to ask for an explanation of it. Hence, it is law, above all, that calls for an explanation (6.12).

In 1902, Peirce suggested that the atomic hypothesis – 'that matter is composed of atoms, all spherical and exactly alike' – by insisting that these atoms are eternal and exactly alike, is inadmissible because it tries to 'explain the phenomena by means of the absolutely inexplicable' (6.173). The argument here is murky, but I take it to be that the theory admits certain ultimate regularities: no explanation can be offered of why there are these atoms, of why they are all alike, of why they have always existed, and so on. We cannot reasonably ask why there are not more, why there are not bigger or of more varied shape, why they cannot be created or destroyed. These have to be accepted as brute ultimate facts about the nature of matter.

We can now begin to trace the route from this assumption about explanation to Peirce's evolutionary metaphysics. In the light of the view of explanation which Peirce defends, we explain laws or regularities by deriving them from the more abstract or general laws. If we know the more general law, the special regularity from which we began would not have been surprising. When we explain a regularity in this way, further explanatory questions can arise, in several ways. First, and most obviously, we need an explanation of the more abstract regularity which is used in the explanation (6.60). If we explain this in the same fashion, we shall invoke a further more abstract law, which itself must be explained. Hence, it seems that, if we accept Peirce's assumptions about anything being explicable, we must expect an infinite hierarchy of ever more abstract laws and generalizations, each introduced to explain laws lower in the hierarchy. There is no end to the new explanatory questions that can arise, and we can never reach the point of having a complete explanation of some phenomenon. This promises an infinite regress of laws and explanations, and it can seem that we can only block this regress by allowing that at some point we reach a law which cannot be explained, which is an ultimate. Nozick speculates that the regress might be blocked by allowing for laws that are self-explanatory, but his discussion is inconclusive and the notion is not one that would be generally adopted (Nozick, 1981, pp. 115 ff). Alternatively, we could claim that the regress is benign, that there is no reason to block the infinite hierarchy of explanations, and no reason to think that why-questions ever receive complete answers. Another possible response is to claim that subsumption under more general laws is not the only means available for explaining laws. We can provide historical explanations of how they arose in the first instance. It is clear that we use such explanations in the study of animal behaviour; we explain a behavioural regularity by showing that, given natural selection, it is not surprising that such a regularity should evolve through time. It is plausible to read Peirce as trying to block the regress of explanations by using this strategy; the evolutionary cosmology provides a framework for understanding laws historically which enables us to block the regress of explanation.

Peirce finds other demands for explanation arising out of the practice of explanation. He often draws attention to the formal and material similarities between laws that govern different sorts of phenomena. These constitute second-order regularities which themselves require to be explained, and, it seems that he thinks that his evolutionary story will help here too – just as the theory of natural selection helps us to understand morphological and behavioural similarities between distinct populations (7.509). Other arguments are more suspect. He says that 'Law is *par excellence* the thing that wants a reason. Now the only possible way of accounting for the law of nature and for uniformity in general is to suppose them the results of evolution' (6.12–13). His argument seems to slide from the reasonable demand that we can ask for an explanation of any particular law to the puzzling claim that we need an explanation for 'uniformity in general'. The demand that we explain why there is law has often, and rightly, seemed hardly intelligible. This does not seem to be a *scientific* question, and certainly is not identical, as Peirce supposes, to the more reasonable claim that it is regularity or uniformity which prompts the search for explanations.

However, I think that a case can be made for Peirce's claim that such an explanation must be provided. One relatively straightforward argument begins from the observation that thirdness (generality) seems to be a ubiquitous, or universal, feature of the phaneron. This is an observable regularity, and since Peirce is not relying upon a simple form of transcendental idealism which would enable him to explain this by reference to the constitutive activities of the knowing subject, he is required to provide a 'scientific' explanation of this regularity. This simply restates some of the points about the relations between metaphysics and the rest of Peirce's philosophy that we mentioned in the introduction to this chapter. A second argument draws more directly on the doctrines about explanation that we have just considered. Suppose that we do accept the evolutionary cosmology as a device for blocking the regress of explanations of laws. Then, it is reasonable to ask for an explanation of this evolutionary process. On the natural assumption that this is a law-governed process, then, the regress of explanations has not been blocked; for we shall want explanations of the laws which govern this process of explanation. Either this explanation is ultimate, or it makes use of laws which are self-explanatory, or it invokes laws which are explained in some further way, or . . . It is very unclear what kind of explanation this could be. I am not yet ready to explain how Peirce proposes to cope with this problem. However, it is clear that he did think that an explanation of how law, in general, evolves has a role in this: he hopes to show that a process of evolution, which does not have to be thought of as a law-governed process, can explain how a law-governed cosmos emerged.

But, we shall leave these topics for the present and turn to some further preliminary themes. The first of these is Peirce's 'Tychism' defended in the second of the *Monist* papers, a paper we discussed in part in chapter VII, 'The Doctrine of Necessity Examined'. The paper provides a sustained attack upon the deterministic doctrine that 'every single fact in the Universe is precisely determined by law' (6.35). It defends the view that there is 'absolute chance' (6.102). It is tempting to interpret Peirce as defending the modern-sounding claim that the fundamental laws of nature are statistical rather than strictly deterministic: they are of the form

The probability of an F being G is p.

The nineteenth century saw the spread of statistical techniques in fundamental science – and we have noticed that Peirce placed a great stress upon the role of such techniques in induction. Moreover, he was one of the first to remark on the statistical basis of the reasoning used by Darwin in *The Origin of Species*. However, when we look more closely at the claims Peirce makes and the arguments that he uses, it emerges that this is not his primary concern. The claim is not one about the *form* of the laws that govern reality, but about the extent to which reality is governed by law at all. The claim appears to be that laws are at best approximately true, that they constrain the course of events but that there is room for chance, spontaneous deviation from them. Laws are not absolutely exact and do not have 'absolute sway in nature' (1.325). In 1903, he distanced himself from those who 'suppose nature to be subject to freaks, who believe in miracles not simply as manifestations of superhuman power but as downright violations of the laws of nature, absolutely abnormal' and scorned the mathematician Newcomb who believed that 'the human will has a power of deflecting the motions of particles, in plain violation of the third law of motion' (6.92). Rather, he holds that 'uniformities are never absolutely exact . . . At the same time . . . even these departures from law are subject to a certain law of probability, and that in the present state of the universe they are far too small to be detected by our observations' (6.91). Hence, he thinks that long-run frequencies only converge *indefinitely* on fixed values in the long run. We can expect the frequency to settle down, oscillating within a certain interval, but not to become ever closer to some exact value.

The support for the doctrine is of two sorts. In spite of Peirce's claim that the deviations from law are too small to be perceived, he thinks that his thesis of 'chance-spontaneity' can be given a precise formulation and empirically confirmed (6.62). His editors regretfully announce that they have found no trace of this confirmation in published or unpublished writings (6.62 n); but I think that we can interpret him as referring to a wide range of phenomena which, he thinks, can only be explained if tychism is true – what else could empirical confirmation mean here? These phenomena are varied, and some have been encountered already. Tychism is a premiss of his evolutionary explanation of law and of 'the regular relationships between the laws of nature – similarities and comparative characters, which appeal to our intelligence as its cousins and call upon us for a reason' (6.64). This explanation also accounts for the 'growth and increasing complexity' which is suggested by reflection upon the life of an individual mind, or a plant, upon the history of states, ideas, languages and institutions, upon what we learn from the palaeontological record, from geology and from astronomy. We naturally assume that 'there is probably in nature some agency by which the complexity and diversity of things can be increased' (6.58). The explanation of irreversible processes of growth will also account for the variety and diversity of the phenomena we find in the world (6.59; 6.64). Hence, Peirce points to a range of phenomena which, he thinks, cannot be accounted for in deterministic terms and proposes a tychistic metaphysics which will account for them. He seeks an evolutionary picture, and tychism provides the element of chance variation which provides new possibilities, which are the materials for growth and change. Notoriously, it is far from obvious that a deterministic theory cannot allow for the growth of variety and law: the fusion of Darwinian natural selection and Mendelian genetics offers to do just that. Peirce does not provide any strong arguments that exclude this possibility.

The arguments that we have noticed so far fit with an understanding of chance as a brute impersonal force, but many of Peirce's comments suggest that he thinks of it in moral or religious terms. For example, he often talks of it as the force of 'life' in contrast to the impersonal constraint of law: it is an expression of freedom or spontaneity. In line with this, he claims that it has an advantage over determinism because it provides for free decision – the necessitarian 'cannot logically stop short of making the whole action of the mind a part of the physical universe.'

> Our notion that we decide what we are going to do, if, as the necessitarian says, it has been calculable since the earliest times, is reduced to illusion. Indeed, consciousness in general thus becomes a mere illusory aspect of the material system. (6.61)

This appears to bring to the surface a conflict between the claim, noticed above, that deviations from exact law conform to probabilistic distributions and the idea that it provides a locus for free decision. Moreover, the claim that a decision was unfree if it could have been predicated has been subjected to a lot of criticism – but it is difficult to evaluate the claim until we have some idea of how decision does take place, and that will be discussed in the following section. Finally, Peirce is eager to view evolutionary change as a process of growth and perfection, as exemplifying the growth of concrete reasonableness. In a letter to William James, he wrote,

> To me there is an additional argument in favor of this theory of objective chance – I say to me because the argument supposes the reality of God, the Absolute, which I think the majority of intellectual men do not very confidently believe. It is that the universe of Nature seems much grander and more worthy of its creator, when it is conceived of, not as completed at the outset, but as such that from the merest chaos with nothing rational in it, it grows by an inevitable tendency more and more rational. It satisfies my religious instinct far better; and I have faith in my religious instinct. (quoted in Wiener, 1949, p. 95)

These positive arguments all rest upon the suggestion that tychism is a necessary component of a powerful explanatory theory, the evolutionary metaphysics. There are other negative arguments. Peirce pours predictable scorn on the claim that pure chance is inconceivable or unintelligible, and points to his own theory of induction to demonstrate that determinism is not a presupposition of science. Moreover, he insists that the observational evidence – although undecisive – favours his own position over the necessitarian alternative.

> Try to verify any law of nature, and you will find that the more precise your observations, the more certain they will be to show irregular departures from the law. We are accustomed to ascribe these, and I do not say wrongly, to errors of observation; yet we cannot usually account for these errors in any antecedently probable way. (6.46)

Attributing them to 'arbitrary determination or chance' is at least as good an explanation as claiming that they must result from some error in observation; for the irregularity is our only evidence that the error occurred.

3 The evolution of reality

As we have just seen, Peirce's tychism holds that the reality that is the object of our investigations is approximately governed by law; it also exemplifies 'chance sportings' which deviate from these laws. Central to Peirce's evolutionary story is the idea that, through time, this chance sporting decreases and law increases its hold upon the course of events. The world comes increasingly to exhibit a rational or intelligible order. This parallels the way in which, through inquiry, we come to form more and more predictive control over our experience: just as we come to understand the world better, so the world becomes more intelligible. The parallel is important for Peirce, and he describes both in terms of 'habit': through inquiry we come to adopt reliable habits of expectation; through the evolutionary process, reality becomes more 'hidebound' with habits, it behaves in a regular and predictable fashion. Both forms of habit-taking have their place in the 'growth of concrete reasonableness'. For the present, I shall leave this parallel aside and look more closely at what Peirce has to say about the ways in which reality 'takes habits'. What are the forces which govern this process? I shall begin by sketching a simplified version of the bizarre story that Peirce tells, and then introduce some of its complexities to show how it is supposed to meet some difficulties. I will not be able to go into all of the details of Peirce's writings on these topics or trace the developments in his views.[2]

This simplified version of the story employs a three-stage history of the evolution of law. In the beginning, all that there is is firstness: a continuous undifferentiated quality of feeling. This qualitative character is not to be thought of as the psychological state of some person or as standing in dyadic or triadic relations to other qualities. Since there is no secondness or thirdness, the world contains no existence or law; rather, the feeling is present simply as a potentiality or possibility. Hence, Peirce sometimes talks of this stage as one of 'Nothingness' (6.215). He seems to think it will involve a continuous spread of feeling along any of the indenumerable dimensions along which feelings can vary (6.201 ff); there is no possibility of feeling which is excluded. The second stage witnesses the arrival of secondness: he speaks of accidental reactions among the events or 'flashes' (1.412). These have to be thought of as singularities in the continuous spread of feeling, they represent discontinuities – certain of the possibilities are excluded by a brute secondness or 'reaction' (6.203 ff). As a third stage, it is claimed that these reactions will give rise to the germ of a 'habit-taking tendency'. Roughly, for there to be such a tendency is for the fact that an event has occurred to make it more probable that similar events will occur in the future; regularities emerge in the reactions which occur in the original feeling. Once this tendency towards generality emerges, Peirce expects that the amount of regularity in the reactions that occur will grow; first, any small regularity will prompt this generalizing tendency to make it more likely that the sorts of things that tend to occur together will do so (6.490); and the tendency will work on itself, so that, with time, it becomes yet more likely that regularities will be transformed into firm habits. Hence, spontaneous, chance reactions provide materials which the generalizing tendency can transform into laws or habits; law and variety grow through time.

The burgeoning generalizing tendency provides a principle that enables Peirce to explain the evolution of law, and, although I shall not discuss these details, he tries to show that he can account for the evolution of time, of space, of substances (which are bundles of habits or laws), and attempts to explain the approximate truth of Newtonian physics within the framework that his cosmology provides. His account is not supposed to lead to the overthrow of currently successful science, but to provide a framework in which it can be understood. I want now to move towards a deeper understanding of this strange doctrine by considering how far it meets the demands which occasioned it.

Gallie has objected that if this account is correct, it is false that Peirce's categories are universal: there was no thirdness before the generalizing tendency got going, and, at the very beginning, no secondness. This would appear to be the consequence of any view which explains the development of existence and reality out of nothingness or potentiality. Moreover, if we can conceive of the starting point, we can conceive of a situation which embodies only firstness, and this seems to be denied by Peirce's phenomenology (Gallie, 1952, p. 225). We might doubt whether Peirce would mind this minimal sacrifice of universality, but, when the position is properly understood, it is not required. Note too another oddity of the evolutionary story. Time does not appear on the scene until the generalizing tendency has been working for a while (sic) (e.g. 6.214). In the early stages, the kind of ordering Peirce has in mind cannot be temporal. He says that it is logical (6.214), and that he is tracing out the beginnings of an 'objective logic' of events, but it is hard to know what to make of that. One important element of the position stressed in the *Monist* papers is that the initial stage before there is any generality is an 'absolute' conception. This term is drawn from mathematics, from the theory of measurement, and is introduced in connection with this issue in 'The Architecture of Theories' (6.27). It explains the strange remark in the passage quoted at the beginning of this chapter that the initial chaos is 'infinitely remote'. Roughly, the idea is that if we were to trace back the history of the universe, we should find less and less order. Although we would never reach the initial chaos of feeling, still we could become arbitrarily close to it if we continued for long enough; the chaos is something that the history would approach as a limit, and we think of it as the limit point of this history. Similarly, Peirce does not think of the totally ordered universe as something that we could ever reach, but thinks of it as what the evolution of the universe is approaching as a limit. In order to find the initial chaos, we should have to trace back the evolution of the cosmos *through* infinity (6.26 ff). Hence, our intellectual grip on the story depends upon our grasping the idea of a growth in order in a cosmos that contains law or habit, chance reaction, and qualitative feeling: we use *mathematical* reasoning to derive the full evolutionary story from this.

This still leaves unexplained what is involved in saying that the early stages of this history present a *logical* sequence, and I want to leave discussion of this until I have considered another difficulty, first raised for Peirce by Paul Carus, the editor of *The Monist*. He complained that the fundamental elements of this story still require to be explained; Peirce presents the initial chaos, the chance reactions, and the tendency to generalize and form habits as explanatory ultimates. Peirce is unworried by this objection, and it is unclear whether he is justified in this. However, some points can be made in his defence, and they will help us to understand why the theory took the form that it did. First, since the reactions which disturb the initial continuous feeling are supposed to occur by pure chance, they stand in no need of explanation: Peirce's tychism provides him with a tool for accepting certain events as brute, unintelligible secondnesses. He is not committed to the claim that it was *inevitable* that secondness should emerge or the generalizing tendency get going, and only has to understand *how* reality evolved (given the empirically secure premiss that it did!). Hence, assigning a role to chance in this process does not conflict with his logical principles. Similarly, the initial chaos – being a state with no existence or reality a state of pure 'nothingness' – is not the sort of thing that needs to be explained. In fact, it is Peirce's claim that only regularity requires an explanation which justifies seeing no need to explain either of the first two stages. Problems arise, however, when we turn to the generalizing tendency: this is a law, the law which governs the evolution of laws. What is its explanation? How can chance reactions have a 'growing virtue'? I am unsure about Peirce's response to this difficulty, but I can see two arguments that he could employ in his defence. So long as the tendency to take habits is thought of as possible – and we can attach empirical sense to the notion through our experience of the present state of the world – then Peirce need provide no further explanation of it. Since he does not think that it was inevitable that reality and law should evolve, the germ of the generalizing tendency could be attributed to chance: the chance occurrence of this tendency to generalize can be accepted as the only explanation of law and the growth of order. However, since this does seem to block the road of inquiry – to posit a law as having no explanation – we should try for something better. And Peirce's insistence that the tendency applies to itself and *grows* may provide the clue. At any time, the regularity involved in the generalizing tendency can be explained by reference to earlier regularities: it results from a weaker tendency to take habits being strengthened by the action of the generalizing tendency. As we trace the evolutionary story backwards, the tendency becomes weaker, but we never reach a point at which it cannot be explained as due to the self-reflexive action of an earlier still weaker generalizing tendency. The state at which the generalizing tendency is absent is thought of as a limit point – the history converges upon it, becomes arbitrarily close to it, but never actually reaches it. Thus, nowhere in the story is there a regularity that cannot be explained by reference to an earlier regularity.

Assuming that this is close to what Peirce has in mind, we must turn to the question: what grounds has Peirce for his choice of primitive notions in this explanation? Why start with feeling and reaction, unless to guarantee that the desired conclusion that the categories correspond to fundamental features of reality is reached? A related question is why we should think of this position as a form of objective idealism, why it shows that matter is effete mind? Peirce has what he takes to be independent arguments for objective idealism. Roughly, he thinks that the hypothesis that there are two independent sorts of substance – the material and the mental – is untenable: Ockham's razor counsels us not to posit an excessive number of fundamental substances, and therefore enjoins us to accept a form of monism. Taking Newtonian physics to characterize the key properties of physical substance, Peirce asserts that, since it cannot account for the properties of *feeling*, for the sensory quality of experience, the doctrine that all that exists is matter cannot be accepted. Consequently, he favours the view that all that exists is mind (6.245). The argument is rapid and unsatisfactory: the assumption that Newtonian physics is the correct sort of account of matter distorts the discussion, and little argument is provided for the denial that it can account for feeling; moreover, the possibility – neutralism – that matter and mind are alike modes of an underlying form of reality which is, in itself, neither mental nor material, is treated very dismissively. However, once this move is made, Peirce looks to the fundamental concepts used in thinking about mind to guide his cosmology. These fundamental concepts, he holds, are feeling, volition and habit: we form habits of action and expectation which order the qualitative character of our experience. Habit-formation proceeds according to patterns of infer-ence, involving hypothesis-formation and inductive testing; through life and inquiry, we acquire habits which provide us with greater control over our experience. The same elements – feeling, reaction (volition) and habit-taking (hypothesis-formation or sign action) are discerned, through the evolutionary cosmology, in reality. Of course, minds (in the normal sense) do differ from matter. But, the difference is one of organization: persons are hierarchically organized in the pursuit of overriding aims, and are more flexible in forming and changing habits than the material world is. The elements, in each case, are the same. Hence, when he criticizes Hegel's evolutionary cosmology for searching for a *necessity* in the development of reality, Peirce does not reject Hegel's use of logical categories in thinking about reality: Hegel wrongly assimilated all development to deductive inference, whereas Peirce models habit-taking on induction and hypothesis (6.218). Talk of habit-taking and hypothetic inference here should not be seen as metaphorical: the forms of sign action involved in the growth of reality and in conscious thought are, in some sense, *the same*.

Having got some idea of how the evolutionary story is embedded in some of Peirce's other doctrines, we can return to the question of how we are to understand the sort of progression that is involved in the stages of the history before time has evolved. I think that his claim that this is *logical* has to be taken seriously: habit-taking is a form of inference, and the appropriate notion of 'priority' is that of premises and conclusion, it is the kind of ordering that can be constructed from a study of the sign relation. Now, it is reasonable to doubt whether logical relations are fruitfully thought of in terms of the kind of temporal metaphor that is provided by the evolutionary idiom. If Peirce's account requires us to think of events analogous to inferrings, which are not temporally ordered, then it is totally obscure what this could mean; the doctrine seems likely to descend into 'meaningless gibberish'. However, there is another way to take it, which is less exciting, but which might make more sense. Just as social contract theories in political philosophy use temporal evolutionary idioms in order to articulate what are, at root, logical analyses, so what Peirce is providing is a logical analysis of the elements of reality. On this reading, the early parts of the history remind us that reality is composed of the three distinct elements – quality or feeling, blind reaction, and thirdness which here appears as a tendency to take habits. The evolutionary story shows us that these elements are sufficient to yield a world which could evolve, through time, into one which is recognizably like the world of our experience. The three stages of the story that we presented are a colourful way of elaborating on the separateness of these categories. But, they do not present what is, in any familiar sense, a story. However, I am not aware of any texts which support this reading, beyond the insistence that the progression in the early stages is a logical one.

From his earliest years, Peirce was a deeply religious man, and the letter to James quoted above will indicate that his metaphysical views were inseparable from his religious outlook. Therefore, I shall conclude this brief, superficial tour of his metaphysics by examining an interesting paper from 1906, 'A Neglected Argument for the Reality of God'. Apart from its independent interest, the views expressed there will enable us to understand more fully both Peirce's view of his metaphysics and the foundations of his logic. It will be apparent that there is a *prima facie* tension between these logical views and the construction of a proof of God's reality: what empirical meaning can we extract from the hypothesis that there is a God when we try to clarify it using the pragmatist principle? How can consensus on God's reality derive from the use of quantitative and qualitative induction? And indeed, there are passages which suggest that Peirce thinks that religious faith must be grounded in instinct (6.500; 6.504) – although, he also says that God is directly perceived (6.613; 6.492-3). Presumably, an inquiry which shows us the reality of God must not be motivated by *practical* concerns; it must be a theoretical inquiry. But it is hard to see what theoretical question could call for the hypothesis of God. These, and other similar considerations, make us sympathetic to those like Goudge who point to Peirce's writings on religion to support their view that his writings show us a man torn between competing and inconsistent intellectual directions. Before asking how consistent these elements of his thought are, I shall sketch the form taken by the 'Neglected Argument'.

The core of this argument is another, simpler one, the 'humble argument', which claims that belief in a deity is a natural product of a form of intellectual activity that Peirce calls 'musement'. He begins with a lyrical description, and recommendation of intellectual play: we allow our thoughts to drift as they will, pursuing whatever appeals to us, simply for recreation (6.458-465). This can involve 'aesthetic contemplation' or 'distant castle building (whether in Spain or within one's own moral training)', or 'considering some wonder in one of the Universes (firstness, secondness and thirdness), or some connection between two of the three, with speculation concerning its cause' (6.458). 'Refreshing enough more than to repay the expenditure', when 'indulged in moderately', this provides Peirce with a form of intellectual activity which is not serving practical goals, yet is not directed towards the discovery of the truth; although it is not scientific activity, it is disinterested. Especially if this play takes the form of 'musement' – reflection upon the three universes of experience, their harmony, perfection and tendency to growth – Peirce thinks it very unlikely that the hypothesis of God's reality will not occur to the thinker. Indeed, he thinks that this hypothesis will be almost irresistible: when belief in God is acquired in this fashion, we are convinced by the 'humble argument'. As he notes, all that this argument can provide is a (strong) abductive suggestion, something analogous to a hypothesis for testing. Thus, the neglected argument builds upon this abduction, clarifying it and testing it in accordance with the method of science. It is worth noting, however, that he often seems to suggest that faith grounded in the natural plausibility of belief, or upon a 'direct perception' of God, is of more lasting value than belief which derives from an argument (6.504).

In order to clarify the hypothesis of God's reality, and to see what it is supposed to explain, we should apply the pragmatist principle and ask what conditional expectations we should form were it to be true. However, Peirce insists that the hypothesis is excessively vague, and no testable precise predictions can be derived from it at all; no small class of observations could warrant the rejection of the hypothesis. But, it does not follow from this that the hypothesis does not have a content of the sort that the pragmatist looks for. In a different paper, we find

> If a pragmaticist is asked what he means by the word 'God', he can only say that just as long acquaintance with a man of great character may deeply influence one's whole manner of conduct . . . so if contemplation and study of the physico-psychical universe can imbue a man with principles of conduct analogous to the influence of a great man's works or conversation, then that analogue of a mind – for it is impossible to say that any human attribute is *literally* applicable – is what he means by 'God'. (6.502)

Peirce seems to be drawing attention to the effects of belief in God upon the believer's life, to the effects of the belief upon his habits of conduct. The believer will desire 'above all things to shape the whole conduct of life and all the springs of action into conformity with that hypothesis' (6.467), and will be provided with 'ideals of conduct'. But in order to make sense of this, we need to understand how belief will colour the believer's perceptions of the world, what difference it can make to his expectations.

Peirce tells us that God is a necessary being (6.452), that He is the creator of all three universes of experience (6.452), that, although He has reality, He does not react with existing things and thus does not exist (6.496), and that He is 'infinitely incomprehensible' (6.466). Such comments do not much help to *clarify* the concept, and do not relate closely to the pragmatist principle. Remarks such as 'Vain as it is to attempt to bring to light any definite meaning from the idea, it is nevertheless true that *all reality* is due to the creative power of God' encourage the suspicion that Peirce has relaxed the standards of clarity and argument that he employs in logic and science (6.505). A central element of acceptance of the hypothesis is that we see the world as growing, as advancing towards a more perfect state, and we shall tend to see this growth as 'purposed': the world appears as subject to self-control moving towards ever greater 'concrete reasonableness', becoming more aesthetically admirable. Indeed, being vague, the hypothesis tends to represent God Himself as growing towards a more perfect state. But, says Peirce, it conflicts with our conception of God that we should think of Him as growing or becoming more perfect – and 'purpose essentially involves growth, and so cannot be attributed to God' (6.466).

But this apparent attribution of growth to God, since it is ineradicable from the hypothesis, cannot, according to the hypothesis, be flatly false. Its implications concerning the Universes will be maintained in the hypothesis, while its implications concerning God will be partly disavowed, and yet held to be less false than their denial would be. (6.466)

Similarly, although God has no purposes, it is less false to say that He does than to deny it! We have to rely upon notions of time, growth, purpose, power and knowledge, to think of a deity to whom none of these concepts can have straightforward application. We rely upon metaphor and analogy to obtain a grip upon the 'infinitely incomprehensible'.

Leaving these vague expressions to one side, just how does belief in God colour one's perception of reality? The believer perceives the world as 'a vast representamen, a great symbol of God's purpose, working out its conclusions in living realities' (5.119). It is perceived as growing in concrete reasonableness: it is ordered in lawlike fashion and becoming more law governed in time; it is aesthetically beautiful and steadily becoming more so; it is available to our knowledge, and through our inquiries, we can contribute to the carrying out of God's purpose; pain and suffering has its place in a progress which is, all in all, good; by acting out of love, motivated to complete His purposes by contributing to the growth of harmony, we can act in the confidence that our efforts will succeed. In general, belief in God grounds an optimistic assurance that our actions in pursuit of our ultimate aims – in action and inquiry – will succeed. It helps us to sustain the ideals of conduct and inquiry which Peirce's investigations in the normative sciences have recommended. The direction of evolution towards a state of beauty, goodness and knowledge is no longer a blind hope on which our inquiries must rest, but a confident belief grounded in religious belief. The evolution is thought of as fated, or purposed. This means that there are (vague) predictions that can be derived from the hypothesis of God's existence: there will be continued growth and progress in the evolution of reality, in the progress of our inquiries, and in the moral goodness of the world. The vagueness of the hypothesis shows up in the fact that nothing could be acknowledged as a *prima facie* falsification of these predictions: we could know, from observation of an event, that there was no such progress only if we were fully aware of the further causal consequences of the event. Otherwise, an apparent evil or setback in inquiry may turn out to be the means to a greater good (6.478–80): the believer would always see it in this fashion. But, what is there to the hypothesis of God's reality beyond these expectations? Could someone hold to these expectations without attributing them to the goodness of

God? If so, can the pragmatist make sense of the additional content that the theistic hypothesis has?

Leaving this problem for the present, let us examine how the humble argument is transformed into the neglected argument. The first stage is simply to *describe* the humble argument: we note that it is natural for people to come to a belief in God's reality in this fashion, and remind ourselves that whatever can convince a normal man must be presumed to be good reasoning. Peirce takes it that the optimistic outlook just described is natural to man, and announces that pessimism – which would prevent its emergence – is a mark of an abnormal 'diseased' mind! (6.484; 6.487). The third stage involves bringing to bear the logic of science, but it is difficult to see what it involves from published materials (6.485; 6.488–91). But it seems that the evolutionary cosmology, which explains the creation of all three universes of experience from nothingness, occupies an important part of this. Peirce complains that in order to present the argument properly, he would need to use principles of logic that 'the logicians have hardly dreamed of', and the strict proof of pragmatism. It is to be an inquiry 'which produces, not merely scientific belief, which is always provisional, but also a living, practical belief . . ' (6.485). So, presumably, it is an argument that brings together the evolutionary cosmology and a secure confidence in the expectations described above. But, what these relations are is unclear.

One way to try to tease out these relations would be to ask whether it would be possible to accept the evolutionary cosmology or act out of the love of truth without believing in God. I think that there is some evidence that Peirce's answer would be negative. First, to think of the cosmos evolving, perfecting itself, moving towards a state of increased reasonableness, simply is to see purpose (see 6.157). The universe, recall, is thought of as mind, and, on occasion, Peirce thinks that the evolution must not be thought of in terms of the blind wasteful mechanisms of Darwinian natural selection, but is rather motivated by a conatus, an urge towards perfection – in 1892, he speaks of 'agapastic evolution driven by purpose or love' (6.13 ff; 6.287 ff). Only if we think of the evolution as purposed have we grounds for confidence that it will continue as it has proceeded up to now. This reflects a Pantheistic tendency in Peirce's thought which is present in his claim that we can directly perceive God. The universe simply is a vast universal mind, developing itself in a logical fashion. Secondly, we noted in the discussion of the normative sciences, that blind regulative hopes seemed a poor basis for a decision that would determine the future course of one's life. How could it be reasonable to pin *so* much on such uncertain foundations? We now find that, alongside the *logical* justification of science, the believer is possessed by a practical certainty that these ends can be achieved. That our ultimate end should be 'to do our little bit in the process of creation' was not metaphor. Although, given the relative positions of logic and metaphysics in his hierarchy of sciences, Peirce needed a justification of the pursuit of knowledge which would satisfy an atheist, he plainly believes himself that an interest in inquiry is motivated by a sense of religious awe. We may reasonably speculate that the project of pure inquiry could only appeal to someone of religious sensibility. At 6.502, Peirce goes further and claims that our ability to obtain knowledge through scientific investigation 'is proof conclusive that, though we cannot think any thought of God's, we can catch a fragment of His Thought, as it were.'

A useful question to raise here concerns the metaphysical explanation of the reliability of our abductive sense. How are we to explain the affinity between mind and nature that accounts for our ability to think of the correct hypotheses quickly enough for cognitive progress to be possible? One possibility is that it results from the fact that knowledge and reality evolve in similar ways, by habit-taking. The truth of objective idealism posits a similarity between the two kinds of development; perhaps this is the affinity that Peirce sought. However, it is hard to see how such an explanation could be adequate at all. Unless the evolutionary cosmology can be brought to yield a detailed theory of the sorts of regularities that can emerge, then it seems conceivable that the sorts of regularities that emerge as reality develops should differ radically from those that appeal to our abductive sense. If it is fated – purposed – that regularity will grow, on the other hand, then it is fated that we will come to knowledge of reality for our taking habits is a part of the general evolutionary progress. Our faith in God, and confidence in continued progress, will assure us that there is a sufficient affinity between mind and nature. I conjecture that this is a necessary move in trying to fill the gaps in the Peircean story through metaphysical speculation. The optimism brought by belief in a deity is a necessary component of the explanation of how knowledge is possible.

I have ignored a lot of Peirce's metaphysical writings, and concentrated upon those that have a bearing upon the logical issues that we have been discussing. Before turning to an evaluation of these views in the next section, I should note that Peirce was probably never satisfied with the form that he gave these doctrines. He returned to religious questions in a number of manuscripts after 1910, but made little progress with them and seemed to be bogged down on foundational issues. My principal concern has been to show that they cannot be divorced from his theories of truth and meaning: at least he tries to use methods in metaphysics which are logically defensible; and the metaphysical doctrines can be seen to answer to explanatory demands which emerge from problems for his account of the life of science, and from logical principles which are defended as ingredients of the scientific method.

4 Conclusion: realism and idealism

After this brief survey of some of the central themes of Peirce's metaphysics, we must turn to an evaluation of his position. I am not going to offer detailed criticisms of particular metaphysical theses, but will rather raise some general questions which will point us towards an assessment of Peirce's philosophical system as a whole. The question to consider is: what reason is there to suppose that the kind of metaphysical inquiry undertaken by Peirce is possible at all? From its systematic importance for his work in logic, it would be natural to think that the discipline is called for by internal features of Peirce's vindication of science. The first point that I wish to make is that this is not so. Recall that we characterized metaphysics by pointing out that its role was to ground the regulative hopes that were adopted at various stages of the route through the earlier philosophical sciences. For example, we hope that phenomenological reflection can reveal to us a set of universal categories because that is a requisite of our having objective standards for the evaluation of arguments; metaphysics provided a description of the structure of reality which showed that the three categories revealed through phenomenological inquiry were indeed universal. It is important to distinguish two claims. First, if our investigations are grounded in the hope that some proposition will turn out to be true, then the loose ends of our philosophical inquiries will not all be tied up until we have shown that that proposition is, in fact, true. So long as that has not been done, we risk our efforts crumbling and coming to naught. This claim is unexceptionable, but Peirce introduces a more restrictive thesis alongside it. He holds that it will not suffice for the regulative loans to be repaid through a scientific investigation. There must be a metaphysics, prior to all of the special sciences, which it is possible to carry out without much difficulty here and now, and which will ground all the regulative hopes.

I remarked in the introduction that Peirce was a conservative philosophical figure. Although we have noticed many themes which will remind us of theses defended by leading philosophers of this century – and, indeed, the pragmatist movement and Peirce himself had a considerable influence upon these later developments – Peirce appears to us as a philosopher from another age. The first of these two claims has a modern ring. Many thinkers attempting to reconcile the objectivity of logic with some form of naturalism may find attractive the strategy of grounding logic in regulative hopes whose truth can be explained scientifically – I shall suggest how this strategy could be developed shortly. It is in the second claim that we find a figure from the past; few philosophers now think it possible to describe the general structure of reality without relying upon the special sciences.

This point can be linked with another curious feature of Peirce's thought, his strict separation of questions of theory and issues of practice, which we discussed at length in chapter II. Consider the following strategy for a vindication of applied science. We require from our logic rules for conducting inquiries to obtain practically useful information. It is one of our common-sense certainties that practically useful information is available. Moreover, we can see that unless we were sure of this, the question of how we should conduct such inquiries cannot arise. So it is reasonable to base the investigation upon the hope that, indeed, we are in a position to acquire practically useful information here and now, to reach the truth in the short run on important issues. We soon see that this requires that we hope that our abductive sense is very reliable in areas of practical concern, and that our sampling techniques do, much of the time, meet the requisite standards of randomness and so on. Having adopted these hopes, we can discuss strategies of practical inquiry. Of course, it is important, subsequently, to show that these hopes are in fact grounded; but we can see how a mixture of psychology, physics and evolutionary biology will do that for us. Hence, our logic of applied science provides fallible, but objective, rules. The strategy parallels the one we have seen Peirce use for pure science. And Peirce's claims about signs and categories could all be applied to carry out the investigation. Moreover, he could continue to ground his investigation in the normative sciences; applicable knowledge can be justified as a worthwhile object for inquiry; the picture of settling what rules ought to be used for the self-control of inquiry or deliberation would retain its application. Given Peirce's desire to ground his logic in ethics and aesthetics, and the related thought that truth is the 'natural product' of inquiry, we might have expected Peirce to move towards a pluralism which stressed the role of inquiry in contributing to the success of practical ventures. He might have held that there were different disciplines working with their own substantive conception of truth, each reflecting different practical concerns and purposes that people can have. Within any discipline, interested, practically oriented yet serious inquiry may easily lead to a fated consensus; each discipline would have its own intelligible conception of truth. If his thought had developed in this way, he would have moved towards a thoroughgoing pragmatism similar to that defended by other 'pragmatists' in this century.

I have already criticized some of the elements in Peirce's resistance to such moves at the end of chapter II. There I complained that he simply asserted with very little argument that investigations in the normative sciences showed that someone who seeks to subject his deliberations to self-control should subordinate himself to the progress of pure science towards the truth. It is useful now to link this view more directly with the claims about metaphysics that I am now querying. According to Peirce, there would be this difference between pure disinterested inquiry and applied science: the regulative hopes required for pure inquiry can be grounded within his distinctive metaphysics, but those required for applied science could only be grounded within the special sciences. This means that we risk not being able to ground the hopes needed for the logic of applied science; but since metaphysics is 'easy' and can be completed in the short run, no similar risk faces the hopes required for the logic of pure science. And this is linked with a central move in his work in the normative sciences: we can adopt something as an ultimate end only if we do not risk being prevented from sustaining it because of contingent properties of our environment or changes in our character. The connections between these unattractive themes in Peirce's thought are evident.

What follows from this, I think, is that there is an input into Peirce's system which has not been fully acknowledged in the earlier discussion. The input reflects a philosophical outlook, or a set of assumptions, which are not *required* by the project of vindicating the objectivity of logic. Indeed, the remarks of the previous few pages are supposed to suggest that there is some tension between this outlook and the positions suggested by the shape of Peirce's logic. It is the source of what is 'traditional' in Peirce's philosophy. We can capture its flavour by sketching three sorts of doctrines which are present in Peirce's writings from the 1860s, which reflect his allegiances to an earlier tradition of philosophy and metaphysics, and which are manifested in the tensions that I have been describing. The first is a belief that philosophy can produce a metaphysical picture of man in the world which will make it possible to reconcile the claims of science and religion: this tendency is as present in the earlier papers in CW 1 as it is in the later metaphysical writings that we have examined here. It is Peirce's response to some of the issues that I discussed in the introduction. Secondly, it is a fact about Peirce that he attached the highest value to the pure scientist who subordinates himself to a larger community of investigators. This rejection of individualism is closely related to the link between science and religion; the scientist is motivated by a religious awe, and is not motivated by secular or temporal concerns. He does his bit in the process of creation, and becomes a part of the growth of concrete reasonableness. This perspective upon scientific activity is lost when the scientist is perceived as an individual preoccupied with issues of 'vital importance'. Thirdly, his work in the normative sciences is coloured by a particular ideal of self-control. If our activities are governed by good ultimate ends then we are completely secure; we do not risk the disappointment or disillusion of finding that our ends cannot be sustained. Self-control is complete; by devoting our lives to completing the work of God in creating a reasonable cosmos we ensure that we cannot be harmed, that we are at one with the process by which reality is developing. The body of thought to which these themes belong is pervasive throughout Peirce's writings – although most markedly in the early 1860s and after 1890.

Although there are points of similarity between what I am saying and Goudge's thesis that Peirce's writings represent an amalgam of 'naturalistic' and 'transcendental' themes which cannot be welded into a system, the underlying point is different. I am not denying that there is systematic unity in Peirce's writings; I find no inconsistency between his metaphysics and the pragmatist principle, and I have no difficulty tying his work in the normative sciences to writings on signs, induction and deductive logic. Rather, I cannot accept his confidence that the results he takes from ethics and the other normative sciences are the correct ones; I cannot agree that he speaks with a universal voice. The unity of the system requires that the outlook described in the previous paragraphs should, as it were, fall out of a serious investigation in the normative sciences. It only seems to do so because of the personal and metaphysical commitments that Peirce brings to the investigation. The proposal that logic be grounded in ethics and aesthetics is more likely to encourage the pluralistic sort of 'pragmatism' described above. And once the investigation moves in that direction, there is just no reason to believe that the sort of metaphysical inquiry that Peirce attempts is possible or desirable at all.

These remarks have, I hope, distinguished the elements in Peirce's thought which prompted Rorty to come to such differing judgments of his importance as those described in the introduction. We shall now turn to a second issue of general interpretation which has been mentioned several times in the course of the book but has not yet been settled.

How should we classify Peirce, is he realist or idealist? Of course, these terms are so imprecise in their meaning – there are so many different kinds of realism and idealism – that no straightforward answer to the question can be given. What is clear to begin with is that he is not a subjective idealist. He believes that we know about objects which are not just states of our own minds, and, through his theory of perception, holds that we are directly aware of external objects. Ordinary empirical objects are real, and their character is independent of the will or opinion of any agents or inquirers. His evident *objective* idealism is consistent with this – those independent empirical objects are best accounted for by adopting a monistic metaphysics which views them as having components and modes of action best thought of as analogous to those found in mental phenomena. When it is claimed that external objects are 'mental', there need be no suggestion that they are parts of, or produced by, the minds of ordinary agents and inquirers. All that is urged is that they *resemble* minds in certain respects. However, once all this is settled, there remains a question about whether Peirce is some form of *transcendental* idealist; does he think that the character of the empirical world reflects the constructive or constitutive activity of our cognitive faculties? In early writings, he asserted that reality was not independent of thought 'in general'; in writings from before 1870, we saw him assert that the character of sensory experience is determined by unconscious inference and thus reflects the nature of our cognitive constitution; in the 'New List', the nature of quality and law was traced through the structure of the process of cognition; and other early arguments for the categories turned to the structure of a logical language for a clue to the categorial structure of reality. All of these arguments saw an internal connection between cognition and reality: since what is real is what is believed in the long run, the structure of reality will reflect the structure of belief. If all propositions contain general expressions, then, Peirce argued, generality is real. It is of a piece with this that Peirce's realist conception of reality saw truth or reality as the 'natural product' of our cognitive activities: there is no scope for doubt about whether our cognitive faculties are so attuned to the nature of reality that whatever beliefs will be cognitively ideal for us – will be stably accepted in the long run – will thereby be true. Peirce's realism, as he acknowleged, bore a more than passing resemblance to Kant's transcendental idealism.

The question that concerns us here is how far the later position – what prompted the grounding of logic in the nomative sciences, the grounding of the theory of the categories in phenomenology, and the propping up of logic with Metaphysics – departed from this transcendental idealism. As I pointed out in chapter III, Peirce's joining Francis Abbot in condemning Kant's 'nominalism' suggests that there was a major shift. Two elements of the new position strongly support this. First, the theory of categories came to be justified by a sort of empirical vindication of a logical language, by showing that such a language was adequate to describe all the elements of the phaneron. Secondly, the metaphysical views discussed in this chapter appear to be a response to a genuine doubt about whether our faculties are sufficiently attuned to reality to enable us to uncover its features. It can seem that Peirce thinks that, unless we can be assured that objective idealism, the evolutionary cosmology and the reality of God can all be established, we cannot rule out the possibility that theories may prove to be cognitively and epistemically ideal to us, but, for all that, not capture the nature of reality. Far from our cognitive constitution being *constitutive* of the nature of reality, rather, one task of logic is to invent a logical language which can be proved to be adequate to the description of a reality whose nature is given independent of the resources that we have for describing or investigating it. We may be persuaded that we have, in Peirce's work, an illustration of Putnam's claim that if we abandon a form of transcendental idealism we shall be forced – if scepticism is to be avoided – to adopt a version of objective idealism which guarantees the attunement of our cognitive faculties with reality (Putnam, 1982a).

There are many passages in the later work which conflict with this interpretation, however. For example, there are approving endorsements of the views defended in the 'New List' and the papers in the *Journal of Speculative Philosophy*; we find the claim that even the nature of the percept involves cognitive elaboration. And, when we look more closely at the structure of the later thought, we can see that Peirce is closer to Kant than the interpretation just described would suggest. Two features of the later position make this especially clear. For all that the categories are defended by a kind of inductive justification, this does not involve measuring the theory against the nature of an independent reality. Rather, they are measured against all that can appear in veridical perception, phantasy, imagination, dreaming, etc. The phenomenological investigation itself is agnostic about the explanation that is to be offered of the ubiquity of the three categories. Subsequent investigation in the special sciences may force us to attribute this to the structure of human cognition. Secondly, the construction of the concept of reality out of the elements uncovered in phenomenology makes essential reference to our capacities for aesthetic pleasure or admiration. Somebody who denied transcendental idealism would attempt to establish what rules of method we should adopt by seeking an independent characterization of truth and asking what rules measure up to that. Peirce does not adopt this procedure, but seeks his characterization of truth or reality by asking what rules for assessing methods it is possible for us to adopt, relying upon our aesthetic sensibilities to establish what ultimate standards can be adopted. Truth is defined as what ought to be assented to.

The point I am trying to make becomes most clear when we consider the precise role of Peirce's metaphysics in shoring up his logical investigations. We saw that the metaphysical theory was required to assure us of a hoped-for attunement between our cognitive nature and reality. A natural way to understand this, which accords with the view that Peirce abandoned transcendental idealism, is that we require an assurance that what is going to seem true to us, in the light of the best means at our disposal, will actually be true. We need to avoid sceptical doubts which may suggest that our substantive conception of truth is seriously flawed. But, I have just suggested that given the way in which the concept of Truth is developed through the normative sciences, *this* sceptical doubt cannot arise; we cannot drive a wedge between what is cognitively ideal for us and what is actually true. In that case, what sort of reassurance do we seek from the metaphysical cosmology?

Some of Peirce's remarks suggest that what is at issue is how determinate reality is, not whether there is any reality at all or whether our substantive conception of reality is adequate. That would be compatible with a broadly Kantian conception of the constitution of reality. But, since he also looks to metaphysics for a justification of his hope that reality will prove to be knowable to us by, for example, explaining the adequacy of our abductive sense, it is easy to suppose that he was worried by sceptical doubts like those just discussed. This would be a mistake. Without questioning the substantive conception of truth developed in the normative sciences, there is scope for the two questions which exercised Peirce: 'Is there any guarantee that a cognitively ideal theory, which brings all of our experience into a harmonious order, exists at all?' and, if there is such a theory, 'What assurance have we that our inquiries will arrive at this theory in a reasonable time?' These are the questions that Peirce's metaphysics is supposed to answer. In that case, there is no basis for denying that Peirce's conception of reality retained a broadly Kantian flavour long after Kant was demoted from being the champion of the realist conception of philosophy to standing as yet one more victim of nominalist illusion.

Notes

Introduction

1 There are a number of useful histories of philosophy in the United States which will amplify this sketch of the intellectual background to the emergence of pragmatism. The more valuable are those by Schneider (1946); Kuklick (1977), which is particularly concerned with the history of Harvard philosophy; Flower and Murphey (1977). Murphey (1968) and Madden (1963) are also useful.

2 In Hookway (1984) there is a comparison of this traditional 'Kantian' structure of Peirce's thought with the naturalistic contemporary pragmatism of W. V. O. Quine.

3 The most detailed study of the development of Peirce's thought, as well as of his biography, has been carried out by M. Fisch. The bibliography lists several papers by Fisch which record some of the results of his researches. His introduction to volume one of the new edition of Peirce's work (CW) contains valuable information on Peirce's early life, and it is likely that the introductions to subsequent volumes will continue the story.

I Logic, mind and reality: early thoughts

1 The most important of the five logic papers is 'On a New List of Categories' (1.545–559), which is discussed in detail in chapter III. The others are 'On the Natural Classification of Arguments' (2.461–514), 'Upon Logical Comprehension and Extension' (2.391–426), 'On an Improvement in Boole's Calculus of Logic' (3.1–19), and 'Upon the Logic of Mathematics' (3.20–44). Versions of the two lecture series are now available in CW1; those of 1865 are at CW1 162–302, and those of 1866 are at CW1 358–504.

2 I have changed Peirce's example slightly here. For the notion of a relative property, see Williams (1978, pp. 243 ff).

3 In his later writings, Peirce's approach to philosophy was less fallibilist. While he denied that we have any grounds for assurance that the special sciences

289

could reach the truth in the short run, he appears to have believed that philosophical issues can be settled here and now. The source of this change in his views will emerge in the following chapter.

4 Peirce continued to present the points in much the same way after he had developed his logic of relations and quantifiers. A clear early treatment of the material is in 2.461 ff.

5 For a useful general discussion, see Laudan (1981).

II Truth and the aims of inquiry

1 A useful discussion of Peirce's views in the early 1870s is found in Altshuler (1980).

2 There is not an extensive secondary literature relating to Peirce's work on the normative sciences. Perhaps the most useful work in this area includes Potter (1967), Bernstein (1971, Part III), and Robin (1964). The most accessible text by Peirce himself is in the Pragmatism lectures of 1903, particularly 5.34–40, 5.108–114, and 5.120–150.

IV Assertion and interpretation: the theory of signs

1 The earliest published version of the theory is found in the series of papers discussed in chapter I; and the argument of the 'New List', discussed in chapter III is an important early discussion of signs. A rich, full treatment from Peirce's later years is found in his letters to Lady Welby, published in SS. Volume 2 of CP and volume 4 of NE both contain a lot of relevant material, and NE iv 235–264 and NE iv 167–184 are both valuable. The 1885 paper published at 3.359 ff is also important.

2 There is an enormous secondary literature on Peirce's semiotic. I have found Ransdell (1977), Brock (1975) and Short (1981) especially helpful in coming to an interpretation of his position. Further material, alternative interpretations, and historical background can be found in Greenlee (1973), Fisch (1978), and many papers in *Transactions of the Charles S. Peirce Society, Semiotica* and elsewhere in journals on semiotics.

VI Mathematical reasoning and the a priori

1 Peirce's writings on the nature of mathematical reasoning are scattered: as the references given in the chapter will indicate, volume iv of NE contains a lot of relevant material, and 4.227 ff is particularly helpful. Useful secondary material can be found in Eisele (1979), Murphey (1961), and the issue of *Historia Mathematica* dated August 1982 (vol. 9, no. 2), which contains useful papers by Eisele, Dauben, Putnam and others.

VII The growth of knowledge: induction and abduction

1 A suitable sample of Peirce's writings on the nature of synthetic reasoning can

be obtained from: three papers from the 1878 'Illustrations of the Logic of Science' found at 2.619–693; the 1883 paper 'A Theory of Probable Inference', at 2.694–754; from 1892, 'The Doctrine of Necessity Examined', 6.35–65; the unpublished 'The Logic of Drawing History from Ancient Documents' (c1901) at 7.162–255 (especially 7.183–222); and, a later manuscript printed at 2.755–760.

2 I have not provided a detailed discussion of Peirce's criticisms of other attempts to vindicate Induction, such as the claim that it rests upon a belief in the uniformity of nature. These views are described and discussed in many places in the secondary literature, for example Goudge (1950, pp. 180 ff).

VIII Pragmatism

1 That there are truths about the actual world which will never be discovered need not conflict with Peirce's claim that rational inquirers are fated to reach a stable consensus on all questions about the nature of reality. *Reality* is the mode of being of laws and general principles. Peirce makes no corresponding claim about *existence*, which is the mode of being of individuals and states of affairs that involve them.

2 I lack the space to present the details of this logical system or to assess its merits as a device for providing a mathematical (iconic) representation of the structure of argument. The reader is advised to consult Roberts (1973) and Zeman (1968).

IX Evolutionary cosmology and objective idealism

1 Volume six of the collected papers contains a large selection of Peirce's writings on Metaphysical topics.

2 Peirce's cosmology has not received any fully adequate treatment in the secondary literature. Murphey (1965) and Turley (1977) provide useful discussions, especially of Peirce's Objective Idealism. Esposito (1980) offers a general discussion of Peirce's views which places his metaphysical concerns at the centre.

References

As well as containing works referred to in the text, the list below includes some works on Peirce which I have found helpful but have not referred to. Where two dates are given, the first is that of original publication and the second that of the reprint or translation employed.

Abbot, F. E. 1885. *Scientific Theism*. Boston: Little, Brown.

Almeder, R. 1980. *The Philosophy of Charles S. Peirce: a Critical Introduction*. Oxford: Blackwell.

Altshuler, B. 1980. 'Peirce's theory of truth and his early idealism', *Transactions of the Charles S. Peirce Society*, vol. 16, pp. 118–40.

Anscombe, G. E. M. 1981. *Metaphysics and the Philosophy of Mind: Collected Philosophical Papers, volume II*. Oxford: Blackwell.

Apel, K.-O. 1981. *Charles S. Peirce: From Pragmatism to Pragmaticism*. Amherst: University of Massachusetts Press.

Ayer, A. J. 1946. *Language, Truth and Logic*. (2nd edition). London: Gollancz.

Ayer, A. J. 1968. *The Origins of Pragmatism*. London: Macmillan.

Bernstein, R. 1964. 'Peirce's theory of perception', in Moore and Robin (eds), 1964, pp. 165–89.

Bernstein, R. 1971. *Praxis and Action*. London: Duckworth.

Boler, J. 1963. *Charles Peirce and Scholastic Realism*. Seattle: University of Washington Press.

Boler, J. 1980. 'Peirce, Ockham and scholastic realism', *The Monist*, vol. 63, pp. 290–303.

Brock, J. 1975. 'Peirce's conception of semiotic', *Semiotica*, vol. 14, pp. 124–41.

Brock, J. 1979. 'Principal themes in Peirce's logic of vagueness', in *Peirce Studies*, vol. 1, pp. 41–9.

Brock, J. 1981. 'An introduction to Peirce's theory of speech acts', *Transactions of the Charles S. Peirce Society*, vol. 17, pp. 319–26.

Buchler, J. 1939. *Charles Peirce's Empiricism*. New York: Harcourt, Brace & World.

Burks, A. W. 1964. 'Peirce's two theories of probability', in Moore and Robin (eds), 1964, pp. 141–50.

Cavell, S. 1976. *Must We Mean What We Say?* Cambridge: Cambridge University Press.

Dauben, J. W. 1982. 'Peirce's place in mathematics', *Historia Mathematica*, vol. 9, pp. 311–25.

Dipert, R. 1981. 'Peirce's propositional logic', *Review of Metaphysics*, vol. 34, pp. 569–95.

Dummett, M. A. E. 1973. *Frege: Philosophy of Language*. London: Duckworth.

Eisele, C. 1979. *Studies in the Scientific and Mathematical Philosophy of Charles S. Peirce* (ed. R. M. Martin). Mouton: The Hague.

Eisele, C. 1982. 'Mathematical methodology in the thought of Charles S. Peirce', *Historia Mathematica*, vol. 9, pp. 333–41.

Esposito, J. 1980. *Evolutionary Metaphysics*. Athens, Ohio: Ohio University Press.

Firth, R. 1949–50. 'Sense-data and the percept theory', *Mind*, vol. 58, pp. 434–65 and vol. 59, pp. 35–56.

Fisch, M. 1954. 'Alexander Bain and the genealogy of pragmatism', *Journal of the History of Ideas*, vol. 15, pp. 413–44.

Fisch, M. 1964. 'Was there a metaphysical club in Cambridge?' in Moore and Robin (eds), 1964, pp. 3–32.

Fisch, M. 1967. 'Peirce's progress from nominalism toward realism', *The Monist*, vol. 51, pp. 159–78.

Fisch, M. 1977. 'American pragmatism before and after 1898', in R. W. Shahan and K. R. Merrill (eds), *American Philosophy*. Norman, Oklahoma: University of Oklahoma Press, pp. 78–110.

Fisch, M. 1978. 'Peirce's general theory of signs', in T. Sebeok (ed.), *Sight, Sound and Sense*. Bloomington: Indiana University Press, pp. 31–70.

Fisch, M. 1981. 'The "proof" of Pragmatism', in Sumner et al. (eds), 1981, pp. 28–40.

Flower, E. and Murphey, M. G. 1977. *A History of Philosophy in America*. New York: Putnam.

Gallie, W. B. 1952. *Peirce and Pragmatism*. New York: Dover Publications, 1966.

Goodman, N. 1952. 'Sense and certainty', *Philosophical Review*, vol. 61, pp. 160–7.

Goudge, T. A. 1950. *The Thought of C. S. Peirce*. Toronto: University of Toronto Press.

Greenlee, D. 1973. *Peirce's Concept of Sign*. Mouton: The Hague.

Guyer, P. 1979. *Kant and the Claims of Taste*. Cambridge, Mass.: Harvard University Press.

Haack, S. 1979. 'Fallibilism and necessity', *Synthese*, vol. 41, pp. 37–63.

Hacking, I. M. 1980. 'The theory of probable inference: Neyman, Peirce and Braithwaite', in Mellor (ed.), 1980, pp. 141–60.

Hempel, C. G. 1950. 'The empiricist criterion of meaning', *Revue Internationale de Philosophie*, vol. 11, pp. 41–63.

Herzberger, H. G. 1981. 'Peirce's remarkable theorem', in Sumner et al. (eds), 1981, pp. 41–58.

Hilpinen, R. 1982. 'On C. S. Peirce's theory of the proposition: Peirce as a precursor of game-theoretical semantics', *The Monist*, vol. 65, pp. 182–8.

Hintikka, K. J. J. 1980. 'C. S. Peirce's "First real discovery" and its contemporary relevance', *The Monist*, vol. 63, pp. 304–15.

Hookway, C. J. 1984. 'Naturalism, fallibilism and evolutionary epistemology', in C. J. Hookway (ed.), *Minds, Machines and Evolution*. Cambridge: Cambridge University Press, pp. 1–15.

Kant, I. 1790. *The Critique of Judgment*, trans. by J. C. Meredith. Oxford: Oxford University Press, 1952.

Ketner, K. L. 1981. 'Peirce's ethics of terminology', *Transactions of the Charles S. Peirce Society*, vol. 17, pp. 327–47.

Kitcher, P. 1979. 'Frege's epistemology', *Philosophical Review*, vol. 88, pp. 235–62.

Kuhn, T. S. 1962. *The Structure of Scientific Revolutions*. Chicago: University of Chicago Press.

Kuklick, B. 1977. *The Rise of American Philosophy*. New Haven: Yale University Press.

Lakatos, I. 1970. 'Falsification and the methodology of scientific research programmes', in I. Lakatos and A. Musgrave (eds), *Criticism and the Growth of Knowledge*. Cambridge: Cambridge University Press, pp. 91–196.

Lakatos, I. 1976. *Proofs and Refutations*. Cambridge: Cambridge University Press.

Laudan, L. 1981. *Science and Hypothesis*. Dordrecht: Reidel.

Lenz, J. 1964. 'Induction as self-corrective', in Moore and Robin (eds), 1964, pp. 122–40.

Levi, I. 1980. 'Induction as self-correcting according to Peirce', in Mellor (ed.), 1980, pp. 127–40.

Lewis, C. I. 1929. *Mind and the World Order*. New York: Dover Publications, 1956.

Madden, E. H. 1963. *Chauncey Wright and the Foundations of Pragmatism*. Seattle: University of Washington Press.

Madden, E. H. 1964. 'Peirce on probability', in Moore and Robin (eds), 1964, pp. 122–40.

Madden, E. H. 1981. 'Scientific inference: Peirce and the Humean tradition', in Sumner et al. (eds), 1981, pp. 59–74.

Mellor, D. H. (ed.). 1980. *Science, Belief and Behaviour: Essays in Honour of R. B. Braithwaite*. Cambridge: Cambridge University Press.

Mill, J. S. 1868. *An Examination of Sir William Hamilton's Philosophy*. Boston: W. V. Spenser.

Mill, J. S. 1891. *A System of Logic*. (8th edition). New York: Harper Bros.

Moore, E. C. and Robin, R. (eds). 1964. *Studies in the Philosophy of Charles Sanders Peirce*. 2nd series. Amherst: University of Massachusetts Press.

Murphey, M. G. 1961. *The Development of Peirce's Philosophy*. Cambridge, Mass.: Harvard University Press.

Murphey, M. G. 1965. 'On Peirce's metaphysics', *Transactions of the Charles S. Peirce Society*, vol. 1, pp. 12–25.

Murphey, M. G. 1968. 'Kant's children: the Cambridge Pragmatists', *Transactions of the Charles S. Peirce Society*, vol. 4, pp. 3–18.

Nozick, R. 1981. *Philosophical Explanations*. Cambridge, Mass.: Belknap Press.

Oehler, K. 1981. 'The significance of Peirce's ethics of terminology for

REFERENCES

contemporary lexicography in semiotics', *Transactions of the Charles S. Peirce Society*, vol. 17, pp. 348–57.

Peirce, C. S. 1929. 'Guessing', *Hound and Horn*, vol. 2, pp. 267–82.

Potter, V. S. 1967. *Charles Peirce on Norms and Ideals*. Amherst: University of Massachusetts Press.

Putnam, H. 1982a. 'Why there isn't a ready-made world', *Synthese*, vol. 51, pp. 141–67.

Putnam, H. 1982b. 'Peirce the logician', *Historia Mathematica*, vol. 9, pp. 290–301.

Quine, W. V. O. 1953. *From a Logical Point of View*. Cambridge, Mass.: Harvard University Press.

Ransdell, J. M. 1977. 'Some leading ideas of Peirce's semiotic', *Semiotica*, vol. 19, pp. 157–78.

Reichenbach, H. 1938. *Experience and Prediction*. Chicago: University of Chicago Press.

Rescher, N. 1978. *Peirce's Philosophy of Science*. Notre Dame: University of Notre Dame Press.

Roberts, D. D. 1973. *The Existential Graphs of Charles S. Peirce*. The Hague: Mouton.

Robin, R. S. 1964. 'Peirce's doctrine of the normative sciences', in Moore and Robin (eds), 1964, pp. 271–88.

Rorty, R. 1961. 'Pragmatism, categories and language', *Philosophical Review*, vol. 69, pp. 197–223.

Rorty, R. 1982. *Consequences of Pragmatism*. Hassocks, Sussex: Harvester.

Salmon, W. C. 1979. 'Why ask "Why?" An inquiry concerning scientific explanation', in W. C. Salmon (ed.), *Hans Reichenbach: Logical Empiricist*. Dordrecht: Reidel, pp. 403–25.

Scheffler, I. 1974. *Four Pragmatists*. London: Routledge & Kegan Paul.

Schneider, H. W. 1946. *A History of American Philosophy*. New York: Columbia University Press.

Sebeok, T. and Umiker-Sebeok, J. 1980. *You Know My Method: a Juxtaposition of Charles S. Peirce and Sherlock Holmes*. Bloomington, Ind.: Gaslight Publications.

Sellars, W. F. 1963. *Science, Perception and Reality*. London: Routledge & Kegan Paul.

Sharpe, R. A. 1970. 'Induction, abduction and the evolution of science', *Transactions of the Charles S. Peirce Society*, vol. 6, pp. 12–33.

Short, T. L. 1981. 'Semiosis and intentionality', *Transactions of the Charles S. Peirce Society*, vol. 17, pp. 197–223.

Skagestad, P. 1981. *The Road of Inquiry*. New York: Columbia University Press.

Strawson, P. F. 1959. *Individuals*. London: Methuen.

Sumner, L. W., Slater, J. G. and Wilson, F. (eds). 1981. *Pragmatism and Purpose*. Toronto: University of Toronto Press.

Thayer, H. S. 1968. *Meaning and Action: A Critical History of Pragmatism*. Indianapolis: Bobbs-Merrill.

Thompson, M. 1953. *The Pragmatic Philosophy of Charles S. Peirce*. Chicago: University of Chicago Press.

Thompson, M. 1978. 'Peirce's verificationist realism', *Review of Metaphysics*, vol. 32, pp. 74–98.

Thompson, M. 1981. 'Peirce's conception of an individual', in Sumner et al. (eds), 1981, pp. 133–48.

Turley, P. T. 1977. *Peirce's Cosmology*. New York: Philosophical Library.

Wiener, P. P. 1949. *Evolution and the Founders of Pragmatism*. Philadelphia: University of Pennsylvania Press, 1972.

Williams, B. A. O. 1978. *Descartes: The Project of Pure Inquiry*. Harmondsworth: Penguin Books.

Wittgenstein, L. 1967. *Remarks on the Foundations of Mathematics*. (2nd edition). Oxford: Blackwell.

von Wright, G. H. 1965. *The Logical Problem of Induction*. (2nd edition). Oxford: Blackwell.

Zeman, J. J. 1968. 'Peirce's graphs – the continuity interpretation', *Transactions of the Charles S. Peirce Society*, vol. 4, pp. 144–54.

Index

297